THE LOSING PARTIES

THE LOSING PARTIES

OUT-PARTY NATIONAL COMMITTEES 1956–1993

PHILIP A. KLINKNER

YALE UNIVERSITY PRESS
NEW HAVEN AND LONDON

Designed by Deborah Dutton.
Set in Times Roman text and Copperplate Gothic types by Marathon Typography
Service, Inc., Durham, North Carolina.
Printed in the United States of America by BookCrafters, Chelsea, Michigan.
Library of Congress Cataloging-in-Publication Data
Klinkner, Philip A., 1963–
    The losing parties : out-party national committees, 1956–1993 /
Philip A. Klinkner.
        p.   cm.
    Includes bibliographical references and index.
    ISBN 0-300-06008-4
    1. Political parties—United States—History—20th century.   2. Democratic
National Committee (U.S.)   3. Republican National Committee (U.S.)   4. United
States—Politics and government—1945–   I. Title.
JK2261.K59 1994
324.273—dc20   94-16353
                                                                              CIP
A catalogue record for this book is available from the British Library.
The paper in this book meets the guidelines for permanence and durability of the
Committee on Production Guidelines for Book Longevity of the Council on Library
Resources.
10   9   8   7   6   5   4   3   2   1

FOR HONORINE

CONTENTS

PREFACE

Political parties and political history have always fascinated me, and, after David Mayhew rescued me from a brief detour into the study of international politics, I began to focus my graduate studies on these subjects. This work exposed me to a variety of theories for explaining the behavior of political parties. While enlightening, I believed that these theories lacked empirical richness and historical context, and, therefore, were often superficial in their explanations. Consequently, this book sets out to examine the causes of party behavior by looking at parties in a more detailed historical setting. I hope that this project and its conclusion— that defeated parties behave according to the dictates of their own unique party cultures rather than as a result of their desire to win elections or to advance a particular ideology—will help to promote a more historical approach to the study of parties.

ACKNOWLEDGMENTS

Several persons greatly assisted this project. Herbert Alexander, John Bibby, Lance Blakesley, David Cameron, Neil Cotter, Robert Dahl, Leon Epstein, Steve Gillon, Paul Herrnson, Robert Huckshorn, John Kessel, David Kinsella, Grant Reeher, and Michal Weinstein provided helpful comments and advice. I am particularly indebted to Rogers Smith, David Plotke, and Steve Skowronek for their advice and support for this project while it was in the dissertation stage. I am also grateful for the assistance provided by the Brookings Institution while I was a research fellow in the Governmental Studies Program during 1990–1991 and as a guest scholar in the summer of 1993. While at the Brookings Institution, I profited immensely from my association with Keith Banting, John Chubb, Tony Downs, Julie Drucker, Chris Foreman, Bill Frenzel, Steve Hess, Charles O. Jones, Bob Katzman, Thomas Mann, Pietro Nivola, Mark Peterson, A. James Reichley, Bert Rockman, James Sundquist, Kent

Weaver and, especially, my fellow research fellows: Bruce Bimber, Tom Sugrue, and Jessique Korn. John Covell and Jane Hedges at Yale University Press were instrumental in bringing this book into existence. David Luke, Deborah Duyan, and Chad Derum were model research assistants. Whatever positive qualities this book possesses stem directly from my association with David Mayhew. Finally, my thanks go to my wife, Honorine, whose love and support give purpose and meaning to this book and to my life.

THE LOSING PARTIES

1

INTRODUCTION

This book examines the question, "How do party organizations respond after losing a presidential election?" This analysis will be limited to the two major parties in American politics, the Democrats and Republicans, from 1956 to the present, with a particular emphasis on the years up to 1984 (see table 1). I believe this span allows for valid comparisons since it covers ten election cycles with adequate variation between parties: six Democratic and four Republican cases. Expanding the number of elections, while allowing for more comparison, would permit a less intensive analysis of each period.

This analysis seems relevant for a variety of reasons. Losing parties act as oppositions and therefore play an essential role in democratic politics. As Robert Dahl states, "Today one is inclined to regard the existence of an opposition party as very nearly the most distinctive characteristic of democracy itself and we take the absence of an opposition party as evidence, if not always conclusive proof, for the absence of democracy."[1] In addition to the importance of opposition parties in democratic theory, parties out of power merit observation because an election loss may exert a strong influence on their ensuing behavior. For example, losing parties are more likely than winning parties to innovate and reform themselves and the party system and to raise new issues. Defeat provides them with a powerful motivation for changing their personnel, organizational structure, internal party procedures, and platforms since past methods have failed to achieve victory.[2] In-parties, following both the need for consistency and the adage "if it ain't broke, don't fix it" seem less disposed to change themselves. Walter Lippmann observed this pattern in New York's Tammany Hall party organization nearly eighty years ago: "Tammany itself becomes rigid when it is too successful, and only defeat seems to give it new life. Success makes men rigid and they tend to exalt stability over all the other virtues. Tired of the effort of willing they become fanatics about conservatism."[3]

In a later analysis of New York City politics, Theodore Lowi

TABLE 1.

OUT-PARTIES, 1956–PRESENT.

Election Period	Out-Party
1956–1960	Democrats
1960–1964	Republicans
1964–1968	Republicans
1968–1972	Democrats
1972–1976	Democrats
1976–1980	Republicans
1980–1984	Democrats
1984–1988	Democrats
1988–1992	Democrats
1992–Present	Republicans

attempted to determine the causes of party innovation. His findings supported Lippmann's observation. According to Lowi, innovation was the function of minority parties—parties that had lost the last several elections. In his words, "A stunning defeat at the polls is more likely to derange [the] structure [of] prevailing interests *and* prevailing ideology."[4]

Along with a greater propensity to innovate, American out-party organizations show greater autonomy, at least at the national level, than in-party organizations. The rise of the modern presidency has meant the consolidation of in-party political activity in the White House. This development has left in-party national organizations with significantly reduced importance and independence.[5] In the assessment of Sidney Milkis, contemporary party organizations are now "neglected or relegated to being personal fools of presidential ambitions and programs."[6] Under such a system, the national organization of an in-party suffers at best benign neglect and at worst outright hostility at the hands of the White House.

From 1956 on, the White House has controlled each incumbent-party presidential campaign. This concentration of party activities in the White House has resulted in campaigns that have focused almost exclusively on reelecting the president and have neglected the rest of the party. The most famous and extreme example of this tendency was in 1972 when Richard Nixon's campaign focused entirely on his own reelection, to the detriment of other Republicans.[7] Even Ronald Reagan, a strongly partisan president who helped to strengthen Republican party organizations during his years in office, made little effort to help other Republicans during his 1984 reelection campaign, despite his large lead over his rival, Walter Mondale.[8]

The incumbent party organization is also forced into a role subordinate to the

White House political operations between quadrennial election campaigns. Such a role has usually entailed a sharp decline in the organizational capabilities of the national party. According to former Democratic National Committee chairman Robert Strauss, "When the party's out of office, you're the head; when a Democrat is President, you're a goddamned clerk."[9] Richard Nixon and Jimmy Carter both oversaw the decline of their party's national organizations, and after the 1964 election, President Johnson "carried out a ruthless attack on the Democratic National Committee beginning in 1965, slashing its budget to the bone and eliminating several important programs, such as the highly successful voter registration division. The President also humiliated Democratic chairman, John Bailey, refusing to replace him, while turning most of his responsibilities over to White House aide Marvin Watson."[10]

Along with the decline of their organizational roles while one of their members occupies the White House, in-parties also lack influence in the formulation of party policies. Once again, both initiative and control in this area are left to the White House. According to James Sundquist, "Adoption of a party position by the 'in' party is a simple process: the party program is what the President says it is."[11]

Out-party national organizations, on the other hand, show no such domination, since no individual has the prestige or power that the president has to control the party. As a result, they play more active and independent roles during campaigns and between elections. Moreover, the greater autonomy of out-parties means that observing them provides a clearer picture of the forces that influence the behavior of party organizations.

A final reason for the study of losing parties is that winners often start out as losers. Ignoring this aspect of successful politicians and parties limits our ability to understand them. One must examine Richard Nixon's early defeats or the Republicans' wilderness years from 1932 to 1968 in order to comprehend their actions when finally in power. Furthermore, many persons and parties have had important influence despite electoral failure. The People's Party never achieved significant success at the ballot box in the 1890s; nonetheless, it had a major impact upon the politics of that era.

For all the apparent relevance of out-parties, political science has been rather neglectful in its treatment of them, particularly for the United States.[12] A glance through the indexes of a random selection of books on American parties yields few mentions of out-parties. Where attention is paid, the treatment is usually cursory at best.[13]

Two possible explanations for this lack of study come to mind. The first is a general disregard for "losers" in American culture and politics. H. L. Mencken once suggested "that all unsuccessful candidates for the presidency be quietly hanged, lest the sight of their grief have a very evil effect upon the young."[14] Vanquished persons and parties in American politics are often considered inconsequential—

forgotten, but not gone. Samuel Lubell described out-parties as pale "moons," illuminated only by the reflected light of the winning party "sun."[15]

A second reason for the lack of attention to out-parties is the presumption of symmetry among studies of American political parties. Democratic or Republican, early or modern, in or out of power, most party scholars have tended to minimize the differences between different types of parties, portraying parties in a variety of circumstances as essentially similar organizations acting in parallel ways. Such portrayals often make for convenient modeling, but, as I have shown, the circumstances confronting an out-party are very different from those facing an in-party. As a consequence, the behavior of an out-party differs significantly from that of an in-party.

DEFINING OUT-PARTY

By "out-party" I mean the party that lost the most recent presidential election. Though the U.S. system of divided and shared powers makes it more difficult to identify in- and out-parties than in a parliamentary system, the importance of the presidency in American politics generally reduces parties not in control of the White House to the role of an opposition, though that party might retain great strength in the Congress and in the electorate. For example, both expert political observers and the general public considered the Democratic party the "out-party" during the 1980s and early 1990s, despite their control of Congress.

The term *party* may refer to various entities: the party in the electorate, the party in Congress, and the party organization, both national and local. This project focuses only on the national party organization. Under the heading of the national party organization, I include the Democratic and Republican National Committees (DNC and RNC), any committees and organizations set up by the national committees, and any national party organizations set up by party elites that influence the national committees. I also include the congressional and senatorial campaign committees and state and local party organizations when the activities of those organizations influence the behavior of the national committee.

There are many reasons for limiting my examination to the national party organizations. First, the party in the electorate is less an objective entity than a collection of opinions and attitudes, and thus does not "respond" or "behave" in as concrete and easily observable ways. The national party organization, on the other hand, offers a tangible unit of analysis. Its membership and activities are known and recorded, allowing it to be more readily observed and analyzed.

Second, while the party in Congress and local party organizations are more concrete and observable entities than the party in the electorate, their status as oppositions does not depend upon the results of presidential elections. Rather, the outcome relies upon the results of House, Senate, state, and local contests. With the national party organization, the result of the presidential election determines its status as opposition or governing party.

Third, the ability and willingness of congressional and local parties to act as a national opposition are limited by institutional and regional circumstances. For the congressional party leaders, their roles as legislative leaders and representatives of local constituencies "may make it very difficult for them to engage in the kind of partisan hell-raising which, from the more narrow context of leadership in the out-party, is necessary to invigorate and arouse the faithful."[16] The specific partisan requirements and parochial interests of local parties prevent them from taking a more active role as part of a national opposition.

Though the national party organizations engage in many activities, their primary functions when out of power are to provide a locus for party activities, to act as a national opposition, and to develop strategies aimed at recapturing the White House. Thus, the national chairperson must fulfill the roles of "image-maker, hell-raiser, and administrator" for the defeated party, putting him or her "in an improved position to determine the meaning of the party in the minds of his fellow partisans and in mass electorate as well."[17]

One objection to limiting the scope of analysis to the national party organizations is that these bodies and their actions are ultimately of little significance. In the classic description provided by Cornelius P. Cotter and Bernard C. Hennessy, the national committees possess "politics without power." Although this might have been the thinking during the late 1950s and early 1960s when Cotter and Hennessy did their research (though in later chapters I will demonstrate that the actions of the national committee were quite significant in this period), more recent examinations of the national party committees stress their large and increasing importance as party rule makers, policy developers, fundraisers, campaign service providers, and as forums for settling factional conflicts.[18] According to one recent analyst, the national committees now possess "power without politics."[19]

THE CATEGORIES AND DETERMINANTS OF
OUT-PARTY BEHAVIOR

My analysis focuses on those activities of the losing national party committee that stem either wholly or substantially from their loss in the previous presidential election. I will not include the activities that are part of the continuing functions of the national committee (for example, the staging of the national convention) or are only weakly related to the election loss. Furthermore, this set of responses will not be limited according to the goals of those responses. For example, I will not just focus on responses that are part of a strategy for winning the next presidential election. I include any responses that are directed at helping the party to compete more effectively in all elections—national, state, and local—or in elections beyond just the next four years. Other responses, such as those intended to alter a party's ideology or its procedures for internal governance, management, or representation, will also be included. In other words, I will include all defeat-caused responses that political analysts see as relevant to the behavior and activity of the parties.

Ordinarily, these responses fall into the following three categories:

Policy Responses—These refer to efforts by a party to change its policies, platform, or philosophy following defeat in a presidential election. This type of response occurs often, but not always, through a policy committee set up by the party to rethink or recast its positions on various issues. Examples include the Democratic Advisory Council between 1956 and 1960 and the Republican Coordinating Committee between 1964 and 1968.

Organizational Responses—These are intended to improve the party's efficiency. Among the responses in this category are improvements in financial operations, media usage, candidate recruitment, polling, issue development, data analysis, and fundraising. Also included here are changes in managerial systems and organization. Two important examples of this response are the organizational revamping of the Republican party from 1964 to 1968 and from 1976 to 1980.

Procedural Responses—These responses refer to changes in a party's procedures for internal governance, choosing its presidential candidates, and selecting the delegates to its national convention. More broadly, they pertain to questions of who will run the party and how. Types of procedural responses include changes in the methods for selecting and apportioning convention delegates, in representation, in the candidate nomination processes, and in the rules and structures of the national committees. The best-known example of a procedural response are the McGovern-Fraser reforms instituted by the Democratic party between 1968 and 1972.

In addition to classifying the various responses of parties, I also analyze the factors that help to determine a particular response. The literature on party behavior suggests three possible explanations for how parties might respond to election defeats. The first school of thought sees parties as rational organizations, with a relatively unified leadership and a consistent set of priorities—primarily winning elections. Though other factors—such as internal party dynamics and concerns about ideology and policy—might exist, these are secondary considerations at best and hence do not significantly influence the behavior of parties.[20]

A second school of thought rejects the notion of parties as unified organizations concerned about policy only for instrumental reasons and devoted almost solely to winning the next election. Instead, parties are portrayed as driven by the desire to maintain and advance their ideological goals. While such parties might still desire to win, they are reluctant to do so at the cost of ideological compromise or programmatic moderation.

A spate of recent writing about political parties tends to support this observation. The work of Ian Budge and Hans Keman offers one example. Budge and Keman conclude that parties do have policy preferences independent of electoral considerations and that they see government as a means by which they might turn these preferences into public policy.[21] Similar findings for the United States have been reported by Henry Chappell, Jr., and William Keech, who claim that "politicians do seem to care about policy as well as winning," and that voter uncertainty allows parties to take positions different from those found at the political center.[22]

A third and less studied school of thought views the behavior of parties in terms of the culture of the party organization. Any organization over a period of time will establish certain rules, traditions, and mores to govern its behavior. Such influences are readily observable in the behavior of businesses, as organizational theorist Alan Kantrow points out:

> Organizations remember—sometimes accurately, frequently not, sometimes with an awareness that that is what they are doing, most often in happy oblivion that their past has any ongoing call on their time or attention. The style of business presentations, the kinds of evidence that tend to sway decisions, the shared sense of what constitutes relevant information about a new market or product, the deep-seated visceral preferences for certain lines of business—all of these characteristics, and a thousand others like them, are the subtle products of memory. In no two organizations are they exactly the same, nor in any two parts of the same organization.[23]

Such cultural factors might also influence party organizations, including how they might respond to defeat, independent of the electoral and ideological concerns portrayed by other theories of party behavior. In the words of William Crotty: "Despite their deceptively similar governing forums, national and local party structures, and even—to the unpracticed eye—apparent unity on such matters as general policy, the two national parties are distinctively separate entities, each with its own traditions, social roots, and organizational and personal values."[24]

Jo Freeman expands upon this point in her study of the Democratic and Republican parties, showing that each party has developed a distinctive culture that governs party structure and intraparty power relationships.[25] Byron Shafer also advances this idea in his analysis of the distinctive cultures evident at Republican and Democratic national conventions.[26]

These distinctive party cultures result from a variety of shared influences and experiences. One such influence is ideology. According to Mildred Schwartz in her study of the Illinois Republican party, ideology provides the central tenets of party culture and thus helps to shape the behavior of the party organization. According to her, the ideological conservatism of the Illinois Republicans provides the party with a reason for being, keeping its members "solidary and committed."[27] Ideology alone, however, does not constitute a party culture. The memory of critical events, prior solutions to problems (both successful and unsuccessful), the preexisting cultural traits of an organization's recruits, and the impact of strong leaders are among the other factors that contribute to the culture of an organization, be it a party or a business firm.[28]

In fact, one is struck by how descriptions of the parties' cultural attributes often contradict aspects of their ideologies. As both Jo Freeman and Byron Shafer point out, the culture of Republicans stresses conformity and deference to hierarchy and authority, in contrast to the party's ideology of exalting entrepreneurship and rugged individualism. On the other hand, the Democrats' culture resists centralization and homogeneity, almost to the point of anarchic tribalism, a sharp divergence from their ideological preference for communitarianism and centralized government leadership.

This project hopes to shed light on this debate over the behavior of party organizations by observing their pattern of responses to election defeats—that is policy, organizational, or procedural responses. Defeated parties acting according to victory-oriented models of party behavior should respond by selecting and implementing the measures most likely to help them adapt to changes in the political environment and to assist them in winning the next election. One characteristic of parties behaving in this manner would be for them to vary their responses across time. Such a pattern would indicate that the parties are attempting to respond to changing political circumstances by using whatever response they deem most efficient.

One would also expect victory-oriented parties to pay close attention to successful responses employed by previous out-parties and to reject responses that had failed in the past. This behavior should be most evident in the aftermath of landslide defeats since imperfect and limited information constrains the ability of parties to act efficiently. Following close defeats, parties are often unable to identify the precise reasons for their loss and therefore to make the necessary changes, but after landslides there is clearer evidence of failed methods and greater ability to make decisive and thorough changes.[29]

Anthony Downs's explanation of parties acting rationally and efficiently posits that they will rely upon policy changes as a response to defeat. One could characterize a party's failure to engage in a policy response as evidence of non-Downsian party behavior, but this would only serve to knock down an analytical straw man. One can criticize Downs for envisioning parties only as promulgators of policy, but such efforts miss his larger point that parties will formulate the most rational and efficient response for winning the next election. Therefore, the absence of a policy response should not necessarily be seen as an indication that the party is less concerned about winning the next election, as long as the response taken by the party—for instance, an organizational response—is the most effective one under the circumstances for achieving victory. Moreover, according to theories of victory-oriented parties, parties employing a policy response would only be aiming at winning the next election if the response is focused on the median voter. A party might employ a policy response, but if it goes against the tide of popular opinion, then it can hardly be classified as attempting to win the next election.

Given the primacy of office-seeking in rational party theories, one would also expect parties to limit their responses to those directed solely at winning the next presidential election. According to these party theories, other responses, such as those geared toward a long-term rebuilding of the party's grass roots or achieving internal party democracy that are only weakly related to a strategy for winning the next presidential election, would occupy a less prominent place in party activities.

Parties motivated primarily by ideology would presumably respond very differently to defeat in presidential elections. Here, one would expect a party to engage in responses that would aim toward electoral success for the party without entailing ideological compromise. For example, an ideological party might emphasize an organizational response as a way of better identifying and mobilizing party stalwarts, and thereby try to win election without having to moderate its message. Ideological parties might also undertake a policy response as a way to better promote or package their views for public consumption, but one would not expect them to engage in the Downsian shifting of policy positions in order to attract more voters.

Parties behaving according to cultural theories should also show very different characteristics in their responses. Here, one would expect to find that responses vary by party. This would show that parties, instead of being symmetrically juxtaposed organizations defined by their common goal of winning, are distinct groupings whose approaches to winning elections are strongly conditioned by the traditions and cultures that result from their divergent histories, memberships, organizations, and ideologies. Furthermore, parties would show a reluctance to adopt the successful responses of the other party, instead relying on those responses that fit their own particular traditions and cultures. One would also expect such a pattern to hold despite the spurs of recurrent or landslide defeats. Finally, responses not immediately directed at winning the next presidential election should play a significant role in the pattern of responses.

RESEARCH METHODS

My analysis of opposition national party organizations relies heavily on detailed historical research. I have examined party documents; contemporary accounts of party affairs in newspapers, magazines, and journals; and secondary documents on party activities and history. I have also interviewed nearly one hundred individuals who were important to the national party organizations during the period of this study, including former national committee chairs, members, and staff; party candidates and elected officials; state party leaders; academics who have worked at the national committees; journalists covering the national parties; and other relevant persons.

Why this type of research? One reason is that substantial histories of the parties, particularly of the party organizations, do not exist. The lack of such histories makes it necessary for me to construct detailed accounts of the party organizations in this period so I can determine the types of responses taken by the parties and the reasons for their selection. Another reason is that, as I mentioned previously, one task of this project is to determine the extent to which culture and tradition might influence the behavior of parties following a presidential election loss. While the existence of party cultures is rarely denied, identifying and assessing the impact of such phenomena is a difficult task. Doing so requires a more qualitative analysis of the parties than can be done through the gathering of simpler or more quantitative forms of data. In the apt description of one student of organizations, observing organizations is like observing icebergs; nine-tenths of what goes on is beneath the surface.[30] Only more qualitative methods allow researchers to probe the depths of party cultures.

Though such qualitative methods are somewhat rare among scholars of party organizations, they are more prominent among those who research business organizations.[31] Such qualitative methods can produce an ethnography of an organization and allow the researcher to "capture the 'feel' of the organization from the inside, the perceptions of individual members, and the community of shared symbols, in addition to the subtleties of everyday routines and rituals as these reveal the quality of life and character of the organization."[32]

This project does contain several possible pitfalls. The most serious of these is determining which, or to what extent, actions of an out-party are truly responses to defeat and which are the result of other influences. There is no sure way to guarantee that one has made the correct determination, but I have taken several steps to maximize the possibility. First, by restricting my analysis to that part of the four-year interelection period before the nomination contenders become prominent, I can help to control for the effects of candidates and focus more specifically on the parties and their responses. Second, the use of interviews together with objective observations and contemporary as well as retrospective accounts of party responses offers a way of confirming or disconfirming a potential party response identified by different sources of data. Third, I concentrate my analysis on those party actions that are most clearly the result of electoral defeat. In this way I hope to err on the side of excluding or minimizing potential responses, rather than falsely identifying party responses or attributing to them a greater role than is warranted.

Chapters 2 through 8 provide a detailed narrative account of how each out-party from 1956 to 1984 responded to its defeat in the previous election. Chapter 9 examines the responses of out-parties from 1984 to the present. In each of these case study chapters, I will examine what factors accounted for the out-party's response and its possible implications for the party. Chapter 10 explores the patterns that emerge from this set of party responses and analyzes the factors that might account for them and the implications of these findings.

2

THE DEMOCRATS,

1956–1960

The Democratic party responded to its defeat in the 1956 presidential election by engaging in a vigorous effort to formulate a strong policy agenda for itself. Under the leadership of chairman Paul Butler, the DNC established the Democratic Advisory Council (DAC) as a policy-making body for the party. This response represents something of a rarity. The DAC offers one of the few cases in the history of American political parties, and the only example in the period covered by this study, of vigorous policy activity by a national party committee. In this chapter I will analyze the factors that led to the development of this response and its implications for the Democratic party.

POLICY FORMULATION IN OUT-PARTIES

Though the party conventions have always played an important role in drafting party platforms, the national party organizations, whether in or out of power, have made little effort and have had even less success in developing party policy. With in-parties, the policy-making initiative is almost always located in the White House, whereas with out-parties, policy formulation is usually seen as the prerogative of the congressional party leadership.

Still, the national party committees have made various efforts to formulate party policy. Few of these efforts, however, had much success. The first significant effort came in early 1920 when RNC chairman Will Hays organized an Advisory Committee on Policies and Platform "to gather facts and data, to invite a full expression of opinion of leading Republicans, and to submit its recommendations . . . to the Resolutions Committee of the National Convention."[1] Hays justified this effort by saying, "If a party platform is to be a mere string of political platitudes, then it can easily be written in forty-eight hours. If it is to be a solemn declaration of a responsible party's real purposes, it deserves the most careful consideration."[2] According to Ralph Goldman, the committee "had Republicans talking to each other on public policy for months before the national convention, practically eliminating any prospect of unexpected or severe convention fights on the party platform."[3] Still, it is very difficult to identify any long-term result of Hays's policy effort.

The next attempt at a party policy council came in the aftermath of Alf Landon's stunning loss to Franklin D. Roosevelt in 1936. The following year RNC chair John D. Hamilton organized a series of regular weekend conferences with congressional Republicans and national committee staff to discuss issues and develop party strategy. Hamilton also called on the party to hold a midterm convention, but the idea was rejected in favor of establishing a program committee to discuss and develop ideas and policies for the 1940 platform. The head of the committee, Glenn Frank, the former president of the University of Wisconsin, said that the committee intended to offer "an utterly honest and objective audit of the New Deal; to restate and reinterpret" what the Republican party stood for; and to "create a comprehensive report of policy."[4] That report, *A Program for a Dynamic America,* issued in February 1940, criticized the New Deal for profligacy and for giving the federal government too much power. Despite the effort put into it by the party, the Frank Committee's report seems to have had little impact.[5]

The failure of the Frank Committee's report did not stop the Republicans from launching another policy committee in 1943. In May of that year, RNC chair Harrison E. Spangler established the Post-War Advisory Council to develop "a realistic peacetime program for American progress." Like the Frank Committee, the Post-War Advisory Council generated little enthusiasm, though it did seem to help council members Arthur Vandenberg and Thomas Dewey to embrace a more internationalist foreign policy.[6]

None of these efforts by out-parties to formulate policy had much success. No significant party positions emerged from these councils, nor did they attract much attention for the party. These failures seem tied to the nature of the national committees in this era. During the first half of this century, few members of the national committee seemed concerned with policy matters. Instead, the major role of most RNC and DNC members was to help ensure the flow of patronage to the state party. Most committee members were given their positions as honorific rewards for service to the party (often in the form of large donations); even if members were interested in policy, they lacked the stature necessary to influence the national party on such matters.[7]

In addition to the weaknesses of the national committee as a policy-making body, there was often little need for policy development outside the congressional party. Since the national party and the congressional party usually agreed on most major policy issues (or were equally divided over the best course of action) the policy councils were reduced to following the lead of the congressional party or issuing bland statements with which everyone in the party could agree.

DEMOCRATIC PARTY CLEAVAGES AND THE
CREATION OF A POLICY COUNCIL

Unlike its predecessors, the DAC emerged as the result of a unique set of circumstances in which the party's ideological division closely matched the organizational division between the national and the congressional parties. Democratic liberals dominated the national committee, while conservative Democrats controlled the congressional party leadership. Additionally, both factions had very distinct notions about the best course for the party to follow in the aftermath of the 1956 election. The liberals of the party's presidential wing sought a more assertive opposition to the Eisenhower administration while the more conservative congressional wing of the party strove to accommodate the president's agenda as much as possible and minimize differences with the Republican party.

The strategy of the members of the congressional wing stemmed from several factors. One of these was their interpretation of why the Democrats had lost to Eisenhower. The congressional wing, led by Senate majority leader Lyndon B. Johnson and House Speaker Sam Rayburn, both of Texas, pointed to Eisenhower's popularity among the public as the reason for his victory. In Johnson's words, "America loved Ike."[8] Johnson claimed that attacking the popular Eisenhower would backfire on the Democrats since it was "like telling children their father was a bad man."[9]

Given Eisenhower's popularity, Johnson and Rayburn believed that the Democratic party's best course of action was to continue their strategy of "responsible opposition." This plan meant working closely with Eisenhower in a spirit of bipartisan compromise and deferring to his agenda on most issues. After the 1956 election, when asked if the Democrats would put forward a legislative program of their own, Johnson said, "No, we'll wait for the President. We'll support him when he's right and oppose him when he's wrong."[10] This strategy, Johnson claimed, offered the best path for the Democrats to regain the White House: "The American people are tired of wrecking crews. They want builders—people who construct. They will entrust their affairs to the party that is constructive. They will turn their backs on the party that is destructive. . . . If we go forward as positive Americans and not negative oppositionists I am convinced that the time is not too far distant when the Democratic Party will again be in the majority."[11]

While Johnson harbored presidential ambitions for himself and may have legitimately believed that this was the best way for the Democrats to win the White House in 1960, other powerful figures in Congress, particularly those conservative southerners who made up the Senate's "Inner Club," were not as concerned about their party's presidential fortunes.[12] Journalist Sidney Hyman explained the reasons for this: "Since they know that men from their section [the South] have been barred from the Presidency for almost a hundred years, regardless of personal talent, they may well ask themselves why they should fight to install a Democrat in the White House when *they* cannot be that Democrat—and when the waging of such a fight might imperil their local position."[13]

Johnson and Rayburn's strategy also reflected their views on the institutional responsibilities of the president and Congress. Both believed that only the president should set the agenda for the nation. According to Johnson biographer Doris Kearns, "In Johnson's view—which many shared—the Presidency was the only institution in the American system capable of consistently initiating major legislation. . . . Congress itself was not, in his view, equipped with the expertise, the time, or the type of coherent organizational structure needed to formulate and initiate programs of action on a regular and systematically related basis."[14]

Johnson and Rayburn also knew that the Democrats had only nominal control of Congress. Conservative southern Democrats in both houses often crossed the aisle to form a "conservative coalition" with the Republicans to thwart passage of liberal legislation. Not only was liberal legislation unlikely to pass, but Johnson and Rayburn also believed that the attempt further alienated southern conservatives from the national party.[15] Moreover, even if such legislation could make it out of Congress, it would face an almost certain presidential veto. Given these circumstances, both men believed that the only way to pass important legislation was by crafting careful compromises among liberal and conservative Democrats and President Eisenhower.

Johnson and Rayburn saw the results of the 1956 election as the vindication of their strategy, which the party had followed since winning back the Congress in 1954. Despite Adlai Stevenson's weakness at the top of the ticket, Democrats in Congress managed to hold their own against the Republicans. They added to their majorities in both houses by picking up two seats in the House and one in the Senate.

Opposing the strategy of the congressional party was the national or presidential wing of the Democratic party, which wanted the party to take a more assertive and partisan stand on important issues. As with that of the congressional wing, the opposition strategy suggested by the presidential wing resulted from a variety of influences. Most important of these was the changing political and ideological orientation of the presidential wing of the party, which was increasingly dominated by political "amateurs." For many years the strength of the Democratic party lay in its control of party machines in the urban centers of the north and in the traditional Democratic loyalties of the rural South. But by the 1950s, a new breed of amateur Democrats began to gain ascendance in the party. These Democrats were more educated and affluent and were motivated less by patronage or the benefits of local one-party dominance or the need to exclude blacks, than by issues and programs. According to James Q. Wilson: "The amateur is one who finds politics *intrinsically* interesting because it expresses a conception of the public interest. The amateur politician sees the political world more in terms of ideas and principles than in terms of persons. Politics is the determination of public policy, and public policy ought to be set deliberately rather than as the accidental by-product of a struggle for personal and party advantage."[16]

The focal points of the amateur Democrats at the national level were the presidential campaigns of Adlai Stevenson, whose eloquence and seeming commitment to a politics of principle provided both leadership and inspiration to the amateurs. It was with Stevenson and his advisors that the amateurs' desire to establish a deliberative process for the determination of policy first took root. In August 1953, Chester Bowles, former governor of Connecticut, wrote to Stevenson suggesting the need for a more vocal opposition to the Eisenhower administration. Later that month Stevenson responded favorably to the idea and expressed his hope that he could get together with Bowles and George Kennan, former director of the State Department's Office of Policy and Planning and ambassador to the Soviet Union, "for some deliberate talks."[17] In September, Harvard economist and Stevenson advisor, John Kenneth Galbraith wrote Stevenson:

> How can we do the most to keep the Democratic Party intellectually alert and positive during these years in the wilderness? We have all told ourselves that mere opposition is not enough. Yet it is hard at the moment to say what the Democratic Party is for. . . .
>
> This situation, if it is allowed to persist, will be dangerous. It is the disease of opposition parties, for initiative and imagination ordinarily lie with responsibility for action. I adhere to the old-fashioned idea that a party should have a program which the people can then accept or reject.[18]

Galbraith went on to suggest the creation of "some organization in or adjacent to the Democratic Party," led by prominent Democratic politicians and intellectuals, to handle issue development.[19] Stevenson, also concerned about the functions of an opposition party, responded favorably to Galbraith's idea. He wrote: "While in Britain I talked to some old friends in the Labor Party, and was impressed with the fact that they are totally becalmed and have exhausted their program and have no present basic objectives except to stop Bevanism. We may be in the same position, and I emphatically agree that now is the time to start to review what has been done and consider what should be done."[20]

On October 3 and 4, Stevenson, Thomas Finletter, secretary of the air force in the Truman administration, Bowles, and Kennan met at Finletter's Connecticut home, marking the beginning of an informal council of Stevenson advisors devoted to discussing ideas and formulating party policies. The leadership of the group rested with Finletter, who had a long-standing interest in the role of parties in a democracy. In 1945, he wrote *Can Representative Government Do the Job?* which stressed the need for stronger and more responsible parties to help American government meet the demands of the postwar world.[21] According to him, "The idea of a 'cabinet,' an organization in opposition, a shadow organization, was in my mind for a long time. I was always horrified at the party in opposition being unable to find out what the policies were and so on."[22] The problem, to Finletter, was particularly acute in this period because, "The Congressional leaders were not leading."[23] Finletter eventually became a prominent member of the reformist amateur Democrats who battled New York City's Tammany Hall in the late 1950s.[24]

Though the Finletter Group, as this policy roundtable came to be known, eventually formed the basis for the Stevenson campaign in 1956, it was still an informal body with no power to set policy for the Democratic party or to develop an agenda in opposition to the Eisenhower administration. That role was left to the congressional party, and many prominent party liberals thought that the congressional party had failed in this task. Many of these liberals believed that Democratic victories in Congress provided evidence of popular support for the Democratic platform, but this had not helped in the presidential campaign because of the failure of congressional Democrats to forcefully point out Eisenhower's faults or to pass a strong Democratic program that the party could present to the nation.[25] In their mind, Johnson's and Rayburn's strategy of "loyal opposition" had only served to blur the distinction between the parties. According to Herbert Lehman, Democratic senator from New York who retired in 1956:

> By hindsight, the election of 1956 was lost before the campaign began. . . . The mistakes that really hurt were mistakes made in Congress during the three-and-a-half-year period from the beginning of 1953 until the summer of 1956. The Democrats in Congress failed to make the issues during the 18 months we were in control. On the contrary, almost everything the leadership did during that time was designed to prevent any controversial issue from being seriously joined or vigorously debated. On the two main issues of our time—civil rights and foreign policy—there was a virtual blackout.[26]

The "presidential" Democrats believed that future success required the Democrats to more forcefully oppose the Eisenhower administration. After his defeat, Stevenson, the nominal leader of the presidential Democrats, said the Democrats must be vigorous in their opposition, "not opposition for its own sake, but opposition of the utmost vigor when we think they're wrong, and a constant attitude of skepticism to keep them [the Republicans] on their toes and make them prove that they are right."[27]

During the 1956 campaign, Stevenson attempted, without success, to point out what he believed were Eisenhower's foreign policy mistakes.[28] This failure led him to state: "I have become convinced through rather sad experience that real issues cannot be developed, nor even effectively presented, during a political campaign. They must be sharpened and clarified largely through the legislative process between elections."[29]

Stevenson echoed this thought in a letter to Senator Paul Douglas written a few days after the election: "The readiest answer would seem to be a more active opposition role in the Congress for the Democrats."[30] According to James Sundquist, "this meant taking a party position, maintaining it against undue compromise, and carrying it to a showdown in the two houses, where the consequence would be either dramatic victory or dramatic defeat to be appealed to the people at the next election."[31]

But Stevenson and other influential presidential Democrats knew that Johnson and Rayburn's strategy of compromise with Eisenhower made this impossible. Journalist Harrison Salisbury wrote to Stevenson on November 17 that he did not believe "that Lyndon Johnson or . . . any of the Congressional Democratic leaders are either prepared to give the country a lead in foreign policy, see a necessity for a lead or have any . . . inclination to come to grips with the problem."[32]

Salisbury's assessment seems justified. Johnson had already rejected a "Democratic Declaration" proposed by liberal Senators Humphrey, Paul Douglas, Patrick McNamara, Wayne Morse, James Murray, and Richard Neuberger. This declaration called on congressional Democrats to enact a sixteen-point "minimum program of liberal Democratic action," which included a civil rights act, reform of Senate rules to limit filibusters (which southern senators used to kill civil rights bills in that chamber), federal aid to education, aid to depressed areas, and repeal of the Taft-Hartley Act. According to the authors of the declaration, "Some of us who have had an opportunity to exchange ideas during the brief interval since the election feel rather strongly that we as Democrats have a responsibility of presenting a constructive, positive legislative program of our own for the 85th Congress, rather than just waiting to see what President Eisenhower suggests."[33]

Lyndon Johnson refused to support the program. Years later he justified this stand:

> The idea that the congressional Democrats have a responsibility for taking the national Democratic platform and program and trying to push it through the Congress is crazy. A political party at a national convention draws up a program to present to the voters. The voters can either accept it by giving the party full power, reject it by taking the party completely out of power, or give it qualified approval by giving one party the Congress and the other party the Presidency. And when we in Congress have been given a qualified mandate, as we were in 1956, it means that we have a solemn responsibility to cooperate with the President and produce a program that is neither his blueprint nor our blueprint but a combination of the two.[34]

Johnson's rejection of the Democratic Declaration foreclosed the possibility of advancing a liberal agenda through the congressional party and forced liberals of the presidential wing of the party to look to the Democratic National Committee as a vehicle for their efforts. The DNC proved a very suitable body for this task. Unlike the congressional party, which was dominated by rural southerners, the DNC was now controlled by the liberal amateurs of the presidential wing who supported a more aggressive opposition strategy, including the establishment of a party policy council, and who were secure enough in their own influence to be willing to oppose the party's congressional leadership if necessary.[35]

Paul Ziffren, national committeeman from California and a key individual in the establishment of the DAC, typified this new breed of national committee member. Ziffren had become involved in politics during the 1952 Stevenson campaign, and he soon rose to prominence as California's national committeeman and as a leader in the Western States Democratic Conference, a liberal group designed to diminish the influence of conservative southerners in the party.[36] Ziffren believed strongly in the need for programmatic and responsible parties, saying, "the party has to stand for something in order to get volunteers. You have to take a firm stand on the issues or you can't attract the kind of person you want into politics. It can't be a Tweedledum and Tweedledee situation."[37]

For Ziffren, this was true at both the state and national levels. According to journalist Sidney Hyman, at the time the DAC was established, "Ziffren was . . . engaged in trying to rebuild California's Democratic Party. Since this task depended for its success on the zeal of volunteer workers and the voters they could win over, he had reason to fear that both were being alienated by the fact that their attitudes were not reflected in the work done by the Democratic Congressional leaders. What he wanted was a national party organ that could formulate and advance the kinds of policies Californians and others on the West Coast would respond to."[38]

David Lawrence of Pennsylvania, another influential member of the DNC, also supported a party policy council. Once again, according to Hyman: "Since the people for whom he spoke shared many of California's political attitudes, arising from a common concern with the problems of urban growth, Lawrence was Ziffren's natural ally. He did not see how the Middle Atlantic bloc of states could be won for the Democrats in a Presidential election, or even how the Democrats there could win major state elections, if all that the local parties had for the standard of performance was the rural-dominated Democratic congressional record."[39]

The idea of a party council also found an enthusiast in Paul Butler, chairman of the DNC from 1954 to 1960. Unlike most past chairmen who had organized policy councils, Butler had strong views about the role of political parties. One factor in his attitude was the report of the American Political Science Association (APSA) Committee on the Political Parties. The committee's report, issued in 1950 and entitled *Toward a More Responsible Two-Party System,* strongly criticized the existing party system for its decentralized power structures and its inability, particularly with out-parties, to offer coherent and specific policy alternatives to the electorate.[40] The report called for reforms to strengthen the national party organizations and make them more responsible, including the adoption of midterm party conventions and the institution of a party council. The report stressed the need for a party council to help coordinate the national party organization, the congressional party, and if the party controlled the White House, the president. The party council would also be responsible for developing party policy by offering a "preliminary draft of the party platform" and "interpret[ing] the platform in relation to current problems."[41]

Butler seemed to take the report to heart, which is not surprising given his existing attitudes toward parties. As a product of both the strong partisanship of Indiana politics and the intense factionalism of that state's Democratic party, he believed in strong parties, but ones that were motivated by more than just the perquisites of office.[42] Thus, while Butler was not an amateur in the strict sense of the term, he did share this group's views on the role of parties.

At the spring 1953 meeting of the DNC's executive committee, Butler, then a national committeeman from Indiana, proposed the adoption of a midterm convention for 1954, as suggested by the APSA report. The draft of Butler's proposal stressed that a midterm convention would attract widespread attention and allow the party to "formulate a simple, comprehensive statement of party policy" for the upcoming congressional elections.[43] In fact, Butler seemed more concerned with the normative goal of creating a responsible party than with short-term political motivations. In a letter he wrote: "Of course, it would be much easier for a Congressman to run in an off-year election without being tied down to a party platform. A good many of them are not much concerned about the improvement of governmental processes through the development of greater party responsibility to the voters."[44]

Butler's suggestion garnered some support among other DNC members, but the DNC's executive committee, citing the cost of such a convention and existing state party regulations, rejected the proposal. It also seems likely that the opposition of Sam Rayburn and other congressional Democrats helped to kill the idea.[45]

Butler also believed strongly in an activist role for the national committee and its chairman. Where most recent Democratic party chairs saw themselves as mediators among the various institutional, sectional, and ideological factions, Butler believed that as the formal head of the Democratic party he had the responsibility to lead the party. In 1959 he said:

> When a party does not have one of its members in the White House, the national chairman, as head of the political organization, becomes the instrument to communicate to Congress what members of the party in all ranks are thinking.
>
> In the absence of a party member in the White House, the national chairman has a duty to remind all Democrats of our pledges. Party officials have the same responsibility to the public that elected officials have.[46]

After becoming chairman in 1954, Butler put into action his views on party loyalty, party responsibility, and the role of the national committee chairman. In

1955 he made an initial effort to locate policy development within the DNC by establishing a Democratic Advisory Committee on Agriculture, led by former Secretary of Agriculture Claude R. Wickard. Originally intended only to make a nonpartisan survey of agriculture issues, the committee delivered a strong critique of Eisenhower's farm policy and advocated a policy of increasing farm price supports, positions that eventually made their way into the 1956 Democratic platform.[47]

Impressed by the work of the agriculture committee, Butler set up three more policy advisory committees in 1956: labor, led by George M. Harrison, president of the Brotherhood of Railway and Steamship Clerks; small business, co-chaired by Senator John Sparkman and Representative Wright Patman;[48] and natural resources, headed by former Interior Secretary Oscar Chapman. Of these committees, only the Natural Resources Committee appears to have made much of an impact.[49]

Butler, who increasingly disagreed with the accommodationist strategy of Johnson and Rayburn, also began to establish a more assertive and programmatic role for the Democrats. One aspect of this was to strongly criticize Eisenhower, despite most Democrats' reluctance to do so and the objections of the Democratic congressional leadership. One of Butler's associates claimed, "Some criticized even the Pope of Rome, but no one dared criticize Ike—except Paul Butler." In early 1955 Butler also wrote Hubert Humphrey that he was "hopeful that agreement may be reached with leaders on the Hill that it is the duty of the chairman to speak out in front of congressional leaders without their thinking he is trying to embarrass them."[50]

Despite the liberal policy views of Butler, Lawrence, Ziffren, and others on the DNC, the split between the presidential and congressional wings was not wholly ideological. After all, Lyndon Johnson was not Willis Robertson and Sam Rayburn was not John Rankin. The differences between these two wings of the Democratic party also had a procedural component to it; *who* would make party policy and *what* would that policy be? Though people like Stevenson, Humphrey, and Lehman often took positions strongly opposing Johnson and Rayburn on many policy issues, they also believed that they were the real leaders of the Democratic party and deserved the policy-making prerogatives that went with such a position. Charles Tyroler, the DAC's executive director, summed up this attitude when he said that those pushing for a policy council were "Goddamned tired of the presidential wing of the party—the liberal, national-oriented wing of the party, stalwarts of it, who controlled 60 percent of the electoral votes—not being listened to in the off-years. Everybody was listening to Sam and Lyndon. Who were they but a couple of Texas politicians?"[51]

THE CREATION OF THE DAC

Confronted with a reluctant congressional party leadership, liberals of the Democratic party's presidential wing decided to mount an aggressive policy response through the branch of the party that they controlled—the DNC. Led by Paul Ziffren and David Lawrence, the executive committee of the Democratic National Committee on November 27, 1956, passed a resolution supporting the Democratic platform and called for Democrats in Congress to "do all in their power to enact legislation to put the platform into effect as speedily as possible."[52] Lawrence told reporters, "If you have a platform you ought to follow it up with a legislative program, not just throw it out after you are defeated in an election."[53]

More important, the executive committee also authorized DNC chair Paul Butler to form a Democratic Advisory Council "to coordinate and advance efforts in behalf of Democratic programs and principles." The executive committee also stated its hope that the DAC would make "Democratic initiative the order of the day so that we can quickly resume social progress at home and save the situation abroad."[54]

Despite the reluctance of the Democratic congressional leadership to mount an aggressive opposition strategy, many in the DNC still hoped that congressional Democrats might be persuaded to join the DAC. One week after the decision to authorize the council, Butler extended invitations to twenty prominent party leaders. Invited to join the DAC were:

Members at Large—Adlai Stevenson, Harry Truman, Eleanor Roosevelt, Senator Estes Kefauver, House Speaker Sam Rayburn, Senate majority leader Lyndon Johnson, ex-governor John Battle of Virginia, Governor Averell Harriman of New York, Governor G. Mennen Williams of Michigan, Governor Luther Hodges of North Carolina, Governor Ernest McFarland of Arizona, and Mayor Raymond Tucker of St. Louis

House Members—Majority leader John McCormack (Mass.), majority whip Carl Albert (Okla.), Democratic Congressional Campaign Committee chairman Michael Kirwan (Ohio), and Representative Edith Green (Ore.).

Senate Members—Majority whip Mike Mansfield (Mont.), Democratic Senate Campaign Committee chairman George Smathers (Fla.), Hubert Humphrey (Minn.), and John Kennedy (Mass).

In addition to these members, persons serving on the DNC's executive committee would act as ex officio members of the DAC. Butler gave the impression that all who were asked had agreed to serve on the DAC, though there is no evidence to indicate he attempted to discuss the matter with the congressional leadership.[55]

Truman, Stevenson, Harriman, Williams, Humphrey, Kefauver, Green, and Tucker accepted their invitations almost immediately, but the DAC quickly ran into serious opposition from Democratic congressional leaders in spite of Butler's denial that the Council was intended to "straighten up" Congress.[56] Soon after Butler's announcement, Rayburn and Johnson conferred over the telephone. Johnson seems to have been originally in favor of the DAC, but Rayburn apparently turned him against it.[57] On December 3, Johnson sent Rayburn a letter, claiming that the Council "opens up a real hornet's nest."[58] Johnson then outlined several objections to the DAC. Among them, Johnson claimed that the Council made the passage of Democratic legislation even less likely:

> With the present narrow divisions in Congress, it is rare that any bill can be passed without picking up a few Republican votes here and there. The Republicans who will vote for certain types of Democratic legislation . . . are highly unlikely to vote for that legislation when they are told that it was advanced by a committee whose sole objective is to sponsor a Democratic ticket that will elect a Democratic Congress in 1958 and Democratic President in 1960.
>
> [The DAC would] do nothing to compensate for the losses [of Republican votes] by keeping the narrow Democratic majorities in line. It is completely powerless to produce any votes. But it is capable of deepening divisions in the Democratic Party.[59]

On December 8 Rayburn told Butler that he believed the House leadership should not serve on the DAC for "fear if we accept a place on any outside committee that it would make many Democrats think we were consulting with outside people and not with them."[60] The following day he wrote Butler to formally decline joining the DAC, saying that the Democratic House leadership believed that it would be a "mistake . . . to join in any program with any committee outside of the House of Representatives."[61]

A few days later, Rayburn wrote to Butler to again state his reasons for declining membership in the DAC. He communicated his belief that the Council would only cause division between the national and congressional parties and therefore he was "firmly of the opinion that this action of the National Executive Committee can cause more harm to the party than any good that might be accomplished."[62] Upon learning of Rayburn's opposition to the DAC, Representative Green withdrew her acceptance.

Johnson also declined membership, claiming, "Legislative processes are already very difficult and the necessity of dealing with an additional committee not created by Federal law before taking action would only cause delays and confusion."[63] He also told Butler, "I trust your group does not go into too much specifics on legislation."[64] In addition to the practical problems he believed the DAC created, Johnson was also opposed on more normative grounds. To him the DAC's call for party responsibility and principle were potentially harmful to the nation's political order. In his view, "The biggest danger to American stability is the politics of principle, which brings out the masses in irrational fights for unlimited goals, for once the masses begin to move, then the whole thing begins to explode."[65]

Along with and influenced by Johnson, Senators Kennedy, Mansfield, and Smathers declined their invitations. So too did Governors Battle and Hodges. McFarland agreed to join the next May but soon resigned. Mrs. Roosevelt declined full membership, claiming her position as a newspaper columnist prevented her from too closely identifying with a party council, but she agreed to serve as a "consultant" for the DAC.[66]

Butler, however, decided to go ahead with the DAC, even without the support or participation of the party's congressional leadership. On December 18, 1956, he called the first meeting for the following month. He also said the DAC was not an "effort to dictate to the Congress or to encroach upon its powers."[67] He regretted that the congressional leadership had declined membership but said that the DAC would not attempt to find other congressional Democrats to fill the vacant positions. Instead, the Council would rely on Democratic governors and mayors. Butler also said that the Council would help the party by offering "progressive and effective political leadership . . . by a continuing study of the inter-convention problems that are constantly arising and suggesting programs to deal with them."[68]

To help allay the fears of the Democratic congressional leadership, Butler wrote Johnson on December 26 to invite them to meet with the DAC and to further explain the purpose of the Council:

> I regret very much that Mr. Rayburn and you and other Congressional
> leaders believe that the functioning of such an Advisory Committee
> would not be in the best interests of our national Party. I believe that this
> committee can be very helpful to our Party. We have a great chance to
> strengthen our Democratic majorities in both Houses in the Congressional
> elections of 1958. There are many problems confronting our Party on
> which the Democratic National Committee will welcome advice and
> counsel not only from our Congressional leaders but also from our Demo-
> cratic governors and mayors and other important and well-informed
> people within the party.[69]

The DAC met for the first time on January 4, 1957. The council issued a statement claiming that it would enable the Democratic party to "present new programs" on a national basis and to "provide a collective voice for the Democratic Party, representing on a year-round basis the millions of Democrats who may or may not be represented in either House of the Congress."[70] Adlai Stevenson added that in order "to be an effective opposition" the party "must have a broader base than the Democrats in Congress."[71] The next day Butler and the DAC met with

Johnson, Rayburn, and McCormack in a show of party unity, but each side indicated it would go its own way.

Ironically, the absence of conservatives and the congressional leadership from the DAC, seen by many at the time as a damaging, if not fatal, blow to the council's chances of success, meant that it could speak with a more forceful and unified voice, something that earlier policy councils had been unable to achieve. As James Sundquist points out, "Instead of an all-party council, it was virtually an all-northern and -western, all-liberal council. It could and did, thus become exactly what most leaders of the presidential wing of the party had wanted—a clear voice for their 'party' that could state positions different from and, if necessary in defiance of, those of congressional leaders."[72]

The DAC wasted no time in providing this voice. On the day before they met with the congressional leadership, the council issued statements criticizing the Eisenhower administration's foreign policy and calling for the Senate to restrict the use of filibusters by adopting "a new realistic rule to limit unreasonable debate."[73] Later that same day the Senate, including a majority of Democrats, voted down an attempt to do so.[74]

On February 17, one day after the full DNC had ratified the formation of the DAC, the council called for statehood for Alaska and Hawaii and once again criticized President Eisenhower's foreign policy. The DAC also asked Congress to enact voting rights and other civil rights legislation.[75] Moreover, the DNC stated its opposition to the Johnson-Rayburn legislative strategy. In a formal resolution, the DNC declared, "The recent election proves the virtual impossibility to have party policy formulated and generally accepted in the brief period from the opening of the Democratic National Convention to the General Election. We can win in 1960 only if we begin now to hammer out a forceful, coherent policy and to keep communicating it to the public."[76]

The DAC's northern, liberal composition and its early stands on civil rights led to an attempt by southern national committee members to restrain its ability to pronounce party policy. At the May 4 meeting of the DNC, these members sponsored a resolution stating that the DAC would need the approval of the national committee before declaring party policy. The full DNC voted down the measure.[77]

At its May 1957 meeting, the DNC also established eight advisory committees to undertake the principal policy work of the DAC. Set up to address a variety of public policy issues, these committees were led by several prominent former Democratic officials and intellectuals. The most important of these were the foreign policy advisory committee chaired by former Secretary of State Dean Acheson, the economic policy committee led by Harvard economics professor John Kenneth Galbraith, and the civil rights committee headed by Eleanor Roosevelt. Other committees established by the DAC were urban and suburban problems, labor, farm policy, health policy, Social Security, natural resources, and science and technology.

In financial terms, the DAC represented a serious commitment by the Democratic party. During its first half year of operation, the DAC spent almost $18,000 and raised more than $50,000. By its final year in operation, June 1959 to June 1960, the council had a budget of $123,400, roughly 15 percent of the budget of the DNC. Funding for the DAC technically came from the DNC, but, according to Charles Tyroler, the DAC was financially independent of the national committee.[78] The council also held its own fundraisers and was heavily supported by New York City supporters of Adlai Stevenson, led by Tom Finletter.[79] The DAC raised $100,000 at a New York City Birthday Dinner for Eleanor Roosevelt in December 1959. In fact the DAC was on sound enough financial footing to have helped the DNC meet its expenses on a few occasions.[80]

THE DAC AND PARTY POLICY

Over the years many claims have been made regarding the substance of the DAC's work. The conventional interpretation is that the DAC offered a vehicle for advancing a liberal agenda for the Democratic party in the areas of foreign policy, economics, and civil rights. While true to an extent, this interpretation overlooks the variations in policy formulation in each of these three areas. Despite the attempts of many liberals to retrospectively inflate their success at establishing a liberal foreign policy agenda, most of the DAC's foreign policy statements were controlled by Dean Acheson and reflected his hawkish views and personal vendettas. On economic policy, liberals battled with one another over what they believed was the proper course in economic policy. Only in the area of civil rights was there substantial agreement on a clearly liberal agenda.

FOREIGN POLICY

From the very beginning the DAC took a hawkish stand on foreign policy that reflected the views of its chairman and vice-chairman, Dean Acheson and Paul Nitze, respectively. Acheson, as secretary of state under Harry Truman, and Nitze, who served under Acheson as director of the State Department's Policy and Planning Staff, were two of the principal architects of the Truman administration's "containment" policy and arch cold warriors.

Acheson, uncertain of the committee's usefulness, seemed at first reluctant to serve. He wrote to Truman, "What the Committee can do still puzzles me, but then if it doesn't do anything it won't do any harm, which for some Democrats these days is a big achievement."[81]

Despite these initial doubts, Acheson threw himself into the work of the committee, in part because it gave him the public voice he had lacked since the Democrats lost the White House, partly because he saw it as a chance to vindicate the policies he had "created," and partly because he sensed an opportunity to refute the charges that he was soft on communism.[82] But above all Acheson believed that the Democrats had lost the 1956 election for want of a more forceful and detailed foreign policy program. According to him: "In foreign policy at least . . . there was not enough conviction among those directing campaign strategy that the American people are capable of adult thought and should have been told forcefully all that should have been done and of the policy of drift."[83]

The first statement put out by the DAC's foreign policy committee reflected Acheson and Nitze's apocalyptic tone. Issued in late October 1957, the DAC's statement damned the Eisenhower administration for "unilateral disarmament at the expense of our national security" and cost cutting in the face of "startling Soviet advances in military capability," concluding, "there is no cheap or easy road to security in the Nuclear Age."[84]

In another statement the following month, the DAC made its first full response to the Soviets' launching of their Sputnik satellite. The Soviets' ability to orbit a satellite well before the United States deeply shook American confidence in its educational, scientific, and military capabilities. Many also saw Sputnik as evidence of a Soviet lead in the development of intercontinental ballistic missiles (ICBMs) and therefore a serious threat to the United States's nuclear deterrent.[85] According to the DAC, "The superiority of the United States in air atomic strength . . . is rapidly being lost. . . . The Russians are ahead in the means of delivery of the future, the intercontinental ballistic missile, and it is plain to everyone that the Russians are well ahead of us in the race to conquer outer space."[86]

Not to put too fine a point on it, the statement went on to say, "The problems we face are the most momentous in our history. They are not merely military problems. It is a question of survival." To meet this challenge the DAC called for an "all-out effort" to reestablish its military and technological superiority over the Russians. Only deep into its document did the DAC try to strike a less militaristic tone: "It must be made plain that it is United States policy that all our armaments are intended only as a shield to prevent war. . . . Unfortunately, this shield is necessary for there is no evidence that the Russians have given up their purpose of world conquest. Nevertheless, the United States must never give up working for peace."[87]

This hawkish tone continued in ensuing foreign policy statements and documents put out by the DAC. These pronouncements spoke of America's "present danger,"[88] "our decline in military power,"[89] and Russian "superiority" in strategic weapons, including a three to one lead in ICBMs.[90]

To meet these dangers, the DAC usually avoided specifics, but called for increased conventional forces to provide more options than the Eisenhower administration's policy of "massive retaliation." "Massive retaliation" or the "New Look," called for the United States to threaten to use nuclear weapons in local conflicts in order to avoid the expense in dollars and lives of fighting limited conventional wars like that in Korea. To Acheson and others on the DAC, such a policy was folly, especially in light of America's allegedly lessened nuclear superiority over the Soviets. The DAC also endorsed a "crash effort to bridge the 'missile gap'" with the Soviets. The council estimated that its recommendations would add $7.5 billion dollars to the defense budget, an increase of approximately 15 percent.[91]

The belligerent tone of the DAC's foreign policy statements partially obscures the division among the members of the foreign policy committee. Many of the committee members believed that Acheson was, according to John Kenneth Galbraith, trying to "out-Dulles John Foster Dulles."[92] Galbraith, Stevenson, Chester Bowles, Herbert Lehman, and Averell Harriman tried to tone down the more extreme positions taken by Acheson and Nitze. In conversations with Arthur Schlesinger, Jr., and Galbraith, Stevenson expressed concern with Acheson's "saber-rattling."[93] Averell Harriman, who possessed cold warrior credentials second to none, seems to have made the most direct efforts to challenge Acheson. At one meeting of the DAC, he asked Acheson, "Dean, do you want to declare war on the Russians?"[94]

Those who challenged Acheson's hard line would later claim great success for their efforts.[95] According to Harriman, "We knocked Acheson out. The DAC kept the Democratic Party liberal. I took the lead in saying the rough things to Acheson that had to be said."[96] This seems hardly possible. First, the disagreements between Acheson and the liberals were more rhetorical than substantive. Almost no one in the Democratic party questioned the need for a military buildup. Also, if the bellicose foreign policy statements issued by the DAC were "toned down," then it is difficult to imagine what the original versions were like. Only in one pamphlet on foreign aid, which was not issued until 1960, did the DAC sound less militarist, but even here, increased economic assistance for developing nations was justified in the Cold War terms of stopping communist expansion in the Third World.[97]

While not successful in restraining Acheson's cold war rhetoric on the foreign policy committee, the more liberal members of the DAC did succeed in developing alternative foreign policy programs through other parts of the council. One of these was the DAC's administrative committee, led by Paul Butler with Charles Murphy, Tom Finletter, Philip Perlman, and Henry Fowler as members. In August 1959, the committee issued a statement blasting the Eisenhower administration for attempting to bypass the United Nations in arms control talks with the Soviets and called for a disarmament commission that would "give representation to the peoples of Asia, Africa, and Latin America."[98]

Another outlet for liberal foreign policy views on the DAC was the Advisory Committee on Science and Technology, led by Dr. Ernest C. Pollard, a Yale University biophysicist. In 1959 and 1960, the DAC issued a series of pamphlets prepared by this committee which spoke forcefully of the dangers posed by nuclear weapons. According to these documents, "a superarms race takes humanity on a course beset with calamitous pitfalls, unsightly detours and genocidal *cul-de-sacs*. . . . Security in the long run requires that there be a universal reduction and control of the methods of widescale destruction."[99] To meet this goal, the committee advocated negotiating bans on testing missiles and nuclear weapons, establishing a National Peace Agency to work for arms agreements, and using science and technology for the advancement of underdeveloped nations.[100]

The DAC's foreign policy pronouncements accomplished several purposes. First, they helped dispel public notions, prominent during the McCarthy Era, that the Democrats were soft on communism. Even one of the most dovish of 1950s Democrats, John Kenneth Galbraith, concedes that Acheson's polemics kept the Democrats safe from these charges in the 1960 election.[101] Further, by forcefully criticizing the Eisenhower administration's foreign policy, the DAC helped build a public case that Republicans, not Democrats, had harmed the national security. Certainly this effort was greatly assisted by the launching of Sputnik and the consequent charges of a "missile gap," but the DAC's activities helped to further publicize these issues and give them a partisan component. Finally, the efforts of some liberals on the DAC to emphasize diplomacy, economic aid, and arms control over military responses kept the party from appearing too belligerent. By doing so, the Democrats could claim, with some justification, that theirs was the party of "peace through strength," a popular electoral position, especially in the late 1950s and early 1960s.[102]

ECONOMIC POLICY

When it came to criticizing the economic policies of the Eisenhower administration, most liberal Democrats agreed that one of the major reasons Stevenson had lost the election was because Eisenhower had won on the issue of prosperity, in part because conservative Democrats in Congress had failed to present a strong liberal, Democratic alternative. Consequently, those on the DAC believed that the party had to make a much more forceful case that Eisenhower's policies were hampering prosperity and that the Democrats' economic proposals would not only invigorate the economy but also provide a more equitable division of its rewards.

Although Democratic liberals agreed on the retrograde nature of Ike's economics, they were not of one mind when it came to formulating an alternative economic policy for their party. One school of thought, led by Leon Keyserling, chairman of the Council of Economic Advisors under Truman, advocated a vigorous growth strategy. The American economy, in Keyserling's view, was operating well below its full capacity because of Eisenhower's insistence on a tight monetary policy and conservative budgets. Keyserling believed that the economy could and should be growing at a rate of at least 5 percent, instead of the 2 or 3 percent average of the Eisenhower years. Beginning in late 1957 and through the recession of 1958, the DAC adopted Keyserling's position.[103] In its first substantive comment on economic matters, the DAC declared: "The first need now is to resume growth—

to get production rising again. Republican policy has stopped expansion. It has made men, plant, and machinery idle. This disease must be arrested before it gets worse. . . . We are committed unequivocally to the principle of a vigorously expanding economy."[104]

The recipe for achieving this growth, according to Keyserling, was for the federal government to follow an expansionary fiscal policy. The DAC echoed this line in December 1958: "Government expenditures, keyed to our vital needs and resource capabilities, are in themselves a key factor in maximum economic growth. Conversely, maximum economic growth is essential to support the necessary level of vital government expenditures."[105]

More specifically, the DAC called for a number of measures to pull the nation out of recession and guide it back onto the path of robust economic growth. It advocated a looser monetary policy by the Federal Reserve and up to an additional $4 billion a year in government spending. Such spending would include increasing the defense budget; allocating $1 billion for school construction and equipment; doubling funds for urban renewal, public housing, and hospital construction; increasing by one-third spending on public works; extending and liberalizing unemployment compensation, and increasing Social Security benefits. The DAC also suggested reducing taxes, especially for the poor and middle class.[106]

Keyserling's views had great appeal for many DAC members, even (or perhaps especially) the foreign policy hawks like Acheson. Not only would they assure prosperity, they would also help to provide the resources for expanded defense spending and the social programs that had been the political bread and butter of the Democratic party since the New Deal. In addition, all of this could be done without requiring the unpopular measures of large deficits or higher taxes. According to historian Iwan Morgan:

> Keyserling claimed that bigger federal budgets could boost annual economic growth to 5 percent without necessitating a long series of deficits. Improved provision for national security and for domestic programs like education, social security, health care, urban renewal, farm income support, highways and natural resource development contributed directly to economic expansion, whether by strengthening the infrastructure of the economy, creating new jobs or increasing individual spending power. In turn, growth-inducing budgets would help to generate the revenue necessary to sustain the continued expansion of defense and domestic expenditure.[107]

The DAC spelled out this plan in early 1958 in a document entitled, "Can America Afford Increased Federal Expenditures for Essential National Purposes?" According to this report, prepared by Henry Fowler, former director of defense mobilization, "a substantial increase in national security programs is possible without interfering with some expansion in productive capacity and some increase in the per capita supply of consumer goods." By inducing a higher rate of economic growth, the report predicted that the share of GNP going to defense could be increased from 10 to 12 percent, without taking anything away from other government programs or increasing taxes.[108]

Not all members of the DAC's economic policy committee agreed with Keyserling's rosy views. Led by John Kenneth Galbraith, chair of the committee, this group insisted that the fundamental economic question was distribution, not growth. For Galbraith and his supporters, most Americans already had the ability to provide for their basic individual economic needs. Further growth would only divert more resources to the consumption of consumer goods. While favoring higher government expenditures, Galbraith favored tax increases so that resources could "be reallocated from the private sector to public services like schools, parks, public safety, hospitals, libraries, slum clearance, natural resource development, environmental protection and scientific research."[109]

The controversy began to take shape in series of letters between Galbraith and Keyserling in the spring of 1958. After a meeting of the Advisory Committee on Economic Policy, Galbraith wrote Keyserling on April 15 to voice his objections to the "growth strategy." Galbraith wrote:

> The emphasis on growth is important, but it tends to be indiscriminate. It almost automatically excludes consideration of the things of which the growth consists. When we examine these things, we find that they contain a great many products from the much maligned tailfins to the deadfalls [casinos] at Las Vegas which have very little to do with national strength or well-being. Indeed, we find that the demand for a great many of these goods only exists if it is elaborately contrived. I have come to the conclusion that growth *qua* growth is not terribly important. . . .
>
> I am deeply persuaded that we must devise some way to effect the massive shifts from the kinds of products of which we are not in urgent need to the kind of which we *are* in great need.[110]

Keyserling replied that he believed Galbraith was ignoring the means necessary to achieve the social ends he desired: "I do not see how anyone can believe that the public or the Government can be brought to accept the specific programs that we ought to have, without being shown how we can pay for them out of our growing resources, how one need can be reconciled with another need, and how the entirety represents a rational program rather than a series of disconnected pies in the sky."[111]

Keyserling's impatience with those opposed to his views apparently reached a breaking point following the April 11, 1958, meeting of the Economic Advisory Committee. On April 30 he sent a lengthy letter to Paul Ziffren blasting Galbraith's views. Keyserling wrote that by ignoring the necessity of economic growth, Galbraith and others on the committee were guilty of "economic irresponsibility" and that it was an "economic truism, derived from all of our history that the problem of economic growth, of maximum employment, and of meeting our great national priorities of need, are inseparably intertwined."[112] Keyserling continued: "From the viewpoint of political strategy, I should hate to think that the Democratic Party might label itself as primarily interested in the distribution of wealth and product, rather than as the Party which stresses that the meaning of our economic and political system involves the bright prospect of balanced progress for all groups, if only we have the brains to *expand* our national wealth and progress at a pace consistent with our capabilities".[113]

Keyserling added that such a strategy was even more dangerous since the Republicans might preempt the Democrats by calling for expanded economic growth. He pointed out that the Rockefeller Foundation had issued a recent report echoing many of his ideas and that Vice-President Richard Nixon, the likely Republican presidential candidate in 1960, had endorsed the report's conclusions.

Though the Keyserling-Galbraith debate continued to reverberate in intellectual circles, economic developments caused the DAC to shift its focus.[114] As the nation climbed out of the 1958 recession, many on the Economic Advisory Committee began to worry that Keyserling's growth strategy, with its emphasis on full employment and deficit spending, was inherently inflationary. Again, Galbraith led the charge against Keyserling, for Galbraith believed that high inflation discriminated most heavily against the types of public services he believed needed nurturing. In his view, Keyserling's strategy of increasing public and private demand would almost certainly trigger higher inflation.[115]

Keyserling discounted the inflationary effects of his policies. In his view, inflation came about when the economy was growing too rapidly, as in World War II, or when it was sluggish, as from 1952 to 1958. Keyserling believed that in an expanding economy, with strictly enforced antitrust laws, businesses would not need to raise prices to assure themselves of healthy profits.[116]

Keyserling, who did not have a doctorate, had spoken what amounted to economic heresy and his views were roundly dismissed by the professional economists on the Advisory Committee.[117] Moreover, political developments made Keyserling's big budget policies seem less acceptable. Following the staggering Republican losses in the 1958 elections, Eisenhower successfully took to the stump to paint the Democrats as inflationary big "spenders," in order to stymie attempts by Congress to increase the budget.[118]

In late 1959 and 1960, the worries about inflation and Eisenhower's political attacks forced the DAC to take a politically safer approach to expanding the economy than the increased spending advocated by Keyserling. The council sought to emphasize a looser monetary policy, which would help stimulate the economy but did not carry the same inflationary stigma of spending increases. Keyserling persisted in his attempts to have the DAC adopt his expansionary fiscal policies at an

April 1960 council meeting to discuss its recommendations for the Democratic platform. But supporters of Senator John F. Kennedy, the likely Democratic nominee, worried that Keyserling's views were too controversial. Charles Tyroler claims that Keyserling had become "a broken record," demanding "'more spending, more spending, more spending' by everybody."[119] Galbraith recruited Yale economist James Tobin to develop a report for the meeting criticizing the Keyserling strategy for leading to inflation and higher deficits. According to Morgan, "Armed with this ammunition, Kennedy supporters were able to persuade the DAC to reject Keyserling's statement."[120]

Despite the DAC's final rejection of Leon Keyserling's economic views, the council did help the Democratic party to develop a position in favor of higher economic growth, though there still existed some debate over how best to achieve this growth. Such a position was popular in both the 1958 and 1960 elections when recessions focused public attention on the nation's economic problems. A growth strategy also allowed the Democrats to provide a means for paying for the higher defense and social expenditures that they and many in the public wanted. In short, the work of the DAC in economic policy helped the Democrats, according to Morgan, discover "a politically effective response to Eisenhower's claim that budgetary restraint was essential for the nation's interests."[121]

CIVIL RIGHTS

One of the least contested areas in the DAC was civil rights. Two factors account for this. One is the absence of strong congressional or southern representation on the DAC. Another is the development after 1956 of a rather coherent attitude among Democratic liberals that a more aggressive civil rights policy was in the best political interest of the party.

Prior to 1956 Democratic liberals were divided on civil rights questions. Some, particularly those associated with Americans for Democratic Action (ADA), had long sought to move the party into a more progressive policy toward race. Others, led by Adlai Stevenson, counseled moderation and patience toward the South. During both his presidential campaigns, Stevenson was viewed as a moderate on race issues.[122] Eleanor Roosevelt summed up the attitude of many liberal Democrats in a letter to Stevenson during the 1956 Democratic presidential primaries: "Somehow I think understanding and sympathy for the white people in the South is as important as understanding and sympathy and support for the colored people. We don't want another war between the states."[123]

This attitude began to change in 1956. One factor was the South's growing intransigence toward any attempt to comply with the Supreme Court's 1954 school desegregation decision in *Brown* v. *Board of Education*. In the spring of 1956, all but three southern senators (Johnson, Kefauver, and Albert Gore of Tennessee) and approximately eighty southern House members signed the "Southern Manifesto" calling for opposition to desegregation. The manifesto raised serious doubt among liberals concerning the effectiveness of a moderate course on civil rights.[124]

A second factor contributing to the liberal shift on civil rights was the meager results gained from the moderate strategy in the 1956 election. Before the election, Hubert Humphrey wrote to warn Paul Butler of the risk the Democrats faced by going too slow on civil rights:

> unless we do something constructive and take a firm forward step our party is going to suffer at the ballot boxes, and it should. The Negro voters in the Northern cities are getting sick and tired of being promised advances in the field of civil rights through the legislative process, and receiving none. . . . Our Republican friends know they are not going to get votes in the South, so they're pushing hard for voters in the North—and I think they are making progress in the cities. . . . I am confident that the trend away from our party in the Negro population will be even greater in 1956, unless we do something.[125]

For all their efforts at holding the South in the party, the Democrats still managed to lose Texas, Louisiana, Tennessee, Virginia, and Florida to Eisenhower. Additionally, some liberal Democrats began to believe that their attempts at moderation cost them more votes among blacks than they gained among southern whites. In 1956 Eisenhower received 39 percent of the black vote, the highest of any Republican candidate in over thirty years.[126] In the black wards of many southern cities, the Republican vote jumped between 13 and 54 percentage points over 1952. These gains among blacks seem to have provided the margin of difference in Tennessee, Kentucky, and Louisiana.[127]

As a consequence of these results, many Democratic liberals began to reassess the political benefits of civil rights moderation. John Kennedy reportedly claimed that the Democrats had lost the 1956 election because of "the compromises of his party on civil rights."[128] Paul Butler took a similar view of the election.[129] A letter from Stevenson aide Newton Minow to James Rowe, Jr., an advisor to Lyndon Johnson, summed up the liberals' frustration: "What good is it to win Senator Eastland's state [Mississippi] and take a beating in all of the Northern big states? More and more Northerners are now convinced that the price the party pays for the Southern extremists has become too high, even during a period of inflation."[130]

Faced with a congressional party that was unresponsive or hostile to civil rights measures, liberal Democrats looked to the DAC as a vehicle for expressing their views. The first policy pronouncement of the DAC called for revising Senate Rule 22, which required a two-thirds majority to end a filibuster—a favorite tactic of the southern segregationists.[131]

The willingness and ability of Lyndon Johnson to steer a moderate civil rights bill through Congress in 1957 did not prevent party liberals from continuing to act through the DAC. In fact, most liberals saw the passage of the 1957 bill as further incentive for the party to take a more vocal position on racial issues. They believed that the bill would lead to a large increase in black voter registration in the South, which would help to balance out any defections by southern whites.[132]

The first indication of DAC's intention to speak out on civil rights came during the Little Rock School Crisis in September 1957, when the Democratic governor of Arkansas, Orval Faubus, decided to thwart the federal court-ordered desegregation of Little Rock's Central High School by calling out the state's National Guard. Faced with a constitutional crisis, President Eisenhower refused to act publicly. Instead, he attempted to negotiate a private settlement with Faubus.[133]

In response to Eisenhower's inaction, the DAC issued a sharply worded statement on September 15 criticizing both him and Faubus.[134] The DAC's action received prominent attention in the media, including front page coverage in the *New York Times*.[135] In its statement, the DAC said:

> The statements which have followed the meeting between President Eisenhower and Governor Faubus are disappointing to all Americans who believe that respect for the law of the land must be paramount.
>
> . . . it is apparent to all that President Eisenhower has failed in his duty to make the principle clear to all of the country that the first responsibility of a Governor is to uphold the Federal Constitution and that Governor Faubus should be using his powers to uphold the orders of the courts instead of using them to bar the Negro students and thereby thwart the law.
>
> President Eisenhower has lost an opportunity to exert leadership on behalf of law and order. He has failed to use the prestige and power of his office to rally the moral force of the country against the defiance of law.
>
> It need hardly be said that the action of Governor Faubus does not represent the position or policy of the Democratic Party.[136]

Governor Faubus's refusal to comply with the desegregation order compelled President Eisenhower to send in federal troops to enforce the court's order. Eisenhower's decision made liberals on the DAC even more inclined to speak out on civil rights. They feared that by sending in the troops, Eisenhower and the Republican party would be seen as the defenders of civil rights and desegregation and that the Democrats would be identified with segregationists like Faubus.[137] As a result, the DAC issued a statement on October 20, charging that Ike's failure "to take an early and firm position" in favor of the desegregation order had caused the crisis. It went on to criticize Eisenhower for inaction in appointing officials to carry out the 1957 Civil Rights Act.[138]

Throughout the next three years the DAC continued to hammer away on civil rights. Typical of the DAC's statements on this issue was one issued in June 1959:

"Questions of civil rights continue to grip the thoughts and emotions of the American people as few issues in our time. It is crucial to the preservation of our democracy and to maintaining our position before the world that these problems be solved so as to secure to all our citizens the full enjoyment of their human rights. . . . Legislation needed now includes provisions for assistance to the States in the transition to desegregated schools and provisions to strengthen the Federal protection of Civil Rights generally."[139]

In March 1960 the DAC recommended that Congress should enact the following "minimum program" on civil rights:

1. Demand conscientious enforcement of existing criminal laws and use of Congressionally-granted civil powers.

2. Place the national legislative branch squarely on record as opposed to racial segregation in public schools on the firm ground that such segregation is a clear violation of the Constitution and laws of the United States.

3. Recognize the right of a person in Federal or State custody to protection by Federal authorities from physical injury or death.

4. Enact additional laws to protect . . . the rights of American citizens to register and vote free of discrimination based on race, color, religion, or national origin.[140]

In addition to such policy recommendations, the DAC also criticized the Eisenhower administration for not doing enough in civil rights. In April 1960, the council claimed, "Presidential leadership [in civil rights] has been totally lacking since 1953." It went on to add a more personal criticism: "We have had too much experience with a Chief Executive who seems to have prided himself on the fact that no one knows how he really feels about racial discrimination. Platitudes about the minds and hearts of men are not enough. Action and positive leadership are required."[141]

Despite the DAC's strong stand on civil rights, some Democratic liberals were still concerned that the party was doing too little. Herbert Lehman and Eleanor Roosevelt were among those especially disappointed in the DAC's performance. According to Charles Tyroler, "At the end of most meetings, Lehman would say, 'Mr. Chairman, one thing we need is a good strong stand on civil rights.' And everybody would cringe. Not because they opposed civil rights, but because they didn't want to beat the issue to death."[142]

Still, there seems to be little evidence to support the claim that the DAC did little of distinction in the area of civil rights.[143] Beginning with the council's statements on the Little Rock Crisis, the DAC helped the Democratic party to identify itself in the public mind with a liberal stand on civil rights. According to Samuel

Brightman, DNC press secretary during the late 1950s, "At the time of the Little Rock school crisis, there was nobody in Congress who was getting any headlines or anybody saying that the Democratic Party was in favor of integration, which was going to be pretty important in the '58 election, until the Democratic Advisory Council put out a statement."[144]

Later statements by the council also helped to move the party away from moderation on racial issues. Though the 1960 Democratic platform, as James Sundquist points out, went further on civil rights than the DAC had advocated, the council still played an important role in making such a stand acceptable, even required, by the party.[145] It therefore seems accurate to agree with one historian's assessment that the civil rights plank of 1960 "was a remarkable tribute to the DAC."[146]

ASSESSING THE RESPONSE

The Democratic party's actions following its defeat in the 1956 election represent a clear example of a policy response. In the immediate aftermath of the election, members of the national party were remarkably consistent in attributing Stevenson's loss to the lack of vigorous policy action by the party, and there was little or no discussion about anything other than a policy response. For Democrats in and around the DNC, the choice was clear—victory in 1960 would come only if the party developed and articulated a strong and clear partisan agenda.

This does not mean that the Democrats did not engage in any procedural or organizational activity between 1956 and 1960. During this time the DNC undertook the "People Predictor" or the Simulmatics Project. Developed by political scientists Ithiel de Sola Pool, Robert Abelson, and William McPhee, the Simulmatics Project used computerized analysis of polling data. Through their connections to various supporters of the DAC, Pool, Abelson, and McPhee managed to interest the DNC in supporting the project. Eventually, the Kennedy campaign made use of various types of polling data produced and analyzed by the Simulmatics Project. All in all, the Simulmatics Project represents one of the first efforts by a national committee to develop and use sophisticated polling data and computerized analysis.[147]

Another example of organizational activity in this period was the Advisory Committee on Political Organization (ACPO), led by Michigan state chair Neil Staebler, which attempted a few organizational innovations. One of these was the creation in 1957 of a Division of Political Organization in the DNC, consisting of six regional representatives who would work with state and county central committees. The Division of Political Organization also undertook various programs to recruit, educate, and train party leaders and volunteers. Other reforms attempted by the ACPO were the Dollars for Democrats dinners and Democratic Party Nights fundraising schemes.[148]

Despite these organizational activities, it would be a great overstatement to say that the Democrats initiated an organizational response in addition to the policy response of the DAC. First, the efforts of the ACPO began in 1955, and its work after the 1956 election represents continuing activity on the part of the DNC rather than a deliberate response to losing the White House. Second, the efforts of the ACPO and the Simulmatics Project pale in comparison to those of the DAC. Moreover, the attention paid the DAC, by the DNC, the press, and the public, far exceeds the attention granted these two activities. Indeed, few of those active in party affairs at the time even recall either the ACPO or the Simulmatics Project. Finally, though the Democrats managed to eke out a narrow victory in 1960, no one has ever attributed this to these organizational activities.

As mentioned earlier, the creation of the DAC also had a procedural component to it, as party liberals, policy differences with Congress aside, sought to assert their leadership within the party. Still, it is impossible to portray the DAC as merely the instrument of a procedural struggle. The differences between the congressional and presidential wings of the party were clear and substantial, and the liberals who created the DAC used it primarily to build and publicize a liberal program for the Democratic party that often differed sharply with the congressional leadership.

What impact did the Democrats' policy response have? One important effect was the ability of the national party organization, represented by the DAC, to influence the development of a Democratic legislative program. As James Sundquist points out, the DAC did not do this alone, but rather in conjunction with liberals in the House and the Senate: "What emerges from a study of Democratic program development in the 1953–60 period is a picture of block-by-block building under the leadership of those making up the activist triangle in the Senate, the House and the Democratic Advisory Council."[149]

Sundquist adds that the DAC was most effective in this process when the normal legislative channels were blocked by southern committee chairmen or the Democratic leadership. Again, Sundquist says, "When the issue could not be forced to a vote, the Democratic Advisory Council, with its national prestige and its official grant of party authority, acted as a legitimating body."[150]

The DAC was not successful in getting many of its proposals passed through Congress and enacted into law, even after the Democratic victories of 1958, due to factional disputes among congressional Democrats and the opposition of President Eisenhower. Despite the lack of short-term success, the DAC did help to make many of these proposals a part of the Democratic agenda and to help ensure their passage during the New Frontier–Great Society Era. Moreover, the DAC served as a training ground and showcase for many of the Democrats who would become important figures in the Kennedy and Johnson administrations.[151] One account claims that nearly one-third of the DAC's participants took positions in the Kennedy administration.[152]

In addition to developing a legislative program and providing training for future Democratic officials, the DAC also gave the presidential wing of the party a high-profile organization for publicizing their views and making them seem, in the public mind, those of the whole party. Most major newspapers gave DAC documents and pronouncement prominent coverage. Following a series of council statements in October 1957, DAC Executive Director Charles Tyroler wrote to Averell Harriman that the council

> had achieved "saturation" coverage in the nation's press. Only a *major* policy statement by the President does as well. . . . News stories on the Council's statements were carried on the front page of virtually every major paper in the United States and . . . well over 75% of the smaller papers also gave them front page attention.
>   Banner front page headlines were frequent. . . .
>   Over 2200 separate new story, editorial and columnist clippings resulted from the meeting. This is a nation-wide average of over 3-1/2 stories per paper.[153]

Even the *New York Times'* Arthur Krock, a critic of the DAC, conceded that the council had a "monopoly of the political publicity market . . . because the national prominence of these citizens [the DAC members] effects widespread and generous use by the newspapers of excerpts, and often the full texts, of the long papers issued under their imprimatur."[154]

Not only did the DAC receive much press attention, but newspapers often described the council in prestigious terms: "the Democratic Party high command," "the policy makers of the Democratic Party," or, "the agency that is the spokesman for the National Democratic Party."[155] Although the DAC had official status as the policy-making body of the DNC, such status usually means very little. But by describing the DAC in such formal terms, the media undoubtedly helped to persuade the public that the DAC spoke for the whole party.

What did this public image amount to? As mentioned previously, by 1960 the Democrats could claim, and were seen by many, to be a party of "peace through strength," increased economic growth, and civil rights progress. Additionally, the DAC also helped to paint the Republicans as the party responsible for a sluggish economy, lethargy in national security, and indifference to civil rights. In his presidential campaign, John F. Kennedy successfully packaged all of these positions together into his call to "get America moving again."

It is, of course, impossible to determine the exact impact of various factors on the outcome of an election, especially for an election that was as narrowly decided as that of 1960. As is to be expected, many of those associated with the DAC claim that its efforts provided Democrats with the margin of victory in 1960. Others, such as historian Herbert Parmet, argue that the DAC had little impact on the attitudes of voters, which were shaped in response to Sputnik and the economy.[156] Another assessment of the DAC asserts that it was part of an unsuccessful and divisive attempt by Paul Butler to reconstitute the Democrats as a "responsible" party.[157]

Each of these assessments contain an element of truth, but none is completely accurate. Without Sputnik and the 1958 recession, the public would have been much less receptive to the DAC's criticisms of Eisenhower and the Republicans, but the council did help the Democrats to use these issues for partisan gain. It would also be hard to argue that the DAC did not further the division in the party between liberals and conservatives and between its presidential and congressional wings. But the sources of this division existed before and after the existence of the DAC, and it hardly seems likely that the Democrats would have been unified in the late 1950s if the council had not been created. The DAC did not win the election for Kennedy, but it did help the party to formulate what was ultimately a successful agenda for the 1960 campaign. Orville Freeman, former governor of Minnesota and a DAC member, is probably accurate in believing that the DAC contributed to "building momentum" for the party's success in 1960.[158]

Why did the DAC succeed when previous party councils had not? The most important reason for this was the unique set of circumstances that influenced the creation and operation of the DAC. In 1956 the ideological division between party liberals and conservatives mirrored the organizational division between the national and congressional parties. This meant that Democratic liberals could not rely on the congressional party, which they did not control, and were instead forced to rely on the national committee, which they dominated.

In any other circumstance it seems doubtful that a party council could have succeeded. If the DNC had been divided between liberals and conservatives, it seems unlikely that it could have developed a successful party council. Even if a divided national committee could have agreed to establish a party council, it seems likely that such a body would have been forced to issue only bland statements of general agreement. Also, if the congressional leadership had been in agreement with the national committee, the DNC would most probably have left the task of policy development to congressional Democrats, since most liberal Democrats believed that the congressional party was usually the best place for the party to develop its policy program.

One must, however, be careful not to overemphasize the success of the DAC. Though its does seem to have aided the Democratic party in the 1960 election and helped the party to develop the agenda that eventually became the New Frontier and the Great Society, it is also possible that the DNC's policy orientation weakened the party in the long run. One possible implication of the DNC's emphasizing policy to the exclusion of organization and procedure was that it failed to develop the organizational strength and autonomy that would have made it better able to resist the organizational decline that they suffered in the 1960s—a decline that, as we shall see in subsequent chapters, hampered the party through the 1980s.

3

THE REPUBLICANS,

1960–1964

Richard Nixon's loss in the 1960 election occurred in the context of the Republican party's worst factional struggle since 1912. In the immediate aftermath of the defeat, Republican liberals and moderates held sway and began to formulate plans to help the party regain its organizational strength in the urban North. This strategy, however, was never fully implemented, for conservatives soon gained ascendance in the party and succeeded in diverting the RNC's organizational efforts from a big city strategy to a southern strategy. Though the successful development of this southern strategy would have further weakened the already declining position of Republican liberals and moderates, these groups, so focused upon organizational politics, failed to consider, let alone attempted to implement, a procedural response that might have increased their voice within the party.

REPUBLICAN FACTIONALISM

Though usually considered much more homogeneous and cohesive than the Democrats, the Republican party has a long history of factional conflicts. These struggles have been as much sectional and cultural as ideological. The party's devastation at the hands of Franklin Roosevelt in the 1930s caused a renewed dispute between Republican factions. On the one side were moderate to liberal Republicans, mostly from the East, who supported an internationalist foreign policy and most aspects of the New Deal. Many in this wing of the party were identified with the business and financial interests of New York City and Wall Street. On the other side were the Republican conservatives, or "Old Guard." Most in this group bitterly opposed the New Deal and advocated the continuation of an isolationist foreign policy. This faction found its home in the Midwest and the Plains states and among small and medium-sized businessmen outside the corporate circles of the East Coast.

Republican moderates managed to control the party's presidential nominations during the 1940s and 1950s by stressing the unelectability of a conservative nominee. In their view, since the Republicans were the minority party, only a moderate candidate who would attract the votes of independents and wavering Democrats could possibly win the White House.

Although many Republican conservatives opposed this strategy as an abandonment of party principles, President Eisenhower, as a sitting Republican president and World War II hero, was able to mediate most issues. Additionally, Eisenhower never made a serious attempt to recast the GOP in his own image of "Modern (read moderate) Republicanism."

This uneasy truce continued through the 1960 campaign. Richard M. Nixon, Eisenhower's vice-president and the Republican nominee in 1960, had long served as a bridge between both party factions. His pragmatic views on domestic issues and support for NATO made him acceptable to party moderates, while his strong anticommunist record won the approval of conservative Republicans.[1]

This truce, however, could not last. Following Nixon's defeat, the party became increasingly polarized. The Republican conservatives, led by Arizona Senator Barry Goldwater, opposed nearly every aspect of the New Deal, supported a militant American foreign policy (particularly in Asia), and were unremitting in their efforts to eliminate domestic communism. According to James Reichley, many of these conservatives were former Democrats from the South and the West who were intensely conservative on economic and social issues, but whose fear and loathing of communism led them to favor an interventionist rather than an isolationist approach to foreign policy.[2]

On the other side were the Republican liberals and moderates, led by New York governor Nelson Rockefeller. This faction supported civil rights, most social welfare policies, and an internationalist foreign policy. They differed from the Democrats in promoting closer cooperation between government and business, stressing the need for sound administration of government programs, and advocating a tougher approach to issues of law and order.[3]

Both sides used the outcome of the 1960 election to bolster their own views; an easy task with such a heartbreakingly close race. The Democratic candidate, Senator John F. Kennedy, won by a margin of 49.7 to 49.5 percent, or 115,000 votes out of the 70 million votes cast in the election. As Leonard Hall, Nixon's campaign manager, told him after the election, "You know, Dick, a shift of only fourteen thousand votes and we would have been the heroes, and they would have been the bums."[4]

Given such a close result, a plausible case could be made for following either a moderate or a conservative strategy. The moderates believed that Nixon had not done enough to win the votes of traditionally Democratic groups—urban dwellers, union members, blacks, and ethnics. They believed that to win back the White House the party needed to emphasize its moderate image and to rebuild Republican party organizations in the large urban areas of the North.

The conservatives argued that Nixon had moderated too much in a misguided attempt to win the votes of liberals and blacks, thereby alienating core Republican supporters in the Midwest and missing the opportunity to gain the votes of conservative southern whites. To form this "union of corn belt and corn pone," the conservatives believed that the party needed to strive for ideological purity and to build a Republican party organization in the South.[5]

THE BIG CITY RESPONSE

BALLOT SECURITY EFFORTS

The RNC's initial attempts to formulate a response to their defeat came hesitatingly and reluctantly. Many on the committee believed that they had actually won the election but that it was stolen from them by the Democrats. The RNC reported receiving 135,000 complaints of electoral fraud in twenty-five states in the month following the election.[6] Most of these complaints focused on Illinois and Texas, two states with long histories of creative vote counting by their Democratic party machines.

Despite these irregularities, Nixon refused to challenge the election outcome. Protesting the election would entail a lengthy recount, which would leave the nation leaderless for a period of months and possibly damage the legitimacy of the eventual winner. It also seems likely that Nixon knew that the Democrats were not the only ones guilty of stuffing ballot boxes. In Illinois the Republican organizations in suburban Chicago and downstate were not averse to padding their vote totals in an effort to swing the statewide outcome.[7] As one Chicago Democratic once told me with only a bit of exaggeration, "They raised all kinds of Hell when Kennedy got over 90 percent of the vote in some Chicago precincts, but nobody batted an eye when Nixon got every goddamned vote in Lake Forest!"

Nixon's refusal to challenge the election outcome effectively closed the issue, but at the January 1961 meeting of the RNC the topic of election fraud was still on the minds of many committee members. Mrs. C. Wayland Brooks, national committeewoman from Illinois, spoke about the irregularities in Chicago:

> It was the most flagrant thing I have ever seen and the election was stolen from us. . . .
>   It is just like living in Russia. I just sat there for days watching this, and we couldn't do a thing about it. You knew this was happening and votes that were for Nixon were just going down the drain. Just like living in Russia.[8]

Despite such charges, the RNC declined to take formal action to challenge the election results. Republican chairman Thruston Morton told the committee: "It isn't good to talk about it [election fraud] after it is over, except for one purpose: to have the facts before us and to rouse individual public indignation so that we do something about it ourselves in the elections that lie ahead."[9]

To prevent future election fraud, some Republicans suggested paying college football players as poll watchers.[10] Thruston Morton described a similar ballot security effort in his home state of Kentucky, saying, "it cost us $50 a piece to get a good man, about 250 pounds, and we broke it up damned fast. They made pretty good poll watchers."[11]

In addition to these rather comical ideas, the RNC appointed a National Recount and Fair Elections Committee, headed by New Jersey National Committeeman Bernard Shanley, to examine ways to improve ballot security. Additionally, in February 1961, the RNC's Women's Division distributed a pamphlet entitled, "Are You a 'Shadow' Voter?" By October 1961, 100,000 copies had been produced and distributed to various educational, civic, and business organizations. The pamphlet described types of voter fraud and recommended solutions for citizens and election officials.[12]

THE COMMITTEE ON BIG CITY POLITICS

Questions of voter fraud pointed to a larger weakness for the Republican party in the 1960 election—their poor showing in most large urban areas—which fit with the interpretation of the election results offered by moderates. The general decline of Republican party organizations in most big cities, particularly in the Northeast and Midwest, meant not only a failure to adequately staff polling places to prevent fraud, but also an inability to mobilize potential Republican voters. In several cases, losses in the cities wiped out large Republican margins in nonurban areas. In Illinois, Nixon's 309,000–vote margin downstate was not enough to overcome Kennedy's 318,000–vote margin in Chicago. In Pennsylvania, the Democratic margin of 330,000 votes in Philadelphia more than compensated for the Republican margin of 215,000 votes in the rest of the state. The same was true in Michigan, New York, and New Jersey—Democratic margins in the cities offset Republican margins in the rest of the state.[13]

Albert B. "Ab" Hermann, the RNC's campaign director, helped support the notion that the Republicans had lost the election in the big cities. Hermann had made his name as a successful party organizer, and he firmly believed in the need for the party to develop strong organizations in urban areas.[14] After the election, Hermann produced an analysis showing that the election had been lost in the big cities.[15]

Hermann's report seems to have formed the basis for Morton's assessment of the election at the January meeting of the RNC.[16] According to Morton, while Nixon was winning fifteen cities with populations over 300,000:

Senator Kennedy was carrying 25 big cities, and the Kennedy big cities
were in swing States with considerable electoral votes, where the election
was really decided—in those swing states. . . .

The Senator racked up a plurality of 2.6 million votes in 12 important
cities, and he only won the election by 113,000 [votes].[17]

According to Morton, it was an "obvious fact that this election was lost for
the Republican candidates in big cities" and that the party should respond to its
defeat by rebuilding its organizational strength in large urban areas.[18] Philadelphia
offers a striking example of this decline in organizational strength. Once the home
of a strong Republican party organization, on election day in 1960, 500 of Philadelphia's 1,623 precincts were unmanned by Republican party workers.[19]

To accomplish this rebuilding, Morton advocated establishing a committee on
big city politics to:

study the practicalities of big city politics, and to use the committee thereon,
and to devise a campaign plan for the maximum Republican impact in these
areas. . . .

This committee will study big city politics; will survey and analyze the
formulas that have been won; will interpret the organizational strengths and
weaknesses in various areas, in order to apply the strengths and avoid the
weaknesses elsewhere; and will tell us what steps have to be taken to erode
the monolithic Democratic big city vote.[20]

Morton recognized that any RNC efforts focused on northern urban areas could
easily exacerbate the party's ideological split. Because of this, he stated that, "this
committee will work on campaign techniques and not on Party philosophy."[21]

The RNC approved Morton's suggestion and established the Committee on Big
City Politics under the direction of Ray C. Bliss, chairman of the Ohio Republican
party. Over the years Bliss had developed a reputation as a mastermind of organizational politics.[22] The 1960 election helped to enhance Bliss's reputation since
Ohio was the only large, northern, industrial state won by Nixon—an outcome
that defied most predictions.[23]

Bliss was viewed as the perfect choice to run the committee. He had a nonideological, organizational approach to party affairs that made him acceptable to
moderates and conservatives.[24] In 1960 Bliss wrote: "Organization is a major key
to success in politics on any level—county, state, or nation. It is the driving force
which gives politics mobility, the bridge that spans the gap between the candidates
and the voters, the source of motivation which binds together all phases of a campaign, the nourishment which keeps the party alive and healthy."[25]

In addition to good organization, Bliss followed the maxim, "Keep issues out
of campaigns."[26] The results of the 1958 election reaffirmed this notion for Bliss. In
that year, Ohio business leaders insisted on putting a right-to-work referendum on

the ballot. Union members mobilized in opposition to the measure and nearly all of the Republican ticket in Ohio went down in defeat.

Bliss brought this organizational, "nuts and bolts," nonideological approach to the Committee on Big City Politics. He appointed subcommittees to deal with various aspects of urban political organization. These subcommittees were Party Organization, Structure, and Candidate Recruitment, led by Congressman Glen Lipscomb; Labor, Business, and Independent Voters, headed by Colorado Senator Gordon Allott; Nationality and Minority Groups, chaired by Congressman Edward Derwinski; and Public Relations, Use of Surveys, and Educational Methods, led by New York state chairman L. Judson Morhouse.

The subcommittee on party organization seems to have been closest to Bliss's heart, and he focused on this subject when he made his preliminary report to the RNC in June 1961. To assess the condition of Republican big city organizations, Bliss surveyed relevant state and local party chairmen, asking specific questions about the level of organization in their area. The results were not encouraging. According to Bliss:

> we find in our surveys a pitiful and woeful lack of adequate staffing in the big cities throughout the nation. . . .
> We found in many precincts in these cities there aren't even committeemen.
> That may seem surprising to some of you; to others not, but there are hundreds of precincts in big city areas where we do not even have a committeeman or a worker, and how are we going to do a job of getting out the vote there unless we do a job of providing people in those precincts?[27]

This was a serious problem, in Bliss's view: "We are competing today in the big cities with paid operations controlled by the Democrats where they can draw on the tremendous manpower, the Democratic machine, in effect, plus a highly efficient . . . and effective, COPE operation."[28]

For Bliss, the establishment of well-staffed and well-financed party organizations provided the key to doing better in the big cities. He believed that improved party organizations would improve candidate recruitment, since good candidates are more willing to run if backed by a strong organization. In Bliss's words, "If you develop a sound organization structure, it is easier to get a candidate. If we have adequate funds to help him, it is easier to persuade a man to run."[29] Better organizations would also help to draw in the votes of union members, political independents, ethnics, and blacks, since the party would now have the means to improve their contacts with these groups.

The final report of the Bliss Committee stressed the need for organizational development and offered a useful primer on organizational tactics. Among the committee's recommendations were the following:

1. Republican Party activities in every big city should be placed on a year round basis.

2. Emphasis should be put on precinct organization and activity, to get precincts manned with dependable workers, to assure concentrations on registration activities, and to establish personal contacts with voters.

3. There should be full-time, paid, professional staffs in city committee headquarters.[30]

THE MORHOUSE CHALLENGE

Bliss's organizational strategy had the virtue of avoiding the party's ideological disputes, but it also overlooked the fact that ideas and policies as well as organizations are crucial for the development of strong parties. This point was not lost on committee member Jud Morhouse, the liberal chairman of the New York Republican party and a close ally of Nelson Rockefeller. Morhouse attempted to convince Bliss and others on the committee that they should deal with issues as well as organization. Bliss refused, so Morhouse used the report of his subcommittee on Republican Relations to blast conservatives and to encourage the party to develop a new and more liberal program that would appeal to the residents of large urban areas. The report stated: "Those who disagree with Republicans may be 'stupid' in the minds of some arch-Republicans, but they still have enough votes to win elections. And it is not enough for Republicans to know what they think of themselves— they must know what the housewife, the truck driver, the farmer and the Democrats think of them. . . . Until the Republican Party listens to the people, it will remain a minority party."[31]

Bliss and the full committee eventually edited this passage out of the report.[32] In response, Morhouse sent a memo to Nelson Rockefeller; George Hinman, Republican committeeman from New York and a close Rockefeller ally; and Harry O'Donnell, publicity director for the New York Republican Party, spelling out the disputes in the Big City Politics Committee:

> Most other members of the committee were determined that we should not discuss "issues." (Representatives of minority groups and labor stood with me.) We were overcome, however, and the committee ultimately made a report which talked about practically nothing but organization—the same subject on which Republican chieftains have concentrated for the past twenty years without any noticeable improvement for the Republican Party. The only exception was the report of a subcommittee on "Public Opinion Polls, Television and Public Relations" which tried to recognize the need to face up to the people's problems, but the parent committee tore up two-thirds of that.[33]

Specifically, Morhouse believed that the party needed to develop programs for medical care for the elderly, federal aid to education, and unemployment. In his view, Nixon had lost the election by not supporting a Medicare proposal.[34] But for Morhouse, the problems in the Republican party went beyond just the lack of discussion of issues. He believed that the Republican party needed fundamental restructuring. His memo concluded:

> 1. The Republican Party nationally (and the Republican National Committee) should be dominated by people from the states which have the big cities—which is not now the case.

> 2. The Republican Party, its National Committee and its elected members must recognize the problems which face people who live in big cities—which it does not now do.

> 3. The Republican Party must run a candidate for President with whose philosophy the people in the big cities can agree and [in] whose honesty of purpose they have confidence—which it is not now inclined to do.

> Somewhere along the line, someone who understands these facts and who is determined to make the rest of the party understand them must break with the existing party structure so that those who want to win can rise out of the lethargic and amorphous slough of defeat and despair to which the Republican Party has fallen.[35]

To achieve these goals, Morhouse proposed restructuring the RNC on a strict population basis, instead of the present system of two seats for each state and a bonus seat for the state party chair in states which voted Republican in the last presidential election, or had a Republican governor, or had a Republican majority in its combined House and Senate membership. Such a system naturally favored the South and the small, conservative, and traditionally Republican states over large industrial states.[36]

Morhouse knew that the conservatives who dominated the national party would never agree to put themselves out of power by implementing these changes. To consider this imbalance, he suggested that liberals, moderates, and Republicans from the large industrial states should boycott the RNC and establish their own counterorganization to promote more liberal policies for the Republican party.[37]

Morhouse's plan eventually came to naught. Rockefeller refused to support it because he was attempting to mend fences with party conservatives in the hopes of securing the Republican nomination in 1964.[38] Other Republican liberals were equally unsupportive, not only for fear of upsetting the increasingly powerful conservative wing of the party, but also because they still held out hope for an organizational strategy such as Bliss's.[39]

THE SOUTHERN STRATEGY

Just as Republican liberals and moderates could look at the razor-thin results of the 1960 election to support their own views of party strategy, so could party conservatives. In 1960 Richard Nixon ran very strongly in the South, carrying 46 percent of the vote and three states, Florida, Tennessee, and Virginia. Nixon's southern vote was only slightly less than Eisenhower's 49 percent in 1956 and 48 percent in 1952, despite Nixon's lack of Ike's war hero status and Eisenhower's dispatch of federal troops to calm the Little Rock Crisis of 1957.[40]

During the campaign, Nixon met with enthusiastic receptions in many areas of the South.[41] Many party conservatives, Barry Goldwater most prominently, believed that Nixon had lost the South and the election by failing to campaign strenuously enough in the region and by moderating his message too much in an attempt to woo Democrats and independents.[42] Goldwater presented this message at the January 1961 meeting of the RNC, the same meeting in which Thruston Morton claimed the election had been lost in the big cities of the North. Goldwater stated, "Only in the South does the presidential election tell the really significant story." This story, according to Goldwater and other conservatives, was that the GOP's best opportunities were in the South.[43]

THE REPUBLICAN PARTY IN THE SOUTH, 1952–1960

A decade earlier, the notion of a Republican opportunity in the South would have seemed fantastic, so it seems worthwhile to describe Republican efforts in the South prior to 1960. Before the 1950s Republican party organizations in the South were next to nonexistent. Areas of Republican electoral strength existed only in the mountains of Virginia, Tennessee, and North Carolina, the German enclave in the Texas Hill Country, the new settlements of northern migrants on the Florida coasts, and the scattered areas where blacks still retained some suffrage rights. In most other areas the party consisted of skeletal organizations interested only in the distribution of federal patronage during Republican administrations. In 1949 V. O. Key described southern Republicanism as ranging somewhere between "an esoteric cult" and "a conspiracy for plunder."[44]

Southern Republican organizations were often viewed as the "rotten boroughs" of the Republican party—vastly overrepresented at the national conventions in relation to their electoral strength for the Republicans in the general election—making them the source of various manipulations by those seeking the Republican nomination. According to Key:

> Presidential aspirants, invariably nonsouthern, are interested in control of
> state organizations only because of the votes they can deliver in national

conventions. Those inside the states are interested in control of the organizations because of the local Federal patronage that they control when their party wins the Presidency. Southern Republican leaders are usually pictured as vultures awaiting the day when the party wins the nation and they can distribute patronage in the South. Meantime, they exert themselves only to keep the party weak in the South in order that there will be fewer faithful to reward.[45]

The Republican National Convention of 1912 offered the most blatant example of this old system at work. In that year, southern delegates controlled 23 percent of the convention delegates, though they had contributed only 7 percent of the Republican presidential vote in 1908. These southern delegates provided President William Howard Taft with the margin he needed to defeat former president Theodore Roosevelt's challenge to his renomination.[46]

The controversy surrounding the 1912 convention led the party to institute a bonus system to reward states that had performed well for Republican candidates. The party increased the bonus system over the years, which helped to reduce southern overrepresentation. Nevertheless, in 1952, the southern states still commanded a disproportionate share of the Republican national convention delegates.[47]

This old system of Republican politics in the South began to change in the early 1950s. In 1952 the Draft Eisenhower movement succeeded in attracting a new corps of conservative activists into local Republican organizations in the South. According to James Reichley, at the 1952 convention: "freshly minted Eisenhower Republicans challenged pro-Taft regular Republican state organizations that existed almost solely to send delegations to Republican national conventions and wait for federal patronage and had generally since the days of Mark Hanna been controlled by the managers of the Ohio Republican machine."[48]

Eisenhower's popularity in the South helped him not only to claim the Republican nomination in 1952 but also to win nearly half of the region's votes in 1952 and 1956. In 1957, RNC chairman Meade Alcorn initiated "Operation Dixie" to help the party build on gains that Eisenhower had made in the region. Alcorn and others believed that the South was ready for a two-party system and that many people in the region would be receptive to moderate, nonracist Republicanism.[49]

I. Lee Potter, Virginia state chairman, national committeeman, and head of the RNC's Southern Division directed the program. Potter faced a formidable task. Many southerners had never seen a Republican, even fewer had voted for one, and almost none had become one. Clarke Reed, former chairman of the Mississippi Republican party, likens Potters travels through the South to sending "missions to China."[50]

One initial effort of Operation Dixie was to gain publicity in order to enhance the Republican party's legitimacy and credibility in the South.[51] To this end, Potter and other Republicans traveled through the region extolling the virtues of a two-party system. These efforts succeeded. According to Potter, "Every time I'd make a speech in which I discussed the South, almost every paper from Florida to Arkansas picked it up."[52] The program also brought in conservative Republicans from outside the South as speakers in order to show southerners that Republicans did not have tails and horns and that the party shared their ideological outlook.[53]

Operation Dixie also recruited activists to staff state and local Republican organizations and run on the Republican ticket. Recruits tended to be young, college-educated, professionally employed. They were, in Theodore White's words, "men between thirty and forty years old, city people, well-bred, moderate segregationists, efficient, more at ease at suburban cocktail parties than when whiskey-belting in courthouse chambers."[54] Many had been World War II veterans, educated by the GI Bill and now part of the South's growing urban middle class.[55] By 1964, the average age of the southern Republican state chairmen was just over thirty-six years.[56]

Few of the older business elites were among those recruited to positions in the party. According to Clarke Reed, most of these people were "fakes"—expressing private support for the Republican party, but refusing to take a public stand for fear of damaging their relationship with the local Democratic party establishments. Younger professionals—especially doctors, lawyers, insurance agents, and owners of construction firms—proved much more willing to become active in the party since they were less attached to the Democratic party and did not have a vested interest in the political status quo.[57]

Women also played an important role in these emerging Republican organizations. According to a former national committeewoman from Mississippi, "Women built the party in the South. Men raised the money, but women did the leg work."[58] Unlike most northern states, where women were usually most active in auxiliary organizations, like the Federation of Republican Women, in the South, the lack of party officials provided women with more opportunities in the regular party organizations.[59] Despite these advances, southern Republican women were still often forced into subordinate roles. Many counties did not have a Republican party chair, only a vice-chair. Although no men were available, women were not allowed to assume the traditional male role of party chair; instead they were forced to remain in the traditional female position of party vice-chair.[60]

Despite Alcorn's and Eisenhower's hopes of building a base of moderate Republicanism in the South, these new activists were strongly conservative. This conservatism focused on national issues and foreign policy. Reed, one of this new breed of activists, says that he and others like him "cut their teeth" on the writings of Whittaker Chambers, the ex-communist writer and accuser of Alger Hiss, and conservative philosopher Russell Kirk.[61]

The open nature of the southern Republican party greatly assisted Potter's recruitment efforts among ambitious, young conservatives. He could easily promise potential Republicans the ability to "come in at the top." Newcomers could quickly (in some cases immediately) become leaders of the Republican party in their states or candidates for state and national offices, while ambitious Democrats faced years of waiting for the opportunity to rise in the party.[62]

Operation Dixie seems to have had some success, as shown by the Republican party's performance in the South in the late 1950s. According to one analyst: "Under Potter's direction the Southern Division provided a center for invigorating and coordinating Republican activity in the South. Each of the eight incumbent Republican congressmen from the South was reelected in 1958 [an otherwise disastrous year for the Republican party]."[63]

As the 1960 election approached, race and civil rights became increasingly important issues. This development underscored the growing dilemma facing the Republican party—whether to jump at the opportunity of pulling the South into the Republican column with a strongly conservative program, including a less progressive position on civil rights, or to project a moderate image to compete for votes, including those of blacks, in the urban areas of the North.

At their 1960 convention, the Republican party chose the latter course. The original draft of the party's civil rights plank was a moderate one, avoiding the specific declarations made in the Democratic platform. But Nixon, facing a potential floor fight over the platform, rejected this moderate plank in favor of a more liberal one favored by Rockefeller.[64]

Nixon's platform shift on civil rights pained Republican conservatives. Barry Goldwater believed that this move cost Nixon the election. One Louisiana delegate complained: "We've lost Louisiana, I tell you, we've lost Louisiana. Lyndon Johnson's going to come across the border now and talk 'magnolia' to them and they'll vote Democratic and we could have had Louisiana, we could of had it."[65]

Even with a liberal civil rights plank, Nixon had enthusiastic support in the South during the campaign. Some 150,000 Atlantans turned out at his campaign kickoff, and he was warmly received at the few other stops he made in the South. Other Republicans, especially conservatives like Barry Goldwater, were also very popular below the Mason-Dixon line. According to Lee Potter, "Demands for Sen. Goldwater to appear before Southern audiences are . . . in such volume that the Senator couldn't satisfy them if he spoke in three cities a day for the rest of the campaign."[66]

As mentioned previously, Nixon ran a very strong race in the South in 1960. Additionally, an analysis of the election by the RNC's Research Division showed that Republican successes were not concentrated at the top of the ticket. According to this report:

> An especially bright spot showing a growth in GOP support was in the five gubernatorial contests in the South during 1960. The Republican candidates for governor increased their vote 105 percent above the 1956 level or by over one million votes.[67]

These results led the report to advise, "Organizational effort at least in selected areas of the Southern states to expand the base of the Republican Party is clearly justified by the 1960 results."[68]

THE REPUBLICAN PARTY IN THE SOUTH, 1961–1964

Despite their initial enthusiasm and the efforts of Bliss and others on the Big City Committee, the RNC did little to implement the committee's report and instead began to upgrade its Southern Division. One reason for this shift was the growing strength of conservatives in the Republican party and in the RNC. Many of them took to heart Barry Goldwater's admonishment at the 1960 convention, "Let's grow up, conservatives! If we want to take this Party back, and I think we can some day, let's get to work."[69] Though Goldwater initially showed much reluctance to run for president, conservatives began to organize to take over the party and to nominate Goldwater for president in 1964.[70] By late 1963, Goldwater supporters had come to control most key staff positions in the RNC.[71]

The rise of the conservatives, as Jud Morhouse knew, was greatly assisted by the malapportionment of seats on the RNC. By 1962, the northeastern states, rich in electoral votes and the base of moderate Republicanism, controlled only 20 percent of the seats on the RNC (see table 2).[72]

Another reason was the surprise victory of Republican John Tower in the May 1961 race to fill the Texas Senate seat vacated by Lyndon Johnson. Though a strong conservative, Tower was aided by the votes and abstentions of liberal Democrats who refused to support the Democratic nominee, the reactionary William Blakely, who had been appointed to fill Johnson's seat. Even so, Tower's victory was taken as strong evidence for the claim that conservative Republican candidates could win in the South.[73]

The RNC's new emphasis on the South was also aided by the resignation of party chairman Thruston Morton and his replacement by New York Congressman William E. Miller in June 1961. Unlike Morton, Miller had no enthusiasm for the big city strategy, and he made few, if any, attempts to implement Bliss's program. When asked what the party was doing to recapture the urban vote, Miller replied, "We adopted a big-city report at a convention in Oklahoma City. Isn't that enough?"[74]

Several reasons may have influenced Miller's favoring of a southern over a big city strategy. Though a New Yorker, Miller was no Rockefeller Republican and had supported Nixon in 1960. His conservative views made him more open to a southern strategy than Morton, who, despite coming from Kentucky, was more liberal than Miller.

Miller, as a House member, also seems to have favored a strategy that promised to help the Republicans gain control of the Congress. He realized that the Republicans were at a severe disadvantage as long as the Democrats were guar-

TABLE 2.

GEOGRAPHIC DISTRIBUTION OF SEATS ON THE RNC, 1962.

South, Seats	Midwest, Seats	West, Seats	Northeast, Seats
Alabama, 2	Illinois, 2	Alaska, 3	Connecticut, 2
Arkansas, 2	Indiana, 3	Arizona, 3	Delaware, 3
Florida, 3	Iowa, 3	California, 3	Maine, 3
Georgia, 2	Kansas, 3	Colorado, 3	Massachusetts, 3
Kentucky, 3	Michigan, 3	Hawaii, 3	New Hamp., 3
Louisiana, 2	Minnesota, 3	Idaho, 3	New Jersey, 3
Maryland, 2	Missouri, 2	Montana, 3	New York, 3
Mississippi, 2	Nebraska, 3	Nevada, 2	Pennsylvania, 3
North Carolina, 2	North Dakota, 3	New Mexico, 3	Rhode Island, 2
Oklahoma, 3	Ohio, 3	Oregon, 3	Vermont, 3
South Carolina, 2	South Dakota, 3	Utah, 3	
Tennessee, 3	Wisconsin, 3	Washington, 3	
Texas, 2		Wyoming, 3	
Virginia, 3			
West Virginia, 2			
Region Total 35	34	38	28
% of U.S. Total (135) 25.9	25.2	28.1	20.7

Source: Memorandum, Jo Good to William Miller, December 5, 1962, State Chairmans Advisory Council Files, 1963–1967, box 91, RNC Papers, National Archives.

anteed 100 southern House seats.[75] Miller knew that the Republicans' only chance to capture the House was to win seats in the South and that a big city strategy offered no such hope. Bliss's plan envisioned raising the Republican vote to about 40 percent, at best, in the big cities. While this was enough to allow Republicans to carry statewide races, it was not enough to elect Republican congressional candidates in urban areas.

Another factor that might have influenced Miller was that the southern strategy was institutionalized into the RNC in the form of Lee Potter and the Southern Division. Though the big city strategy had its supporters at the RNC, it was never institutionalized into the structure of the RNC as the Southern Division had been in the late 1950s. As a result, Ray Bliss, the mastermind of the big city strategy, was in Ohio, not down the hall from Miller as Lee Potter was.[76]

Whatever the reasons, beginning in late 1961, the RNC began to invest more attention and resources into implementing the southern strategy.[77] By 1964, Miller claimed that the RNC had spent $500,000 on Operation Dixie.[78] Though this seems small in comparison to the amounts spent by today's national committees, at the time this was a very large sum of money. In 1963 the RNC's total expenditures were only $1.7 million dollars.[79]

In April 1962, Potter hired Hal Dunham to handle public relations for the Southern Division. Dunham began a newsletter for the division in June of that year: *The Republican Southern Challenge*. The newsletter started out in June 1962 with four pages and a circulation of 5,000. Two years later it had grown into a monthly release with a distribution list of 39,000 people. According to one observer of the RNC at the time:

> In both format and editorial care *Southern Challenge* became a more stylish, more expensive, and probably more effective publication than any of the others which the national committee distributed widely.
>
> Editorially, the publication emphasized "conservatism," and it pushed hard for a two-party system in the South. . . . The publication argued that the Democrats from the South betray their constituents by supporting the liberal policies of the Democratic White House and of their Northern Democratic colleagues. The paper carried much news and many names related to Republican organizations and organizational drives in the South, as would certainly be the function of such an organ.[80]

The RNC also ran political advertising in the South as a means of creating publicity and support. One typical effort of the Southern Division depicted the Democratic party as a sleeping donkey, neglectful of the South's needs. Other ads pointed out the liberalism of the national Democratic party and claimed that many southern Democrats were not as conservative as they portrayed themselves.[81]

In addition to its publicity efforts, the Southern Division also embarked on a major organizational effort. In November 1961 the RNC sponsored a conference of southern state party chairmen in Atlanta. The purpose of this first-time conference was to help train local party workers in the techniques of precinct organization, political research, and public relations. A second conference was held in Charleston, South Carolina, in November 1963. Both conferences brought much regional and national press attention.[82]

The RNC also sponsored numerous training seminars and conferences for the individual state organizations in the South. One of these training course was Mobilization of Republican Enterprise (MORE), a training course for party workers. Though originally designed for use as part of the Big City Program, MORE was used most extensively in the South. MORE was credited with helping John Tower's 1961 Senate victory and in 1963 the program was used to train 1,300 party workers in Alabama.[83]

Another aspect of the increased organizational efforts of the Republican party in the South was its ability to raise funds. To do this, many of the state parties relied on innovative fundraising techniques. Several southern state parties used a "United Republican" fundraising method of deducting contributions from the paychecks of party supporters.[84]

Through these efforts, the Republican party in the South began to develop the organizational depth that it had previously lacked. One measure of the growing organizational strength of the southern Republican parties is in the number of counties with a Republican party chair and vice-chair. By 1964, more than 87 percent of the counties in the South had people in these positions. Only in Louisiana were the Republicans significantly unorganized (see table 3).

The RNC, along with the Republican Congressional and Senatorial Campaign Committees (the latter headed by Barry Goldwater), had great hopes for Republican advances in the South in the 1962 elections and focused their efforts on this region.[85] The party sought to pick up as many as sixteen House seats and two Senate seats in the region. To achieve these goals, the party put up sixty-one congressional candidates in the region's 113 House districts. This contrasts with 1958, when the Republicans had managed to find only twenty-nine House candidates.[86]

Republican hopes for the 1962 election were not fulfilled. The party managed to add only four House seats in the South, while losing two in the North for a rather disappointing net gain of two seats. The seats won in the South were in North Carolina, Florida, Texas, and Tennessee. The North Carolina and Tennessee seats were in the mountain areas of those states, historically more supportive of Republicans. The Florida seat was in the Orlando–Cape Canaveral area, home of many transplanted northerners. Only the Texas seat, in the El Paso, Midland, Odessa area, could be considered a strong Democratic area. But even here, the election turned more on the incumbent Democrat's association with corrupt businessman Billie Sol Estes than on any realignment toward the Republican party.[87]

Still, conservatives pointed to what they believed were significant gains for the party in the South. In addition to the four House seats, South Carolina Republican Senate candidate William Workman managed to gain 43 percent of the vote against incumbent Democrat Olin Johnston. In Alabama, Republican James D. Martin came within 7,000 votes of unseating incumbent Democratic Senator Lister Hill, winning thirty of the state's sixty-seven counties.[88] In North Carolina and Georgia, Republicans elected their first state senators since the end of Reconstruction. North Carolina Republicans also managed to defeat the incumbent Democratic speaker of the state House of Representatives. Overall, the Republicans increased their congressional vote in the South by 244 percent over 1958, as opposed to 41 percent for the Democrats.[89]

The RNC greeted these results enthusiastically. Lee Potter called the GOP's southern gains "impressive" and described the 1962 election as "the most historic . . . of modern times in the South."[90] As for the future, he claimed, "The tide is

LEVEL OF REPUBLICAN ORGANIZATION IN THE SOUTH, 1964.

State	Total Counties	GOP Organized	% Organized
North Carolina	100	98	98.0
Tennessee	95	93	97.9
Virginia	131	128	97.7
Arkansas	75	73	97.3
Alabama	67	64	95.5
Texas	254	237	93.3
South Carolina	46	42	91.3
Florida	67	59	88.1
Mississippi	82	71	86.6
Georgia	159	122	76.7
Louisiana	64	15	23.4
Total	1140	1002	87.9

Source: George L. Grassmuck, "Emerging Republicanism in the South" (Paper delivered at the 1964 Annual Meeting of the American Political Science Association, Chicago, Illinois), 13.

coming in now in the South."[91] William Miller backed up this prediction by saying that Operation Dixie would become "increasingly intensive" with a "major penetration" of the South in 1964.[92] In his report to the RNC after the election, Miller listed the Southern Division as the first priority of the RNC's Campaign Division. His report stated:

> In view of the progress made at the Southern States at the grass roots level since 1957 as I reported this morning, our plan is to enlarge activities within this Division.
>
> 1. Appointment of additional field workers.
>
> 2. Increase the circulation of our "Southern Newsletter" from its present circulation of 7,000.[93]

In the same report, Miller paid lip service to the Big City Program but failed to provided any specific plan to implement it, as he did with Operation Dixie.[94]

The amount of resources devoted to Operation Dixie in relation to similar activities offers another indication of the program's priority in the RNC's efforts. In December 1962, Miller reported that Operation Dixie was spending approximately $40,000 per year, for a total of $250,000 since 1957, not counting salaries. This was more than twice as much as any other activity of the RNC's Campaign Division and ten times the expenditures for the Big City effort (see table 4). The following October, *Congressional Quarterly* reported that while most divisions of the RNC were "starved for funds. . . . The exception was Operation Dixie, which appeared to be fully funded and more active than any other division."[95]

The success of the southern strategy depended not only on the commitment of resources, but also on the Republican party writing off the votes of northern blacks and taking a strongly conservative stand on civil rights in order to attract white southerners. Barry Goldwater spelled out this strategy in 1961 at a meeting of southern Republican state party chairmen in Atlanta, "We're not going to get the Negro vote as a bloc in 1964 and 1968, so we ought to go hunting where the ducks are."[96]

To attract these ducks, the Republican party relied on a distinctly conservative and segregationist call. Since most southern Democrats were staunchly opposed to civil rights, Republican efforts in the South focused on linking local Democrats with the Kennedy administration, which was now highly unpopular in the region because of its support for black Freedom Riders in 1961 and the integration of Ole Miss in 1962. In the 1962 U.S. Senate race in South Carolina, Republican candidate William Workman, author of *The Case for the South,* a segregationist tract, claimed, "The need of the hour is to defeat [Democratic Senator Olin] Johnston, not simply because of his 'liberalism,' but because he is the man that the Kennedys want in the Senate."[97]

The Republican U.S. Senate campaign in Alabama was even more overtly segregationist. Republican candidate James Martin addressed the state Republican convention and called for" a return to the Spirit of '61—1861, when our fathers formed a new nation . . . God willing, we will not again be forced to take up rifle and bayonet to preserve these principles. . . . Make no mistake, my friends, this will be a fight. The bugle call is loud and clear! The South has risen!" Martin continued this theme during the campaign, labeling Hill a "Kennedycrat" and "the most complete supporter of the President in Alabama today."[98] A Martin advertisement promised "vigorous action . . . to forestall collusion between the government and the NAACP to integrate schools, unions, and neighborhoods."[99] Only in Georgia did the Republican party, led by Robert Snodgrass, attempt to steer a moderate and nonsegregationist course.[100]

The RNC denied relying on racist appeals. In an April 1963 letter to the *New York Times,* Potter wrote, "The issue of civil rights . . . has nothing to do with our gains. Our impressive victories in the 1962 Congressional elections were in districts in which Republicans offered "moderate" candidates. Our strength is in the cities of the South, not in the rural areas, where the 'diehards' are found."[101]

Somewhat more honestly, Miller claimed that the RNC had nothing to do with the selection of local candidates or the issues that they ran on.[102] He also complained that the Republicans were the victim of a double-standard: "As long as the

TABLE 4.

RNC CAMPAIGN DIVISION EXPENDITURES, 1962.

Activity	Expenditures
Southern Division	$40,000
Special Events	$20,000
Labor Division	$18,000
Minorities Division	$18,000
Business and Professional Groups	$15,000
Arts and Sciences Division	$15,000
Senior Citizens Division	$13,000
Nationalities Division	$10,000
Big City Panel	$ 4,000

Source: Minutes of the RNC Executive Committee, December 6, 1962, Washington D.C., *Papers of the Republican Party*, pt. 1: Meetings of the Republican National Committee, 1911–1980; Series B: 1960–1980, Paul L. Kesaris, ed. (Frederick, Md.: University Publications of America), reel 2, frames 484–486.

Democrats control Congress by electing a Jim Eastland in Mississippi and an Adam Powell in New York and win a national election with a ticket like Kennedy and Johnson, I'm damned if I see why I should apologize for the differences within the Republican party."[103]

Even today, many of those associated with Operation Dixie play down the role of race in their efforts. Clarke Reed believes the party received a "bum rap on race." In his view, southern Republicans only pointed out the "excesses" of the civil rights movement. While not necessarily taking a progressive stand on race, Reed claims most southern Republicans in this period were not racists and did not rely on seg-regationist appeals, rather, they emphasized a broader ideological conservatism and national issues. According to Reed, the White Citizens' Council types were Democrats and stayed Democrats. "We would have taken them, no mistake about that," says Reed "but they were Democrats."[104]

This claim seems unlikely. If Reed and other southern Republicans did not actually burn crosses and parade in sheets, they actively recruited and supported candidates like William Workman, James Martin, and Rubel Phillips, the Republican candidate for governor of Mississippi in 1963, who ran with the following promise: "Rubel Phillips is a staunch segregationist. He condemns the use of federal power or threats of reprisals to force integration of Mississippians to curry favor with the minority voters in the big Northern and Eastern cities. As governor he will fight for genuine racial harmony in keeping with Mississippi traditions."[105] If such appeals did not win the votes of racist whites, it was not for lack of trying.

By 1963, most members of the RNC tolerated and supported a southern strategy and the racism of many southern Republican party officials. Journalist Robert Novak, then as now, hardly a political radical, observed the following at a conference of state party chairmen in Denver in June 1963:

Item: During one closed-door session of Republican state chairmen at the Denver Hilton Hotel, two Southern state chairmen carried on a boisterous conversation about "niggers" and "nigger-lovers" while Negro waiters were serving lunch. "The amazing part of it was," an eastern state chairman recalled later, "that nobody criticized them for doing it and only a few of us were uncomfortable."

Item: Some of the biggest headlines produced by the Denver meeting came from a press conference held by Wirt Yerger, the fire-eating young segregationist who was Mississippi's Republican state chairman and head of the Republican Party's Association of Southern State Chairmen. Yerger blandly accused Kennedy of fomenting that spring's racial violence in the South in order to win the election.

Item: The "omnibus resolution" adopted by the National Committee as a matter of routine came close to implicit support for Yerger's outrageous claim. The resolution's only provision dealing with civil rights condemned the Kennedy Administration for "its failure to deal effectively with the problems of civil rights and to foster an atmosphere of understanding and good will in which racial conflict can be resolved." Though the nation then was embroiled in the worst racial crisis since the Civil War, the Republican National Committee officially had no word of support—not even a lukewarm word of support—for the Negro movement. . . .

All of this pointed to an unmistakable conclusion: A good many, perhaps a majority of the party's leaders, envisioned substantial political gold to be mined in the racial crisis by becoming in fact, though not in name, the White Man's Party. "Remember," one astute party worker said quietly over the breakfast table at Denver one morning, "this isn't South Africa. The white man outnumbers the Negro 9 to 1 in this country."[106]

THE RISE OF DIRECT-MAIL FUNDRAISING

At the same time that the RNC was developing a new base of voter support in the South, it was also developing a new base of financial support. Richard Nixon's defeat in 1960 put the RNC in serious financial difficulty; it had no money on hand and was running deficits of $16,000 to $20,000 a month, not counting service on a debt of $700,000.[107] Future prospects looked bleak, as the party had just lost the White House and would not have the same amount of political clout available to gather funds.[108] In 1961 the RNC was only able to raise 60 percent of its budget, requiring sharp cuts in staff and programs.[109]

To relieve this situation, the RNC decided to experiment with a new means of fundraising—direct mail. Though both parties had attempted various small contributor programs over the last fifty years, none, according to Alexander Heard, "demonstrated sufficient success, . . . to become an established part of either party's campaign apparatus."[110] In the aftermath of their 1960 loss, the Republicans succeeded in reversing this experience and were thereby responsible for one of the most important developments in modern party fundraising.

The program began in March 1962, when Republican National Finance Committee (RNFC)[111] director, Hamiliton W. Wright, and William Warner, executive director of the RNC, began sending mass mailings to potential contributors. The letters, signed by the national chairman, the heads of the congressional campaign committees, and the RNFC director, asked for a $10 annual contribution to the party.[112] The RNFC began with a test mailing of 30,000 letters to three states. The addresses were drawn from the RNC's records of 500,000 addresses. The trial mailing generated a very good response (see table 5) and the RNFC decided to expand the program.

Additional mailings were sent to twenty-eight more states, mostly in the South and the West, and again the response was favorable.[113] By the beginning of December 1962, the program had raised $110,000, at the rate of about $10,000 a week.[114] The RNC then sent mailings to the remaining states and the program ended the year having raised $700,000 for the RNFC from more than 67,000 contributors. This figure represented more than 20 percent of the RNFC's total receipts in 1963.[115]

The success of the sustaining membership program continued and expanded over the next two years. Those who contributed in 1962 were tapped again; 70 per-

TABLE 5.

REPUBLICAN NATIONAL FINANCE COMMITTEE SUSTAINING MEMBERSHIP
PROGRAM TEST, MARCH 1962.

Test State	Solicitations	Memberships	Amount
Missouri	10,581	606	$ 6,055
Montana	6,552	555	$ 5,533
New Jersey	13,601	667	$ 6,682
Total	30,734	1,828	$18,270

Source: "Report on the Sustaining Membership Program," Minutes of the RNC Executive Committee, December 6, 1962, Washington D.C., *Papers of the Republican Party,* pt. 1: Meetings of the Republican National Committee, 1911–1980; Series B: 1960–1980, Paul L. Kesaris, ed. (Frederick, Md.: University Publications of America), reel 2, frame 494.

cent of whom renewed their membership in 1963.[116] Addresses were purchased from a variety of commercial sources, including lists of credit card holders, members of Disabled American Veterans, business magazine and newspaper subscribers, persons who had mail-ordered Richard Nixon's book, *Six Crises,* brokerage firm clients, and buyers of Kozak Auto Drywash cloths.[117]

In 1963, the expanded direct-mail program sent out nearly three million letters, which produced over 108,000 contributions for a total return of nearly $1,108,000. In 1964, the party mailed more than five million letters, resulting in more than 188,000 contributions for a total of more than $2.3 million. This figure represented more than 46 percent of the total funds raised by the RNFC in 1964 (see table 6).

The new sustaining membership program not only increased the amount of funds available but also helped to change the structure of power within the Republican party. In his study of political finance in the 1950s, Alexander Heard commented that the subservience of the national party organizations to the state and local parties was directly related to the financial dependence of the former on the latter. He wrote: "The national leadership has on occasion rejected the demands of important state and local party leaders, but the paucity of its independent financial resources, along with other factors, circumscribes its freedom and denies it a potential source of stability. The cumulative effect pushes the center of gravity further down in the party structure than it need otherwise be."[118]

TABLE 6.

REPUBLICAN NATIONAL FINANCE COMMITTEE SUSTAINING MEMBERSHIP PROGRAM, 1962–1964.

	1962	1963	1964
Letters Mailed	2,400,000	2,900,000	5,205,364
Returns	67,660	108,629	188,577
Amount Raised	$700,000	$1,107,957	$2,369,340
Rate of Return	2.8	3.7	3.6
Average Contribution	$10.35	$10.20	$12.56
Total RNFC Receipts	$3,299,426	$2,759,512	$5,094,380
% of RNFC Receipts from Direct Mail	21.2%	40.2%	46.5%

Source: Figures compiled from "Report on the Sustaining Membership Program," Minutes of the RNC Executive Committee, December 6, 1962, Washington D.C., *Papers of the Republican Party,* pt. 1: Meetings of the Republican National Committee, 1911–1980; Series B: 1960–1980, Paul L. Kesaris, ed. (Frederick, Md.: University Publications of America), reel 2, frame 494; "Report on the Sustaining Membership Program," Minutes of the RNC Executive Committee, January 8, 1964, Washington, D.C., *Papers of the Republican Party,* pt. 1, reel 3, frame 264; and document from the Republican National Finance Committee Meeting, January 21, 1965, Chicago, Illinois (photocopy).

The rise of its direct-mail program helped the RNC to overcome this constraint by making it much less reliant on large contributions and state party contributions than it had been in the past. In 1956, the party received more than 74 percent of its individual contributions in gifts of more than $500, but in 1964 these gifts represented only 28 percent.[119] In 1956, the RNFC obtained 46 percent of its funds from state and local party contributions, but by 1964 these contributions had declined to only 15 percent.[120]

The diminished influence of large contributions and state quotas meant a consequent decline in the intraparty influence of the moderate, "establishment" Republicans. These Republicans had the resources to contribute in large sums, and they also controlled the parties in states like New York, Pennsylvania, and Massachusetts, which were among the largest contributors to the national party.[121] The decline in the share of Republican money originating from the East Coast can be seen in table 7. Between 1960 and 1964, the amount of contributions over $500 from the mid-Atlantic states declined by over $500,000. This decline meant that the share of total contributions over $500 from the mid-Atlantic states fell from 42.7 percent in 1960 to just 24.5 percent in 1964.

According to J. William Middendorf, treasurer of the RNFC from 1964 to 1968, the rise of direct mail "broke the back" of eastern establishment influence in the Republican party.[122] Stephen Hess and David Broder support this claim, arguing that the development of the sustaining membership program "liberated" the party "from whatever degree of financial control the small group of financial angels imposed. . . . The continued increase in numbers of small contributions in response

TABLE 7.

REGIONAL DISTRIBUTION OF CONTRIBUTIONS OVER $500, 1960–1964.

Region	1960 Contributions ($)	% of 1960 Total	1964 Contributions ($)	% of 1964 Total	Change in Contributions ($)	Change in % of Total
New England	206,000	6.7	288,500	9.3	82,500	2.6
Mid-Atlantic	1,304,300	42.7	763,500	24.5	-540,800	-18.2
Border	201,300	6.6	255,300	8.2	54,000	1.6
South	331,100	10.8	485,700	15.6	154,600	4.8
Midwest	714,600	23.4	844,700	27.1	130,100	3.7
Mountain	25,500	0.8	171,600	5.5	146,100	4.7
Pacific	273,000	8.9	307,700	9.9	34,700	1.0
Total	3,055,800	100.0	3,117,000	100.0	61,200	0.0

Source: Herbert Alexander, *Financing the 1964 Election* (Princeton, N.J.: Citizens' Research Foundation, 1966), 232–36.

to direct-mail solicitations and the success of the televised appeals during presidential campaigns frees the party from any veto power over a nominee by a specific number of its principal contributors."[123]

LIBERAL COUNTER-RESPONSES

CRITICISMS OF OPERATION DIXIE

The southern strategy was not without its detractors in the Republican party. One source of criticism was the liberal Republican journal *Advance,* which persistently called for Republicans to take a progressive stand on civil rights and to denounce those who supported segregationist appeals. In November 1962, the journal carried the following editorial criticizing the political merit of a southern strategy:

> Before Mr. Potter begins the 1964 campaign, for instance, it would be well if the party would face the facts of the 1962 election: 1) that the Republican campaign machinery is disproportionately geared to the right-wing, frøm the petty and parochial Congressional Committee Newsletter to "Operation Dixie"; 2) that the Republican campaign in 1962 was an overall failure in the Senate, where the official bias toward the right wing—particularly in the South—was most pronounced; 3) that the Southern House victories and Senate improvements, though significant, were not as auspicious as Messrs. Potter and Goldwater would have us believe.[124]

Black Republicans also opposed the southern strategy. One was Grant Reynolds, special assistant to RNC chairman William Miller. Reynolds came to the RNC in 1961 and set out to reinvigorate the committee's Minorities Division by establishing better public relations with the black media, recruiting more black Republican candidates, and registering more black Republican voters.[125] The RNC, however, showed little support; Reynolds was prohibited from publicizing historic Republican support for civil rights or current Republicans who supported civil rights. He and others in the Minority Division were not invited to attend important party gatherings.[126]

What few efforts the RNC took to appeal to blacks were feeble or patronizing or both. According to journalist Meg Greenfield, one of these projects:

> was the publication of one of the saddest comic documents on the political scene—a pamphlet entitled, "Who Is George Lewis?," which was meant as a rejoinder to a Democratic listing of important Negro government appointees. Lewis, as it turned out, was the librarian at the Republican National Committee offices; he and a collection of other Negro employees there—many of them on the mailroom staff—were lavishly photographed and more lav-

ishly characterized. "Electronics," for example, was the job description given to a Flexo-writer operator.[127]

Reynolds claims that Miller refused to discuss the merits of the southern strategy with him. According to Reynolds, Miller told him that he had other people to advise him on political strategy and did not need his input.[128] In Reynolds's description, the Minorities Division "was simply window dressing."[129]

Other, more prominent, Republicans also questioned the southern strategy. Former RNC chairman Meade Alcorn, who began Operation Dixie in 1957, claimed that the party was abandoning its commitment to civil rights in order to attract the votes of segregationist whites. Others in the party also spoke out. New York Senator Jacob Javits said, "I feel the Republican Party should be the fighter for civil rights . . . I do not see that this role should be compromised by an effort to win the South on the basis of outsegregating the segregationists."[130] Kentucky Senator John Sherman Cooper was another who warned the Republican party against taking this course: "If our party uses the expedient argument of States' rights with respect to constitutional and human rights—in an effort to secure convention or electoral votes—it is possible we might win a few Southern States in 1964. But in the long run, such a position will destroy the Republican Party, and worse, it will do a great wrong because it will be supporting the denial of the constitutional and human rights of our citizens."[131]

Despite the efforts of Senators Javits and Cooper, most liberal and moderate Republicans in this period did little to retain their influence in the Republican party. Though Javits and Cooper publicly denounced the southern strategy, few other Republican liberals did. Grant Reynolds complained about the RNC's southern strategy to John Lindsay and other Republican liberals in the House "Wednesday Group," but they failed to support him. In fact, Lindsay told Reynolds to leave the RNC alone and concentrate on attacking the Democrats.[132]

THE KEATING PROPOSAL

One is struck by how most liberal and moderate Republicans made only the most halting of efforts to alter the party's course on policy or organizational strategy. One proposed counter-strategy came from moderate New York Senator Kenneth Keating, who called for the RNC to create a party policy council. According to Keating, his proposed "All-Republican Committee" would be composed of thirty-five members—ten senators, ten representatives, ten public members, Presidents Eisenhower and Hoover, Vice-President Nixon, Henry Cabot Lodge, Nixon's running mate, and the RNC chairman. In his view, the committee would help "shape, but not dictate party policy." Jacob Javits also called for the creation of a "shadow cabinet," made up of prominent Republicans in various fields of expertise, especially former members of the Eisenhower administration. These proposals called to mind the Democratic Advisory Council, but Keating claimed that his idea was modeled after the Committee on Program and Progress, a Republican policy council headed by Charles Percy in 1959.[133]

The Keating proposal fell upon deaf ears. Conservatives denounced the idea, fearing that it would give party liberals, like Keating and Javits, added influence in determining Republican policies. Barry Goldwater responded to the idea of a party council by saying, "We do not need a fancy advisory group such as the Democrats have."[134] Republican congressional leaders opposed the formation of a group that would infringe upon their ability to set party policy.[135] Others in the party believed that Nixon's near victory showed support for the Republican program and that there was no need to reformulate party policy. In his assessment of the election results at the January 1961 meeting of the RNC, party chairman Thruston Morton said:

> In my opinion, we do not particularly need another Mackinac Island Conference [a Republican policy council of the 1940s]. We do not need any kind of new party manifesto. We do not need any shift in philosophy.
>
> As I see it, we don't really need any new kind of declaration. We have able leaders in the Congress . . . and in the State Houses, eminently equipped to help the party progress.
>
> We have our platform of 1960 . . . . Far from being rejected, this platform is supported by half of the American people, at least.
>
> We have the long-range guidelines of the excellent 1959 report of the Republican committee on program and progress. We also have—in the legislative messages of President Eisenhower over the past years—an affirmative Republican solution . . . for every problem that faces us at home and abroad.[136]

Later in the meeting the RNC took up the Keating proposal. Again Morton expressed his view that a party committee was unnecessary at best and divisive at worst: "We don't want to get ourselves into the situation in which the Democrats found themselves, with an advisory committee which was at loggerheads with the leadership of the Democratic Party in the Congress."[137] Though a few members expressed support for the Keating proposal, the RNC killed it by calling for further study of the idea.[138]

THE REPUBLICAN CITIZENS' COMMITTEE

President Eisenhower also attempted to counter the rightward drift of the Republican party. In May 1961 he sponsored a meeting of his former administration officials with the idea of establishing a body both to criticize the Kennedy administration and to help the Republican party form policies.[139] Encouraged by Walter Thayer, moderate Republican publisher of the *New York Herald Tribune,* Eisenhower decided to broaden this group into the Republican Citizens' Committee. Ike hoped that the group, composed mainly of former members of his administration and prominent Republican business leaders, would help to broaden and moderate the increasingly conservative GOP, through research and consultation with party officials, just as the Citizens for Eisenhower organizations had done in the 1950s.[140] In his view, the citizens' committee would help to "build a bridge between the Republican Party on the one hand and the Independents and the dissatisfied Democrats on the other so that these latter people may eventually find themselves more comfortable living with Republican policies and personalities."[141]

The Republican Citizens' Committee was kicked off on June 30, 1962, at the All-Republican Conference held at Eisenhower's farm in Gettysburg, Pennsylvania. Attending the conference were Eisenhower, Richard Nixon, William Miller, Senate minority leader Everett Dirksen, House minority leader Charles Halleck, and other current and former Republican officials.[142] At the conference, Eisenhower presented the case for a unified and moderate party and called on Republicans to reject those who strove for ideological purity.[143]

Just about every portion of the Republican party apart from Ike's immediate family opposed the citizens' committee. The RNC believed that it would siphon off funds from potential contributors. The party's congressional leadership believed that it would infringe on their power to set party policy. Even some liberals like Nelson Rockefeller were opposed to the committee since they thought it was a front to support Richard Nixon or George Romney for the 1964 Republican nomination.[144]

Republican conservatives were the most opposed to the citizens' committee since they believed that it would increase the influence of the moderate, "establishment" wing of the party. The *National Review* called it the "least appealing mess of modern Republicanism since Harold Stassen ran last."[145] Barry Goldwater exploded in a letter to William Miller, claiming that the people behind the committee were "the same people who have caused most of our trouble. It is unthinkable that they should be given another opportunity to lead us down the path to political destruction."[146]

In spite of the opposition it engendered, the citizens' committee went ahead with its efforts. In 1963 the group established a Critical Issues Council, headed by Milton Eisenhower, the former president's brother. Despite this activity, the committee had low morale and never managed to generate much interest or enthusiasm.[147] The RNC and other Republican officials ignored the citizens' committee for the most part. "It can drop dead," said one RNC member.[148] By 1964 the Republican Citizens' Committee had receded into oblivion.

The fate of the policy responses suggested by Keating and Eisenhower is interesting since the Republicans paid very little attention to the Democrats' response over the previous four years, despite the belief of many political observers at the time that the DNC's policy response had helped the party to regain the White House in 1960. Perhaps a policy response was inappropriate for the Republican party after 1960, but what is striking is how quickly the RNC reached that conclusion and with so little discussion of the possible merits of such a strategy. The RNC's almost single-minded focus upon a nonideological, organizational strategy seems to have prevented them from engaging in a more thorough and objective analysis of possible responses.

ASSESSING THE RESPONSE

What did the RNC's response to its party's defeat in the 1960 consist of? Four activities stand out: the ballot security measures, the Big City Program, Operation Dixie, and the direct-mail program. Each of these was clearly a response to the 1960 election. Other than Operation Dixie, all were started after the election and each corresponded to some perceived problem related to the 1960 defeat. Operation Dixie, though started in 1957, can also be considered a response to defeat since the program took on new importance and energy as a result of the 1960 election.

The RNC's response in this period can be categorized as an organizational one. All four of the previously mentioned efforts were directed at improving or upgrading the party's organizational capacity, from rebuilding Republican party organizations in the large cities, to building new ones in the South, to improving the RNC's fundraising capacity. The RNC did consider various ideas for procedural and policy responses—the Morehouse plan, the Keating proposal, and the Republican Citizens' Committee were discussed by the party—but each was quickly rejected in favor of the organizational strategies. Though the citizens' committee did manage to establish itself, the RNC had little to do with this other than providing the staffing for the Gettysburg Conference. After the conference the RNC's attitude toward the citizens' committee can best be described as hostile neglect. Finally, while these organizational changes ultimately had a great impact upon the policies of the Republican party, that impact was an indirect one. The primary emphasis of these efforts was organizational rather than ideological.

Both factions in the Republican party saw their internal party strategies in organizational terms; liberals advocated rebuilding the Republican party in the North, whereas conservatives favored building Republican organizations in the South. Neither side seems to have given serious consideration to implementing a procedural or policy response to help them control the party's destiny. Even in this period of often bitter division, a norm of emphasizing organization over procedure and policy seems to have constrained the outlook of both Republican liberals and conservatives.

This behavior seems most striking for the Republican liberals and moderates, since the party's emphasis on organization in this period, primarily Operation Dixie and the direct-mail program, vastly reduced their power and influence within the Republican party and made the nomination of a moderate or liberal candidate extremely unlikely. Prior to 1964, liberal and moderate candidates could and needed to rely upon substantial southern support. In fact, in the three competitive Republican nomination battles before 1964 (1940, 1948, and 1952), southern delegates at the national convention divided their votes nearly evenly between the liberal and conservative nominees (see table 8). In each of these years, the more liberal candidate(s) managed to get at least 40 percent of the southern delegates.

Operation Dixie changed all of this. Southern Republicans would no longer be under the influence of party moderates. Tom Stagg, Jr., a RNC member from Louisiana, best typified this new attitude when he said in 1961, "I just hope to God that for once my party has the guts to say to hell with carrying New York. I hope for once we have the guts to say to hell with those eastern liberals."[149] By 1964, this attitude predominated among southern Republicans as they gave over 97 percent of their convention votes to the conservative nominee, Barry Goldwater.

Operation Dixie not only helped Republican conservatives to defy liberals and moderates with regards to the party nomination, but it also helped them to say it with regards to the general election. Previously, Republican moderates could argue that without the Solid South, any Republican nominee would have to compete for electoral votes in the more liberal Northeast. Operation Dixie meant that a conservative Republican nominee could win the presidency without the electoral votes of the more liberal Northeast, by winning the South and the traditional Republican areas in the West and Midwest. Finally, the establishment of the RNC's direct-mail program freed the party from its dependence upon the money of its more liberal, Wall Street wing.

Fixated upon organizational strategies, few on the left wing of the Republi-

TABLE 8.

CONTESTED REPUBLICAN NATIONAL CONVENTIONS: FIRST BALLOT DIVISION OF SOUTHERN DELEGATE SUPPORT.

	Liberal Candidate(s)	*Conservative Candidate*	*Other*
1940	*Dewey/Wilke*, 41.4%	*Taft*, 44.4%	14.2%
1948	*Dewey/Stassen*, 43.8%	*Taft*, 45.4%	10.8%
1952	*Eisenhower/Others*, 51.8%	*Taft*, 48.2%	
1964	*Rockefeller/Scranton*, 2.9%	*Goldwater*, 97.1%	

Source: Congressional Quarterly, *Guide to U.S. Elections*, 2d ed. (Washington, D.C.: Congressional Quarterly Press, 1985), 201–6.

can party seemed to understand these changes and the problems that they created for their position within the party. Among them, only Jud Morhouse seems to have understood the danger that they faced by focusing exclusively upon organization. It seems doubtful that his proposal for sweeping procedural changes, or the policy recommendations made by Keating and Eisenhower, would have succeeded, but given that it offered liberal Republicans perhaps their only chance to stop the growing influence of the conservatives, one would expect that these proposals would have gained more support than they did. Only the organizational strategy of the Big City Program generated much enthusiasm among Republican liberals and moderates.

The futile position of the Republican liberals and moderates became apparent when Thomas Dewey, the leader of the Republicans' moderate establishment, attempted to gather support for Pennsylvania governor William Scranton in a last-minute effort to prevent the 1964 Republican nomination from going to Barry Goldwater. According to James Reichley:

> Dewey gathered some of his old lieutenants and began making calls around the country from a boardroom in downtown Manhattan. But the structure of the Republican party, and indeed the financial structure of the United States, had changed since 1952. Banks and law firms in the South and the West were no longer so responsive to calls from Wall Street, and most of the backcountry politicians who at earlier critical moments had aligned themselves with the establishment were retired or dead. At the end of the afternoon, Dewey rolled down his sleeves and said, "Boys, it's not going to work. I'm going home."[150]

4

THE REPUBLICANS,

1964–1968

In 1964, Republican presidential candidate Barry Goldwater led his party to one of its worse defeats. Goldwater's opponent, President Lyndon B. Johnson, won 61.1 percent of the vote, the largest percentage in American history. Goldwater managed to win only his home state of Arizona and the states of South Carolina, Georgia, Alabama, Mississippi, and Louisiana in the Deep South. In addition to their dismal showing in the presidential election, the Republicans also lost thirty-eight House seats and two Senate seats, giving the Democrats their largest margins in Congress since 1936.

In the aftermath of this disastrous showing, the Republican party fashioned a vigorous organizational response. This effort can be seen in the struggle to replace the conservatives ideologues who headed the RNC during the 1964 campaign with Ray Bliss, a pragmatic, nonideological, "nuts and bolts" political technician. Once in office, Bliss instituted a series of measures to rebuild Republican party organizations across the country.

In addition to its organizational response, the RNC also mounted a secondary policy response in the form of the Republican Coordinating Committee (RCC). The RCC had three purposes. One was to furnish the party with a policy council that would allow it to reestablish a more moderate image than was created by the 1964 platform. Second, the RCC gave the party a vehicle through which to criticize the Johnson administration and to develop Republican approaches on a variety of issues. Finally, the RCC provided Republicans with an internal forum for achieving consensus among various factions.

THE STRUGGLE FOR BLISS

The damage to the Republican party inflicted by the 1964 election went beyond its losses at the polls. The party was rent by the conflicts between its conservative and liberal wings. While some moderate and liberal

Republicans, like William Scranton and Charles Percy, loyally endorsed Goldwater, many others, such as Kenneth Keating, Nelson Rockefeller, George Romney, and Jacob Javits, refused to do so, and others, including Thomas Dewey, went so far as to help the Johnson campaign.[1]

On the other hand, Goldwater conservatives had taken over the national party apparatus, to the exclusion of nearly everyone else. The conservatives viewed the RNC as the base through which they could continue to dominate the Republican party, whether or not Goldwater won the election. In July 1964, an unnamed Goldwater aide said, "I know we probably won't win in November and I don't give a damn. Winning control of one of the two major parties is victory enough for me."[2] Karl Hess, a member of Goldwater's campaign staff, later wrote that conservatives believed that "if Goldwater could win the candidacy, he would also win control of the Republican National Committee and that this, for the future of the party, would be secondary in meaningfulness only to an electoral victory."[3]

Following his selection by Goldwater as RNC chairman at the 1964 convention, Dean Burch and his executive director, John Grenier began a wholesale restructuring of the RNC. Burch and Grenier reshaped the RNC's executive committee by replacing moderate and liberal members with conservatives. They also fired or demoted RNC staff members who lacked the proper conservative credentials and replaced them with persons of purer ideological beliefs. Ironically, one of those demoted in the RNC was Lee Potter. Despite having played an instrumental role in the development of the southern Republican organizations which were so crucial to Goldwater, Potter was assigned the inglorious task of coordinating advance work for Richard Nixon's and Dwight Eisenhower's campaign appearances.[4]

If the shake-ups in RNC personnel were not enough to damage staff morale, Burch and Grenier instituted a regime that demanded both secrecy and loyalty to the conservative cause. Staff members were issued memos discouraging them from talking to the press and journalists were denied access to RNC headquarters. Grenier ordered that only pictures of Goldwater and William Miller (his running mate) be displayed in RNC headquarters and initially instructed an RNC staffer to remove portraits of Lincoln and Eisenhower; he later relented. As morale plummeted, bitter humor developed among many longtime RNC staffers; making the rounds at the RNC was a bumper sticker that read, "Better LBJ than John Grenier."[5]

Even more disturbing to party regulars than the shake-up at the RNC was Grenier's plan to replace or take over existing Republican organizations with the more conservative Citizens for Goldwater–Miller groups. This plan was described by Stephen Shadegg, a Goldwater campaign aide, in a manual for conservative political activity. Shadegg advocated guerrilla warfare against regular Republican organizations where a conservative "cell group" of "enthusiastic, knowledgeable Goldwater supporters . . . able to infiltrate centers of opposition support, keep us informed of opposition tactics, disseminate information, enlist other supporters, and to do all these things completely unnoticed by the opposition."[6]

By mid-October 1964 it was becoming increasingly apparent that Goldwater would lose the election and by a very large margin, so Republican liberals and moderates began to take steps to return the RNC to a more neutral footing.[7] This shift would serve the goals of moderate Republicans by reducing the power of the conservatives within the party. Additionally, such a move would help to reunify the party and signal to the public that the party was no longer in the hands of extremists—two of the principal reasons for Goldwater's defeat.

By election day this effort was in full swing. As soon as the polls closed, Michigan national committeeman John Martin called for Burch's removal.[8] Martin's call was soon echoed by other Republicans. Kentucky Senator Thruston Morton, a former RNC chairman, stated, "We have got to change the national committee and we have got to change the party's image, by broadening the base of the party's appeal." To achieve this, Morton suggested recruiting a new RNC chairman less identified with an ideological faction.[9] Pennsylvania Senator Hugh Scott, himself purged as RNC chairman after Thomas Dewey's defeat in 1948, said, "The present party leadership must be replaced—all of it." He added that Burch and Grenier "ran this campaign with no intention to win but to rule over the ruins."[10] Another former RNC chairman, Meade Alcorn, came to a similar conclusion, stating, "We cannot hope to shape future party victories if that rebuilding job is entrusted to the leadership of the Goldwater organization, which has brought us the most devastating defeat the party has ever suffered."[11]

Despite these criticisms, Burch refused to resign and Republican conservatives insisted that he remain. Three days after the election, Goldwater praised Burch for doing "a very, very commendable job" as RNC chairman and recommended that the party "keep him because for the first time in memory we finished the campaign in the black."[12] Goldwater's statement referred to reports that the RNC had finished the campaign with a $1.2 million surplus.[13] Many moderates and liberals, however, used this report to criticize Burch, claiming that the money had been withheld from liberal and moderate Republican candidates.[14] The following week, Goldwater told the press that the job of RNC chairman "is contracted for four years and I would expect the Republican party to live up to that contract."[15]

Despite Goldwater's opposition, influential Republicans began a behind-the-scenes campaign to oust Burch and regain control of the RNC.[16] One of the principal players in this drama was Donald R. Ross, RNC member from Nebraska. Though a solid conservative and a Goldwater supporter in the general election, Ross, in conversations with other Republican party officials, primarily from the Midwest, came to the conclusion in October 1964 that Goldwater would lose the election and that it was imperative for the party to unite itself.

To that end, Ross traveled from Nebraska to New York City on election day to meet with George Hinman, national committeeman from New York and a close political advisor of Nelson Rockefeller. Ross and Hinman discussed how to unite and rebuild the party. Both men agreed that Burch would have to go, but that any moves against him had to be carried out with the utmost delicacy. The Goldwater campaign had recruited many conservative activists and contributors, many of whom were deeply embittered at the eastern Republican "establishment" for abandoning Goldwater. In order to keep these people in the party, Hinman and Ross realized that efforts to remove Burch had to operate out of the more conservative Midwest. If eastern Republicans were seen as leading the anti-Burch effort, conservatives would view it as a liberal takeover, further polarizing the party.[17]

Additionally, Hinman and Ross believed that Burch's replacement would have to be acceptable to both wings of the party. The two decided that the best candidate for the RNC was Ray Bliss, the chairman of the Ohio Republican party. In 1960 Bliss described his approach to managing a political party: "Methods used by state chairmen vary considerably, each geared specifically to particular state situations. At some time nearly every state chairman must make a basic decision as to whether he will be an office chairman, managing the party affairs from state headquarters, or be a speaking chairman, traveling over the state day in and day out making public appearances. There are both types. I have chosen to be primarily an office chairman."[18]

Hinman, Ross, and others in the party believed that Bliss's nonideological "office chairman" approach was ideally suited to calm the turbulence in the Republican party. Unlike Paul Butler, a "speaking chairman" par excellence who strove to lead the Democratic party on policy issues, they knew that Bliss would devote himself to the less controversial role of managing the "nuts and bolts" (a favorite expression of Bliss's) of the Republican party.[19]

The next day Ross began contacting other RNC members. Some were reluctant to take action against Burch, believing that it was the party nominee's prerogative to appoint the national committee chairman. Others worried that removing Burch would, according to Ross, "disenfranchise 28 million Republicans who voted for Goldwater" and alienate many of the conservatives Goldwater had brought into the Republican camp. But most of the RNC members Ross spoke with knew that "28 million wasn't enough" and that removing Burch was necessary for the party to begin to unify itself.

Outside of the RNC, the moderate-dominated Republican Governors' Association, also called for Burch's removal. At their December 5 meeting in Denver, the governors voted unanimously to issue the following statement: "The first step in marshaling Republican party strength for the future must be the uniting of Republicans themselves. Any policy of exclusion must be changed and cannot be tolerated. We strongly recommend to the national committee that, in determining its leadership at the forthcoming meeting in January, it adopt leadership which clearly represents a broad view of Republicanism and practices a policy of inclusion, rather than exclusion."[20]

Though Burch was not named directly, most understood the statement as a call for his removal. "If it isn't, you can shoot me," claimed Nelson Rockefeller.[21]

George Romney added: "Dean Burch is a symbol of disaster. It would be impossible for the Republican party to unify and broaden and strengthen itself under his direction. . . . Dean Burch should be removed or resign as national chairman."[22]

In spite of the governors' statement, Goldwater refused to budge. In December, he wrote to each of the 132 members of the RNC in an effort to shore up support for Burch, saying, "I feel the removal of Dean Burch would be a repudiation of a great segment of our party, and a repudiation of me."[23] Goldwater also made rumblings that if he did not get his way he would consider a conservative third-party movement. He stated that there were approximately 10 million conservative activists in the country which he thought was "something like 12 times as much as any so-called third party or outside party ever started with."[24]

Meanwhile, Ross continued with his efforts in the RNC. In late December he called a meeting of midwestern RNC members. Most at the meeting believed that Burch had to go, and they were willing to work actively to achieve that goal. Though traditionally conservative and therefore seemingly reluctant to oust a conservative from the RNC, they were also pragmatic. Midwestern Republicans had suffered heavily in 1964. Not only had Lyndon Johnson swept this traditionally Republican region, but nineteen of the thirty-eight House seats lost by Republicans in 1964 came from the Midwest. Seventeen of these seats had been held by conservatives.[25] In Iowa (which, it was said, would go Democratic "when Hell went Methodist"), Republicans lost five of the six House seats that they had controlled in 1964. Political survival in the region necessitated a new direction for the party.

From this base in the Midwest, Ross and others began to gather support for Burch's ouster. Ross also attempted to persuade Ray Bliss to declare himself a candidate, but Bliss, who abhorred controversy, declined. He insisted that he would not accept the chairmanship if the party was divided—an unlikely prospect given the current state of the GOP.[26] Ross knew that Bliss was the only acceptable alternative to Burch and that his refusal to expressly declare his interest in the RNC chairmanship complicated efforts at unifying the party.

According to Ross, the effort to remove Burch reached a critical stage during a series of meeting in Washington in early January 1965. On January 4, Bliss, Goldwater, and William Miller met and discussed the condition of the party. Goldwater insisted on keeping Burch, but he realized that Republican party was in serious difficulty and that something had to be done. The next day Ross, Bliss, Goldwater, Miller and Burch met at the Mayflower Hotel. The meeting started cordially, but Burch soon became upset and caustic, criticizing Bliss and Ross for attempting to damage the party. Goldwater then stepped in, saying, "Let's not get into a pissing match" and defended Ross for supporting him during the election.

Burch and Ross then argued over the next several hours. Burch claimed that removing the RNC's conservative leadership would be a disservice to the party, making it only a bland echo, not a real choice. Ross countered that the party was deeply divided and needed new, less ideological leadership.

Ross asked Bliss several times to state his feelings on the issue, but each time he refused. Ross worried that Bliss's unwillingness to take a stand would make Goldwater think that Bliss was weak and unwilling to fight for the chairmanship. As the meeting broke up, Ross once again asked Bliss to state his views, saying, "Ray, I really think you owe it to Senator Goldwater to say what your feelings are." Bliss finally admitted that he would take the position, but only if there was a vacancy.

Ross then began working to convince Goldwater that he would lose a fight in the RNC and that he should go along with the Bliss-for-Burch switch. After leaving the meeting, Ross told Miller that he had the names of seventy-one RNC members willing to dump Burch. The next day Ross met with the midwestern RNC members and produced a letter with thirty-one names (about 75 percent of those attending) saying that Burch had to go. Bliss, however, told Ross to hold off sending the letter because Miller was working with Goldwater to reach an agreement.

By now Goldwater must have realized that he was fighting a losing battle. Not only was he aware of Ross's efforts, he had also corresponded with numerous RNC members after the election. Though divided on the issue, most RNC members who wrote to Goldwater stated their belief that Burch should go. Vermont national committeeman Edward Janeway told Goldwater that fighting to keep Burch would "destroy the hoped for unity that you both [Goldwater and Burch] so loudly proclaim."[27] North Dakota's national committeeman called on Goldwater to use his "good offices to see that it will not be necessary for us [the RNC] to vote no confidence in Mr. Burch." He added his belief that if it came to a vote, Burch "would lose rather decisively unless there are more liars in this party than I think there are."[28] Stanley Hathaway, Wyoming's national committeeman, wrote to Goldwater:

> I have no quarrel with Dean Burch or with the operation of the National Committee during the recent campaign. I think that he did a commendable job under the circumstances. However, I feel that Dean has become too controversial to continue to work effectively as National Chairman. . . .
>
> In my humble opinion, it is a mistake for you to jeopardize your position of leadership by tying it to the question of whether or not Dean Burch remains as National Chairman. I respectfully urge you to take the lead in recommending to the National Committee a new chairman who is not presently controversial and who can have some hope of uniting all segments of the party.[29]

Knowing that at best Burch would retain his position by a narrow margin, an outcome which might possibly rupture the party, Goldwater finally agreed to ask Burch to resign and to have Bliss take over the RNC. Goldwater invited Bliss to his Phoenix home to announce the decision. Bliss, ever cautious, worried that Goldwater might back out of the agreement and make him look foolish, but he finally decided to go after consulting with Don Ross. Even so, Bliss did not let word of his trip get out until after his plane was in the air.

The episode finally ended on January 12, 1965, as Goldwater, Miller, Bliss, and Burch announced to the press that Burch would resign and that Bliss would take his place. As a face-saving effort, Burch was allowed to stay on until April 1. Goldwater praised Burch but acknowledged "that without having the support of the committee he could not do his job or himself justice."[30]

The decision to replace Burch with Bliss then had to be approved by the RNC, which met in Chicago on January 21. Many RNC members, especially on the more conservative executive committee, protested angrily over what they perceived as a liberal coup. One national committeewoman commented: "For thirty years it's been the conservatives who had to make the concessions. If the others [nonconservatives] feel sincerely about unity, why don't they make concessions once in a while?"[31]

Despite these complaints, the RNC still voted unanimously to accept Burch's resignation and to elect Bliss to replace him. Some of the bitter feelings and third-party thoughts of conservatives were allayed by Barry Goldwater's and Dean Burch's speeches to the committee. Burch said that it was "absolutely vital" to unify the party and, "A party that is splintered is nothing but a sect." Goldwater accepted full blame for the defeat and said he "would resist any third-party movement in this country and never allow my name to be associated with such a movement."[32]

The maneuvering to replace Burch with Bliss illuminates a pervasive reaction within the Republican party. Until 1964, Republican liberals and moderates held sway over the Republican party, but the nomination of Barry Goldwater marked a dramatic end to that influence and showed that the balance of power within the Republican party had shifted to the conservatives. Yet, in response to this shift, liberal and moderate Republicans once again focused on an organizational response (the selection of Ray Bliss as RNC chairman), seemingly oblivious to the fact that the party's focus on such tactics had helped to diminish their influence over the previous four years and that such a response offered little hope for them to regain their past influence.

BLISS COMES TO THE RNC

Unfortunately for Bliss, when he took over the RNC in April 1965 he found that the factional battles of the previous year had undermined both its morale and effectiveness. Within the RNC, conservative staff members left over from the Burch regime were suspicious of both Bliss and his plans. Outside the RNC, ideological splinter groups on both the right and left were cropping up and threatening to undermine the authority and the effectiveness of the committee.

One of the principal nonparty organizations set up following the election was the Free Society Committee, established by Barry Goldwater and Denison Kitchel, Goldwater's 1964 campaign manager. Goldwater claimed that the association would in "no way be a third party movement" and instead would merely "attempt to educate more and more American people into the values of the Republican party."[33] Bliss, however, took exception and issued an uncharacteristic public denunciation of the Free Society Association and other splinter groups, saying, "All such groups are destructive of party unity."[34]

Bliss's attempts to deal with these factional problems blew up in his face. Soon after starting at the RNC, it came to his attention that Frank Kovac, RNC finance director and a Burch holdover, was selling the RNC's contributor list to assorted right-wing groups. Bliss ordered Kovac to stop; when Kovac persisted, Bliss asked for his resignation. Kovac sent his letter of resignation on May 26, but it did not take effect until July 1.

In the meantime, a computer tape of RNC contributors turned up missing. Bliss, worried that Kovac had taken the tape to give to the Free Society Association, ordered one of his assistants, William Cody Kelly, to break into Kovac's desk to find the tape. On the night of June 18, Kelly and an assistant forced their way into Kovac's desk. During the raid, Kelly is alleged to have said, "Kovac is a phony from way back. He is out to cut us up with his new Goldwater outfit."[35]

Several members of Kovac's office staff witnessed the event and it soon became public. Bliss was then forced to fire Kelly, who then told the press that Bliss had approved the break-in. The whole fiasco only served to highlight the factional tensions in the RNC and also to undermine Bliss's leadership less than two weeks before his first meeting of the RNC since he had become chairman.

Despite the negative fallout from the Kovac-Kelly affair, Bliss went ahead with his organizational plans for the RNC, which he unveiled at the June 29 meeting of the RNC. In his speech Bliss stressed what he believed were the four cornerstones of an effective political party operation: adequate financing, strong organization, good candidates, and the right party image.[36] As chairman of the RNC, Bliss worked to improve the party in each of these areas.

FINANCE

Despite having ended the campaign in the black, by the time Bliss took over, the RNC was in financial difficulty. Of the approximately $1 million left over from the campaign, the RNC controlled only about $300,000. The Citizens for Goldwater-Miller Committee controlled most of the remainder. The RNC struggled fruitlessly to take possession of these funds, which the Goldwater organization spent to advance various conservative efforts, often at variance with the purposes of the RNC.[37]

Moreover, fundraising prospects looked bleak as potential contributors hesitated to give money because of the party's poor showing and internal divisions. The Republican National Finance Committee (RNFC) also lacked a chairman following Ralph J. Cordiner's resignation after the election. Finally, the Republican party's coordinated fundraising program had broken down during the 1964 campaign as the Republican House and Senate Campaign Committees began their own fundraising efforts.

In spite of these financial difficulties, one of Dean Burch's last acts as chairman was to submit a highly unrealistic $4.7 million "victory" budget for 1965. At the time the RNC could not raise enough funds to cover the $200,000 a month necessary to keep the doors open, let alone the $400,000 a month required under Burch's budget.[38] By April 1965, the RNC had only enough money for another two months of operation.[39]

Bliss's plans for the RNC required an adequate financial base, or as one of his aides put it, "His brick by brick rebuilding of the party has got to be cemented together with money."[40] As a result, Bliss set out immediately to improve the party's financial picture. He cut costs by implementing drastic economy measures and reestablished administrative control over RNC activities, which had collapsed since the election.[41] Bliss also persuaded former General Lucius D. Clay to become chairman of the RNFC. This was not an easy task for Bliss since Clay initially insisted on having some control over where the money would be spent. Bliss, already beset by numerous conflicting pressures, refused and finally persuaded Clay to concentrate solely on raising funds.[42]

Clay, the commander of the Berlin airlift and an imposing figure, was well suited to the task of restoring order and prestige to the RNFC.[43] Also, as a partner in the Wall Street brokerage firm of Lehman Brothers and a member of numerous corporate boards, Clay could help bring back those members of the Republican business establishment who had abandoned the party in 1964.[44]

Bliss and Clay set out to recentralize party fundraising. Though unable to reestablish the system that had existed prior to 1964, in June 1965 they did persuade the Republican Congressional Committee to combine its lucrative ($400,000 in the first six months of 1965) Boosters Program of $1,000 contributors with the RNFC's own $1,000 contributors program. In return, Bliss and Clay agreed that C. Langhorne Washburn, director of the Boosters Program, would serve as Clay's assistant at the RNFC and that the money would be used to support Republican challengers in the 1966 House elections.[45]

Clay also used his Wall Street and business connections to help keep the RNC afloat in 1965. Soon after coming to the RNFC, he sent out personal letters to large contributors, many of whom had refused to support Goldwater in 1964, asking for $1,000 donations to the party. By the end of August, Clay's appeal drew 237 responses.[46]

Despite the success in increasing large contributions to the RNC, the party's principal means of income remained the direct-mail program. Since its origin in 1962, the program had grown tremendously, raising almost $6 million for the party and the Goldwater campaign in 1964.[47] Though some attributed the success of the direct-mail program to enthusiasm for Goldwater and predicted that it would decline after the election, the RNC maintained and expanded the direct-mail program after the 1964 election. In 1965 the party sent out more than 3 million solicitation letters which generated a return of $1.7 million dollars, more than 40 percent of the total funds raised by the RNFC that year.[48] The direct-mail program continued to be successful in following years (see table 9). By 1966 the direct-mail program was raising enough by itself to cover the routine costs of running the RNC.[49] According to RNFC Treasurer J. William Middendorf, the party "lived off small contributors" in this period.[50]

The total fundraising efforts of the RNFC during the Bliss era reaped great rewards. The party raised far more funds than in the previous four years (see table 10). Another indicator of the success of Republican fundraising in this period is that the RNFC raised $5.1 million in 1967, whereas the DNC only brought in $2.2 million, despite controlling the White House.[51]

Bliss and Clay's fundraising efforts put the party into a very solid position for the 1968 election. The RNC had $700,000 in available cash in January 1968 and nearly $1.5 million in August 1968 for the Nixon campaign to use.[52] This money undoubtedly contributed to Nixon's narrow victory in November.

TABLE 9.

REPUBLICAN NATIONAL FINANCE COMMITTEE INCOME, 1965–1968.

Year	Direct-Mail Income ($)	Total Income ($)	% From Direct Mail
1965	1,700,000	4,200,000	40.5
1966	3,300,000	7,100,000	46.5
1967	3,500,000	5,100,000	68.6
1968	6,600,000	29,600,000	22.3

Source: Data compiled from Minutes of the RNC Executive Session, January 31, 1966, Washington, D.C., *Papers of the Republican Party,* pt. 1: Meetings of the Republican National Committee, 1911–1980; Series B: 1960–1980, Paul L. Kesaris, ed. (Frederick, Md.: University Publications of America), reel 5, frame 54; minutes of the RNC Executive Session, January 23, 1967, New Orleans, Louisiana, *Papers of the Republican Party,* pt. 1, reel 5, frame 740; Herbert Alexander, *Financing the 1968 Election* (Lexington, Mass.: Heath, 1971), 148; Alexander, *Money in Politics* (Washington D.C.: Public Affairs Press, 1972), 109; and Robert B. Semple, Jr., "Skill Replaces Ideology at G.O.P. Headquarters under Bliss," *New York Times,* February 1, 1968, 24.

Note: The figures for 1968 represent the total raised by all party and campaign committees in that year. The discontinuity in the figures for 1968 represents the inordinate number of large contributions raised by the Nixon-Agnew Campaign Committee.

TABLE 10.

REPUBLICAN NATIONAL FINANCE COMMITTEE INCOME, 1961–1968.

Year	Total Income ($)
1961	1,658,368
1962	3,299,426
1963	2,759,512
1964	2,069,500
1965	4,200,000
1966	7,100,000
1967	5,100,000
1968	5,673,000

Source: Data compiled from document from the Republican National Finance Committee Meeting, January 21, 1965, Chicago, Illinois (photocopy); minutes of the RNC Executive Session, January 31, 1966, Washington, D.C., *Papers of the Republican Party*, pt. 1: Meetings of the Republican National Committee, 1911–1980; Series B: 1960–1980, Paul L. Kesaris, ed. (Frederick, Md.: University Publications of America), reel 5, frame 54; minutes of the RNC Executive Session, January 23, 1967, New Orleans, Louisiana, *Papers of the Republican Party*, pt. 1, reel 5, frame 740; Herbert Alexander, *Financing the 1964 Election* (Princeton, N.J.: Citizens' Research Foundation, 1966), 172; Alexander, *Financing the 1968 Election* (Lexington, Mass.: Heath, 1971), 148; and Robert B. Semple, Jr., "Skill Replaces Ideology at G.O.P. Headquarters under Bliss," *New York Times*, February 1, 1968, 24.

Note: The amounts for 1964 and 1968 represent pre-convention income only.

ORGANIZATION

Under Bliss, the RNC took a no-nonsense approach to achieving victory for the Republican party. As the RNC's Research Division pointed out, the 1964 results destroyed the "myth" that "there exists a huge, silent vote which had not voted previously but which, under the right conditions, would emerge as a new balance of power in Presidential elections."[53] Instead of chasing this myth, the RNC under Bliss concentrated on political organization, which he described as "the dirty, ditch-digging job that must be done if we are to succeed."[54]

Perhaps more than any other modern national party chairman, Ray Bliss believed in the importance of organization for political success. In a handbook for state party chairmen, he claimed: "In modern American politics, the primary [role] of the state chairman . . . is to build a party organization. . . . Whether his party wins or loses an election, a state chairman should build and maintain an effective year-round organization. . . . A political organization must be a continuous thing. It must be an alive, alert, and aggressive operation. . . . Organization is a major key to success in politics on any level—county, state, or national."[55]

True to form, Bliss began to reinvigorate the Republican party organizations at the national, state, and local levels. At the national level Bliss expanded the staff of the RNC, but his real emphasis was on winning state and local offices, which he believed were "the heartbeat of a local political organization."[56] "We are rebuilding from the basement up, not from the roof down," Bliss stated.[57] As chairman he promised that the RNC would try to "build a solid Republican Party organization that goes right down to the precinct level."[58]

To accomplish this, Bliss instituted a series of training seminars, an idea that he had championed earlier as Ohio state chairman and as head of the Republican State Party Chairmen's Association.[59] By January 1966, Bliss had developed a staff of more than fifty specialists to act as speakers and consultants at various workshops.[60] In 1966 and 1967, the RNC sponsored three workshops for party research personnel, four seminars for campaign managers, a conference for public relations staff, and several "Countdown '66" training sessions for party workers in state and congressional campaigns in the 1966 election.[61] These workshops concentrated on teaching state, county, and city party workers and congressional campaign staffs the techniques of polling, data processing, vote analysis, fundraising, advance work, scheduling, volunteer organizing, campaign headquarters management and media usage.[62]

The RNC's party-building activities went beyond just holding workshops. The RNC developed numerous manuals on political techniques for state and local parties. In 1966 Bliss instituted a state legislative division in the RNC to help coordinate efforts to win these seats. Bliss viewed this effort as crucial, telling the RNC: "Just never forget who redistricts the congressional districts and makes our job tougher—the state legislatures. That's important. Who passes laws that affect the businessmen we ask to give contributions? Not this congress—the state legislatures."[63]

Bliss also instituted a novel program where four regional field workers would act as a liaison between local campaign organizations and the RNC. In the past, local party officials had been reluctant to allow RNC representatives to meddle in their affairs, but this program was well received since the services offered by the RNC were useful and because it was well known that Bliss, a former state party chairman, was not out to centralize power in the RNC.[64]

As a major component of his party-building activities, Bliss dusted off the recommendations of report of the Committee on Big City Politics, which he had chaired in 1961 and 1962.[65] Beginning in early 1966 Bliss began to implement many of the report's recommendations.[66] He called a meeting of Republican chairman from the nation's seventeen largest cities to discuss the party's problem in urban areas, consider ideas for the future, and learn more about various political techniques. Most considered the session a success and two more sessions were held in March 1966.[67] Bliss also increased RNC efforts to recruit more black and union support for the GOP and he eventually appointed a field director for the big cities program.[68]

Though an emphasis on big cities could have exacerbated the ideological division in the Republican party, Bliss managed to avoid such a trap. He made sure that the emphasis on cities was geographically balanced and that organizational efforts were equally strong in the North and the South.[69] Bliss also tried to avoid ideological struggles by making sure that the training seminars concentrated purely on political techniques. According to observers of these sessions, they were "how to do it" sessions devoid of ideological content. Also, the factional battles of the previous four years and Goldwater's stunning loss seem to have both exhausted and disappointed many in the party by 1965, making them more than ready for Bliss's "nuts and bolts" approach.

CANDIDATES

The third cornerstone in Bliss's party building efforts was the recruitment of good candidates. In 1960 he wrote: "A state chairman can work endless days and nights in building a fine organization, but all his effort goes for naught if he fails to make provision for a constant flow of good candidate material. A party without competent, appealing candidates is pretty much like a large automobile agency without cars to sell."[70]

As chairman of the RNC, one of Bliss's first tasks was to seek out and recruit good candidates, regardless of ideology. This he did in the spring of 1965 when he helped persuade Republican Congressman John Lindsay to run for mayor of New York City. Bliss reportedly told Lindsay that fielding a strong Republican candidate in the race would greatly help the party's rebuilding efforts across the nation. He also offered to help Lindsay with fundraising.[71] Many took Lindsay's victory that fall as evidence of improved Republican fortunes.

Bliss also encouraged A. Linwood Holton to run for governor of Virginia in 1965. Though Holton lost the election, he ran a strong race and helped to show that Republicans need not embrace segregation to do well in the South. Holton managed to build upon this effort and won the governorship four years later.[72]

Bliss's recruitment efforts also bore fruit in the 1966 elections. He dissuaded several older ex-Congressmen who had lost in 1964 from attempting to win back their seats. In their places, he helped to recruit a younger and more attractive crop of challengers.[73] According to David Broder: "Instead of mouthing platitudes about the need for good candidates, Bliss went out and found them himself. The winners of no less than six of the [1966] election upsets—one Governor and five Representatives—were picked right from the ranks of his colleagues, the Republican state chairmen."[74]

PARTY IMAGE

The image of the Republican party in the aftermath of the 1964 election was, to put it mildly, tarnished. Many voters viewed the party as riven with ideological struggles and controlled by conservative extremists. Though much of this image was a distortion created by Democrats during the campaign, it was not a wholly inaccurate description of a party whose platform called for liberalizing control over nuclear weapons and whose candidate said, "Extremism in the defense of liberty is no vice."[75]

Efforts to moderate the party's image began soon after the election. The most significant attempt at this task was the Republican Coordinating Committee (RCC). The RCC grew out of the December 1964 meeting of the Republican Governors' Conference. In addition to calling for Dean Burch's removal, the governors' statement also called for a party conference to "reflect the opinions of all elements of the party" and the development of a "responsible executive committee, capable of expressing party policy, positions and programs promptly and constructively during the intervals between national conventions and meetings of the national committee."[76]

The governors' call was taken up by the Republican congressional leadership. On January 11, 1965, Senate Minority Leader Everett Dirksen and House Minority Leader Gerald Ford announced the establishment of the RCC. While asserting that policy-making authority for the party remained with the congressional party, Dirksen and Ford acknowledged that the party's other elected officials, former presidents and presidential candidates, members of the RNC, and state party chairmen offered "an additional repository of advice and counsel" that "must be channeled into party policy formation."[77] The RCC would examine party policy and research various issues and would be composed of the following members: former President Eisenhower; former presidential candidates Alf Landon, Thomas Dewey, Richard Nixon, and Barry Goldwater; five Republican governors; eleven congressional leaders; and the chairman of the RNC, who would also chair the RCC. Under pressure from the RNC, the RCC's membership was changed to include five additional members from the RNC. Eventually the RCC included sixteen congressional leaders (seven from the Senate and nine from the House) and a representative of the Republican Legislators' Association.

The RCC met in Washington on March 10, 1965, for the first time and issued the following statement of purpose: "The Republican Coordinating Committee was created (1) to broaden the advisory base on national party policy; (2) to set up task forces to study and make recommendations for dealing with the problems that confront the people of our nation; and (3) to stimulate communication among the members of the party and others in developing a common approach to the nation's problems."[78]

The RCC soon set to work by establishing task forces on the topics of human rights and responsibilities; foreign relations; federal, state, and local relations; and fiscal and monetary policy. Later, the RCC created task forces on job opportunities and welfare, senior citizens, national defense, and crime and delinquency; and two special study groups on revenue sharing, urban education, and national emergency strikes. The RCC also issued statements of its own on a variety of topics.

Unlike the Democratic Advisory Council (DAC) established by the DNC in 1956, the RCC strove to achieve unity within the party rather than to advance the programmatic goals of one faction of the party.[79] Because of this, the statements issued by the RCC tended to be less hard hitting than those of the DAC. The RCC did issue some controversial statements. For example, in December 1965, it denounced the John Birch Society and other right-wing extremist organizations, but these statements remained exceptions.[80] The typical statement by the RCC was a bland analysis of a domestic policy issue or a partisan blast at the Johnson administration.[81]

The RCC, moreover, tended to be much less divisive and controversial than the DAC, due to the active participation of all segments of the party. Unlike the DAC, the RCC insured a strong role for the congressional leadership from its inception. Senators and representatives made up the bulk of the committee and the congressional leadership exercised control over both the selection of the issues addressed by the committee and the conclusions of the RCC's statements and reports.[82] Bliss, ever cautious and deferential to the party's elected leadership, was a key person in helping the congressional leadership keep control.

The RCC also managed to avoid serious ideological disputes. One reason for this was that the presence of Eisenhower and other prestigious party leaders tended to keep the discussions calm and moderate. Also, Bliss, acting as chairman of the RCC, ruled with an iron hand to make sure that disputes did not get out of hand. Finally, Barry Goldwater chose not to use the RCC as a battleground for the conservative cause.[83]

Even so, heated discussions took place on several issues. In these situations Thomas Dewey, for so long the bête noir of Republican conservatives, was often able to find common ground for all factions to agree. According to Don Ross, who became vice-chairman of the RNC in 1965, after much argument Dewey would say, "Isn't what we all mean this . . . ?" and then present a consensus that most members could agree upon.[84]

The RCC was a reasonable success during its short life from 1965 to 1968. The committee managed to avoid most of the controversies resulting from a party policy council. The RCC also provided an internal forum for discussion between party factions and thereby helped to unify a badly divided party. Finally, the committee also produced a steady flow of reports and statements spelling out constructive, if not exciting, Republican positions on the issues and criticisms of the Johnson administration.

In addition to moderating the party's image with the RCC, the RNC also worked to improve the quality of its political research by substantially upgrading the RNC

Research Division. From 1961 to 1964, the Research Division produced less than a dozen major reports for the RNC, but from 1965 to 1968, the number increased to 116. These reports covered a variety of topics, from analyses of elections to surveys of public opinion polls to compilations of Republican and Democratic positions on various issues.[85]

The final aspect of Bliss's push to improve the image of the Republican party was the development of the RNC radio program, "Comment." This program, begun by Fred Morrison, director of public relations for the RNC, sent out five-minute recordings of various Republican officials speaking on different issues to radio stations around the country. Many stations, starved to fill airtime, eagerly broadcast the weekly tapes. Since the program was run as news, there was no cost to the RNC other than the costs of tapes and mailing. "Comment" started in June 1965 with 160 stations. One year later, the number of stations had risen to 1,200. By the end of 1966, 1,700 stations were playing the RNC tapes.[86]

ASSESSING THE RESPONSE

The RNC's activity between 1964 and 1968 can clearly be labeled an organizational response. During these years the RNC made significant efforts to repair the damage done to its national, state, and local party organizations by the 1964 election. First, the RNC's controversial conservative leader, Dean Burch, was removed and replaced with the more stable and ideologically neutral Ray Bliss. Second, under Bliss and Lucius Clay the RNC worked to upgrade the fundraising apparatus that had broken down as the result of the 1964 election. Finally, the RNC undertook a major effort to rebuild Republican party organizations across the country.

In addition to its organizational response, the RNC also fashioned a policy response. With the RCC as the principal mechanism, the RNC helped to unify a party that had been badly divided by the 1964 election and to moderate its image among the public. Though an important part of its activities in this period, the RNC's policy response was distinctly secondary to its organizational efforts. As chairman of the RNC, Bliss was far more interested in organizational work than in policy leadership. In addition, the RCC was largely an instrument of the Republican party's elected officials as well as the RNC.

As mentioned previously, the RNC's response to the 1964 election is somewhat remarkable given the factional disputes within the Republican party at that time. For most Republican liberals and moderates, selecting an organizational response offered little prospect of reversing their declining fortunes within the party. The RCC's policy response did offer a vehicle for liberals and moderates to use in their factional battle against the conservatives, much as the DAC's response did for Democratic liberals after 1956. But, it seems that no one on the left wing of the Republican party was willing to use the RCC for this purpose; instead, those responsible for the running the RCC used it as a forum for settling factional disputes.

One possible explanation for the rather passive behavior of Republican liberals and moderates in this period is their recognition that nothing could have returned them to their former position and that an organizational response was the best they could hope for given their diminished influence. Yet at the time the mortal wounds of the liberal and moderate Republicans were less apparent than they have become with hindsight. Furthermore, little or no discussion was given to a possible procedural response similar to the one Jud Morhouse proposed four years earlier, even though the dire future for liberal and moderate Republicans that he had predicted was now coming to pass. Just as after 1960, the Republican party's emphasis on organizational matters seems to have precluded the selection of a different response, despite the adverse consequences that such an action had on an important segment of the party.

5

THE DEMOCRATS,

1968–1972

When the Democratic party lost the 1968 election, the belief was that the party, divided over the nature of its nominating process, had not been able to achieve the unity necessary for Humphrey to win. The DNC had already established the McGovern-Fraser Commission on Party Structure and Delegate Selection, and many of the reasons for its establishment were independent of the election outcome, but this procedural response was the DNC's primary response to the 1968 election.[1]

In addition to its primary procedural response, the DNC also engaged in some organizational and policy activity. The Democratic Policy Council (DPC), established in 1969 as a conscious attempt to emulate the Democratic Advisory Council of 1956–1960, and a program to improve the DNC's direct-mail fundraising were both instituted after the 1968 election. These efforts were, however, of a much lower priority than the party reform commissions.

THE ORIGINS OF THE PROCEDURAL RESPONSE

While questions of representation have a long history within the Democratic party, the immediate origins of the Democrats' procedural response after the 1968 election reach back to the 1950s and the rise of the "amateur" Democrats who were devoted to both liberal policies and internal party democracy. In fact, as James Q. Wilson points out, many amateurs saw the latter as a necessary condition for the former. According to Wilson, the amateurs of the Lexington Democratic Club in New York had "three major demands: the democratization of the party machinery, an improvement in the caliber of party leaders and candidates, and an emphasis on program and principle in attracting both party workers and voters. Of these, the first was clearly of greatest importance. . . . The reformers were convinced, by and large, that if the first goal (democratizing the party apparatus) were attained, the other two would follow almost as a matter of course."[2]

The amateurs' call for internal party democracy gained strength in the 1960s. The struggle for civil rights, the movement to end the Vietnam War, and the burgeoning influence of the baby boom generation unleashed a variety of forces that came into conflict with many established institutions, compelling these institutions to become more inclusive and participatory. The Democratic party first felt the impact of these forces in 1964. Throughout that summer, civil rights workers, often facing jail, beatings, and death, conducted a campaign to register black Mississippians into the Mississippi Freedom Democratic Party (MFDP). The MFDP hoped to send a delegation to the 1964 Democratic National Convention to challenge the all-white delegation selected by the segregated regular Mississippi Democratic Party.

Fannie Lou Hamer presented the MFDP's case before the convention's Credentials Committee. In her moving testimony, Hamer described the beating she had suffered for attempting to exercise her right to vote and said that the MFDP sought only "to register, to become first class citizens, and if the Freedom Democratic Party is not seated now, I question America. Is this America the land of the free and the home of the brave?"[3]

President Johnson worried that the appeals of Hamer and other MFDP members might upset his nomination and election plans. Johnson, aware that many Democratic liberals distrusted him, feared that in a fit of emotion the convention might attempt to draft Robert Kennedy. Ignoring the MFDP might provide a rallying point for such a move. But Johnson also knew that his Republican opponent, Barry Goldwater, strongly appealed to white southerners and that giving in fully to the MFDP might further alienate southern Democrats. Thus, the president sought a compromise on the issue.

Johnson's representatives first offered the MFDP only floor privileges and then, after Hamer's testimony, two at-large votes and the promise that for the 1968 convention state parties must establish procedures allowing "voters in the State, regardless of race, color, creed, or national origin, . . . to participate fully in Party affairs."[4] The MFDP refused to accept the compromise. "We didn't come all this way for no two seats!" declared Hamer.[5] The Mississippi whites also balked at any deal, walking out of the convention in protest.

1968: THE DEMOCRATIC SCHISM

The controversy over the MFDP merely foreshadowed the conflicts that would overtake the Democratic party four years later. The party, divided over the Vietnam War, saw both Eugene McCarthy and Robert Kennedy challenge President Johnson for the 1968 nomination. After a poor showing in the New Hampshire primary, Johnson withdrew from the race, leaving Vice-President Hubert H. Humphrey as the choice of most party regulars.[6]

Humphrey's announcement in April 1968 came too late for him to enter any of the remaining primaries, leaving these battlegrounds to McCarthy and Kennedy. Here Kennedy gained the upper hand, scoring important wins in Indiana, Nebraska, and California. Kennedy hoped to use these victories to persuade party leaders to support him at the convention, but his tragic death following the California primary prevented that. Though Senator George McGovern served as a stand-in candidate for Kennedy delegates who refused to support either McCarthy or Humphrey, the race narrowed to the latter two candidates.[7]

Despite much popular support, McCarthy failed to mount a serious challenge to Humphrey since the delegate selection process presented a serious hurdle to McCarthy supporters in many states. Only fourteen states held primaries in 1968, and in only a few of these states did the primary outcome significantly influence the composition of the state's delegation. At the 1968 convention, only 40 percent of the delegates came from states with primaries.[8]

The other 60 percent of the delegates came from states where party regulars controlled the selection process with varying degrees of power. The least participatory was Georgia, where the state chairman, with the governor's approval, could handpick the delegation. In many others the state central committee named one-third to one-half of the delegates. In some places the selection process began months, even years before the start of the nomination campaign, often in secret or unannounced meetings closed to public participation or scrutiny. Finally, several states employed a unit-rule, whereby the candidate with the majority of support won control of the entire state delegation, effectively denying representation to other candidates.

Given this selection process, McCarthy, an anathema to the party regulars who controlled the process in most states, stood little chance of winning the nomination. Though he won nearly 40 percent of the vote in primary states, McCarthy received just 16 percent of the delegates in nonprimary states. On the other hand, Hubert Humphrey received just over 2 percent of the primary vote, but he still managed to win 67 percent of the convention delegates. Of Humphrey's 1759 delegates, 76 percent came from nonprimary states.[9]

In many nonprimary states, party regulars blatantly disregarded McCarthy supporters. In New York, McCarthy received a majority of the 125 elected delegates, but only 15 of the 65 additional delegates appointed by the state party's central committee.[10] Even in primary states, support for McCarthy was often underrepresented. For example, in Nebraska, McCarthy's 31 percent in the primary translated into only 20 percent of the delegates. The worst, however, was in Pennsylvania, where McCarthy's whopping 71 percent in the primary gained him but 21 of Pennsylvania's 130 convention seats.[11]

Their experience with the delegate selection procedure outraged many McCarthy supporters. In June 1968, a group of McCarthy activists in Connecticut, angered over what they believed was unfair representation in that state's delegation, decided to organize a committee to investigate the national party's delegate selection procedure and to recommend reforms for the party to consider at its convention in Chicago.[12] Iowa's governor Harold Hughes agreed to chair the ad hoc commission, which eventually produced a report, *The Democratic Choice,* outlining many of the abuses in the delegate selection procedure and calling on the convention to appoint a reform commission.

The Hughes Committee report formed the basis for a minority report of the 1968 Democratic Convention Rules Committee. Though Humphrey had the votes to defeat the minority report on the convention floor, he decided not to do this. The vice-president knew that the Democratic party was badly divided and that he would need the votes of McCarthy supporters to win in November.[13] He decided to leave the decision on the minority report to the delegates as a token gesture to the defeated McCarthy forces. Without Humphrey's active opposition, the minority report passed by a vote of 1,350 to 1,206.[14]

Even though Humphrey had not killed the reform proposal, McCarthy and many of his supporters still refused to endorse the vice-president after the convention. Their intense commitment to ending America's involvement in the Vietnam War, their frustrations with the Democratic party, and their abuse at the hands of the Chicago police during the convention made it too difficult for them to cast aside their objections to Humphrey, whom they saw as Lyndon Johnson's puppet. Only later in the campaign, after Humphrey began to distance himself from Johnson by calling for a halt to the bombing of North Vietnam, did many liberals begin to drift back toward the Democratic nominee.[15] Though endorse would be too strong a word, McCarthy finally and petulantly came out in support of Humphrey in the final days of the campaign.[16]

Still, many McCarthy activists refused to support Humphrey. One group, consisting of McCarthy's student coordinator, Sam Brown; press secretary and speechwriter for the campaign, Paul Gorman; co-chairman of the campaign's finance committee, Martin Peretz; deputy campaign manager, Robert Pirie; and Harold Ickes, co-chairman of the McCarthy organization in New York, released a statement claiming: "When a Democrat who bears responsibility for so much tragedy and error is nominated by undemocratic procedures for the Presidency . . . the time has come for that faction of the party which won all the major primaries to refuse to be taken for granted. If it does not do so now, it may never do so."[17]

In addition to these and other McCarthy lieutenants who failed to endorse Humphrey, many rank-and-file McCarthy voters also did not vote for the Democratic nominee. A poll taken by the Nixon campaign shortly before the election showed that only 40 percent of the three million people who had voted for McCarthy in the primaries were planning to vote for Humphrey. The other 60 percent represented enough voters to have easily have tipped the balance of an election decided by only 500,000 votes. Most of these people probably sat out the election, but many also went to Humphrey's opponents.[18]

The split between the Humphrey and McCarthy camps denied Humphrey not only the votes of McCarthy supporters, but also the equally important resource of party activists and money. According to one account of the campaign:

> "The people who were most disenchanted with Humphrey," as one staff man recalled it, "were desperately needed. Not because of their votes—there weren't many of them—but because they are the people who work and write and get active in campaigns: graduate students, young professors, lawyers, upper-middle-class housewives, the elite of the Negro community. They are also the journalists and the people the journalists talk to." It is, of course, this edge which the Democrats have among the educated bourgeoisie that normally countervails the Republicans' advantage in financial muscle. And Humphrey didn't have it.[19]

Many of the wealthy liberals who had bankrolled the McCarthy campaign also sat on the sidelines, vexed over Humphrey's position on the war and the flaws in the nomination process. The most notable example of this was Stewart R. Mott, heir to the General Motors fortune and a prominent supporter of liberal causes. In 1968, Mott gave upwards of $200,000 to the McCarthy campaign and served as a finance coordinator for the campaign. On October 13, Mott, writing for himself and a group of other McCarthy fundraisers, stated that while Humphrey seemed the only alternative to "a conservative martini (four parts Nixon, one part Wallace)," he was:

> still not convinced that I should give money and time to your campaign, especially when the "peace" candidates so urgently need help.
> . . . the least we on the McCarthy Finance Committee could do for you would be to give you a hearing . . . in order to question you about our own view of the nation's future and what it ought to be. . . . We would "like" to be able to support you, but we certainly do need to be convinced. . . .
> If we become "turned on" and enthusiastic towards your candidacy, we have the capacity to give $1,000,000 or more to your campaign—and raise twice or three times that amount. But we will each make our own individual judgements on the basis of how you answer our several questions and how you conduct your campaign in the coming weeks.[20]

Humphrey, though badly in need of funds, refused to attend the meeting and Mott kept his money.[21]

THE NEED FOR ORGANIZATIONAL REFORM

As fated as the DNC's procedural response seems in hindsight, there were compelling reasons for the Democrats to mount an organizational drive in response to their narrow loss, just as the Republicans had in 1960. Certainly the 1968 election showed the organizational weakness of the national Democratic Party. Lyndon Johnson had abused the DNC over the previous four years, hobbling it as a campaign and fundraising organization.[22] The DNC was in debt and disarray; no money existed to run Humphrey's media campaign and the DNC's organizational efforts were poor at best. Humphrey staffer William Welsh claims that the DNC "was useless to Humphrey."[23] It was late September before the DNC managed to scrape up enough money to buy campaign buttons, and what field operations the party mounted were run by the few state parties that had the capacity to do so or by labor unions. According to Theodore White, only this massive intervention by organized labor, headed by the AFL-CIO's Committee on Political Education (COPE), saved the Humphrey campaign from disaster.[24]

The Democrats' loss was also due in part to the RNC's organizational prowess. Though an election as close as the one in 1968 turns on many factors, the programs developed by Ray Bliss at the RNC since 1965 almost certainly helped provide Richard Nixon with his razor-thin margin of victory. Not only were the Republicans able to vastly outspend their opponents, they also had the benefit of the party building and training programs in which the RNC had invested heavily since 1965.[25]

A final reason why an organizational response might have been useful was that the DNC was heavily in debt. In addition to its own deficit of $6.2 million, the DNC also agreed to assume the debts of the Kennedy and Humphrey prenomination campaigns, each totaling approximately $1 million. In the aftermath of most campaigns, it is common to negotiate a repayment of only some fraction of what is owed, but federal laws prevented a reduction in much of this amount since it was owed to federally regulated phone and airline companies.[26]

Such a large debt placed a staggering burden on the DNC, requiring it to allocate the bulk of its receipts to pay off creditors and leaving little money for operating costs or campaign activities. Moreover, the Democrats were out of the White House for the first time in eight years and could no longer rely upon many of the large donors who had funded them while in power.[27] Given this rather dire situation, a major attempt to build a fundraising apparatus along the lines of the RNC's direct-mail program would certainly have been a plausible strategy for the DNC.

Despite this rather compelling set of factors, the DNC did not opt for a strong organizational response. One indication that organization was not a high priority in the DNC was the selection in January 1969 of Oklahoma Senator Fred Harris as chairman to replace the departing Larry O'Brien (O'Brien would return as chairman in 1970). Harris, though a dynamic politician, had no particular organizational talents and as a sitting Senator he was unable to offer the full attention necessary for the type of "nuts and bolts" rebuilding that Bliss had devoted himself to as chairman. In addition, Harris made it clear to Hubert Humphrey, the titular head of the party and the man who chose Harris to lead the DNC, that his first priority was procedural reform and not organizational rebuilding.[28]

Harris did attempt to take some steps to reduce the DNC's debt, but the effort was halfhearted and produced meager results. Moreover, evidence suggests that Harris did not direct his early financial efforts toward debt reduction and organizational rebuilding, but rather toward securing adequate funding for the reform commissions.[29] According to Verrick "Vick" French, executive director of the DNC at the time, one of Harris's first moves after becoming chairman was to find a way of raising funds and sequestering them so that they could be used for the reform commissions rather than for paying off creditors. Harris contacted his friend Herbert Allen, a prominent Democratic contributor, and persuaded him to run a series of small fundraisers to help support the reform commissions. These events raised approximately $200,000, which Harris then sequestered to be used to pay the staff of the reform commission.[30]

Later in Harris's tenure at the DNC, he began a direct-mail effort to broaden the party's financial base and, he hoped, to copy the RNC's success with such programs. But even here, one of his motivations was to find a new source of funds for the reform commissions.[31] In late 1969, Harris hired Olga Gechas, former director of UNICEF's direct-mail campaign, to run a similar program at the DNC, but she found progress to be extremely difficult. Gechas told Harris that she "had never seen mail talk back like ours does," since so many of the fundraising appeals came back not with money, but with angry responses from party members still bitter over the experience of 1968.[32]

The angry tone of the letters eventually subsided, but the program still failed to generate much income. According to Gechas, more pressing needs prevented Harris from using the profits of the direct-mail profits to expand the list of contributor names.[33] Herbert Alexander reiterates this view, claiming that between 1969 and 1970: "receipts from the program increased, but without the seed money to enlarge the mailings, and without the ability to reinvest all receipts from the program in further mailings, there are limits to the revenue from this source."[34]

The failure of the direct-mail program, in addition to the defection of many of the large donors who had given to the party while it was in power, plunged the DNC further into debt. By early 1970 the committee owed $9.3 million and was accumulating new debt at the rate of $100,000 per month. The situation came to a crisis in February 1970 when a Miami Beach fundraising event, which had been expected to raise as much as $2 million, brought in less than $300,000, most of which came from a group of wealthy Texans flown in on a plane chartered by Dallas lawyer and businessman, Robert Strauss.[35] Disappointed at the event's result, Harris decided to resign as DNC chairman.[36]

To help alleviate the party's desperate financial situation, Larry O'Brien, who replaced Harris in March 1970, appeared on "Meet the Press" and asked for viewers to send in contributions. This brought $100,000 to the DNC in five days, but provided only a temporary respite from a continuing problem.[37] O'Brien and Bob Strauss, who had recently become DNC treasurer, managed to put the DNC on a pay-as-you-go basis by the end of 1970, but they failed to retire any of the debt or to significantly increase the take from small contributors.[38]

In 1972 the DNC made two more attempts to increase small contributions. The first was a full-page advertisement in the *New York Times* on February 7. The ad stated that "the Democratic Party needs your help!" and asked readers to give money to help ensure "the survival of the two-party system."[39] In July the DNC engaged in another novel fundraising effort when it sponsored a nineteen-hour telethon prior to its 1972 convention. John Y. Brown, the wealthy owner of Kentucky Fried Chicken, masterminded the program which featured an array of Hollywood celebrities.[40] The program grossed nearly $4.5 million in pledges and netted $2 million after subtracting expenses and unhonored pledges.[41] Despite this large sum, the telethon proved to be an inefficient mechanism for fundraising, since its ratio of income to costs was two to one, while other fundraising methods operated at a ratio ranging from fifty to one for some direct-mail appeals to four to one for fundraising dinners.[42]

PROCEDURAL REFORM AND THE SEARCH FOR UNITY

Despite these rather halfhearted organizational initiatives to revamp party fundraising, the DNC's primary response to the 1968 election was a procedural one embodied in the Commission on Party Structure and Delegate Selection (CPSDS). Why this response? The simplest answer is that the 1968 convention mandated the reform commission. Yet the convention's mandate did not require the DNC to devote as much energy, attention, and money as it eventually did. And the convention's mandate certainly did not prevent the DNC from mounting a more serious organizational or policy response than it did.

Another answer is that the reform response was preordained, that the Chicago convention laid bare the abuses of the regular Democratic party and made reform inevitable, whatever the outcome of the election. This interpretation, usually advanced by McCarthy supporters and other reform advocates, is predicated on the notion that the insurgents had control of the DNC and could carry out their plans for reform with little interference.

This, however, was not the case. As Byron Shafer's account of the Democrats' reforms shows, the DNC was in the hands of party regulars, who, while not totally unsympathetic to many of the reformers' goals, certainly did not wish to carry reform as far as many of the reformers did. If the Chicago convention had been the crucial event and if party reformers had been in control, then one might presume that serious reform efforts would have begun much sooner, between the convention and the election. But this was not the case. As William Crotty notes, "Party reform took second place to a lackluster general election campaign in the fall," since the regulars who controlled the party were far more concerned with running the campaign than with reforming the party. He adds that it took Humphrey's defeat "to trigger a profound transformation of Democratic party procedures."[43]

The DNC could have treated the CPSDS much as they did the Commission on Rules, another reform body mandated by the 1968 convention. The DNC appointed Congressman James O'Hara, a competent but colorless parliamentarian, as chairman of the Commission on Rules. The O'Hara Commission labored in near obscurity and produced a set of necessary and important, but mostly limited and noncontroversial, reforms governing the apportionment of delegates among states and procedural rules for the national convention.[44]

By contrast, the story of the CPSDS concerns how the reform coalition persuaded the party regulars to acquiesce to their sweeping program and what role was played by the Democrats' loss in 1968. In the minds of many of those who ran and influenced the DNC, Humphrey's loss resulted from the division in the party, and they saw the CPSDS as a vehicle for healing that rift. In other words, the DNC's primary response to the party's loss in 1968 was to help unify the party by enacting procedural reforms.

This response is evident in the establishment of the CPSDS. Following the election, DNC chairman Larry O'Brien took steps to set up the CPSDS. As Byron Shafer points out, the need for party unity in the aftermath of Humphrey's loss was an important motivation for O'Brien:

> Negotiations over the membership of the two commissions were nevertheless resumed in mid-November, on the down-side of a losing election, with Chairman O'Brien himself taking the lead role. O'Brien was intensely aware of the party split which had come to focus on these two promised bodies, and his general approach was to try to make a virtue of necessity. He intended to appoint major spokesmen for the various and unhappy factions within his party to both commissions and to use the commissions themselves to hammer out a modus vivendi within the party as a whole.[45]

Though O'Brien left the DNC in January 1969 before he could accomplish this task, the effort to reunite the party through procedural reforms also motivated other actors who helped the DNC continue on the path of reform. According to Bill Welsh, who served at the DNC after the election, Humphrey, the titular head of the party and the man to whom it fell to find a replacement for O'Brien, favored reform for many reasons, one of which was the hope that the reform commissions would bridge the chasm that had helped to cause his defeat.[46] To accomplish this task, Humphrey named Senator Fred Harris of Oklahoma as O'Brien's replacement, who he knew, as mentioned previously, was strongly committed to the reform effort.[47]

Harris, though supportive of reform for a variety of reasons, also saw the establishment of the CPSDS the same way as O'Brien and Humphrey. In addition to having a normative attachment to internal party democracy and his hope that by supporting reform he could develop a national constituency for a future presidential bid, Harris also believed that Humphrey's loss in 1968 was related to the exclusive nature of the party's nomination procedures, which made it difficult to bring the supporters of McCarthy and Kennedy back into the party.[48]

Motivated by a desire to use the CPSDS as a vehicle for party unity, Harris appointed a commission heavily slanted toward the reformers, but not overtly so. One key appointment was that of the commission's chairman. The obvious choice was Harold Hughes, who had led the ad hoc reform effort prior to the 1968 convention. Hughes, however, was mistrusted by both Harris and Humphrey, the titular leader of the party, since he was too closely identified with the reform faction. Instead, Harris appointed George McGovern, a man much more acceptable to the various factions of the party.[49]

The desire to use procedural reform to unify the party also influenced McGovern. He believed that Humphrey's loss "verified the judgement of the 1968 convention" and "fortified the [party's] resolve" to revamp their delegate selection procedures. In McGovern's view, the nomination process embittered McCarthy's supporters and kept many of them from unifying around Humphrey, resulting in the latter's "painful" and narrow loss in November.[50]

Thus intended as a vehicle for reuniting the party in response to the 1968 election, the CPSDS went about its work. The commission and its staff, both dominated by reformers, produced a set of sweeping recommendations in November 1969. Among them were the following:[51]

1. Requiring state parties to take "affirmative steps" so that representation of blacks, women, and youth would bear "a reasonable relationship to the group's presence in the population of the State."

2. Instructed state parties to adopt written rules for the process of delegate selection, uniform times and dates for meetings concerning delegate selection, and adequate public notice of those meetings. These rules effectively eliminated the ability of party organizations to select delegates through "closed caucuses."

3. Prohibited the unit-rule, but deferred the question of how to treat California's winner-take-all primary until the 1972 convention.

4. Banned the use of proxy voting in the delegate selection process.

5. Established a standard for apportioning delegates within states by congressional district and required that convention states select 75 percent of their delegates at or below the district level.

6. Capped the number of delegates appointed by a state party committee at 10 percent of the state's delegates, but recommended that this practice be eliminated in the future.

7. Forbid ex officio delegates in caucuses and conventions at any level.

One impact of these reforms and others was to ban two important tactics by which party regulars had influenced the delegate selection process. The first was the closed caucus, where only party officers met to select the delegates. The second was the delegate primary, in which delegate candidates ran under their names only, leaving voters with little way of knowing which presidential candidates they represented.[52]

The recommendations of the CPSDS required the approval of the DNC before they could be implemented. Though many on the committee were skeptical of the reforms, O'Brien, in his second tenure as chair, played a crucial role in persuading the DNC to approve the changes. O'Brien could have easily led the DNC in a successful effort to quash the reform proposals, but he did not, knowing that such an action might further divide the party—a potential catastrophe for a party deeply in debt and looking toward the midterm elections of 1970 and the presidential election of 1972.[53] Instead, O'Brien, responding to the events of 1968, focused on maintaining party unity. According to Shafer: "Larry O'Brien may have been especially sensitive to the divisions within the national Democratic party, and thus to the apparent, associated need for unity that underlay his entire strategy. His most recent experience in party politics, after all, had been the divisive 1968 Convention and the disastrous presidential campaign that followed."[54]

In his memoirs, O'Brien writes of how he viewed unity as the Democrats' preeminent concern when he returned to the DNC:

> Even more serious than our financial plight was the deep division within our party, the worst I had ever seen. The problem encompassed far more than our loss of the 1968 election. We had lost in 1952 and 1956 and remained reasonably united. But in 1970 the bitter divisions of 1968 still existed— hawk versus dove, liberal versus conservative, reformer versus regular—and no reconciliation was in sight.
>
> The National Committee was, I thought, the proper forum, indeed the only forum, through which the party might be united.[55]

In O'Brien's mind, unity offered the Democratic party the chance to heal the party's division and restore the victory that had been lost in 1968. In his 1971 year-end report, O'Brien stated: "If a significant number of young people, women, minorities, and others alienated by traditional political institutions are actively involved in the nominating process, a revitalized and recharged Democratic Party almost surely will emerge in the general election campaign. I have no doubt that these votes—when combined with more traditional sources of Democratic strength—could spell the difference between victory and defeat in November 1972."[56]

Unity, for O'Brien, meant going along with the reformers. Shafer quotes Vick French on this point: "O'Brien also saw that after the reformers had gotten as far as they did, to undo it would have instantly created open warfare. There was no other way to go, at that point. His internal party position was impossible otherwise. He was too smart and polished a pol not to know that."[57]

Seeking to avoid a split in the party over the implementation of the reform proposals, O'Brien brought the power of his office, his persuasive skills, and his extensive network of personal ties and friendships to bear on the members of the DNC. Though many on the committee were skeptical of the reforms, they approved, with O'Brien's urging, the reform recommendations of the CDSDS on February 19, 1971.[58]

TOWARD A POLICY CONSENSUS

The split within the Democratic party was based not only on disagreements about procedure, but also on divisions over policy. The 1968 election saw the party shattered into a variety of factions covering the whole spectrum of views on the issues of race, law and order, and foreign policy. In order to help the party bridge these differences and to provide a vehicle for criticizing the Nixon administration and for stating party positions on the issues, the DNC established the Democratic Policy Council in January 1969.[59]

The creation of the DPC owed much to the legacy of Paul Butler and the Democratic Advisory Council. Facing out-party status for the first time in eight years, many Democrats remembered how the DAC had, in their view, helped the party regain the White House in 1960. Both Fred Harris and Hubert Humphrey, an original member of the DAC, favored the creation of a party policy committee for this reason.[60]

Still, it is not possible to say that Harris was as devoted to a policy response as Butler had been. According to Vick French, Harris supported the DPC because it seemed the obvious thing to do since Butler had done it the last time the party was out of power. In French's view, the DPC was far less important to Harris than the reform commission, "On a scale of one to ten, the Policy Council was about a two or a three, but the reform commission was a nine."[61] John Stewart, who served as executive director of the DPC, echoes French's view, stating, "Much more money and attention were paid to the reform commissions," than to the Policy Council.[62]

In addition to Harris's lack of enthusiasm, the DPC's size also hampered its effectiveness. By early 1972, the DPC had 119 members, including such different figures as Gloria Steinem and Marvin Mandel, while at the same time lacking an executive committee that could help to focus the group's work.[63] According to Arthur Krim, a former DNC finance chairman and a member of the DPC, the council "became a Tower of Babel."[64] By contrast, the DAC had only 31 members in 1960 and was run by an administrative committee of 5 people.[65] The DAC's small size meant that its membership had a relatively homogeneous set of policy views, making the council's statements clearer and more forceful. On the other hand, though the DPC was overwhelmingly liberal in its orientation, the group's large size forced it to issue statements that were, for the most part, Democratic party boilerplate.[66]

The liberal composition of the DPC points to another problem with the council. In 1968, George Wallace drew almost ten million votes, most of them from nominal Democrats disturbed by many of the party's liberal policies, particularly those regarding civil rights and foreign policy. This fact should have disturbed those Democrats concerned with winning elections; for good or ill, these Wallace voters held the balance of power in presidential elections and it behooved the party to find a way to keep them in the fold. Certainly any party acting according to Downsian rationality would have done so. But such questions were not raised within the Democratic party at the time and the DPC aimed primarily at reestablishing consensus among the liberal elements of the party.

Despite these handicaps, the DPC had some successes. Hubert Humphrey seems to have believed in the council's purpose and brought some enthusiasm to his role as its chairman. Humphrey, who well remembered the battles between Butler and Rayburn and Johnson, tried to make sure that the council did not further divide the party. Though the Democratic leadership in Congress was initially skeptical of the DPC, Humphrey, who was known and trusted by most of the party leadership, managed to avoid antagonizing Democratic leaders on the Hill by going out of his way to consult them.[67]

The DPC's most significant work came in the area of foreign policy, particularly on the issue of the Vietnam War. Averell Harriman, who headed the DPC's Committee on International Affairs, helped the council stake out a strong stand against the war. Moving away from the rather hawkish position adopted in its 1968 platform, the DPC issued a position paper in February 1970 demanding "a firm and unequivocal commitment" to withdraw all American forces from Vietnam over the next eighteen months.[68] The council stated, "Our national interests require that the war in Vietnam be brought to a close at the earliest practical moment. The loss of life, the diversion of resources from critical domestic needs, and the disunity of our country must be ended." The statement criticized the Nixon administration for linking troop withdrawals to a winding down of the war, claiming that the decision to withdraw, "affecting American lives and resources, should not be dependent upon either North Vietnamese or South Vietnamese actions. Our schedule of withdrawal should not be dependent upon the progress of the Paris peace talks, the level of violence, or the progress of so-called Vietnamization [Nixon's plan to shift the burden of the war from American to South Vietnamese forces]. It should depend primarily upon the interests and policy of the United States."[69]

By May 1972, the DPC's statements on Vietnam had taken on an even starker tone. In its recommendation to the Platform Committee of the 1972 convention, the DPC stated: "Indochina represents a continuing waste of billions of dollars but even that pales into insignificance when compared to what it is doing to our society, the Vietnamese people and to the respect for our judgement and decency which once pervaded the international community."[70]

The statement harshly criticized President Nixon for escalating the war in 1972 by resuming the bombing of Hanoi and Haiphong and mining North Vietnam's harbors in response to increased North Vietnamese attacks:

> President Nixon, seeing his Vietnam policy about to collapse, chose to lash out in reckless frustration—and men, women, and children, pilots and civilians have died for no purpose. The increased bombing will inflict very heavy civilian casualties. The mining raises the fearful possibility of confrontation with the Soviet Union and China and will jeopardize our complex negotiations with the Soviet Union. The moral position of the United States has eroded further. More and more decent people around the world will regard our misuse of our vast power as a prime threat to peace.[71]

In addition to its stand on the Vietnam War, the DPC also made important statements on arms control issues. The DPC's Committee on Arms Control and Defense Policy, headed by Paul Warnke, strongly favored an agreement with the Soviets to halt the testing and development of MIRV (Multiple, Independent, Reentry Vehicle) missiles, an issue that the Nixon administration had not taken up with the Soviets at the Strategic Arms Limitations Talks (SALT).[72] In February 1970, the DPC issued a statement claiming that "steps should be taken now to bring about reciprocal restraint in testing and deploying new nuclear missiles with improved warheads, such as MIRV. Only by such steps can we keep open the option of negotiating an effective and verifiable agreement on nuclear arms control."[73]

The DPC's position was a prescient one; MIRV technology vastly increased the size of the superpowers' nuclear arsenals. Since the Soviets possessed larger missiles which could carry more MIRV's, the development of this technology allowed them to increase their arsenal of warheads relative to the United States, creating the so-called window of opportunity, that many conservatives believed gave the Soviets the ability to launch a successful first-strike attack against the United States. Ironically, though liberal Democrats had first raised the issue, it was used with great effect by Ronald Reagan during the 1980 presidential campaign.

Despite its positions on the war and on arms control, the DPC did not amount to much. According to Stewart, while the DPC "made some news" and had some influence on opinion leaders and journalists, "not all that much impact" resulted from the Council's work. At best, Stewart claims, the DPC offered the party "an internal forum for thrashing things out and healing wounds that needed to be healed" in the aftermath of the 1968 election.[74] In his view, "The Policy Council gave a lot of groups within the party an opportunity to be heard, but it also represented an attempt to contain and channel the debate."[75]

ASSESSING THE RESPONSE

In the wake of Hubert Humphrey's defeat in 1968, influential Democrats used the Commission on Party Structure and Delegate Selection to accommodate the liberal reform wing of the party and thereby heal the party split that they believed had caused Humphrey's defeat. This reconciliation seems to have been an important motivation for Larry O'Brien and Fred Harris, the DNC chairmen during this period; Hubert Humphrey, the party's titular leader; and George McGovern, who headed the reform commission.

There can be no doubt that the reform commission was the DNC's primary response from 1968 to 1972. Despite serious organizational and financial handicaps, the DNC made only limited efforts in this period to improve its organizational capacities. In addition, Fred Harris's early fundraising efforts were directed, not at reducing the DNC's debt or upgrading its campaign services, but at financing the reform commissions. Furthermore, the policy efforts of the DPC were, for the most part, of little consequence and a low priority of the DNC and its chairmen.

The Democrats' selection of a procedural response has several interesting aspects. First, in spite of what could be described as an organizational and financial meltdown during the 1968 campaign, the DNC still chose to concentrate on procedural reforms. Furthermore, the idea of selecting a party chairman who had expertise in the area of party organization or who was committed to organizational renewal, does not seem to have been a consideration in the minds of many Democrats following the 1968 election.

Second, though the DNC during its previous experience as the out-party had relied on a policy response, they did not do so after 1968. Paul Butler's legacy influenced the creation of the Democratic Policy Council, but this effort never reached the same priority level that the reform commission did. The notion of the Democrats relying upon a policy council as a response to defeat seems to have been rather short-lived, perhaps indicating that the DAC resulted from a series of factors unique to that period, rather than any more enduring characteristics of the party.

Third, this procedural response did nothing to help bring Wallace voters back into the Democratic party. Instead of implementing a policy response that might have reached out to the ten million people who voted for Wallace for ideological reasons, the Democrats focused on a procedural response that would accommodate that portion of the three million McCarthy voters who had stayed at home or voted for Humphrey's opponents because of their dissatisfaction with the nomination process. This behavior seems to indicate that the Democrats saw procedural concerns as a higher priority than reforming party policy to appeal to a majority of the electorate.

Finally, by comparing the Democrats' experience after 1968 with the Republicans' after 1964, one can better see how the two parties chose to respond to similar defeats. One can view both losses as policy rejections, since in 1964, the majority of the electorate saw Barry Goldwater and the right-wing of the Republican party as dangerously conservative, while in 1968 millions of conservative Democrats left their party to vote for George Wallace. According to theories of victory-oriented parties, the parties should have undertaken policy responses to steer them back to the political center. This, however, did not happen; both parties chose to view their defeats as something other than an ideological rejection and, consequently, to implement something other than a policy response: an organizational response for the Republicans, even though organizational weakness was not a problem for Goldwater, and a procedural response for the Democrats, even though far more voters were alienated by party policies than by party procedures.

Both parties were also torn by factional disputes in 1964 and 1968. To overcome the divisions created by the 1964 campaign, the Republicans brought in Ray Bliss to mount a neutral and nonideological organizational campaign that would appease both factions of the party. This response occurred even though the RNC following Goldwater's defeat was far better off organizationally and financially than the Democrats were four years later. The Democrats in 1968, however, chose to try to heal the split in their party through procedural reforms, with little thought given to the organizational renewal that was far more necessary for them than it had been for the Republicans four years before.

In 1964, no thought was given to altering the balance of power within the Republican party through procedural reforms, even though Republican moderates and liberals found themselves increasingly marginalized in the RNC and the national convention. Even if the Republican liberals had been as persistent as the Democratic reformers, one doubts that the factional balance of power would have been altered. For that to happen, the Goldwaterites and more moderate conservatives who controlled the RNC would have had to agree to yield power to the Republican liberals who had abandoned the party in 1964. Imagine Barry Goldwater, Ronald Reagan, John Tower, and Richard Nixon agreeing to revamp party procedures so that Jacob Javits, Nelson Rockefeller, John Lindsay, and Edward Brooke would have greater power within the Republican party!

Such was not the case with the Democrats in 1968. The party's procedural reforms were ultimately carried out by the established party regulars who, as

Humphrey's nomination showed, still firmly controlled the party machinery. This group had little if anything to gain from extensive procedural reforms and, as ultimately transpired, they stood to lose much of their power and influence within the party. Yet, the desire to make the party less exclusive and more representative of all Democrats, even those liberals and reformers who had contributed to Humphrey's loss, exerted a powerful influence over their actions.

6

THE DEMOCRATS,

1972–1976

After its defeat in the 1972 election, the Democratic party again selected a procedural response. Though DNC chairman Robert Strauss made strong organizational efforts—developing campaign services and working strenuously to reduce the party's debt—the principal activity of the DNC in this period was attempting to restore party harmony and reduce factional feuding between the liberal/reformist and conservative/regular wings of the party. This accommodation was worked out in the Mikulski Commission on Delegate Selection and the Party Charter Commission and Conference, which modified the more controversial of the McGovern-Fraser reforms to appease their critics. Still, the reformers were also satisfied since their basic accomplishments were maintained and institutionalized by the commissions. Strauss also established an issues council, but its purpose was less a policy-oriented attempt to modify the party's program than a procedural effort to increase the representation of elected officials within the party.

1972: DIVISION AND DEBACLE

Following the 1972 election, the Democratic party found itself defeated and divided, as it had in 1968. The reforms of the party's delegate selection process, which had come about in reaction to the divisions of the 1968 nomination and election campaigns, proved crucial to the nomination of George McGovern, leader of the liberal, reform wing of the party. But, just as the old procedures, which allowed Hubert Humphrey to secure the nomination in 1968, had divided the party by excluding many Democratic liberals and reformers, the new delegate selection process aided McGovern at the expense of excluding many party regulars.

The new reforms had opened up the nominating process, bringing into the convention many of the insurgents who had battled the party regulars in 1968. Not only did the reforms ban the use of closed caucuses, the unit rule, and delegate primaries—all of which had helped to assure control of delegate selection by party regulars—they also, though not explicitly, required the use of quotas so that the number of blacks, women, and youth in each delegation would "bear a reasonable relationship to group presence in the state as a whole."[1]

Not only did the reformers and regulars often disagree ideologically, they also represented very different cultural backgrounds. The regulars tended to be older white males, with long involvement in state and local party affairs or with labor unions. The insurgents, however, were mostly novices at party politics, coming instead from the "New Politics" of social movements, and had a much greater representation of blacks, women, and young people. The complaint of one regular delegate at the 1972 convention aptly summed up the differences between these two groups, "There is too much hair and not enough cigars at this convention."[2] AFL-CIO President George Meany put it even more bluntly in his comment about the New York delegates: "What kind of delegation is this? They've got six open fags and only three AFL/CIO people on that delegation! Representative?"[3]

Moreover, the presence of these insurgents often meant the exclusion of the party regulars who had controlled the party for so long. The most notable example of this exclusion was the convention's vote to unseat a portion of the Illinois delegation that was composed of members of Chicago's Democratic party machine and led by Mayor Richard Daley. Taking its place was a group of insurgent delegates, led by liberal reform activist William Singer and black civil rights leader Jesse Jackson.[4]

Obviously the reforms that allowed such changes to take place were extremely unpopular with party regulars in Chicago and elsewhere. The regulars' complaints about the new nominating system focused on George McGovern, who not only was the beneficiary of these reforms, but, as the head of the Commission on Party Structure and Delegate Selection was also one of the principal architects of the new rules. McGovern also had to carry the additional burden of being perceived as far to the left of the party's ideological mainstream. Despite his attempts at reconciliation with party regulars after the convention, many of the more traditional elements of the party refused to support McGovern in the general election. David Hill's comment about Grover Cleveland in the election of 1888, "I am a Democrat still—very still," best describes the attitudes of disaffected regulars toward their party's nominee.

Saddled with these divisions, it was unlikely that McGovern would have been able to mount a successful challenge to President Nixon in 1972. But tragedy soon turned into farce as the Eagleton fiasco destroyed any hopes that the Democrats could avoid a landslide. In the end, McGovern carried only Massachusetts and the District of Columbia, losing by a margin of 60.7 to 37.5 percent.

THE CHAIRMANSHIP BATTLE

In the aftermath of McGovern's defeat, party regulars were intent on reestablishing their influence within the party. This meant revising, perhaps even eliminating, the reforms of the last four years. As William Crotty states: "The outcome of the [1972] election was predictable. From the beginning the Democratic nominee—whoever he was—would be the underdog. The Democrats would lose. But what stunned party members was the magnitude of the defeat. The party had been humiliated and party members were angry. The party became wracked by dissension. And the scapegoat for the party's frustrations became the reforms. The reforms had 'created' McGovern, and McGovern's ineptitude had caused the election debacle. Or so the dominant argument ran."[5]

In the view of these regulars, the reforms had allowed the party and its nomination process to be captured by a small, ideologically and socially unrepresentative group of elites. This case was made most clearly by Congressman James O'Hara, the chairman of the reform Rules Commission but also a party regular with strong ties to organized labor:

> I submit to you the reason we suffered the terrible reverse we did in 1972 is that we lost the support of the casual Democrat, the uninvolved Democrat, the Democrat whose only real attachment to our party is that once every two years, perhaps only once every four years, he is in the custom of walking in to a voting booth and pulling the Democratic lever. That is his only connection with our party. He wasn't represented at the last Convention. Our candidate and our program did not appeal to him, did not win his support.
>
> Of course, you say, "O'Hara, how could he be represented, you define him as a fellow that doesn't participate in the delegate selection process." Well, I submit to you that he has been represented imperfectly, but nevertheless represented at the past conventions prior to '72. He was represented by the professional powers, by the Democratic office holders, by the county and district leaders, by the state chairmen, by the elected Democratic labor leaders, by the elected Democratic farm leaders, by the elected Democratic civil rights leaders: people whose very business it was to know the problems, the aspirations, the hopes, to know the mood of these lightly attached Democrats, these Democrats that do not ordinarily participate, and who went to that Convention with the idea of coming back with a candidate and a platform that they could sell to these Democrats whose support was essential to us in the November elections.
>
> And I think that was the difference between the last Convention and the Conventions that nominated Franklin Roosevelt and Harry Truman and Adlai Stevenson and John Kennedy and Lyndon Johnson. That was the difference.[6]

One unidentified party regular put the matter more bluntly after the election: "It's a crime against democracy that we had a candidate who didn't represent the Democratic party, and we don't want that to happen again. We want the party organization and machinery to reflect the party, not a fraction of the party. We don't want a party that consists of Bella Abzug on one hand and Jesse Jackson on the other."[7]

The first step for the regulars was to reestablish control of the party and that meant removing Jean Westwood, the McGovern-appointed chairwoman of the DNC, and replacing her with a candidate more in tune with their thinking. Though Westwood herself had done little to offend party regulars—journalist David Broder commented that she was "about as radical as your average forest ranger"—she was the most obvious symbol of McGovern's influence in the party and thus replacing her became the focus of the counter-reformers.

The desire to see Westwood removed united many Democrats from all sections of the party. On the extreme right was Alabama governor George Wallace, the acknowledged leader of the party's conservative southern wing. Following McGovern's loss, Wallace claimed, "I want to see the party taken back and given back to the average man."[8]

Perhaps the most adamant members of the anti-Westwood coalition were the more conservative leaders of organized labor, principally Meany and COPE Director Alexander Barkan. Both men vehemently criticized the the "New Politics" reforms in general and McGovern's nomination in particular, which they saw as a slap in the face for the Democrats' most loyal and important ally—organized labor. As a result, the two had made sure that the AFL-CIO refused to endorse McGovern in the general election.

McGovern's nomination and subsequent defeat were disturbing developments for labor, which traditionally had close relations with the Democratic party. But, as David Broder notes, "Labor learned something from its 1972 experience. And from the moment of McGovern's defeat, big labor has been back in the Democratic Party with both feet, using every bit of its considerable leverage to be sure, as Alexander Barkan, the head of the AFL-CIO Committee on Political Education (COPE), says, that 'never again are we left in a position where neither party nominates a presidential candidate we can support.'"[9]

Labor's first move in rolling back the changes of the previous four years was to insist that Westwood ("that broad" or "Gravel Gertie" as Barkan referred to her) be removed. In Barkan's words, "The crazies have got to go."[10]

Those who wanted to see Westwood replaced also included many moderate to liberal Democrats, such as Senator Edmund Muskie and Representative Thomas "Tip" O'Neill.[11] Even some of McGovern's associates, dispirited by the election results, wanted to see Westwood step down. McGovern himself gave her only tepid support.[12] In William Crotty's view, "many of the reformers themselves had been thrown into self-doubt. Seemingly the very worst predicted by the critics had come to pass. Maybe a return to something approaching the old ways was called for."[13]

George Mitchell, DNC member from Maine and an associate of Senator Muskie, was the choice of many of these moderate and liberal Democrats as Westwood's successor. Mitchell had served on the McGovern-Fraser Commission and was seen as acceptable to all factions within the party. Also drawing some support from this group of Democrats was Charles Manatt, the California Democratic party chairman.

Labor's choice for the chairmanship was Robert Strauss, a Texas lawyer and businessman who had served as DNC treasurer between 1970 and 1972. In addition to labor, Strauss also had the endorsement of eighteen Democratic governors from the South and the West, some members of the Chicago Democratic party, and a scattering of others.[14]

Though Strauss had the most support of any of the alternatives to Westwood, he was also the candidate most opposed by Westwood and her backers. Strauss was an associate of Treasury Secretary John Connally, former governor of Texas and a conservative Democrat who headed "Democrats for Nixon" in 1972. According to the liberal *Texas Observer,* "As one jaundiced Texas political watcher has put it, 'I wouldn't say that Connally and Strauss are close, but when Connally eats watermelon, Strauss spits seeds.'"[15] Connally was, at best, unloved by most moderate and liberal Democrats, and Strauss's relationship to Connally made him unacceptable to them. Ralph Yarborough, a former senator from Texas and a long-time Connally foe, claimed that the campaign to elect Strauss as chairman was part of a larger effort to make Connally the Democratic presidential nominee in 1976.[16]

Strauss's role as the candidate of Meany and Barkan also raised objections among liberals, since the two had actively opposed McGovern. McGovern campaign assistant Frank Mankiewicz said that Meany and Barkan "should be disqualified" from party councils and that, "I don't think we should turn the party over to the people who tried to wreck it."[17]

Mankiewicz also threatened to withhold the campaign's list of 600,000 contributors until the leadership battle was over.[18] This list had provided a financial gold mine for the McGovern campaign, raising a net sum of over $10 million and giving McGovern the honor of becoming the first Democratic presidential candidate since Franklin Roosevelt to end his campaign in the black.[19] The financially strapped party did not take Mankiewicz's threat lightly; one New England state chairman commented, "I'm not so sure that we can afford to kick her out if it costs us the McGovern contribution list."[20]

Rather than simply give in, Westwood decided to fight to keep her position, for fear of it going to Strauss.[21] Westwood had hoped to avoid such a battle, proposing that both she and Strauss withdraw for an alternative candidate, but Strauss and his allies refused the offer.[22] To help her retain her position, Westwood mobilized a corps of McGovern campaign workers. These volunteers worked to identify Westwood supporters on the DNC and to help persuade any undecided committee members.

The showdown over the Westwood chairmanship came at the meeting of the DNC on December 9, 1972. Westwood claims that prior to the meeting she had had enough votes to defeat the measure offered by the Strauss supporters declaring the chairmanship vacant, but this majority fell apart when several members of the black caucus switched their votes at the last minute, swayed by promises made by the Strauss forces.[23] Westwood then contacted Mayor Daley, with whom she had developed a working relationship. Daley agreed to switch enough votes to West-wood so that she would win, but only if she would then resign her position. West-wood won the vote by a margin of 105 to 100 and then announced her resignation.[24] The hope that a more liberal alternative to Strauss might emerge did not come true as he won the chairmanship on the first ballot.

THE SILENT DOG OF COUNTER-REFORM

In the eyes of both reform critics and proponents, the bitter fight over leadership of the DNC and Strauss's subsequent election set the stage for an attempt at repealing the McGovern-Fraser guidelines. Early on, it appeared that both sides were mobilizing for just such a battle. Soon after Strauss's election, Marvin Madeson, vice-chairman of the New Democratic Coalition, an organization of liberal and reform Democrats established in the aftermath of the 1968 Chicago convention, warned the new chairman in a letter to the *New York Times,* "Liberals are waiting . . . and working . . . and watching . . . closely."[25]

Another liberal organization looking over Strauss's shoulder was the Democratic Planning Group (DPG). Set up soon after Strauss's election by Alan Baron, Westwood's administrative assistant at the DNC, the DPG intended to pressure the new chairman not to roll back the reforms. According to Baron, the DPG was financed by progressive unions, like the Machinists and the Communications Workers of America, and by liberal activists, such as Stewart Mott, who favored the continuation of the reforms.[26]

Party conservatives were also organizing in an effort to shift the party away from the reforms. Soon after McGovern's defeat, a group of moderates formed the Coalition for a Democratic Majority (CDM). The members of the CDM read like a who's who of soon-to-be neoconservatives: Ben Wattenberg, an associate of Senator Henry Jackson; Max Kampelman, an advisor to Hubert Humphrey; and Democratic intellectuals Jeanne Kirkpatrick, Nathan Glazer, Seymour Martin Lipset, Michael Novak, Norman Podhoretz, and Midge Decter. The CDM did, however, include some notable liberals such as Representatives Richard Bolling and Thomas Foley, Patricia Harris, and Bayard Rustin.

The CDM hoped to move the party back to the center and was openly disdainful of the "New Politics." In a direct-mail fundraising appeal in late November 1972, the CDM attacked the "New Politics" as:

> a politics new in its contempt for the very people and institutions on which the Democratic Party has built its electoral strength. It is a "New Politics" that has derided the organized labor movement, driving it from its traditional place in the vanguard of the Democratic coalition. It is a "New Politics" that has sneered at the greatness of America. It is a "New Politics" that has dismissed as morally unworthy the long-range values and daily concerns of tens of millions of ordinary people. And finally, and tragically, it is a "New Politics" that has allowed the Republican Party—a party so long and so accurately known as the party of privilege—to represent itself for the first time as the champion of such values and concerns.[27]

Despite the expectation of a bitter intraparty battle between these two groups, such a conflict never came to pass. As the emotions engendered over the past year during the convention, the election campaign, and the chairmanship battle began to subside, both factions of the party—with the conspicuous exception of organized labor's most conservative elements—began to take more realistic and less absolutist approaches to the reforms. Despite its harsh initial rhetoric, the CDM recognized that the bulk of the reforms were both just and useful. Only on the matters of quotas and the representation of party and elected officials, whom the CDM felt represented broad categories of average Democrats who themselves did not have the ability to participate, did the they insist that changes be made. According to Crotty: "In general, the coalition was supportive of the balance of the guidelines. Most of these rules dealt with less contentious procedural matters. The differences the CDM chose to emphasize are significant, and directly reflected the belief that the reformers entertained a prescribed bias, and an elitism that shortchanged the common man—the blue-collar worker, the ethnic, the elderly, and anyone else not included among the economically and educationally favored middle classes."[28]

In addition to the mellowing of the CDM, it soon became apparent that Bob Strauss was not hell-bent on overturning the reforms. Though he was the candidate of disaffected party regulars, Strauss did not use his position to launch their hoped for counter-reformation of the Democratic party. According to Robert Keefe, DNC executive director from 1972 to 1976, Strauss instead sought to "to bring some harmony out of this mess." Keefe adds that Strauss saw the party as composed of "several disputing groups, all important to the party" and focused on finding some way to accommodate them all, including the liberals and reformers who had initially distrusted him so much.[29]

To do this, Strauss focused on using his position as chairman to rebuild the party's center, something that he and his associates at the DNC believed had been lacking since 1968.[30] Without such a center, the party had been racked by disputes between its left and right wings, with no element in the middle that could seek out some accommodation between the two extremes. As chairman, Strauss hoped to play the role of an independent arbiter who could find some common ground between the party's warring factions and interests. Strauss spoke of this role in his acceptance speech after winning the chairmanship, telling the DNC, "I belong to no man; I am owned by no organization. I am a centrist, a worker, a doer, a putter-together, and those talents belong to you."[31]

Strauss brought many qualifications and assets to this role of party unifier. Because he did not have a strong ideological orientation, he was willing to be accommodating.[32] Strauss was also known for his personal charm and negotiating ability. Prior to his election as DNC chairman, liberal Texas journalist Molly Ivins wrote: "There is one thing about Robert Strauss that no one has ever questioned and that is his enormous charm. He charms men as well as women (and does he ever charm women). He charms liberals as well as conservatives. He flatters and cajoles and agrees with whoever is in his company at any given moment. Regrettably, one Democratic honcho has called this charm 'the ability to talk out of both sides of his mouth.' But in fact, Strauss seems to suffer from an inability to be unkind about anyone."[33]

As DNC chairman, Strauss used this charm to reach out to all party factions, including some of his old enemies from Texas. Billie Carr, a liberal DNC member from Texas, stated, "It's absolutely not like the Connally days. He now speaks to me and talks to me sometimes."[34] Strauss also brought a sense of humor to the position, something that the party had seen little of over the previous four years. "Goddamn! Let's make this party a place where you can have a laugh and a drink again," he declared after his election as chairman.[35]

Nevertheless, some elements in the party remained committed to purging the reformers and their works. The principal advocate of such a tactic was Al Barkan of COPE, who had a "bloodlust for revenge," according to Mark Siegel, Strauss's assistant on procedural matters. Siegel adds that Barkan, whom he refers to as "the monster on 16th Street," became enraged when Strauss did not push hard enough to undo the reforms.[36] Eventually Barkan was quoted as saying that helping to engineer Strauss's election was "the worst political mistake" he had ever made.[37] Such criticisms, however, only helped Strauss gain the trust of the reformers.[38]

With the realization that Strauss, the CDM, and most party regulars did not want to turn the clock back to the days of corrupt party bosses and "smoke-filled rooms," the reformers also began to moderate their stance in an attempt to find some way of accommodating their critics. In addition, many of the reform supporters had also come to question many of the same guidelines that so disturbed the party regulars—quotas and the lack of input by party leaders.

George McGovern, seen by both supporters and critics as the architect of the reforms, reflected this new attitude in his statements before the first meeting of Party Charter Commission. McGovern told the Commission: "We need not pretend that the reforms were written in stone. Every sound law must be informed and improved by experience. Human rules will fail sometimes, for human beings are frail always. And the reform rules were not without some defects or errors of inter-pretation even as they are properly judged a general success."[39]

McGovern added that the reforms were "an innovation, a voyage on an uncharted sea—and they can be improved." He specifically asked that the reforms be rewritten to abolish quotas and to increase "the participation of senior party leaders" in the delegate selection process.[40]

In spite of these important accommodations by the pro- and antireform fac-tions, many substantial differences remained, but, as Crotty indicates: "Opponents and supporters were now arguing from a reform base. . . . Both camps were con-ceding that reform had become an accepted fact of life. In effect, the more signifi-cant battle was not only over, it never took place. The questions debated were on the content of the rules, not their existence."[41]

This compromise by the reform critics shows that all but the most extreme of the party's more traditional elements were willing to acknowledge the basic legit-imacy of the party's procedural reforms. The regulars did so despite the fact that these reforms had caused them to be either alienated from or locked out of the 1972 convention, the most important mechanism that they had to influence the national party. Additionally, the reforms had at least partially contributed to the worst Democratic showing in a presidential election since 1924, and still the regulars, theoretically those most concerned with winning elections, were willing to go along with them for the most part. All of this seems to contradict theories of victory-ori-ented parties. In this case, those Democrats, the regulars and professionals, who one would think would be concerned only with winning elections, were in fact quite open to appeals to procedural fairness—even in the face of massive electoral defeat and sharp reduction of their influence within the party.[42]

UNITY THROUGH PROCEDURE

Despite the movement away from the extremes by both factions within the party, the period between 1972 and 1976 was no love fest. Both groups cast a wary eye at one another and important differences remained on procedural matters. Accommo-dation was the outcome of a continual and often contentious process that threatened to explode at various times. Often what one side viewed as a reasonable and just compromise, the other side considered an all-out attack on a matter of principle.

Such a situation placed a heavy responsibility on Bob Strauss as he attempted to seek positions that would allow for compromise between the party's factions. Throughout his tenure as chairman, Strauss maneuvered continually to find some position that might satisfy the grievances of the party regulars, but would also keep the liberals and reformers from walking out of the party. One example of this strategy concerned representation on the DNC. At the time of Strauss's election, there were twenty-five new at-large seats on the committee to be appointed by the chairman and approved by the full committee. Having won with 106.5 votes, only 2 more than a majority, Strauss might have used these appointments to stack the DNC in his favor. Instead, he used these appointments to accommodate the party's various factions. Among the twenty-five names recommended by Strauss and approved by the DNC, ten were representatives of labor unions, but liberals were also satisfied with the appointments since they included eight women, eight blacks, and two Hispanics.

Strauss also used these DNC appointments to placate George Wallace. During the 1972 Democratic primaries Wallace had shown substantial support before an assailant's bullet ended his campaign. Though now confined to a wheelchair, he still spoke for many conservative white Democrats on both sides of the Mason-Dixon line. Aware that keeping Wallace and most of his followers in the party was crucial for its future success, Strauss traveled to Alabama to meet with him on December 21, 1972. Prior to the meeting, he included Wallace in "the real leadership of the Democratic party," and stated that "he represents a large and important constituency."[43] At the meeting, Wallace expressed his desire to remain a Democrat and to work within the party. According to Strauss, "He told me that he didn't want any special treatment from the party; he just wanted to be treated like everybody else. And I told him his support among Democrats all over this country entitled him to a seat at the table; I told him I'd put him there, but it was up to him how much of the chicken he got to eat. We understood each other perfectly."[44]

Wallace's seat at the table took the form of one of the twenty-five at-large positions on the DNC and an appointment to the twenty-five-person DNC Executive Committee for Wallace's aide, Michael "Micky" Griffin. Wallace also kept up his end of the bargain. He stayed with the party, and Griffin was, according to Strauss, able to "function well" on the DNC.[45] In David Broder's assessment, Griffin and other Wallace supporters were "cooperative, conciliatory, and notably non-combative."[46]

THE MIKULSKI COMMISSION

In addition to these DNC appointments, Strauss used party reform commissions as vehicles for restoring unity. Though these commissions were mandated by the 1972 Democratic National Convention—and therefore not formally initiated in response to McGovern's loss—their membership, their deliberations, and their final results were strongly shaped by the results of the 1972 election. The first of these bodies was the Commission on Delegate Selection and Party Structure, also known as the Mikulski Commission for its chairperson, Baltimore City Council member Barbara

Mikulski. The 1972 convention, well aware of the controversies created by the McGovern-Fraser reforms, authorized the establishment of this commission to review the reforms, especially the provisions regarding "affirmative action," and to develop new guidelines for the 1976 convention.[47]

Charged with establishing this new commission, DNC chairperson Jean West-wood appointed members to the commission who were sure to protect the reforms. Westwood also made a nominal attempt to appease those who criticized the reforms for excluding labor and ethnic minorities by appointing as chair and co-chair (with only nominal vice-chair responsibilities), United Auto Workers president Leonard Woodcock and Mikulski, respectively.[48] Although Woodcock was certainly a labor leader and Mikulski a member of an ethnic minority, they were both liberal and proreform, and their appointments did not satisfy party regulars who were thinking more along the lines of Frank Rizzo and the head of a construction workers' union.

Before the work of the commission began, Woodcock, citing pressing union business, stepped down as its chairman in January 1973. Woodcock's departure created both problems and an opportunities for opponents of reform. The problem for the counter-reformers was that with Woodcock out of the way, the most natural move was for Mikulski to assume full responsibility for the commission. According to Mark Siegel, Strauss's liaison to the reform commissions, this prospect horrified many party regulars, who saw Mikulski as "a radical reformer" or even as "a wacko, feminist crazy."[49] Passing over Mikulski not only would have prevented her from controlling the commission, but would have provided Strauss with the opportunity to appoint someone willing to roll back the reforms. Such a move was not without precedent. In late 1970 when George McGovern stepped down from the CPSDS, DNC chairman Larry O'Brien passed over commission vice-chairman Harold Hughes and instead appointed Congressman Donald Fraser.[50]

Yet passing over Mikulski was not without political costs for Strauss. Appointing someone else would have angered, not only reformers, but also the DNC's Maryland delegation and many female DNC members. Replacing Woodcock with someone committed to rolling back the reforms might well have split the party wide open. Faced with these considerations, Strauss eventually decided that appointing Mikulski was the best available option.[51]

Though he appointed Mikulski, Strauss did not take a hands-off approach to the commission. Pressured by Barkan and the CDM, he announced the addition of twenty-one new members to the fifty-one-member panel. Strauss claimed that this move was only to ensure that each of the fifty states was represented on the panel, but many saw it as an attempt to shift the ideological makeup of the commission.[52] Alan Baron of the DPG claimed at the time that Strauss was trying to make the commission a "rubber stamp" for repealing the reforms.[53] In reality, Strauss was not attempting to gain control of the commission but rather to increase the membership to better reflect the views of the reform critics.[54] According to Mark Siegel, Strauss saw the commission, not as a vehicle for counter-reform, but merely as "a forum" to hash out the various issues.[55] As a result, the full DNC, which for the most part shared Strauss's accommodationist strategy, agreed to increase the size of the Mikulski Commission.

Despite these additions, the Mikulski Commission retained its proreform orientation. The commission's support for reform, however, was tempered by both the less strident attitude of the reformers and the knowledge that the commission could only go so far before it would run into opposition from Strauss and the DNC. At times, Strauss helped remind the Mikulski Commission that there were limits on what the regulars would accept. In September 1973 he pointedly publicized a legal opinion that he had solicited from former FCC chairman Newton Minow, declaring that the commission's recommendations were "subject to review and adoption by the Democratic National Committee."[56] Minow's opinion strengthened Strauss's influence over the Mikulski Commission since he and the other regulars had control over the DNC. Though some reformers disagreed with the ruling and wanted to go to court to challenge Strauss, cooler heads prevailed. Addressing the commission, Mikulski emphasized the need for unity rather than for a favorable court opinion, saying, "the important thing is not what legal opinion prevails, but the nature of our work—and [what] I can't stress enough today is our whole concept of unity in formulating the consensus report because the debate is not over jurisdictional perimeters, what the debate should always be on is what should be the rules of the delegate selection. And if we can't have an overwhelming majority from this body; and an overwhelming support of the Democratic National Committee, we would be in difficulty, regardless of what opinion was there."[57]

The commission met in a series of regional hearings and in Washington, D.C., throughout 1973. Though marked by an unending series of seemingly petty disputes, the commission eventually produced a set of guidelines that, although maintaining most of the McGovern-Fraser reforms, went a long way toward meeting the objections of the reform critics. The first of these concerns was quotas, which the commission abolished. During the presentation of the final draft of the report, Robert Vance, the liberal Alabama party chairman and one of the report's authors, stated: "The entire concept of quotas, we undertook to the degree that any draftsman could do so, to put it to rest. The overwhelming majority of the Drafting Committee wanted it clearly understood that the quota system was rejected in its entirety, either de facto, de jure, explicit or implied, in all respects. Substituting for this type of device, to ensure broad participation, was a new—not really a new—but a greatly reinforced concept of affirmative action."[58]

The new guidelines, in addition to clearly banning quotas (except for the equal division of all delegations between men and women), set up a series of affirmative action models for the state parties to follow in selecting convention delegates: the numerical representation of various groups would be "considered relevant evidence" in any credentials challenges, but "composition alone shall not constitute prima facie evidence of discrimination" and, "if a state party has adopted and implemented an approved Affirmative Action Program, the Party shall not be subject to challenge based solely on delegate composition or primary results."[59] In addition, the Mikulski Commission rules placed the burden of proof on the challengers, not on the state parties, to show that there had been discriminatory intent in the delegate selection process.[60]

The Mikulski Commission also attempted to meet the criticism that the reforms had removed party regulars and professionals from the delegate selection process. Ex officio delegates were still forbidden, but convention "privileges, except voting rights," were extended to all "Democratic Governors, United States Senators, United States Representatives, and members of the Democratic National Committee."[61] The commission also revised the McGovern-Fraser rules by increasing the number of delegates who could be appointed by the state party committee from 10 to 25 percent.[62]

Finally, the Mikulski Commission eliminated the McGovern-Fraser ban on slate-making activities by state and local parties (one reason for the removal of the Chicago delegation at the 1972 convention), as long as the slate did not receive preferential treatment on the ballot and its candidate preference or uncommitted status was clearly indicated on the ballot.[63] Yet, this rule eventually did little to increase the power of the party regulars since the commission also permitted the presidential candidates to approve all delegates listed as committed to him or her. As David Price points out, this rule "brought back slate-making with a vengeance, but this time the power to select delegates was given to the candidate organizations rather than to party leaders."[64]

Though these new guidelines were a step back from the McGovern-Fraser reforms, in some areas the Mikulski Commission went beyond its predecessor. The McGovern-Fraser Commission had mandated only that the delegate selection procedures "provide fair representation of minority views," but it did not specify any particular method for meeting this requirement.[65] As a result, California was allowed to keep its winner-take-all primary in 1972. The Mikulski Commission, however, established a system of proportional representation for the allocation of delegates based on that state's primary or caucus results for all candidates receiving more than 10 percent of the vote.

The only exceptions to this rule were in the so-called loop-hole primaries of Illinois, Pennsylvania, New York, Ohio, and New Jersey, where delegates were directly elected at the congressional district level. This type of primary approximated winner-take-all ones since voters were unlikely to split their votes between the delegates of two candidates, thus allowing the candidate with the most support to pick up all of the delegates. In addition, a candidate with enough support distributed evenly across the state could often win the delegates in most of the congressional districts, even with only a plurality of the statewide vote.[66]

The final innovation of the Mikulski rules was the establishment of the Compliance Review Commission (CRC). In the past, challenges to state delegate selection procedures were contested in the politically charged atmosphere of the Credentials Committee or on the floor of the Democratic convention. Such a system no longer seemed appropriate given the reformers' emphasis on procedures based upon laws and regulations as opposed to political conflict. According to the Mikulski Commission report:

> For the past two decades, this party has taken remarkable steps toward the creation of a body of national party law. In doing so, however, we have too often ignored the need for a mechanism to fairly enforce these rules and laws. For laws to be meaningful, they must be enforced in a manner which all recognize to be uniform, predictable, even-handed and politically neutral. Systems of law enforcement generally strive toward fair application of laws through the promulgation of laws that are clear, unambiguous and concise, and through the establishment of an impartial judiciary, free from the political pressures of the moment. To achieve the latter, an impartial judiciary, in the context of National Convention delegate selection rules requires "depoliticization" of the credentials certification process. In 1972, the most obvious weakness of the McGovern-Fraser Commission Rules was the inherent conflict between the judicial functions assigned to the Credentials Committee and the political nature of its selection, composition and primary role, i.e. acting as delegates for a particular nominee, at the Convention. Accordingly, the Committee's decisions are unavoidably influenced by the political ramification of a challenge, rather than the merits of the dispute.[67]

The CRC was intended to function as this "depoliticized" Credentials Committee. Some party regulars had wanted the DNC, which they controlled, to oversee compliance, but most saw the CRC as a reasonable compromise. According to Bob Vance, "Both sides are suspicious and neither can control it. So it must be fair!"[68] The CRC allowed party regulars, who were often uncertain about what the new rules did and did not allow, to verify that the delegate selection procedures that they had established were in accordance with party rules. Moreover, they could do this well before the convention, allowing them to make adjustments in time to avoid politicized credentials fights or expulsion from the convention—like Mayor Daley.[69]

Though the idea for the CRC had support from nearly everyone, the composition of the group was an extremely contentious issue. The Mikulski Commission originally proposed a seventeen-member CRC: Mikulski and the two vice-chairs of the commission, five members appointed by Strauss, five by Mikulski, and one member each appointed by the Senate and House majority leaders, the chairman of the Democratic Governors' Caucus, and the president of the Association of Democratic State Chairmen.[70] Mikulski's choices for the CRC were all liberals and included no representatives of labor. In addition, Mikulski actively campaigned to be named chair of the CRC.[71]

These developments disturbed Strauss and the regulars since they had hoped for a CRC that would be more accepting of the state parties. To their minds, Mikulski's plan was inadequate; the proposed size was too small to allow adequate representation for party regulars, and Mikulski's choices for appointments were too slanted toward the reformers. In January 1974, Strauss announced former New York City Mayor Robert Wagner as his choice for CRC chairman. He also advocated increasing the size of the CRC from seventeen to twenty-five, saying, "I have no quarrel with any of the five people she has selected as an individual, but the make-up of her appointees does pose some problems for me. I have to come up with a balance. Affirmative action plan is the name of the game for 1976. It's not child's play. We've got to come up with a balanced group. We need lawyers, people who have served as mediators, going into these states. There is no representation of labor; if we're going to win in 1976, we need to have it. There's no Chicano, no representative of Wallace . . . I don't have enough spots."[72]

Though one might accuse Strauss of cynically turning the reformers' arguments on their heads in order to stack the CRC, this statement shows that the regulars at least paid lip service to the notion that the bodies which conducted party affairs should be broadly representative of the various groups within the Democratic coalition.

Another controversial issue concerned proportional representation. Party regulars and the CDM opposed proportional representation. Penn Kemble, CDM's executive director, claimed, "It will prevent a coalition building process. We'll end up going to the convention with a host of independent, disputative groups. The leadership will tend to be more separatists."[73] Alan Baron of the DPG disagreed, stating that a winner-take-all apportionment method "causes disunity and division. The minority is locked out and the party often remains bitterly divided."[74] Mikulski also opposed changing the requirement, declaring, "These rules are like a sweater. You try to unravel one thing and the whole damn thing will fall apart."[75]

On this issue, Strauss once again played the role of the neutral compromiser, hoping only to find the position that would keep both sides happy:

> My personal feeling is that we would be better off if we had proportional
> representation at the congressional district level, rather than at the precinct
> level, just for the purely mechanical reason that it is so hard to enforce and
> to carry out and it's going to make for some additional contests and dis-
> agreement that we shouldn't have. This doesn't have anything to do with phi-
> losophy, because you find people on the left who agree with me and people
> on the right who disagree with me. It just depends on how they feel their
> own particular ox is going to get gored. I'm not prepared to say, if we left it
> as it is now, it would make me sick. And if they changed it, I wouldn't say a

great victory had been won by anybody. I just want whatever is reasonable. I could take it anyway.[76]

In March 1974 Strauss finally brokered an agreement on the issues of the CRC and proportional representation. According to Billie Carr, a leader of the DNC's liberal wing and a proponent of the Mikulski reforms:

He [Strauss] came up to me and said, "Billie, what is it you want?" I told him we wanted the Delegate Selection Commission report adopted as it was. He told me he only wanted two changes [increasing the threshold for winning any delegates from 10 to 15 percent and expanding the CRC from 18 to 25 members]. I told him we could live with the 15 percent on proportional representation but I'd like to know who the 25 members of the CRC would be. He turned to an aide and said "give her a list." I took it to our caucus and we went over it and decided it was fair. . . . We got 85 percent of what we wanted.[77]

The experience of the Mikulski Commission once again confirms that, despite much bickering, the party's reforms were never seriously challenged. All but the staunchest critics were willing to accept the vast majority of reforms and to find some compromise on the others. This was true even of the party regulars who presumably would have had less interest in notions of adequate representation and procedural fairness.

THE CHARTER COMMISSION

In addition to the Mikulski Commission, the 1972 convention had mandated the creation of a commission to write a party charter. In the spring of 1972, the McGovern-Fraser and O'Hara commissions had worked together to develop such a document for acceptance by the national convention. The intention of this effort was to develop a written body of law to govern the various activities of the party, just as the McGovern-Fraser guidelines had done in the area of delegate selection for the national convention. The draft document put out by the two commissions outlined a more centralized, disciplined, mass-based Democratic party, along the lines of various European Social Democratic parties. According to *Congressional Quarterly,* the proposed charter: "called for a national, dues-paying membership to help finance the party; establishment of seven strong regional party organizations, and yearly calls to national or regional Democratic conferences. The salaried national chairman would have been elected to a four-year term each even-numbered year between presidential elections. The national party staff would have been composed of professionals under a merit system that would permit dismissals 'only for just cause.'"[78]

The initial response of party regulars and elected officials to the proposed charter was extremely negative; the House Democratic Caucus said that it was "not in the best interests of the Democratic Party."[79] Faced with this reaction, the McGovern forces at the 1972 convention, not wanting to further alienate party regulars, put off consideration of the charter until after the election by creating a special commission to finish the document and establish a midterm party charter conference to approve the final document.[80]

The Charter Commission began its work the following March. Commission chairman Terry Sanford, former governor of North Carolina and a moderate Democrat, quickly scrapped the earlier recommendations for a dues-paying membership, telling the press with vast understatement that it "is an idea I don't think you could sell." Sanford also rejected any efforts to make the party tightly centralized by saying that he did not want "any effort to clamp down one system on all 50 state" parties.[81]

Strauss further reduced the Charter Commission's reform potential by appointing an additional 55 members to the 105-person commission in March 1973.[82] In a manner similar to his padding of the Mikulski Commission, Strauss claimed that the new appointments were only to ensure greater geographical representation, but in reality he intended to increase the number of moderates and party regulars on the body to make sure that their views were adequately represented.[83]

The Charter Commission met in relative harmony over the next year and produced a draft proposal for debate and approval at the December Charter Conference. First presented in March 1974, the draft charter established the national party as superior to the state parties, and it formalized party law on the size, composition, and operation of the national committee. The document also incorporated the McGovern-Fraser and Mikulski guidelines on delegate selection into party law, applied the Mikulski rules on affirmative action to all party affairs, and authorized a National Education and Training Council to help the party in the "furtherance of its objectives." Finally, the charter established a judicial council to rule on party disputes, called for mandatory midterm conferences, and formalized the tenure of the national committee chairman.[84]

These latter points remained contentious ones for many party regulars, so the commission put off final consideration until its last meeting in August 1974. At this meeting, the commission would decide whether the midterm conventions would be mandatory (as the reformers wanted) or optional (the choice of the regulars), whether to establish a judicial council (the wish of reformers) or to continue to solve disputes through the more political bodies of the DNC and the national convention (the regulars' preference), and whether the DNC's chairman should be elected for a four-year term between conventions (the reform option) or should serve at the discretion of the party's presidential nominee (the regulars' option). Despite these differences, neither the reformers nor the regulars considered these issues of great importance.[85]

Over the summer, Strauss, under pressure by Barkan, made sure that the regulars would prevail on these questions. He encouraged commission members who would not be at the August meeting to resign, allowing him to appoint more conservative replacements. Strauss's actions disturbed party reformers, who boycotted the DNC Executive Committee meeting which had to approve the replacements to the commission. Strauss still managed to achieve a quorum at the August 15 Executive Committee meeting that ratified his appointments. Donald Fraser, a strong reformer and member of both the Charter Commission and the Executive Committee, criticized the chairman's heavy-handed tactics and charged that Strauss's victory came at a "high cost of bitterness within the party."[86]

Despite the bad feelings caused by this incident, both Strauss and the reformers expected the last meeting of the Charter Commission to proceed smoothly. Though it now seemed that the regulars would prevail on the remaining issues, the reformers were not wholeheartedly committed to these proposals. According to David Broder, the issues involved were "of such exquisitely small significance that even the most theological of the Democratic factionalists could not really work up a sweat about it."[87] As a result, when the commission convened on August 17, the regulars prevailed decisively on each of the three issues. They made the midterm convention optional, left the choice of the national chairman to the party's nominee, and eliminated the judicial council, proposing instead that the DNC consider authorizing a much weaker body.[88]

Had the regulars stopped there, they would have won the battle. Instead, under the direction of COPE's Al Barkan, they overplayed their hand and nearly split the party. Aware that they had enough votes to dominate the proceedings, the next day representatives of labor, led by Congressman Thomas Foley and Barkan's lieutenant John Perkins, revised the charter in three sensitive areas. First, they deleted the charter's provision that the goal of affirmative action is to "encourage participation by all Democrats as indicated by their presence in the Democratic electorate," claiming that the latter phrase required "implied quotas." The move enraged the commission's black members, who threatened to walk out until a compromise was quickly arranged that put the matter off until the Charter Conference in December.[89]

Seeming not to recognize the nerves that they were touching, representatives of labor then offered an amendment that would have gutted the McGovern-Fraser and Mikulski reforms by prohibiting the DNC from establishing rules governing participation in primaries and other party proceedings, restoring the unit rule, removing the requirement for proportional representation in delegate selection, and allowing the delegate selection process to begin in the calendar year before the presidential election.

The meeting exploded. Commission member Hodding Carter of Mississippi accused those sponsoring the amendments of "making what's left of this charter a sham. You're killing 10 years of reform and 18 months of work by this commission." Donald Fraser questioned "why anyone would want to revive the discredited unit rule unless they are so obsessed with turning back the clock they've lost everything else."[90] California State Assemblyman Willie Brown then declared, "I am walking out. This is a travesty on the whole process. . . . This is the nail that closes the coffin on the Charter Commission." With Brown went the other black commission members, who were soon followed by the white reformers. The walk-out succeeded in denying a quorum, thus preventing the commission from conducting any further business.[91]

What might have been an uneventful meeting had exploded into controversy. Though Strauss was not a direct participant, his role in this incident bears examining. If he had been instrumental in the attempt to roll back the reforms, then it would have indicated that not only he, but the vast majority of party regulars and centrists that he represented, were also interested in eliminating the reforms. At the time, several reformers blamed Strauss for engineering the fiasco.[92] Crotty supports this view, but he provides no direct evidence.[93]

Strauss did help to appoint the replacements (including the woman who introduced the fateful resolution) to ensure that the regulars would prevail on the meeting's original issues, but there is no indication that he foresaw or sanctioned the actions of the regulars. Accounts of the meeting suggest that Strauss's representative at the meeting, Mark Siegel, recognized that the regulars were playing with fire but was unable to restrain them.[94] Even Alan Baron, a principal advocate of the reforms, does not believe Strauss directed the effort.[95]

In fact, Strauss, along with most other regulars, opposed rolling back the reforms. The principal voice of the regulars, the CDM, although not overjoyed by the charter, seemed satisfied that the document was no longer attempting to establish a strongly centralized, European-style party.[96] The counter-reform effort did not even have the support of the many regular state chairmen who were in attendance and took exception to the efforts to undo the reforms, such as New York's Joseph Crangle.[97]

Instead, it seems that the incident resulted from the overzealousness of COPE's representatives, who, sensing this was their chance to regain control of the party, decided to dismantle the reforms they so detested. (One must also remember that at the time, Tom Foley, the floor leader of the antireform effort, was not the even-handed moderate liberal he is today, but rather the protege of "Scoop" Jackson, well known for his antireform views and close ties with the AFL-CIO.) David Broder offered this same interpretation at the time:

> But once the labor forces proved they were in the saddle, no one—not
> Strauss or Siegel or the "regular" state chairman—could hold them back.
> And what was revealed was the essential difference between the Barkan
> view and that of the Strauss forces.
>
> Strauss has been practicing the politics of conciliation . . . trying to
> patch the opposing demands of the diverse elements in the Democratic

coalition. Barkan and Meany don't want conciliation; they want control of their party back from those who, in their view, usurped its franchise when they nominated George McGovern in 1972.

Some of the older labor union staffers swarming around the charter commission meeting here compared the fight to their battle against the Communists in the labor movement decades ago. In their minds, the opponents must be "purged," or they will subvert the organization.[98]

Whatever his role in the explosive end of the Charter Commission, Strauss now faced a situation that threatened to destroy his efforts to unify the party. Consequently, he would have to find some way to broker a compromise on the issue, or face a bitter Charter Conference that would likely leave a divided party. Over the next three months, Strauss, working closely with Democratic elected officials and party regulars, engineered a compromise.

The key step toward a compromise came at a November 18 Democratic governors' meeting. In a statement worked out by Ohio governor John Gilligan and Florida governor Reuben Askew, the governors endorsed a compromise charter similar to the one presented before the August explosion. The compromise made the midterm convention optional but did establish the judicial council. The governors also kept the charter provision giving the national party the power to set delegate selection guidelines, in effect formalizing the McGovern-Fraser and Mikulski Commission rules. Finally, the governors' proposal restored the affirmative action compromise worked out by the Mikulski Commission.[99]

This compromise quickly received the support of Strauss, the DNC's Black Caucus, party regulars, and even George Wallace.[100] Still, many in labor, principally COPE's Barkan, remained opposed. They feared that the Mikulski language did nothing to prevent implicit quotas.

Yet even Barkan's bite was reduced. The reform issue divided labor, with several progressive unions—the machinists, and the communications workers in particular—supporting the reforms and the liberalized Democratic party that they had created. According to Alan Baron, the leadership of several of these unions went over Barkan's head to George Meany, who ordered Barkan to back off.[101] This action by Meany, certainly no fan of the reforms, might seem strange, but he, perhaps reflecting his AFL background, took a much less partisan interest in politics than Barkan, who had come up through the CIO unions that had traditionally had a symbiotic relationship with the Democratic party.[102] Meany was also well aware that the debate over the reforms had divided the labor movement and that further divisions would only help reduce its already diminishing influence.[103]

With Democrats being Democrats, no internal party compromise could last long. This time it was the Black Caucus's turn to try to change the language at the last minute. On Thursday, December 5, two days before the start of the Charter Conference, the Conference Rules Committee voted to endorse the Mikulski Commission's language on quotas and affirmative action that had been worked out by the governors. Though the leaders of the Black Caucus had originally endorsed the compromise, it became apparent that evening that many caucus members were unhappy with the provision and wanted to delete the final section of the proposal, which stated that racial composition alone would not "constitute prima facie evidence of discrimination, nor shall it shift the burden of proof from the challenged party." The caucus members feared that unless this language were removed, it would be too difficult to challenge instances of discrimination. Joe Reed, chairman of the Alabama Democratic Conference, declared, "With that language in there, affirmative action is an empty promise."[104]

The leaders of the Black Caucus went to Strauss the next evening, demanding that he change the language or face a walkout by black delegates. Strauss refused to back down and accused them of going back on their promise to support the governors' compromise. Rebuffed by Strauss, the black leadership then convinced several governors, most notably Reuben Askew of Florida, to back them on the issue. On Saturday afternoon, Askew and DNC Treasurer Edward Bennett Williams then hammered out a compromise that removed the offending language.[105]

Strauss then acted to make sure that the rest of the convention would accept the new language. He asked Mayor Richard Daley to help sell the compromise to party regulars. Daley, the epitome of the party regular and someone who had seen his own power greatly reduced by the reforms, agreed, not only to support the resolution, but also to work the floor in favor of it. Strauss then treated the convention to the sight of him kissing "Hizzoner."[106] Through the efforts of Daley and Strauss, the conference passed the new language along with the rest of the charter. The Democratic party had managed, though just barely, to adopt a charter without destroying themselves in the process.

The Charter Commission's significance is similar to that of the Mikulski Commission: both efforts showed that attempting to roll back the reforms instituted since 1968 lacked broad support in the party. In fact, the only support for such an effort came from the most conservative faction of organized labor, and their efforts were quickly repudiated by the other elements of labor, party regulars, Mayor Daley, and even George Wallace! Once again, even in this more conservative and traditional wing of the party, there existed concerns for procedural fairness, even at the expense of political expediency.

STRAUSS'S ORGANIZATIONAL EFFORTS

In addition to his principal focus on restoring unity to the party by resolving various procedural controversies, Bob Strauss also attempted to strengthen the DNC's organizational apparatus. His first task was to reduce the party's debt and place the party on a better financial footing. In this effort, Strauss needed all the help he could get. Raising money for a party that has just lost the presidency by a landslide is difficult in any circumstances, but Strauss had the additional burden of managing the party's $3.5 million debt and paying for the Mikulski and Sanford commissions and the Charter Conference, both of which were mandated by the 1972 convention.[107]

In many ways, Strauss was the ideal chairman to help the party financially. As Mark Siegel puts it, as a Texan, a Jew, a lawyer, a businessman, a moderate, and a former DNC finance chairman, Strauss was well connected to the party's traditional sources of funds.[108] By 1976, he had made substantial headway, reducing the debt to $2 million and coming up with enough money to fund an expansion in DNC programs and staff.[109]

It is often claimed that, under Strauss, DNC fundraising relied heavily on big contributors and that the party failed to develop a direct-mail base of small contributors using the lists of contributors to the McGovern campaign. According to journalist Robert Kuttner: "Robert Strauss . . . made a public display of scrapping the 600,000-name McGovern donor list, and cultivating the PAC's. 'We had a list about three times the size of the Goldwater list that started the Republican direct mail,' says a former DNC official, 'but Bob Strauss threw the McGovern list out the window because he wanted to build a party dependent on his network of wealthy contributors, people who really didn't share the philosophy of the national party.'"[110]

It is indisputable that Strauss increased the DNC's take from large contributors, but there is no evidence that he sacrificed attempts to solicit small donations. In fact, under Strauss the DNC made important strides in developing a sustaining base of small givers. Accounts such as Kuttner's overlook that Strauss was the principal supporter and developer of the DNC Telethons. Though begun by Strauss while he was DNC finance chairman in 1972, he expanded the program when he became chairman. The DNC sponsored three telethons from 1973 to 1975, and though their production costs were high, they did succeed in raising large sums of money for the party (see table 11). In addition to the money they raised, the telethons also served as a source of new names for direct-mail solicitations (see table 12). A survey of the 1973 telethon contributors showed that almost half of those who gave had not made a contribution to the party in the previous year, while a survey of the 1974 telethon contributors showed that two-thirds would not have given to the party without the telethon.[111] Finally, the telethons also gave the party substantial television exposure and helped it to project a positive image to the public.

In addition to the telethons, and in direct contradiction of the claims of Kuttner and others, Strauss did place a heavy emphasis on the direct-mail program and did use the McGovern campaign's contributor list. The return from these contributors was mediocre at best, however, because the DNC was but one of many groups that were soliciting funds from the McGovern donors.[112] In addition, the success of McGovern's direct-mail program rested heavily on his ideological appeal. Like

TABLE 11.

DNC TELETHON INCOME, 1973–1975.

Telethon	Net Receipts	Production Costs	Net Income	DNC Share	DNC Net
1973	$4,215,215	$2,273,237	$1,941,978	50%	$970,989
1974	$5,403,672	$2,555,839	$2,847,833	33%	$949,278
1975	$3,661,107	$2,751,336	$ 909,771	50%	$454,889

Source: John W. Ellwood and Robert J. Spitzer, "The Democratic National Telethons: Their Successes and Failures," *Journal of Politics* 41 (August 1979): 836–38

Note: The money that did not go to the DNC went to the parties in the states and localities where it was raised.

TABLE 12.

DNC TELETHON CONTRIBUTIONS.

Telethon	Net Receipts	Total Contributors	Mean Contribution
1973	$4,215,215	260,888	$16.16
1974	$5,403,672	389,679	$13.87
1975	$3,661,107	209,344	$17.49

Source: John W. Ellwood and Robert J. Spitzer, "The Democratic National Telethons: Their Successes and Failures," *Journal of Politics* 41 (August 1979): 837.

Barry Goldwater and George Wallace, the first presidential candidates to use direct-mail successfully, McGovern took ideological positions that a great many people believed strongly in and were willing to support with their money. Such contributors, however, were less willing to support the more general purposes of the DNC. In the words of Bob Keefe, the McGovern contributors "were prepared to support a candidate, not a party."[113] Still, the McGovern list was moderately successful for the party, with a return rate of approximately 2 to 4 percent—enough to show a small profit, but far below what is usually expected from a list of previous contributors.[114]

The names from the McGovern list, the DNC's own direct-mail file, and the lists of telethon contributors provided the DNC with a direct-mail file of more than a million names by the beginning of 1974.[115] Overall, during Strauss's tenure the DNC received about 50 percent of its total income from direct mail and 80 percent from donations of less than $100.[116] The income from these small contributors paid for upwards of 80 percent of the DNC's fixed operating costs, such as salaries and infrastructure.[117]

Although some might argue that direct mail should have accounted for a larger share of the DNC's income under Strauss, this was not for lack of effort and especially not because he was opposed to the party's relying less on big contributors. Those who wish to find fault with the DNC's fundraising operations from 1972 to 1976 must look elsewhere. One factor is that the DNC had a smaller base of potential contributors than did the RNC. Another is that the DNC's debt prevented the financial investment necessary for developing a truly sustaining direct-mail program. Also, the DNC, unlike the RNC, did not yet have the base of technology and expertise necessary to mount a successful direct-mail effort. Finally, as we shall see later, the DNC was committed to spending the bulk of its resources on procedural reform efforts, thus limiting its ability to develop the fundraising organization that it needed.

Along with these financial programs, the DNC under Strauss began to provide campaign services to candidates around the country. The idea originated with executive director, Bob Keefe, who proposed that the DNC begin, as the Republicans had under Ray Bliss, to focus on doing more for Democratic candidates and institutionalizing campaign services into its operations. According to Terry Straub, the DNC's director of National Field Operations, "Strauss didn't know shit about campaigns, but he was willing to support our notions" about campaign services. Consequently, early in 1973 the DNC sent out teams of campaign consultants to work on various special elections to Congress.[118]

The Democrats managed to win most of these races and the support of the DNC staffers seemed to be an important factor. One aspect of this support was the polling done by the DNC, which showed that Watergate was a powerful issue at the local level. Previously, Strauss and many other Democrats were unsure that hitting Republicans on Watergate would play well in congressional races and were reluctant to use the issue, but these surveys helped convince them otherwise.[119]

Strauss eventually institutionalized the campaign services program under the leadership of outgoing Georgia governor Jimmy Carter and his assistant Hamilton Jordan. Carter, who had recently decided to run for president, put great effort into the job, since it offered him the opportunity to meet and to help Democratic candidates and party officials around the country. Carter seems to have done an outstanding job in the position, devoting himself to the task of making sure the program ran effectively.[120] In Straub's assessment, "He worked it, he really worked it."[121] Had a less ambitious person run the program, one can easily imagine that it would not have proven so effective.

In addition to offering direct assistance with field operations, the program also developed manuals to help candidates and their staffs mount more effective campaigns. With this goal in mind, the DNC assembled a group of Democratic campaign technicians who developed manuals describing how to perform the various tasks involved in a campaign—phone banks, fundraising, get-out-the-vote drives, polling, field operations, and several others. The idea was to establish a standardized and simple approach to campaign tasks that could be used by candidates around the country.[122]

Despite the DNC's efforts in finance and campaign services under Strauss, one cannot call their response in this period an organizational one. Clearly more attention was paid and greater resources were allocated to the attempt to unify the party through procedural means. Strauss made this much clear in his 1974 report to the DNC:

> We inherited, in 1973, from the 1972 Democratic National Convention, a commitment to spend our most fundamental resources to the continuing process of structural reexamination. Although our Commission expenses have totalled approximately $600,000, and we can look forward to the additional expenditure of at least another $800,000 for the 1974 Conference on Party Organization and Policy, these inherited expenses, *although taxing to our resources and to our fundamental responsibility to elect Democrats on all levels,* was [*sic*] a necessary commitment to the future of our Party and our Nation's political system.[123]

Strauss's comments provide further confirmation of the DNC's emphasis on procedural reform, even at the expense of short-term electoral necessity and despite his evident preference for spending the money elsewhere.

ISSUE DEVELOPMENT

By most accounts, Bob Strauss is a man of considerable ambition and energy, so it seems appropriate that as DNC chairman he would also attempt some form of policy response in addition to earlier mentioned procedural and organizational activities. Yet even Strauss had his limits. In February 1973, he appointed the Democratic Advisory Council of Elected Officials (DACEO). The panel consisted of sixty-one members, all elected officials. Strauss also appointed Arthur Krim, chairman of United Artists and a major Democratic party fundraiser, to chair the DACEO. The group seldom met and had minimal impact. The only statement issued by the council to have received much attention was one on energy policy in 1975, but it is remembered for little else.[124] David Broder notes that "its pronouncements were universally, and justifiably, ignored by the press," and Bob Keefe claims that the DACEO was "never of strong significance."[125]

The failure of the DACEO is attributable to Strauss's basic indifference to policy matters. When asked what the Democratic party stood for, Strauss answered, "Hell, I don't know. That's not my worry."[126] Yet he knew that the party was deeply divided on several issues and, according to Mark Siegel, he wanted to "stop liberals from using the DNC as a platform committee."[127] Strauss also did not want an issue council that might serve as a platform for liberals. This concern grew out of what Strauss incorrectly believed was the experience of the Democratic Policy Council (DPC) from 1969 to 1972. According to John Stewart, DPC director, "He knew the DNC couldn't simply walk away from policy activity, but he wanted a more stable, predictable structure."[128] Therefore, Strauss relied on a body composed only of elected officials, whom he believed would take more responsible, centrist, and noncontroversial stands on the issues.[129]

Still, the DACEO might have served a useful role, much as the Republican Coordinating Committee did between 1965 and 1968, by allowing different party factions to discuss their positions on the issues. But even this was not to be. In essence, Strauss created the DACEO, not to develop issues and programs, but rather to provide a vehicle through which elected officials could reinvolve themselves in party affairs.[130] Even Arthur Krim agrees that Strauss never thought the council could succeed as a policy generator and describes the DACEO as an "exercise in keeping the National Committee as a centrifugal force."[131] Thus, even with the DACEO, the effort was directed more at procedural than at policy matters.

ASSESSING THE RESPONSE

Though the nomination, campaign, and landslide defeat of George McGovern created deep bitterness among many in the party's traditional wing concerning the reforms that had helped McGovern, there was no widespread effort to roll back these reforms. Yet such an outcome was at least theoretically possible. A majority of the DNC elected Bob Strauss chairman, thus showing that the regulars were in control of that body and could have taken more aggressive steps at counter-reform. But, with the exception of labor's more conservative elements, the regulars made no concerted effort to repeal the McGovern-Fraser reforms. In fact, only in the area of quotas and the representation of party officials did the regulars seek important changes; in other areas the reforms were institutionalized and written into party law. For the most part, the DNC's activity between 1972 and 1976 can be characterized as the institutionalization of reform, not counter-reform.

Why was this so? Certainly one aspect of the regulars' attitude in this period was political expediency. They realized that rolling back the reforms would divide, if not destroy, the party. For the sake of party unity, they were willing to tolerate reform.

Such a motivation was an important one, but it seems incomplete. Rather, one senses that the bulk of the reforms had widespread support within the party and that even the party regulars—those politicians who are usually focused solely on electoral gain—recognized that procedural fairness and broadened participation and diversity were important values for the Democratic party. This made them willing not only to tolerate the reforms but also to support and institutionalize them.

Evidence for this widespread support comes from two sources. First, comments made at the time by the CDM, which stressed the need for fairness—but not special considerations—in the nomination process.[132] Second, interviews with several of Strauss's associates at the DNC indicate that they, along with Strauss and most of his supporters, also supported the reforms' basic goals, if not all of their specific applications.

What did this emphasis on reform mean for the party? Obviously it involved a diminution of organizational and policy efforts. Though Bob Strauss made important strides in the area of finance and campaign services, the high cost of the DNC's procedural projects (the Mikulski and Stanford commissions, the Charter Conference, and the Compliance Review Commission) drained resources from other DNC projects, particularly organizational ones. As a result, when Strauss left the DNC in 1977 its heavy debt burden continued to jeopardize the party's financial and organizational future. Moreover, the DNC did not have the capacity to provide services to its candidates on the same scale that the RNC could at the time, a disparity that would drastically increase over the next four years.

Despite this organizational handicap, the most important consequence of the DNC's focus on procedure in this period was a neglect of policy reevaluation. Strauss had no interest in policy, and his only effort in this direction, the DACEO, was intended not for policy results, but rather for the procedural purpose of ensuring the participation of elected officials in party affairs. The DNC's lack of attention to policy in this period was noted at the time. In the fall of 1973, Patricia Derian, a DNC member from Mississippi, sent Strauss a public letter warning of the consequences of failing to focus on policy:

> Democrats have been absorbed with problems of organization, delegate selection, fund raising. . . . Our party is balkanized; each elected official stands on his own plank, works in his own area of interest. . . .
>
> We cannot wait until the next presidential campaign to propose some alternative to the Nixon form of government. We are not obliged to focus on one individual before we can devise a program for this country. We can take responsibility as a party. . . .
>
> I know the argument that we have a party so diverse that we cannot bind campaigning Democrats to a party line. I have heard people say that the only reason for having a party is to get Democrats elected. But what does it mean to anyone any more to be a Democrat? If it only signifies one is not a Republican that is not enough . . . .
>
> We know our glorious past. . . . Grand yesterdays and a good feeling that we'd be dependable and right for the country if we were in charge don't cut any ice with the voters. . . . And while we might slide by the next congressional elections by not being Republicans, that state of affairs won't last

long. And it's not the point; we haven't got three years to wait to influence the direction of this country.

This is an emergency of the first order. We can feud our intraparty feuds another day. Now, we must set about saving this country.[133]

David Broder also made a consistent point of taking the Democrats to task for failing to develop an agenda, claiming in 1974, "Unless the Democratic Party sweeps the mental cobwebs out of its mind before 1976, Republicans may have the issues field to themselves again. . . . The Republicans are well into issues politics." He added that while the Democratic party was still standing, "What remains to be seen is whether it will stand for something."[134] In 1975, he commented:

> The Democratic Party under Strauss has spelled out its rules and procedures in mind-boggling detail. But it has said virtually nothing about its goals, its policies, and its programs. It will be little short of amazing if the Democrats do not pay a price for this neglect.[135]

Though the Democrats managed to win the next presidential election, one can argue that they ultimately did pay a price for their neglect of issues. Jimmy Carter ran and won his campaign less on the issues or his agenda than on the appeal of his "trust me" personality. Once in power, the party found itself with a president who shared few common goals with the congressional wing of the party, itself divided into contending factions. The result was both the perception and reality of a party unable to develop a governing agenda with which to lead the country. Though the party did not pay for this neglect of a policy agenda until 1980, the eventual cost was high indeed.

7

THE REPUBLICANS,

1976–1980

After controlling the White House for eight years, the Republican party again found itself out of power following the 1976 election. Though President Gerald Ford had only narrowly lost the election to Jimmy Carter, the party fashioned an organizational response very similar to its response to Barry Goldwater's landslide defeat in 1964. Under chairman Bill Brock, the RNC rebuilt its financial and organizational capacities, copying many of the same programs and methods employed by Ray Bliss from 1965 to 1968. The RNC also engaged in a policy response in this period, but, just as during the Bliss era, this effort was secondary to the RNC's organizational activities.

Republican fortunes were at a low ebb after the 1976 election. Not only had the party lost the White House, but in Congress it had failed to recover any of the ground lost in the 1974 elections, leaving the Republicans in control of only 143 House seats and 38 Senate seats. Republicans confronted an equally bleak picture at the state level: only thirteen governors were Republican, and the party controlled just four state legislatures. Only a quarter of the population identified itself as Republican.

The Republican party once again found itself divided between its moderate and conservative factions. In 1976, former California governor Ronald Reagan mounted a strong conservative challenge to President Ford, who only narrowly won renomination despite the powers of incumbency. Though the party managed to unify itself for the general election more than in 1964, both factions were wary of one another following the election. Some conservative intellectuals even suggested that their cause would best be served by abandoning the Republican party and building a new, conservative third party.[1]

The Republicans' weaknesses in this period were the subject of much commentary in the national press, with some even predicting that the party might be following in the footsteps of the Whigs. The *New York Times* reported: "Most of its [the GOP] national leaders are either defeated, discredited or too old for any claim on future political influence, the political observers say. The no longer Grand Old Party has lost the White House, barely preserved apparently irreducible minorities in Congress and clings to governorships in 13 of 50 states, many of them small and politically impotent."[2]

Many Republican officials also shared this pessimistic attitude. Morale among Republicans had fallen so low that many in the party, including Ronald Reagan and North Carolina Senator Jesse Helms, suggested that the party might even consider changing its name.[3] At the January 1977 meeting of the RNC, John East, then national committeeman and later senator from North Carolina, also suggested that the Republican label had become an albatross and that the committee should consider changing the party's name. Though nothing came of these proposals, they underscore the sense of near desperation many Republicans felt after the 1976 election.[4]

THE LEADERSHIP STRUGGLE

In 1976 the leadership struggle for the RNC took a somewhat different course from the contest that followed the 1964 election. Because he had won his party's nomination, President Ford and the more moderate wing of the Republican party retained control over the RNC. This control, however, came into question soon after Ford's defeat. In November 1976 RNC Chairwoman Mary Louise Smith, despite requests from Ford and Vice-President Nelson Rockefeller to continue on the job, announced her intention to step down from the position in January 1977.[5]

Smith's announcement intensified the RNC's ongoing leadership struggle. Many conservatives had already called for Smith to resign, claiming that by losing the election, Ford and other Republican moderates had lost their mandate to lead the party and that conservatives should assume control of the RNC. One Reagan supporter stated, "The Ford people have had their chance. They had the national committee, they had the Administration, but they didn't do much with the Presidency or with Congress."[6] Jesse Helms declared, "Now more than ever, the Republican Party must be transformed to a broad-based conservative party" by taking control of "the machinery of the party, from the chairman of the Republican National Committee on down."[7]

Moderate Republicans quickly organized to prevent the Reagan forces from gaining control of the RNC. A group of fifteen to twenty moderate Republican senators and House members, mobilized by Michigan governor William Milliken, met in Washington following Smith's announcement. No candidates emerged from this meeting, but most moderates began to line up behind either James A. Baker, President Ford's campaign manager; Thomas Milligan, Indiana state party chairman; or Robert Carter, party chairman and national committeeman for the District of Columbia.[8]

The conservative leanings of most RNC members hampered the efforts of these moderate Republicans. The conservatives, however, were also divided and could not agree on a single candidate. John Connally, the former Democratic governor of Texas, who switched parties after becoming secretary of the treasury during the Nixon administration, was one conservative who expressed interest in the position, but only if the RNC lifted its rule requiring a full-time chairman. Connally seems to have been unwilling to give up his lucrative law practice in order to become head of the RNC, which paid only $42,000 a year.[9] While Connally had the support of several southern conservatives on the RNC, many others on the committee opposed his candidacy for a variety of reasons.[10] Supporters of Ronald Reagan disliked Connally for endorsing Ford before the 1976 convention, and they also did not want to enhance the presidential ambitions of a potential rival to their candidate. Others were wary of so recent a convert to the party and viewed Connally, recently tried for influence peddling, as exactly the wrong person to lead the party as it tried to escape the stigma of Watergate. Finally, most on the RNC, believing strongly in the need for day-to-day supervision for robust organizational efforts, seemed unwilling to change its requirement for a full-time chairman.[11]

As the Connally candidacy died on the vine, conservative support coalesced around two candidates: Richard Richards, national committeeman from Utah and a strong supporter of Ronald Reagan, and Bill Brock, Republican senator from Tennessee who had been defeated for reelection in 1976. At first a reluctant candidate, Brock's Senate staff eventually persuaded him to run for the position, and he soon mounted an intensive campaign.[12]

With the Republican party in such a weakened state and no clear leader for the position, the selection of a new RNC chairman had the potential for further dividing the party. Many party leaders recognized this possibility and began to call for the selection of someone in the mold of Ray Bliss—a nonideological chairman, devoted to organization renewal rather than ideological positioning. House Minority Leader John Rhodes of Arizona called for the RNC to select "a practical technician" with "expertise in nuts and bolts organization at the grassroots level. If he or she can talk articulately, it will be frosting on the cake." Ronald Reagan echoed Rhodes's call, saying that the RNC needed "a full-time technician, not a party spokesman."[13]

Ford, Rockefeller, Reagan, and Connally met at the White House on December 9, 1976, and January 5, 1977, to try to find a compromise choice for RNC chairman. These meetings failed, however, to produce an agreement. Reagan ended up endorsing Richards, while Ford backed Baker. A week before the election, both Baker and Milligan, dropped out of the race, presumably for lack of support for a moderate candidate.

The race then essentially became a contest between Richards and Brock. According to one associate of Brock's, the Brock forces mounted a heavy campaign before the RNC's vote, working the RNC meeting like a political convention.[14]

On January 14, 1977, the RNC selected Brock as its chairman on the third ballot by a vote of 90 to 46.[15]

How did Brock become chairman of the RNC? One factor was his perceived skill as a political technician. From 1973 to 1974, Brock had served as chairman of the Republican Senatorial Campaign Committee, and many hoped he could help to coordinate the efforts of the RNC and the congressional campaign committees.[16] Brock's Senate office was also well known for its organizational sophistication, particularly its computer and direct-mail systems, and his Tennessee campaigns were marked by significant grass-roots organization.[17] These were not insignificant attributes given the Republican party's propensity for organizational innovation.

A second factor was his perceived ideological centrism (relative to the spectrum within the Republican party). With the demise of the candidacies of moderates Baker and Milligan, many moderates saw Brock as an acceptable alternative to the more conservative Richards. Brock, however, had a voting record in the Senate that was conservative enough to make him palatable to conservatives on the RNC and his southern roots helped him win the votes of conservatives from this region.[18] According to John East, "Brock came through as a neutral, while Richards came through as a Reagan man. It cost Richards centrist votes, while Brock ended up being everyone's second choice."[19]

A final, and somewhat related factor, was that Brock's conception of his role as chairman appealed to the self-interest of the RNC. According to Brock's associate, Ben Cotton, Brock actively campaigned for the chairmanship by stressing that as chairman he would employ a "tactical" approach of party building that would help to increase the RNC's institutional power. Brock contrasted this "tactical" approach with a "political" approach, whereby the RNC merely served as an arena for intra-party factional competition.[20]

Brock tried to link Richards to this "political" approach, telling a group of RNC members, "You can't take this job if you are interested in your own candidacy or if you are interested in the candidacy of somebody else. If you do, you'll never do anything again."[21] Brock seems to have succeeded in this effort. Many committee members viewed Richards as too closely linked to Reagan to effectively and independently lead the RNC.[22]

Brock's distinction between "tactical" and "political" approaches to party building mirrors the difference between an organizational and a policy or procedural response. Moreover, it is informative that Brock (correctly, as it turned out) saw merit in using the "tactical" label in describing his own leadership agenda, perhaps recognizing that the Republican party was more receptive to the organizational efforts inherent in this approach than to the more ideological emphasis of a "political" approach.

BROCK'S LEADERSHIP APPROACH

With the exception of Paul Butler, Bill Brock seems to have been one of the only national party chairmen in recent years to have seriously considered the potential role of the national committees in American politics. Butler saw the role of the national committee as a programmatic one, developing and publicizing a party agenda. Brock believed that the RNC had abandoned its traditional party building role in the decade prior to his selection as chairman and was now lacking any meaningful purpose. As a result, he believed that the Republican party was increasingly divided between its "elected" wing of elected officials and its "political" wing of volunteer activists.[23]

This disjunction had not always been a problem. From 1964 to 1968 Ray Bliss's party-building activities made great strides in uniting these two wings of the party, but following his election in 1968, Richard Nixon proceeded to undo much of what Bliss had achieved. Not only did Nixon replace Bliss, he also made sure that Bliss's successors placed their first and only loyalty with the White House. While the national party organizations traditionally recede into the background when a member of their party occupies the White House, the Nixon experience offers the most extreme example of a president dominating their national committee. According to one analyst of the period: "The precise nature of President Nixon's plans for the RNC were unclear, and it is doubtful whether he had even fully formulated them. His main concern appeared to be ensuring its loyalty and subordination to the White House. In truth, Nixon rapidly lost interest in the official party; in so far as the RNC meant anything, it was a potential rival for power."[24]

In the view of many, inside the party and out, Nixon's actions had the effect of making the Republican party a top-down organization. The party's image and organization became increasingly centered around its control of the White House. This strategy culminated with the 1972 campaign, where the RNC and most state and local Republican parties were effectively shunted aside by the Committee to Re-Elect the President, which avoided using the Republican name or image. As a result, though Nixon won a huge landslide, the party performed anemically.

Following Nixon's resignation in 1974, it was obvious to all that the Republican party faced deep difficulties. To rectify this situation, President Ford and RNC Chairwoman Mary Louise Smith, appointed by Ford in 1974, attempted various party-building measures, but these proved ineffective in the face of financial difficulties, factional feuding, and the White House's eventual focus on Ford's reelection campaign.[25]

As a result of Nixon's abuse of the RNC, Watergate, and the losses of 1974 and 1976, when Brock took over at the RNC, the Republican party bore little resemblance to the robust and vital organization it had been in 1968. As Ray Bliss pointed out in 1977: "The ideological problem was worse in 1965, but erosion at the bottom is worse this year. . . . I had good fortune when I was chairman. . . . We had a sensational comeback. But when Nixon came in, he and his people went back to the old pattern of building up the party at the top."[26] As Senator Robert Dole of Kansas, the party's 1976 candidate for vice-president and a former national chairman noted, "We are a 'top-down' party instead of a 'grass-roots-up' party."[27]

Stepping into this situation, Brock believed that his task was twofold. First, he had to disabuse the party of any lingering confidence in a top-down strategy, whereby Republican success at the presidential level would trickle down to the state and local parties. This approach had failed miserably in 1976; though President Ford came close to winning, Republicans failed to make gains at any other level.

A top-down approach to elections, Brock believed, had also helped to erode the "political" wing of the party. As he told the RNC in his acceptance speech: "The party is in shambles in some of our states. Where we survive, it is often in a defensive posture, shutters closed, all ports battened down. We have become too dependent upon the presidency, oriented too much to the top of the ticket and thereby assuring our own ultimate destruction as we ignore our eroding base in precinct and state legislature, in community and county government."[28] Brock's efforts to dissuade the party from concentrating on the top of the ticket even included a slide show, "A Close Encounter in Political Survival": "Set in the year 2001, the drama shows a man reading a book titled 'The Death of the Republican Party.' The narrator relates that Republicans paid too much political attention to the White House and gradually gave up control of governorships and state legislatures until gerrymandering helped eliminate the party."[29]

The second aspect of Brock's approach was to revitalize the "political" wing of the party through vigorous party-building efforts at the local, state, and national levels. In his acceptance speech Brock saluted the "too often forgotten men and women" who worked for the party in their communities. He added:

> They really do count. They deserve better. More importantly, it is essential that we understand that these people constitute our roots, and we must restore that foundation if we are going to rebuild on solid ground. . . .
>
> That is what we have got to do with these individuals and these people. Every resource must be utilized to achieve this objective of rebuilding this party in the community from the bottom up.[30]

Much of Brock's effort mirrored RNC activities under Ray Bliss, but the two chairmen differed on the ultimate purpose of their activity. Bliss, unambitious to a fault and always a state party chairman at heart, used his party-building efforts to reinforce the state and local parties without attempting to concentrate and centralize power within the RNC. The more ambitious and entrepreneurial Brock, however, recognized that extensive party-building activities, paid for and run by the RNC, would help to centralize power and influence within the national committee.[31] In order to better compare and contrast Brock's and Bliss's activities, I will explore the RNC's activities from 1976 to 1980 using Bliss's four cornerstones of an effective political party operation: financing, organization, candidates, and party image.

FINANCE

Unlike Ray Bliss, and due in no small part to his efforts, Bill Brock took over an RNC that was on stable financial footing. Despite the abuse it received from the Nixon administration, the RNC still received a steady and significant flow of funds from its direct-mail program. As a result, during the 1976 presidential election campaign, a period when the national committees usually drive themselves into debt, the RNC actually managed to improve its financial position from $986,000 in January to $1,398,000 by year's end. By April 1977, the RNC had a surplus of more than $2.6 million.[32]

Despite possessing financial resources far in excess of the Democrats', Brock recognized that the party-building activities he envisioned would require raising vast amounts of money.[33] To accomplish this goal, Brock focused on direct mail. Without the White House, the party faced a more difficult task in wooing big contributors. Moreover, the recent implementation of campaign finance reforms limited the maximum individual contribution to a party to $20,000. Brock also believed that emphasizing the small contributor–oriented direct-mail program would help the shake the image of the Republicans as a party beholden to the rich. In addition, expansion of the RNC's mailing list produced a list of potential volunteers for the party's grass-roots efforts.[34] Finally, as opposition party, the Republicans could better use the negative attacks that work most effectively in direct-mail fundraising. Two of the more successful Republican mailings were letters attacking United Nations Ambassador Andrew Young and the ratification of the Panama Canal Treaties.[35]

To expand the party's base of givers, Brock assigned all funds not needed for current expenses to prospecting for new contributors. This plan had many risks, but, as Brock recognized, "There really was no other way to build an effective national party."[36] The gamble did not initially pay off; some of the early prospecting letters were not as successful as hoped and according to Brock's aide, Jack Faris, "We were running on a thin string. There were no raises, and we had to borrow money then."[37] Eventually Brock's strategy succeeded. During 1977, the RNC expanded its base of contributors from 250,000 to 350,000. That base grew to 510,000 in 1978, 550,000 in 1979, and in 1980 a phenomenal 1.2 million people contributed to the RNC.[38] These contributions, averaging around $25 each, increased RNC net receipts from $12.7 million in 1976 to more than $26 million in 1980 (see table 13.)

In addition to expanding the base of its direct-mail program, Brock also man-

TABLE 13.

RNC DIRECT-MAIL FUNDRAISING, 1976–1980.

Year	Contributions	Net Receipts
1976	250,000	$12,700,000
1977	350,000	$ 7,300,000
1978	510,000	$10,100,000
1979	550,000	$12,000,000
1980	1,200,000	$26,480,000

Source: Timothy B. Clark, "The RNC Prospers, the DNC Struggles as They Face the 1980 Elections," *National Journal*, September 27, 1980, 1618; and Herbert Alexander, *Financing the 1980 Election* (Lexington, Mass.: Heath, 1983), 300.

aged to make the solicitation more efficient. Though able to raise huge sums of money, direct mail is a very costly method of fundraising. By targeting mailings to zip codes with high rates of Republican voting and registration, the RNC managed to improve its rate of return on prospecting letters (letters sent to solicit new contributors) from ten to seventeen contributions per one thousand letters sent.[39] According to Herbert Alexander: "Although promotional mailings to recruit new contributors are generally viewed as a break-even activity, 1980 the RNC grossed $7 million from such mailings and netted $1.3 million while adding approximately 400,000 new names to its contributor files."[40]

Also, the overhead costs on the RNC's direct-mail program were significantly reduced in 1978 when Congress enacted a law allowing the parties to use the non-profit bulk mailing rate of 2.7 cents per letter instead of the commercial rate of 8.4 cents.[41] These changes, in addition to placing the RNC's finance committee on a budget for the first time (in previous years the finance committee raised what it could, spent what it wanted, and gave the remainder to the RNC) allowed the RNC to reduce its direct-mail costs by 19 percent.[42]

Fundraising letters were also scrutinized from a political standpoint for the first time, as the RNC made an effort to coordinate fundraising appeals with the party's political appeals. For example, letters attacking organized labor were limited since the party was making a strong effort to woo blue-collar Democrats.[43]

The RNC did not rely solely on direct mail to solicit contributions. It also tried short television appeals accompanied by a toll-free phone number to encourage viewers to contribute using their credit cards.[44] The RNC also launched a campaign to increase its take from large contributors through its Republican Eagles Program—those who had contributed $10,000 or more to the party. The program began in 1978 with 211 donors and grew to 365 in 1979 and to 865 in 1980.[45] The RNC also established a "Victory '80" program that raised more than $1 million dollars in donations of $500, $1,000, and $2,500.[46] Despite the success of the Eagles Program and other programs directed at large donors, 73 percent of the RNC's funds in 1980 came from contributions of less than $500, the bulk of which came from direct-mail and phone solicitations with an average contribution of $25.[47]

By the late 1970s, campaign finance reforms had greatly increased the number of political action committees (PACs). Though these groups, representing various ideological, business, and trade interests, created a major new source of political contributions, the RNC under Brock made only minor efforts to solicit PAC money. In 1980, only $330,000, or about 1 percent, of RNC funds came from PACs.[48] Since the RNC already had a very successful financial base, it had little need to go after PAC money, which was tied to special interests. Also, the new campaign finance laws made PAC money more effective when channeled directly to campaigns rather than through party organizations, so the RNC made efforts to facilitate the flow of PAC funds to Republican candidates.[49] According to Ben Cotton, it did this by attempting to educate PACs on issues of importance to the Republican party, arranging access to PACs for Republican candidates, and by indicating to PACs which were the best Republican candidates.[50] The RNC also sought, with only limited success, to convince business and trade association PACs that their political contributions should be geared more toward their ideological interests (that is, Republican candidates) instead of trying to obtain access to and win the influence of important members of Congress (that is, Democratic incumbents).[51]

Brock's financial efforts at the RNC were remarkably successful. From 1977 to 1980, the RNC became a financial powerhouse, raising unprecedented amounts of money for Republican party-building and campaign activities and dwarfing the efforts of the DNC (see table 14). This money not only gave the RNC a clear advantage relative to its Democratic counterpart, but also through the financing of party-building activities and contributions to candidates increased the RNC's influence within the Republican party.

ORGANIZATION

The RNC put these funds to work in an extensive variety of party-building activities. As he indicated in his acceptance speech, Brock's efforts focused this rebuilding on state and local parties. To aid in this effort the RNC employed up to fifteen regional political directors (RPDs) to assist the state chairmen in improving state party organizations. The RPDs also served as a liaison between the state parties and the RNC to better help the states gain access to RNC services. Through the RPDs, the RNC in 1978 encouraged each state to devise its own election plan;this would enable the states to achieve realistic goals in an efficient manner and allow the RNC to better allocate its resources to crucial state and local contests.[52]

TABLE 14.

NATIONAL COMMITTEE FINANCES, 1976–1980.

Year	RNC Contributions	DNC Contributions
1976	$19,000,000	$ 7,300,000
1977	$10,700,000	$ 5,200,000
1978	$14,500,000	$ 5,100,000
1979	$17,000,000	$ 3,700,000
1980	$36,400,000	$12,300,000

Source: Data compiled from Xandra Kayden and Eddie Mahe, Jr., *The Party Goes On: The Persistence of the Two-Party System in the United States* (New York: Basic Books, 1985), 73; and Herbert Alexander, *Financing the 1980 Election* (Lexington, Mass.: Heath, 1983), 325.

Note: These figures understate the financial disparity between the parties since much of the money raised by the DNC was used to pay off its debt, while the RNC figures exclude funds raised in conjunction with state and local party committees. If such funds had been included, the RNC figure for 1980 would actually have been $46.5 million. See Alexander, *Financing the 1980 Election*, 300.

The RNC also established a series of task forces to encourage state parties to develop campaign plans for state and local elections. RNC staff members and Republican state chairmen made up these task forces. The groups visited twelve states to evaluate and advise the state parties.[53]

Similar to the RPDs was a program of regional finance directors to aid local and state party fundraising. Brock appointed four regional finance directors to help the states develop a sustained fundraising program geared toward long-term state party development. The regional directors also made sure each state had a federal account, which allowed it to contribute the maximum possible to federal elections, and helped the states comply with Federal Election Commission guidelines.[54]

In 1978, in addition to these regional efforts, Brock also established a program of organizational directors for each state. Financed jointly by the RNC and the state organization, the ODs allowed every state party to have an on-site expert to aid its organizational efforts. Many states, however, could not afford to pay the OD's travel expenses, causing many of them to stay at the party headquarters working on fundraising and administration. The RNC estimated that the ODs worked well in one-third of the states, moderately well in another third, and not at all in the other third. The program's mixed record and high cost led the RNC to scrap it in 1979.[55]

Because state legislators were important in congressional redistricting and as training grounds for future state and national candidates, the RNC made special efforts in state legislative races. To improve Republican fortunes in these races, the RNC established the Local Elections Campaign Division (LECD) in 1977. Led jointly by Joe Gaylord and Charles Bailey, the LECD initially employed fifteen field coordinators and a Washington staff of seven.[56] By the 1980 elections, the LECD had grown to thirty-one staff members and fourteen field coordinators.[57]

LECD's major task was recruiting and training both the candidates and staffs of state legislative campaigns. In 1978, the candidates and staffs of 2,800 state legislative campaigns participated in LECD seminars.[58] From 1977 to 1980 the LECD conducted 150 seminars that helped to train more than 4,000 candidates and campaign managers.[59]

The emphasis on training arose because Brock and others in the RNC believed that Republican campaigns were forced to rely more heavily on amateur and volunteer help than the Democratic campaigns did. A Republican campaign worker (in this era before the explosion of political consultants) had nowhere to go after the end of an election cycle, whereas the labor union organizers and staff members who ran Democratic campaigns could go back to their union jobs following the election, or so their thinking went. To make up for this perceived disadvantage, the RNC placed a special emphasis on the training of amateur party workers at its Campaign Management College.[60]

The LECD also encouraged the state parties to develop campaign plans targeting key districts. For example, in 1978 the LECD helped the Alabama state party identify state legislative districts that had been over 50 percent Republican in the 1976 presidential election. The LECD also gave services valued at $30,000 for state legislative contests and helped to persuade the Alabama GOP not to run any statewide candidates, whose sacrificial efforts would have drained resources from more competitive legislative campaigns.[61]

The RNC also targeted key states. In 1980 it made a particular effort in Ohio, where the Democrats held a three-seat margin in the state senate. The RNC provided technical support and $20,000 in five targeted races, of which the Republicans won four, giving them control of the Ohio Senate.[62]

The LECD represented a significant investment on the part of the RNC. The program had a budget of $1.7 million during the 1978 election, with $1 million allocated to direct financial aid to candidates and the rest to support services. In 1980 the LECD gave $1.7 million in direct support and $1.3 million in services.[63] In certain key races, the LECD provided almost all the campaign resources, including campaign management, preparation of direct-mail pieces, planning and distribution of campaign literature, development of campaign plans and budgets, and assistance with public appearances and advertising.[64]

In cooperation with the Republican Governors' Association, the LECD also assisted the Republican gubernatorial challengers. RNC staffer Richard Thaxton was appointed as the director of campaign services for the association, and he oversaw the work of several campaign technicians provided by the RNC.[65] The RNC also made large financial contributions: $350,000 to fourteen Republican candidates in 1978, and $500,000 plus a variety of campaign services to thirteen candidates in 1980.[66]

For the 1980 campaign, the RNC, along with the Republican House and Senate campaign committees and the Republican Governors' Association was instrumental in creating GOPAC, a political action committee devoted to electing more Republican state legislators. GOPAC provided a means to funnel corporate contributions into state legislative races, something the RNC and the other Republican campaign committees were prevented from doing by federal election laws.[67] During the 1980 campaign, GOPAC raised approximately $1.5 million for state legislative candidates.[68] Though nominally independent, the RNC had a significant amount of influence over GOPAC's activities. Bill Brock served on GOPAC's board of directors, and GOPAC's executive director, J. E. B. Carney, was a former RNC staffer. Throughout the 1980 campaign, Carney worked closely with LECD director Joe Gaylord and the 300 to 350 districts targeted by GOPAC closely matched those selected by the LECD.[69]

Brock also improved the technical services RNC provided to various state and local campaigns and parties, giving those organizations access to sophisticated technology at a low cost. At Brock's insistence, the RNC purchased its own computer network (REPNET) and made its services available at minimal cost to state and local organizations. REPNET gave the state and local parties programs for accounting, word processing, direct-mail generation, mailing list maintenance, donor information, get-out-the-vote (GOTV) efforts, and political targeting.[70]

The RNC also provided polling services and media consulting to many Republican campaigns and party organizations. During the 1980 campaign, the RNC's survey research staff helped over 130 campaigns to develop, conduct, and analyze polls for as little as $250. If provided by private political consultants, such assistance can cost thousands of dollars.[71] The RNC also established a media training school and made its service available to all Republican candidates at a nominal cost.[72]

The RNC did not concentrate exclusively on local elections; it also made significant efforts to expand and improve the operation of the national party organization. From 1976 to 1980, the RNC's staff grew from 200 to 350 employees.[73] To improve the prospects for its presidential candidates, Brock appointed liaisons to work with each of the Republican contenders. He also asked each of the campaigns what the RNC could do that would benefit all of them, a request that led the RNC to provide each of the candidate organizations with voter lists in various states and opposition research on the Democrats.[74]

Brock also laid the groundwork for a generic party campaign for whichever candidate won the 1980 nomination. This effort, "Commitment '80" sought to contact and recruit a nationwide network of volunteers for the 1980 presidential campaign. The program succeeded in attracting over 500,000 volunteers and became a major part of the 1980 Reagan-Bush effort.[75] The RNC also conducted five national polls and analyzed the data from 175,000 precincts to help determine the most efficient use of campaign resources.[76]

In addition to this vast array of expertise and services, the RNC also provided significant cash assistance to various Republican campaigns and party organizations. In 1977 the RNC made a $650,000 loan to the National Republican Senatorial Campaign Committee to help it start its own direct-mail fundraising system.[77] Along with the previously mentioned direct contributions to gubernatorial and state legislative candidates, the RNC spent $4.6 million on behalf of the 1980 Reagan campaign (the maximum allowed by law), and over $800,000 directly on Republican House and Senate candidates. The RNC gave another $800,000 in indirect coordinated expenditures (see table 15).[78]

CANDIDATES

The development of an effective political organization requires strong candidates to run for office on the party ticket. To assist in the recruitment of effective candidates and party staffers, Brock instituted a series of "Concord Conferences." Developed by then governor of Delaware, Pierre (Pete) du Pont, the program established weekend gatherings for young professionals and party leaders. The conference attendees were tutored on how to plan local campaigns and motivated to become involved in politics.[79] In 1980, over 600 people participated in five Concord Conferences.[80]

Once people decided to run for office, the RNC ran a series of training seminars for the candidates, sometimes even attended by primary opponents. The seminars offered advice on various aspects of an effective candidate: improving public-speaking skills, managing the stress of the campaign, following professional advice rather than that offered by friends and relatives, dressing appropriately for different types of campaign events.[81]

In addition to training available candidates, the RNC sometimes gave direct support to individual candidates, even if they had primary opponents. Usually the RNC tried to do this in conjunction with the wishes of the state party organization,

TABLE 15.

RNC CONTRIBUTIONS TO CONGRESSIONAL CAMPAIGNS, 1980.

	Direct Contributions	Coordinated Expenditures	Total Contributions
House	$766,212	$538,390	$1,304,602
Senate	$ 69,813	$309,703	$ 379,516
Total	$836,025	$848,093	$1,684,118

Source: Paul S. Herrnson, *Party Campaigning in the 1980s* (Cambridge, Mass.: Harvard University Press, 1988), 66–69.

but according to Ben Cotton, the RNC, at times "bit the bullet" and opted to support one candidate over the wishes of the state party.[82]

Needless to say, such actions by the RNC caused great controversy. Such was particularly the case when the RNC-selected candidate lost in the primary, as when Roger Jepsen beat the RNC-supported Maurice Van Nostrand in the 1978 U.S. Senate primary in Iowa. Jepsen then went on to beat Democratic incumbent Dick Clark in the general election.[83] Most state and local parties resented these efforts by the RNC to interfere in their affairs. As a result, the party passed a rule at its 1980 convention prohibiting the RNC from assisting a primary candidate without the consent of the state party chairman and that state's national committee members.[84]

PARTY IMAGE

The final aspect of Brock's rebuilding of the RNC involved improving and broadening the party's public image. According to Michael Baroody, director of public affairs under Brock, in the aftermath of the 1976 election, the Republican party was beginning to take on all of the characteristics of a minority group—defensiveness and exclusiveness. The close vote in 1976 also showed the party could not afford to write off any portion of the electorate, or as one Urban League official commented, "If Ford had gone to black churches in Ohio, he still might be president."[85] As a result, Brock and those around him saw a strong need to develop a positive image and broader appeal for the party.[86] In 1980 Brock talked about how the party would do this: ,"You've got to not only open up the party to new groups, but reach out and bring them in. There's a difference between the two. If you are going to try to attract women, young people, working people, blacks and ethnics and other minorities, you do it by talking about the issues that they are concerned about. And you also create the kind of process that they can participate in when they decide to come in to you."[87]

In this effort, the RNC sought to broaden the party's base and to make it more open and accessible to minorities and women. The Democrats had undertaken a similar effort with the various reform commissions that grew out of the 1968 election, eventually establishing informal quotas for the representation of various groups at their national conventions. The Republicans, however, rejected such an approach to opening up the party. While the party did establish a series of reform commissions between 1968 and 1976, these came mostly in reaction to the changes forced upon it by implementation of the Democratic reform rules by the Democratically-controlled state legislatures, and the party categorically dismissed any mandatory or enforceable representation requirements for the RNC or convention delegates.[88]

The RNC's reluctance to engage in procedural reforms stems from several factors. One is the perception that despite their win in 1976, the Democratic party's reforms had created more headaches than they were worth. Also, the more homogeneous Republicans had less of a need than the Democrats to accommodate the representational demands of such groups as women, labor, youth, and blacks and other minorities. Finally, to conservatives on the RNC, party reform in the form of representational requirements was both ideologically and politically unacceptable. Representational requirements were considered the type of "quotas" and "special preferences" that they had recently come to oppose. Moreover, any meaningful representational requirements might begin to chip away at the confederal structure of the RNC, which had been so important to conservative influence within that body and thus in the larger party.

Instead of traveling down the procedural path taken by the Democrats, the Republicans under Brock attempted to increase diversity within the party through organizational efforts. In 1977 the RNC put $640,000 into an effort to recruit more black support for Republican candidates.[89] To lead this effort, the RNC hired the black political consulting firm of Wright-McNeill and provided $140,000 to establish the Black Republican Council to help build stronger organizations for black Republican candidates. Finally, the RNC purchased advertising time on a black public affairs program and distributed it to black civic and social groups for public service appeals.[90]

Blacks were not the only group to receive the blandishments of Republicans. After polling data showed that women ran strongest in particular districts, the RNC, led by Co-Chair Mary Crisp, mounted an intensive effort to recruit women to run for office.[91] Many saw the RNC's selection of Detroit for its 1980 convention as an effort to attract the votes of blacks, ethnics, the poor, and union members.[92] In 1980 the party platform committee, chaired by Brock and Senator John Tower, held a series of public hearings in ten cities across the country as a means of showing the Republicans as "a party of the people" through the exposure and inclusion of various groups in the platform writing process.[93]

The RNC also tried to bring more evangelical Christians into the party by establishing links with prominent church leaders, the Moral Majority, and the National Association of Religious Broadcasters. According to Ben Cotton, Brock and others on the RNC saw the evangelical churches as a "distribution system" for disseminating Republican information and as an institution for mobilizing voters.[94]

Under Bill Brock, the RNC also focused on policy development. The idea for some sort of a party policy council came soon after the 1976 election when President Ford, a key architect of the post-1964 Republican Coordinating Committee, called for the establishment of a similar organization.[95] Ford submitted his plan to the RNC at its January meeting. His proposal called for a thirty-five -member committee, composed of prominent Republican elected and party officials and supported by a dozen task forces.[96]

Ford's ideas for a policy council meshed with those circulating through the

RNC at the time. According to Roger Semerad, an associate of Brock's who later became director of the RNC's policy councils, both he and Brock discussed the need for a "serious and substantive vehicle" for policy discussion within the party. Such a policy group would bring various points of view into a "common working environment" with the intention of providing the party with a coherent policy statement for the 1980 campaign.[97]

Brock and those around him decided that the RNC could formulate party policy better than the congressional wing of the party. According to Baroody, the RNC believed Congress was too involved in the day-to-day routine of legislation, while the RNC could take a more exclusive approach to reorienting party policy. He adds that the RNC could also engage in policy development free of the parochial political interests that were more prevalent in Congress.[98] Semerad echoes this idea, claiming that the RNC staff believed "we had greater freedom than elected leaders" to set policy for the party.[99] Eddie Mahe, another RNC staff member in this period, goes even further, claiming that the congressional party had been in the minority so long that they were incapable of formulating a governing strategy for the Republicans.[100]

The thinking of the RNC regarding the establishment of a policy council parallels the reasoning found in the DNC prior to the creation of the Democratic Advisory Council. Twenty years earlier, Paul Butler and many other Democrats also believed that the congressional Democrats were incapable of formulating an effective party policy. They too saw their party's congressional wing as too willing to compromise in order to reach the agreements necessary for the day-to-day work of the legislative process. Moreover, these Democrats also believed that the Democrats in Congress—hamstrung by the seniority system that inflated the power of conservative southerners—were not representative of the national party's interests.

Early in 1977 the RNC established five advisory councils on the topics of natural resources, human concerns, national security and international affairs, general government, and economic affairs. The advisory councils and their thirty-six subcommittees involved more than 400 people. The councils had a small budget of approximately $100,000 (the members paid their own expenses). The councils also wrote their own papers, so the support staff was small—Semerad plus two or three assistants.[101]

Any policy effort by a national party committee will inevitably overlap with the congressional party's perceived prerogatives in that area. Brock, however, succeeded in minimizing the friction between the congressional party and the RNC on this matter. The congressional leadership knew and trusted Brock, a former member of the Senate and House, and gave him more freedom in policy areas than they might have given a chairman with a different background.[102] Brock reciprocated by making sure the Republicans in Congress were adequately represented on the councils.[103] Even so, the congressional wing of the party did not control the effort. One RNC official claimed that while there was "a substantial congressional presence . . . the Councils weren't dominated by the congressional leadership."[104]

According to Semerad, the advisory council meetings provided a forum for Republicans of all ideological stripes and contained "exhaustive discussion and argument" on a variety of issues.[105] Baroody adds that the councils "broadened the circle" of debate and exposed the party to new ideas.[106] Supply-side economics, principally the proposal to spur savings and investment by lowering taxes, was perhaps the most important idea to gain acceptance in the Republican party through the advisory councils.[107] This policy, which eventually formed the cornerstone of the Reagan administration's economic agenda in 1981, gained credence through discussions on the Advisory Council on Economic Affairs. Here the idea, originally supported by only a small circle of conservative economists, was explained to a wider range of scholars, business and financial leaders, and elected officials, helping it to gain acceptance.

The advisory councils played an important role in formulating the 1980 Republican platform. One reason was that there was a substantial overlap between the members of the advisory councils and the platform committee. Roger Semerad, director of the policy councils, also served as executive director of the platform committee. Michael Baroody, who edited the policy council reports, served as editor-in-chief for the platform committee. Congressional Republicans and their staffs also had a substantial representation on the platform committee, but, according to Semerad, "the Hill staff had to contend with the RNC."[108] Also, many of the Congressmen of the platform committee had been members of the advisory council. Two in particular were Representatives Jack Kemp and David Stockman, who acted as whips during the floor debate over the platform.[109] Reagan campaign advisors Richard Allen and Martin Anderson also reviewed the proposals drafted by the platform committee, but, in Michael Malbin's analysis of the development of the platform, "the platform remained a party statement that Anderson and Allen cleared, as opposed to a Reagan document."[110]

To further contribute to the discussion of ideas within the Republican party, the RNC began publishing *Commonsense* in 1978. *Commonsense* was a "Republican journal of opinion and thought" intended for both substantive and symbolic purposes, according to editor Michael Baroody. The journal had the substantive purpose of providing a policy discussion forum for Republicans and the symbolic purpose of promoting the Republican party as "the party of ideas."[111] Since the 1930s, Republicans were often portrayed as hidebound, parochial, anti-intellectual naysayers and the RNC saw *Commonsense* as a means to help change that image. To a certain extent, this effort succeeded. The journal received generally favorable reviews from the media and the intellectual community. Baroody also claims that Daniel Patrick Moynihan, Senator from New York and a well-known Democratic intellectual, held up a copy of *Commonsense* at a meeting of the California Democratic party and cited it as evidence that the "party of ideas" label had shifted from the Democrats to the Republicans.[112]

The journal, unlike most party publications, had a high standard of editorial quality and published important pieces by a range of intellectual and political figures, both Republican and Democratic. It was eclectic, covering topics from welfare reform to synthetic fuels policy, and it was similar to such journals as the *Public Interest* or the *American Prospect* in terms of its format and its emphasis on policy discussion.

A continuing concern of *Commonsense* was rethinking the ideology of the Republican party in an attempt to offer a credible governing alternative to New Deal–Great Society liberalism. As Baroody saw it, the debate over the role of government had, since the 1930s, been cast in terms of the individual versus government, a debate the Republicans had, for the most part, lost. The Republican party began to reevaluate the terms of this debate with the help of two articles published in the original issue of *Commonsense*. These articles, by sociologist Peter Berger and by Michael Novak, discussed the concept of "mediating structures," such as family, neighborhood, community, and voluntary associations, as an alternative to the unsuccessful Republican rhetoric of individualism and as a new basis for Republican policies. Baroody claims that these articles helped the party reshape the political debate to the Republicans' advantage, from individual versus government to government versus the mediating structures of family, work, and neighborhood.[113]

The themes of family, work, and neighborhood became prominent in the rhetoric of the Republican party. Beginning in 1978 Ronald Reagan incorporated these terms, along with peace and freedom, into his speeches. In his acceptance address at the 1980 Republican convention, these terms provided the thematic framework and the basis for a broad appeal to Democrats and independents: "a party ready to build a new consensus with those across the land who share a community of values embodied in these words: family, work, neighborhood, peace and freedom."[114] At the end of his speech, Reagan came back to these themes: "Everywhere we have met thousands of Democrats, Independents and Republicans from all economic conditions and walks of life bound together in that community of shared values of family, work, neighborhood, peace and freedom."[115]

These terms also provided the basis of the 1980 Republican platform, which Baroody edited. In language that seems drawn from the dialogue in *Commonsense,* the platform states:

> We seek to restore the family, the neighborhood, the community, and the workplace as vital alternatives in our national life to ever-expanding federal power. . . .
>
> For too many years, the political debate in America has been conducted in terms set by the Democrats. They believe that every time new problems arise beyond the power of men and women as individuals to solve, it

becomes the duty of government to solve them, as if there were never any alternative. Republicans disagree and have always taken the side of the individual, whose freedoms are threatened by the big government that Democratic idea has spawned. Our case for the individual is stronger than ever. . . .

But we will redefine and broaden the debate by transcending the narrow terms of government and the individual; those are not the only two realities in America. Our society consists of more than that; so should the political debate. We will reemphasize those vital communities like the family, the neighborhood, the workplace, and others which are found at the center of society, between government and the individual. We will restore and strengthen their ability to solve the problems in the places where people spend their daily lives and can turn to each other for support and help.[116]

To aid the party in creating this new and positive image for itself, the RNC began an expensive program of "institutional" or "genre" advertising. This type of advertising, as opposed to candidate-oriented ads, sought to create a positive appeal for the entire Republican party and to highlight the differences between the parties. The need for this was clear to Brock, who stated in 1980: "There was a time just a few years ago when many people said there wasn't a dime's worth of difference between Republicans and Democrats. Our position on issues wasn't clearly defined, and most voters felt that there was no real difference between the two parties."[117]

This effort began as a rather low-key attempt to create a more positive image for the Republican party. Polling showed that the public ignored Republican issue appeals because of the party's poor image and low credibility, so in 1977 the RNC began a series of short spots, entitled, "America Today," featuring Republican elected officials speaking on what they were doing for various human concerns, such as cardio-pulmonary resuscitation or the disabled. The following year the RNC sponsored an "Issues of the '80s" series featuring Republican statements on policy matters.[118]

In 1980 the RNC ran a hard-hitting advertising campaign attacking the Democrats and offering a Republican alternative.[119] The ads declared, "Vote Republican. For a Change." The message harkened back to the party's slogan in 1946, "Had Enough? Vote Republican," but it also borrowed heavily from the British Conservatives' more recent media campaign that Brock had observed and been impressed by during visits to England.[120] The Republican campaign consisted of six ads focusing on the failures of congressional Democrats. One of the ads featured an unemployed factory worker who asked, "If the Democrats are so good for working people, then how come so many people aren't working?"[121] Another featured a pair of hands counting out money at the government's spending rate of "a million dollars a minute" while another showed a dollar bill shrinking in size due to the effects of inflation.[122] The most famous of the ads depicted a look-alike of House Speaker

Thomas "Tip" O'Neill continuing to drive a car despite repeated warnings that it was running out of gas while the narration claimed, "The Democrats actually passed laws that cut back energy exploration here at home, and made us dependent on foreign oil."[123]

The RNC initially put $5 million dollars into the campaign, and the spots ran in all major media markets during February, April, and June.[124] RNC polls concerning the ads showed that the public had a high rate of recall for them and that they had substantially increased the number of voters who were aware that the Democrats controlled Congress. The RNC also believed that the ads contributed to a decline in the percentage of voters planning to vote Democratic for Congress. Consequently, it continued the campaign into the fall. The additional spots ran in early September, early October, and just before the election. The "Vote Republican. For a Change" campaign cost a total of $9.4 million, of which the RNC contributed $6 million.[125]

BLISS AND BROCK: A COMPARISON OF EFFORTS

The chairmanships of Ray Bliss and Bill Brock possess many similar characteristics, especially since Brock consciously attempted to implement many of the same programs first begun by Bliss. Most important, both men led the RNC during periods of rapid organizational growth.

The two periods, however, are not identical. The RNC's efforts under Brock dwarf those undertaken by Bliss. Differences in financial resources offers one reason for this disparity. Although Bliss succeeded in putting the RNC on a sound financial footing (no easy task in those days) and in expanding and initiating a variety of programs, the RNC in the late 1970s had access to an unprecedented amount of funds. For example, in 1967 the RNC raised $3.5 million, while in 1979 it raised more than $17 million, a vast disparity even accounting for inflation.[126]

But the distinctions between the party-building efforts of Bliss and Brock differ not only in scale, but also in scope. Where Bliss saw the rebuilding of state and local parties as an end in itself, Brock saw it as a means to increase the power of the RNC by making it the central organizational structure on which all other parts of the party, from state and local parties to presidential nominees, would depend.

Candidate recruitment offers the most vivid example of the difference between the two men's strategies. Bliss preached the need to recruit good candidates and made many efforts to do so. His wooing of John Lindsay for the New York mayoral race was the most important example. But from all accounts, Bliss would never have had the RNC support a candidate in a major primary contest, such as the RNC attempted to do under Brock. For Brock, favoring a particular candidate over the wishes of the state and local party organization grew naturally out of his desire to concentrate power within the RNC.

In addition to the differences in their organizational strategies, they also had very different attitudes toward policy matters. Bliss's heart and soul were caught up in the day-to-day detail of running a political organization, the "nuts and bolts," to use his favorite phrase. Policy was a distinctly lesser interest for him. Though most observers justly credit Bliss as an efficient chairman of the RCC, this task was never an important concern of his. He was not involved in creating the RCC, and he strove mostly to keep it from saying too much, rather than too little.

Brock, while also devoted primarily to organizational politics, took a very strong interest in policy matters. He centered the debate among Republican intellectuals within the RNC and played an active and important role in that debate. Roger Semerad describes Brock as the "intellectual as well as political leader of the party."[127]

To a great extent, Brock succeeded in his effort to "nationalize" the Republican party by upgrading the RNC's organizational capacities.[128] The principal reason for this accomplishment was that under his tenure, the RNC was awash in money (and the campaign services that money can buy), a very useful commodity for acquiring political power. As the *New York Times* observed in a 1978 comparison of the two party chairmen: "Money, as Californian Jesse Unruh once said, is the mother's milk of politics, and the fact that Mr. Brock has it and Mr. White [DNC Chairman John White] does not makes Mr. Brock immediately more of a force in his party than is his opposite number."[129]

The money and resources available to state parties through the RNC were invaluable, giving them a level of organizational sophistication they had never before enjoyed. According to one Midwest state chairman: "Bill Brock has changed the whole concept of the National Committee. The field people we had helping us were the best I've seen. They gave us staff, resources, and money. In the last two years, we've had more help from the National Committee than in the whole time I've been around."[130]

By providing them with this organizational and financial prowess, Brock made the state and local parties willing to accept, even to encourage, the centralization of power within the RNC. As one state chairman stated, "I figure that I should go along with Bill Brock and the National Committee as much as possible, because I want as much of their money as I can get for my state."[131]

In addition to the state and local parties, the RNC became an important factor for candidates. Republican candidates now make contacting the RNC one of their first steps.[132] As Paul Herrnson has shown, many of the innovations first developed by Brock have led House and Senate candidates to view the national party committees as an important influence upon their success.[133]

The RNC's increased influence extended to the top of the party. During the 1980 campaign, Brock demonstrated his staying power and that of his work through 1980 despite opposition from the party's dominant conservative faction and the traditional prerogatives of the party nominee over the RNC. After Ronald

Reagan secured the 1980 nomination, many conservatives, led by Nevada Senator Paul Laxalt, a close Reagan supporter, and Reagan campaign aide Lyn Nofziger, called for Brock's removal. These conservatives believed that by having won the nomination, they had the right to appoint an ideological soul mate as RNC chairman. Also, Brock had angered many conservatives by refusing Laxalt's request to have the RNC fund a national campaign against the Panama Canal Treaties and by selecting Detroit for the 1980 convention, a choice *National Review* publisher William Rusher called "an intrinsically wrong-headed move."[134]

But Brock's work on the RNC had created strong support for him among state and local party officials and according to the *New York Times,* "Mr. Reagan received an avalanche of mail and phone calls from party regulars, urging the chairman's retention."[135] Reagan decided to keep Brock through the fall campaign. Following the party's victory in November 1980, Brock received an important administration job as a reward for his work, and, even more important, Reagan did not dismantle the RNC's organizational apparatus as Nixon had done after 1968.

ASSESSING THE RESPONSE

Following their defeat in 1980, the RNC sought a chairman who would emphasize the organizational upgrading of the Republican party. In doing so, the RNC rejected the procedural reform path followed by the Democrats over the previous eight years, despite the fact that the Democrats had beaten them with a candidate produced by those reforms and a public image of the Republican party as narrow, elitist, and exclusive.

In addition to its organizational activity, the RNC engaged in a vigorous effort at policy formulation, perhaps the most important and successful example of party policy formulation since the Democratic Advisory Council. But this policy effort still remained secondary to the RNC's organizational emphasis. Organizational activities far surpassed the RNC's policy programs in funding, staffing, and attention. In addition, one could view these policy efforts as symbolic rather than substantial. Although the RNC genuinely wanted to help the party develop a new agenda, it was also motivated by the desire to be seen as "the party of ideas," regardless of the substantive results.

8

THE DEMOCRATS,

1980–1984

The 1980 presidential election traumatized the Democratic party. Its candidate, Jimmy Carter, was the first elected incumbent president to be defeated since Herbert Hoover in 1932 and the first Democratic incumbent since Grover Cleveland in 1888. In addition to losing the White House, the party also lost the Senate for the first time since 1952 and saw its margin in the House substantially reduced.

This defeat caused the Democratic party to develop an organizational response. The DNC undertook a number of activities designed to improve its finances and to make it organizationally more robust. The party, however, could not shake its concern with procedural matters as it once again revised its rules with the Hunt Commission. Moreover, these procedural concerns went beyond just the rewriting of party rules and influenced many of the DNC's organizational activities.

BEYOND REFORM

How best to respond to this loss was a point of confusion for the Democratic party. The party's initial reactions to the defeat pointed in the direction of policy and organizational responses. Proponents of the former saw the Democrats' defeat as a rejection of liberal doctrines that had grown stale over the years and could not offer an alternative to an ideologically energized Republican party. Journalist Tom Wicker described the Democrats as "a party that has let itself become the proponent of political orthodoxy and elephantine bureaucracy."[1]

This attitude was not universally shared within the party. Joseph Rauh, a long-time liberal activist, argued that the Democrats needed to reclaim their commitment to liberal principles that he and others on the party's left believed President Carter had abandoned: "The Democratic Party has been a middle-of-the-road, non-ideological mush. The only hope is in a coalition, which is still there among intellectuals, liberals, labor, minorities, women and the handicapped."[2]

This view, however, seemed to be in the minority. Most observers believed that ideological renewal entailed a shift to the center. They took the defeat of such prominent Senate liberals as George McGovern, Frank Church, John Culver, Gaylord Nelson, Warren Magnuson, and Birch Bayh as strong evidence that the Democrats' traditional liberalism no longer reflected the views of the electorate. Congressman Charles Stenholm, a conservative Texas Democrat, stated: "First, we have to redefine our ideology. The middle-class—the small businessman and the working man—traditionally has been the heart and soul of the Democratic Party. That's where the votes are. But we lost their support. The liberal direction of the party has been devastating. We've got to modify our image to regain a majority plus one."[3]

DNC chairman John White echoed Stenholm, advocating a new and more centrist agenda for the party: "The political needs of our traditional supporters—white ethnics, urban dwellers, labor, blue-collar workers, small businessmen—have changed but we haven't changed with them. We must realize this is a new America, with new constituents and a new culture. . . . Blue-collar workers have moved into the same middle-class bracket as white-collar workers and have the same concerns about taxes, the environment, schools. . . . For us to write off that segment of society would be a mistake. We have to capture the center. But that doesn't mean we have to be less compassionate or progressive."[4]

In addition to the conservative Stenholm and the moderate White, ideological renewal also had the support of more liberal Democrats like Senators Gary Hart and Paul Tsongas. Both of these men advocated retaining the party's traditional commitment to liberal goals—civil rights and economic justice—but insisted that Democrats must develop new formulas for achieving these goals that did not rely on higher taxes or more government regulation and bureaucracy. Even Carter's vice-president, Walter Mondale, long-identified with the party's traditional liberal, labor wing, saw the defeat as a chance to reconsider what the party stood for: "One of the virtues of losing is that it gives you time to think again, and to refresh yourself. . . . We . . . have a priceless opportunity now, a chance to use this time to really focus on . . . the central questions."[5]

The party was uncertain about how best to achieve this ideological renewal. One prominent idea was to establish a party policy council, similar to the Democratic Advisory Council established by Paul Butler in 1956. Chairman White, Congressmen Michael Barnes and Henry Reuss, and New York lieutenant governor, Mario Cuomo, all advanced this idea at various times and in various forms.[6] Senator Daniel Patrick Moynihan of New York also called for the party to consider publishing a journal of opinion, similar to the RNC's *Commonsense*, to help develop new ideas.[7]

Others, while not necessarily denying the need for a policy response, emphasized the party's need for organizational renewal. In their view, the procedural and factional struggles of the previous twelve years had so occupied the party that it had become organizationally noncompetitive. Proponents of this approach pointed to Bill Brock's financial and organizational accomplishments at the RNC over the previous four years. According to Anne Campbell, a former head of the Association of State Democratic Chairs: "The 1980 election was a referendum on national party structure. We were outspent, out-targeted, and outpolled. The RNC did a superlative job. The Democratic Party should hold its head in shame."[8]

Much of the support for an organizational response mirrored that expressed in the Republican party after 1976—the party had become a top-down operation, with a national committee that focused almost exclusively on the presidential race and that offered little or no aid to congressional, state, or local candidates. And like the Republicans in 1976, the Democrats saw organization as a way to help ameliorate the factional divisions remaining from the nomination fight between President Carter and Senator Edward Kennedy.[9] Finally, the Democratic defeats at the local, state, and congressional levels were the worst in nearly thirty years, and many in the party began to see the need for increased organizational and financial support from the DNC if the party was to remain competitive.

With this in mind, the Association of Democratic State Chairs passed a resolution in November 1980 urging the party to select a chairman who would concentrate on organizational and financial support for the state parties.[10] The following month, a group of fifteen Democratic governors stated their interest in finding a DNC chair who would better serve the needs of state and local parties. According to North Carolina governor James Hunt, "As governors we want to do what we can to focus on the party's effort at the state and local level."[11]

Democratic members of Congress were also eager to see the party concentrate on organizational rebuilding. Like the state party chairs and the governors, they attributed the party's losses to the Republicans' organizational edge. In December 1980, Congressman Don Pease of Ohio and Montana Senator Max Baucus wrote a letter signed by more than 140 House and Senate Democrats calling on DNC Chairman White to seek a new chairman who was skilled in management and fundraising and who would cooperate closely with the House and Senate campaign committees and the state parties.[12] Upgrading the DNC's organization was also a high priority for House Speaker Thomas "Tip" O'Neill. According to his aide, Kirk O'Donnell: "The Democrats have been delivered quite a blow and felt they needed structural support from the national committee . . . in such areas as fund raising, direct-mail operations, polling and institutional advertising. We had neglected these basic political techniques, and the Speaker assigned me to look into what was happening at the DNC."[13]

In addition to those who emphasized the need for policy and organizational renewal, there were also calls for the party to reform their delegate selection procedure. Most statements stressed the need to increase the participation of Democratic party and elected officials in the presidential nomination process.[14] Still, in the immediate aftermath of the election, the party paid relatively little attention to a procedural response in comparison to policy or organizational responses. In fact, there seems to have been a general sentiment that the party had spent too much of its attention, energy, and resources on procedure in the past twelve years, to the party's organizational and ideological detriment.[15] "We've reformed ourselves right out of business," stated Suellen Albrecht, the vice-chairman of the Wisconsin Democratic party.[16] John White also criticized the party's recent emphasis on reform, stating, "We have become too occupied with fringe issues."[17] Speaker O'Neill saw the party as moving past the reform era, declaring, "In the 1970s, the preoccupation was with procedural concerns, opening the process and making it more democratic. In the 1980s, ideology and regionalism will be a greater concern."[18]

THE SEARCH FOR ORGANIZATIONAL LEADERSHIP

As the Democrats began to cast about for a successor to outgoing Chairman John White, the need for organizational renewal quickly became their highest priority. "First thing, the party has to elect itself a chairman. Then, he has to find a good, professional staff and raise money."[19] This advice of former DNC chairman Robert Strauss was echoed by Richard Moe, an aide to Vice-President Mondale, who stated that a new chairman "will have to build a professional staff committed to the party's goals rather than to any prospective candidate. Everybody is in agreement there must be closer and more effective coordination between the DNC, the congressional campaign committees, governors and other elected officials so that we're not competing with ourselves or duplicating efforts."[20] Indeed, as Adam Clymer of the *New York Times* reported, "there is widespread agreement that the new chairman should have fund-raising and organizational ability, take an interest in helping the party in the states, and not be allied with a potential Presidential candidate like Mr. Mondale or Mr. Kennedy."[21]

Four contenders for the DNC chairmanship quickly emerged: Charles Manatt, chairman of the DNC's finance council and former California state chairman; Charles Curry, a Missouri state party official; and two former New York Democratic party chairmen: Joseph Crangle and Patrick Cunningham. Each man stressed his intention to mount an organizational response for the party. In Manatt's view, "The first priority must be to work with each state party in building its organization, recruiting candidates and developing the largest possible expertise." If elected, Curry offered to provide "greater assistance to state party committees and better campaign services for our candidates, Congressional, state and local in 1982." Cunningham declared, "We must return the term 'organization' to respectability." And Crangle stated that "renewal must start at the bottom and filter upward."[22]

Though each of the contenders offered very similar prescriptions for the party, Manatt was the acknowledged front-runner for the chairmanship. Moreover, he campaigned intensively, spending $75,000 for buttons and leaflets and traveling to meet with DNC members.[23] Curry and Cunningham, the two lesser-known candidates, soon dropped out of the race, leaving it to Manatt and Crangle. Crangle, facing almost certain defeat, also withdrew at the last moment. On February 27, 1981, the DNC unanimously elected Manatt as its chairman.

Though many criticized Manatt for his excessive ambition and self-interest, his experience as a party fundraiser and as California state chairman (at a time when the California Democrats were also in opposition to Ronald Reagan) received high marks and seem to have been instrumental in his election.[24] In Adam Clymer's assessment: "The election of Mr. Manatt . . . does not indicate whether the Democrats are, like the earlier victims of landslides, to rebound, to languish, or to vanish. What it does signify is an intention to maintain the franchise they have tended to so carelessly of late—to operate as a national political institution in the era of computers, direct mail, and polling, to which the oldest political party in the world has not yet adjusted."[25]

In her analysis of the Democrats in this era, political scientist Caroline Arden agrees with Clymer: "Apparently the Democratic Committee saw in Manatt, who had formerly held the post of the Party's finance chairman, a shrewd financier, a manager who would bring strong organizational skills to the national party headquarters of the Party and one who would seize every opportunity to put himself and the Party forward. He was, in effect, the very textbook model of a modern party chairman. The Party needed strong administrative leadership."[26]

Manatt set out to meet these expectations. In his remarks to the DNC after his election, Manatt stated, "We have been out-conceptualized, out-organized, out-televised, out-coordinated, out-financed, and out-worked." More specifically, he promised to establish a policy council to develop "a new American agenda," an increased emphasis on direct-mail fundraising, and a program of increased cooperation with state and local parties in the areas of candidate recruitment, political training, and voter registration.[27]

One of Manatt's first priorities as national chairman was to start rebuilding the party's organizational apparatus. The 1980 defeat and the recognition of the RNC's great strides in party building seem to have woken Manatt and other Democrats up from their organizational slumber. In 1982, Manatt commented: "We must institutionalize the Democratic party. The Republicans are way ahead of us in that regard. For many years, things were so easy for us that we didn't have to set up our party in any institutionalized way."[28]

In Manatt's view, the 1980 election defeat had been instrumental in pointing out the costs of the party's organizational lethargy. In his assessment, inadequate funds, poor communications, and a disorganized campaign had handicapped the party.[29] As chairman, he therefore set out to improve the DNC's direct-mail fundraising, upgrade its use of communications and computer technology, and increase the services provided to parties and candidates at the state and local levels.[30] The programs Bill Brock had instituted at the RNC over the previous four years served as a conscious model for Manatt.[31] In 1982, he declared, "My goal is to do the kind of job that Bill Brock did."[32]

REFORM REDUX

The Democratic party's focus on an organizational response following the 1980 election corresponds to the behavior one would expect from a victory-oriented party. This defeat caused the party to engage in a fair amount of soul-searching regarding the causes of their defeat and to analyze the merits of all three types of possible responses: policy, organizational, and procedural. By selecting an organizational response, the Democrats also demonstrated their willingness to venture beyond previous responses to select one successfully used by the Republicans.

Yet, old habits die hard, and despite his intention "to do the kind of job Bill Brock did," Manatt led a very different party from Bill Brock's. Though there was an almost universal recognition of the need for organizational renewal within the Democratic party and though the party had selected a chairman committed to such a program, the Democrats' chronic concern with procedural matters once again emerged as one of its chief priorities. According to Caroline Arden: "Manatt, the opportunist pragmatist, the organization man who knew 'where the tools' were, set about once more to tinker with the party machinery . . . the reforms would have to be reformed."[33]

The 1980 Democratic National Convention had mandated the creation of yet another commission to reconsider the party's delegate selection process. Technically then, the commission itself was not a response to the 1980 loss, but like other convention-mandated reform commissions, the development and product of this commission would be strongly influenced by the party's reaction to its 1980 defeat. According to David Price, who served as the staff director of the commission, the 1980 defeat gave an added "impetus" to the commission's work.[34] He has also written: "The 1980 Democratic National Convention passed two vaguely worded resolutions mandating a review of the presidential nomination process. Had President Carter been reelected, the rules review probably would have been a low-key affair, perhaps carried out entirely within the Democratic National Committee. As it happened, however, the rules became a focal point for those attempting to diagnose the troubles of 1980 and wishing to 'do something' about the party's condition."[35]

Manatt faced the question of what to do with this new reform commission. The body had been established by the convention, and John White had already appointed a chairman, North Carolina governor James Hunt, but it was up to Manatt to appoint the commission's full membership. If Manatt had chosen to, he could have given the Hunt Commission a narrow mandate and filled it with members cer-

tain to keep it out of the limelight. Instead, Manatt chose the opposite path, selecting commissioners who took their jobs seriously and giving them a sweeping
mandate "to undertake a complete review of the presidential nomination process
for the purpose of making specific recommendations to the Democratic National
Committee."[36]

Why did Manatt choose to put so much emphasis on reform? According to
Price: "Manatt had a healthy skepticism about the tendency of Democrats to place
excesses of both blame and hope on party rules. But faced with widespread expectations that a rules-writing commission would and should be named, and finding
commission posts useful bargaining chips in his own election bid, Manatt carried
White's plans forward."[37]

This, of course, raises the question of what the party hoped to accomplish with
the Hunt Commission and how it related to the results of the 1980 election. From
the start, those responsible for the Hunt Commission saw it as a means to further
involve elected and party officials in the presidential nomination process. Such an
idea was not new; it had been one of the principal issues facing the Mikulski Commission eight years earlier. But the idea had taken on new urgency in the aftermath
of Carter's defeat.

Most Democrats blamed their party's electoral failures in 1980 on the political
failures of Jimmy Carter. Carter won the Democratic nomination in 1976 as an out-
sider—an outcome greatly influenced by the party's new procedures. These procedures, which replaced party and elected officials with activists tied only to a
particular candidate, allowed Carter to win the nomination without the support of
its organizational leaders and elected officials.

Once in office, however, Carter had great difficulty working with Democrats in
Congress or in the party establishment. Neither he nor congressional Democrats
had needed the other to get elected, and this lack of interdependence left the
Democrats without an effective governing coalition. According to Bill Sweeney,
deputy chairman of the DNC in 1981, Manatt and others in the DNC thought that
Carter had lost because he "lacked the capacity for effective policy or political
responses to circumstances because he had no position in the party."[38]

The experience of a president isolated from the congressional Democrats
greatly influenced the work of the Hunt Commission. Those involved in the commission hoped to restructure the nominating system to give greater representation
to elected and party officials in the hope that this might help the party to establish
a broader, party-based governing coalition. In his assessment of what the DNC
hoped to accomplish with the Hunt Commission, Sweeney comments, "The party
under Carter was the party of Carter. We tried to make it the party of the party."[39]
Lanny Davis, National Committeeman from Maryland and a member of the Commission made the point most forcefully in a paper presented to the other members
of the Hunt Commission:

Ultimately it was the way Jimmy Carter won and retained the nomination in 1976 and 1980, and the way he conducted his Presidency, which led both party regulars and elected officials and traditional reform elements to the same realization that new reforms were needed at this time to prevent the Carter-type of candidacy from happening again. Liberal-reformers realized that the same rules which made it easier for a liberal-insurgent like George McGovern to get nominated could be used successfully by a southern-conservative-insurgent, which is the way they perceived Jimmy Carter. Democratic party leaders and elected officials (particularly in Congress) believed that many of Carter's problems as President were a direct result of their own diminished role in the nominating process, encouraging Carter's indifference and insensitivity to them after his inauguration. All agreed that the party organization—and the liberal-reformers now saw themselves as in the mainstream of the party apparatus and not as insurgents—needed to play a more important role in the process.[40]

Obviously, the Hunt Commission would have had to show more circumspection in criticizing the party's most recent president, but one can still discern a similar sentiment in its final report: "Recent years have seen an electorate too often pulled to and fro by the issues and personalities of the moment. Executives and legislators alike have too often chosen to 'go it alone' electorally; their accountability to the broad electorate and the overall coherence of government have suffered accordingly."[41]

In addition to bringing back party leaders and elected officials (PL/EOs in the parlance of the Hunt Commission) to correct the flaws in the nominating process, the Hunt Commission also saw the inclusion of PL/EOs as a means of helping to restore the state and local party organizations. According to its report:

> The adversities of 1980 have fired our determination to build our strength from the precincts up, to mobilize our voters, to articulate our convictions and aspirations with a new clarity. Signs of the party's organizational, financial and philosophical renewal abound. We have seen the work of our Commission in this broader context. We know that recasting rules and procedures is only a small part of the overall task of party renewal. But it is a critical part, and we have thought it important to scrutinize each proposed change in light of its implications for the Party's organizational strength and for its capacity to campaign and govern effectively.[42]

Such an attitude on the part of the Hunt Commission is interesting. In their view, procedural changes were a small but critical part of the process of rebuilding organizational strength. This strikingly contrasts with the Republicans, who focused exclusively on the financial and technical aspects of organizational renewal. For the Democrats, however, it was not enough for the state and local parties to have financial and technical resources; these organizations would also have to have increased voice and representation within the party's internal procedures.

The mechanism the Hunt Commission established for increasing the voice and representation of the party organizations was the inclusion of the so-called super delegates. The Hunt Commission called for the addition of 550 unpledged, ex officio delegates to the 1984 convention. Constituting 25 percent of all convention delegates, the super delegates would be drawn from the members of the House and Senate Democratic caucuses, with the remainder appointed by the state parties, including the state chairs and vice-chairs. The super delegates would be in addition to the 10 percent of pledged delegates who were appointed by the state parties under the old rules.[43]

Along with increasing the representation of PL/EOs, the Hunt Commission, despite its "counter-reform" inclinations, also moved to further ensure the participation of various groups in the delegate selection process. The commission formally incorporated "sexual orientation" (in addition to race, sex, age, color, national origin, religion, ethnic identity, and economic status) as one of "the forbidden bases of discrimination."[44] The Hunt Commission also changed the wording of the party's affirmative action requirement that demanded participation of various groups in "reasonable relationship to their presence in the population" to "participation of target groups to a degree commensurate with 'their presence in the Democratic electorate.' "[45]

The change in wording seems slight, but in many states this meant substantially increased representation for various minority groups. For example, in many southern states where the party systems are polarized along racial lines, this move meant that blacks would be represented far in excess of their percentage of the population. Significantly, this move shows that the Hunt Commission, while ostensibly interested in moving toward a system with increased influence for those whose principal identification was as party leaders, was at the same time willing to enact other reforms that undercut this goal by increasing the participation of people whose first commitment was not necessarily to the party.

FINANCES

Along with its attempt to rebuild the party organizations through the Hunt Commission's procedural reforms, the DNC began a significant effort at providing the party with the financial and technical resources necessary for a Republican-style organizational renewal. The most important aspect of such an effort was placing the DNC, as Ray Bliss and Bill Brock had done with the RNC, on a stable financial footing. In fact, the RNC's financial largesse had played a crucial role in its organizational renewal and Manatt knew that a similar organizational effort by the DNC would entail a vastly improved fundraising effort.

In 1980, the DNC was financially noncompetitive, raising only $12.3 million to the RNC's $36.4 million.[46] The disparity between the Democratic and Republican congressional campaign committees was equally large. Nor did the future look any rosier. The DNC had incurred a large debt during the 1980 campaign and, after losing the election, it could not look forward to the support of many of the large contributors that had been willing to help while the party held the White House. Michael Steed, special counsel to Manatt at the DNC, describes the situation the chairman faced upon his election: "On the day that Manatt was elected, the good news was that in the morning we had $250,000 in the bank. The bad news was that by that afternoon, the $250,000 in the bank had been attached and that other bills were still showing up."[47]

The only financial bright spot for the party was that its debt from the 1968 campaign, once totaling $9.3 million, had been reduced to approximately $600,000 by 1981.[48] Through the purchase of an annuity, the DNC managed to pay off this remaining amount in June 1982, but the party still owed more than $500,000 in current operating debts and another $640,000 in debts remained from the 1980 Carter campaign.[49]

Any attempt to improve DNC finances meant building a direct-mail fundraising program. Though Robert Strauss had endeavored to develop such a program during his tenure as chairman, with a Democrat in the White House, the party once again began to rely heavily on contributions from large donors. According to Herbert Alexander, the percentage of DNC contributions from "major contributors and fundraising events" went from 54 percent in 1976 to 61 percent in 1980.[50]

Also, as the incumbent party the Democrats were less able to employ the sharp, often negative attacks that work best with direct-mail appeals. This was especially true since the party was led by Jimmy Carter, an ideological moderate who choose not to employ negative fundraising appeals. In 1977, direct-mail expert Roger Craver, whom the DNC had hired to help with their program, produced a letter appealing for funds to help the DNC fight the growing influence of the New Right. President Carter, however, thought the letter too extreme and refused to let the DNC send it to potential donors.[51]

The DNC's neglect of direct mail during the Carter years meant that by 1979 the program was losing between $200,000 and $300,000 a month, causing DNC Treasurer Peter Kelly to sharply limit the program.[52] In 1980, direct mail accounted for only 20 percent of the DNC's income. In that same year, direct mail provided 73 percent of the RNC's income.[53]

When Manatt began his attempt to improve the DNC's direct-mail fundraising, he was essentially starting from scratch. In June 1981, the DNC's direct-mail list included only 27,500 names in comparison to the 1.2 million names on the RNC's list.[54] The DNC hired Roger Craver's firm—Craver, Matthews, Smith, & Co.—to run its direct-mail program in May 1981.[55] Though contracting out for their direct-mail operation entailed higher costs, the DNC had no other choice. It lacked both the technology and the extensive contributor lists necessary for a successful program and developing them alone could take years. By going to the outside, the DNC could begin its program immediately by using Craver's technology and the extensive contributor lists that his firm had compiled while raising funds for a variety of liberal causes and campaigns.[56]

The direct-mail program started very slowly since the DNC did not have a sizable list of previous contributors (a "house list" in direct-mail terminology), which forced them to reinvest most of their direct-mail receipts back into the program in a search for more contributors. In previous years, the DNC was either unable or unwilling to make this reinvestment. Instead, it took all of the returns from the program to pay for more immediate expenses. Ann Lewis, DNC political director, stated, "Like a faltering railroad, we paid out dividends without paying for reinvestment."[57]

Manatt, however, was willing to make the sacrifices necessary for the successful long-term development of a direct-mail program. In 1981 the program raised a total of $2.7 million for the DNC, of which $2.1 million was reinvested into prospecting mail.[58] Foregoing this income was not easy, and as a result, according to Bill Sweeney, "We starved."[59] In July 1982, only three months prior to the critical midterm elections, budget constraints, resulting in part from the need to reinvest direct-mail proceeds, forced the DNC to lay off fifteen people from its ninety-member staff and to cut back on travel expenses in order to free up needed funds for political operations.[60]

The sacrifices eventually began to pay off, and by January 1982 the contributors' list had grown to 100,000 names.[61] In ensuing years the program slowly kept developing momentum. With Craver's help, the DNC began to develop the type of sharp, ideological attacks that work best in direct mail. In late 1981, one DNC consultant commented: "The approach the DNC used to take—mealy-mouthed, general letters—got nowhere. People give because they're angry or alarmed. The New Right knows this, and we're learning.[62]

The most effective of the DNC's direct-mail appeals came out in September 1981. It clobbered the Reagan administration for proposing cuts in Social Security. The letter was sent out in what looked like an official government envelope, bearing only a Washington, D.C., address and the words, "IMPORTANT: SOCIAL SECURITY NOTICE ENCLOSED." The enclosed letter from Chairman Manatt was dire indeed:

> Social Security is no longer secure. Unless you and I act—and *act immediately*—Social Security benefits could be drastically reduced or destroyed. . . .
> The New Right Republicans say it's time to "get tough" on expenditures. But who do they choose to "get tough" with?

NOT giant corporations . . .

NOT consulting firms . . .

NOT big oil companies . . .

No, they chose to get tough with the most vulnerable people in American Society—the elderly. . . .

Because you care about your community, the society you live in, and your future, I hope you will help us in the *CAMPAIGN TO SAVE SOCIAL SECURITY*.[63]

The letter was highly controversial and Republicans accused the DNC of using demagogic appeals to scare the elderly. Reagan aide Ed Meese called the DNC to protest the letter.[64] Social Security Commissioner John Svahn described the letter as "blatantly misleading" and claimed that it "generated undue anxiety among the 36 million Social Security beneficiaries." He called on the U.S. Postal Service to investigate the letter as a possible violation of mail fraud laws, but nothing ever came of the request.[65]

Those responsible for the letter acknowledge that their methods were less than pure. "We knew that we were scaring them [the elderly] and we intended to scare them," says Michael Steed.[66] But they saw such methods as necessary. According to Roger Craver, "Sometimes you have to turn the temperature up, because the stakes are high."[67] The DNC did, however, contact anyone who gave more than $100 to make sure that they could afford the contribution.[68]

Ironically, the letter's best responses did not come from the elderly. Peter Kelly, who served as chairman of the DNC's Finance Council from 1981–1985, claims that in a case of "selective incompetence," Craver once sent out the Social Security letter to the names on the environmentalist list and a letter from Idaho governor Cecil Andrus attacking James Watt (Reagan's unpopular secretary of the interior) to the names on the elderly list. The Andrus letter managed to draw the normal return, but the Social Security letter pulled in about eight times what the DNC expected.[69]

For all its controversy, the letter raised little money for the DNC, but it did add thousands of new names to the DNC's contributor list.[70] By the beginning of 1983, direct mail was bringing in nearly $500,000 a month to the DNC and the contributor list had grown to 230,000.[71] By the end of 1984, the DNC had raised nearly $13.5 million from direct mail and its contributor list had topped 600,000 names.[72] Though the Democrats were still far behind the Republicans, they had begun to narrow the gap. In 1980, the DNC raised only $2.5 million in direct mail to the RNC's $26.5 million, a ratio of more than 10 to 1. By 1984, the RNC was still ahead of the DNC, but only by a ratio of 3 to 1.[73]

Along with the new emphasis on direct mail, the DNC also retained many of their old fundraising methods. Under Manatt, the party resurrected the fundraising telethon, which it had last used in 1975. In 1983, Manatt decided to hold another telethon over Memorial Day weekend. The DNC initially hoped to raise more than $7 million, but the event quickly turned into a fiasco.[74] RNC chairman Frank Fahrenkopf sent out a mass mailing urging Republican activists to jam the telethon phone lines to "help to combat the Democrat smear campaign aimed at President Reagan and the entire Republican Party."[75] The DNC also had trouble rounding up Hollywood celebrities to perform on the seventeen-hour show.[76]

The program turned out worse than expected. Republican supporters flooded the phone lines with criticisms of the Democrats and hoax pledges.[77] The show itself appears to have been less than entertaining and according to *Washington Post* television critic Tom Shales, it "was enough to make a television viewer long for the sight of Jerry Lewis and his Vitalisized head."[78] When it ended, the DNC claimed the telethon could net as much as $3 million, but in reality the party lost $4.5 to $5 million on the show.[79]

Despite the emphasis on small donors, Manatt did not give up on large donors. During his tenure, the DNC established a variety of councils to help solicit large contributions: the Democratic Business Council, the Democratic Labor Council, the Democratic Small Business Council, and the Democratic Women's Council. The first two of these bodies were the most important. Membership in the Democratic Business Council (DBC) cost $10,000 per year for individuals or $15,000 for PACs. In 1981, the DBC provided nearly $300,000 to the DNC, and by 1984 the council's contribution was more than $3 million.[80] In 1981 the DNC established the Labor Council, consisting of twenty labor union presidents whose organizations, according to a *Washington Post* report, had given "substantial financial and political support to the party."[81] In its first year, the Labor Council gave $730,000 to the DNC; by 1984 it was contributing more than $1 million to the party.[82] The DNC's total income from large contributions in 1984 amounted to just over $15 million— a 100 percent increase over 1980.[83]

One might view the DNC's fundraising efforts in this period as an indication that the party, after years of organizational lethargy and emphasis on internal procedure, had been jolted awake and was now beginning to copy the organizational techniques of the more successful Republicans. Certainly the Democrats were attempting to copy what the Republicans had done, but their experience does not suggest an easy transformation into a quasi-Republican, organizationally oriented party. Instead, the DNC's fundraising operation, much more so than the RNC's, was fraught with the same questions of voice and representation that had permeated the controversies over procedural reform since 1968.

For Manatt and others, the purpose of fundraising was not just to raise revenue but also to incorporate various interests within the Democratic party. According to Mike Steed, the DNC established the new fundraising councils to help include "the constituencies that had not felt a part of the party . . . there was every reason to have them at the table." In his characterization, the councils "formalized" a process by which these groups could make contributions *and* have a policy input.[84]

Finance chairman Peter Kelly agrees, claiming that he and Manatt saw the councils as a "methodology of involving people."[85]

This process was highly controversial, and it led to charges that the party was under the influence of elite special interests who sought to move it to the right on economic and foreign policy issues. According to journalist Robert Kuttner:

> In rebuilding the national party, Manatt pushed hard both to develop direct mail and to reach out to organized business. He encouraged young entrepreneurs to run for Congress, and created a Democratic Business Council, 350 members strong, headed by his friend and fellow Californian Irv Kipnes. For a contribution of $10,000 a businessman could join the council, and presumably influence party affairs. Manatt was pursuing the old game of separating fat cats from their money, but with one new wrinkle. Rich people were being asked to get involved, not just as well-to-do individuals who happened to be Democrats, but as business leaders articulating a business viewpoint.[86]

Political scientists Thomas Ferguson and Joel Rogers paint an even more critical portrait of a party coming under control of such interests as defense contractors and international banks:

> Like most other business Democrats, Manatt wanted to strengthen the party's ties with the business community, rather than with blacks, community organization, or the poor. To that end, he and his allies deliberately sought out millionaires and other wealthy business figures to run as candidates. They also tried to shore up the party's desperately straitened financial condition. . . . Major banks, including Bank of America and Chase, helped float the loans, which prominent business leaders of the party guaranteed. . . .
>
> The most important step Manatt and his allies took to reform the party finances, however, was their organization of the Democratic Business Council (DBC). Originally promoted by Byron Radaker (chief executive officer of Congoleum, the huge New Hampshire holding company whose Bath Iron Works subsidiary has been a major naval contractor since the days of Admiral Alfred Thayer Mahan), the DBC required annual contributions from each member of either $10,000 of the member's own money or $15,000 from the member's company. In return, the party invited members to participate in a regular series of task forces and study groups to develop party policies, as well as "quarterly meetings of a substantive nature held in Washington" and elsewhere, "where members can share their respective business, professional, and political interests with the political leadership of America."[87]

Kuttner and Ferguson and Rogers believe that business's increased financial involvement in the party translated into increased political and policy influence. Kuttner claims that business helped to persuade Manatt to "use his party position to lobby Democratic members of Congress to retain 'safe harbor leasing,' one of the most egregious and economically inefficient gimmicks of the 1981 tax act."[88] Kuttner also quotes Kipnes as saying: "For the first time in 20 years [during the 1984 campaign], the Democrats were not beaten over the head on the defense issue. I take some pride in that. The defense contractor members of our Business Council worked very hard on that. So we had some real insider knowledge and input on the defense issue."[89]

Peter Kelly, who was instrumental in establishing the DBC, agrees that the effort was not just an attempt to raise funds but also to move the party to the right. According to him, "Money was the weight that put the argument over. But the intention was to move the party." Kelly, however, saw nothing wrong in this effort, saying, "Some people said, 'We don't need two Republican parties today.' My answer was 'We don't need two Communist parties.'"[90]

Despite this evidence, one is hard-pressed to argue that business elites came to dominate the DNC in this period. Even Kelly, who helped set up the DBC and strongly intended for it to help move the party to the right, acknowledges that it had little influence on party policy.[91] Furthermore, most accounts make it clear that organized labor, and not business, became the special interest with the most influence over the party in this period. Though the relationship between organized labor and the DNC had been strained during the 1970s, in the aftermath of the 1980 election and with the passing of the old Meany-Barkan leadership to the more liberal Lane Kirkland as AFL-CIO president and John Perkins as head of COPE, labor sought to involve itself much more in the Democratic party.[92]

Labor's first foray into the DNC came with the process of selecting a new chairman. Manatt, intent on becoming chairman, and labor, intent on increasing its influence in the DNC, quickly struck a bargain; in exchange for the support of the AFL-CIO, Manatt would give labor approximately fifteen of the twenty-five open at-large positions on the DNC.[93] This move gave labor something that the DBC sought, but for all their purported influence, was never able to attain—formal representation on the DNC.[94]

Once in office, Manatt continued this symbiotic relationship with labor. According to Mike Steed, "It was clear that labor was supportive of Chuck and he was supportive back."[95] Manatt turned to labor for support since the party desperately needed money and technology—two things that labor had to offer. According to Bill Sweeney, "They were the only part of the coalition that had the resources and the willingness to get involved in the party."[96]

Despite the claims of Kuttner and Ferguson and Rogers, in the first year of Manatt's tenure, it was labor rather than business that propped up the DNC. In 1981, labor provided approximately $1 million to the DNC.[97] This sum represented 16 percent of the DNC income and more than half of its total income from large contributions.[98] In addition to money, organized labor and the DNC also consulted with one another to plan strategies and share information regarding elections and reapportionment.[99] Moreover, Sweeney claims that turning to labor was the only alternative, since business did not offer enough resources. According to him, "There was nothing else to do. Period."[100]

Though by 1984 the DBC was contributing more to the DNC than the Labor Council, this did not translate into increased influence within the party.[101] Labor seems to have been far more active, interested, and adept at using its influence within the DNC. Steed claims that organized labor was much more attuned to the political environment than business and that labor's centralized leadership made it easier for them to act quickly and efficiently. As a result, the DBC, relative to labor, could never effectively use what influence it had in the DNC. In Steed's words, "Labor is organized when it comes to this, business is not. Business was not organized when it came to participating."[102]

One incident seems to bear out this assessment of the DBC's lack of skill in the internal matters of the Democratic party. The following remarks come from the transcript of DBC chairman Byron Radaker's first appearance before the DNC's Executive Committee:

Before I make a few comments about the specific report, I would like to share an experience with this group. . . .

Well, last night on the elevator, going to my room, it was very crowded, and on the third or fourth floor I noticed that my elbow had been rubbing against the breast of a beautiful lady there, and I thought, now's the time to turn a phrase, and I said to her, Madame, excuse me, but if your heart is as soft as your breast, you'll forgive me. She said, young man, if the rest of you is as firm as your elbow, I'm in room 1411.

(Scattered chuckles.)[103]

Though one can read too much into this incident, it does give some indication of the problems business elites, especially ones attempting to emulate a Las Vegas lounge act, face when dealing with a party that takes its politics and its liberal attitudes very seriously.[104]

Along with business's lack of skill (not to mention tact or humor) in internal party affairs, there also seems to have been a lack of interest. According to Bill Sweeney, business "doesn't give give a shit about the internal workings of the party." He claims that other than support for safe harbor leasing and the appointment of one of their members to the 1984 platform committee, the DBC never had or cared to have influence within the party. In his assessment, the only involvement business wanted was giving money; it had no desire to participate more fully.[105]

Sandra Perlmutter, DNC assistant secretary in this period, supports Sweeney's assessment. According to her, nothing regarding policy ever went to the Business Council, but the DNC always made sure to clear important decisions with labor's representatives. Furthermore, labor had direct input into the writing of DNC policy resolutions or wrote them themselves, something that never occurred with the DBC.[106]

Finally, the alleged domination of the DNC by business elites seems to have gone unnoticed by labor, an remarkable occurrence since one would think that organized labor would have been the group most attuned and most likely to take exception to such a development. According to Frances Kenin, who served as the DNC's labor liaison, labor never thought that business was gaining too much influence with the DNC. In her words, business's influence in the DNC was "not a problem at the time" for labor.[107]

Therefore, even if one accepts the arguable claim of Kuttner and Ferguson and Rogers that the business elites involved with the DBC sought to move the party to the right, their desire to do so was not strong enough to have persuaded them to have taken a more active role within the party. While the DNC did attempt to give big business a greater voice in the party, it also made similar efforts for small business, labor, women, and minorities. Furthermore, there is no evidence that business exerted excessive policy influence on the DNC in this period. Though Manatt did urge congressional Democrats to support safe harbor leasing, if this was the extent of business influence on the party, then it was small indeed. And as for Irv Kipnes's claim that the DBC moved the party to the right on defense and thus prevented Republican attacks on this issue, one is left with the impression that his assertion is an attempt to inflate the perception of his own influence, rather than an objective evaluation of the 1984 presidential election campaign ("There's a bear in the woods. . . ."). All in all, any rightward move by the DNC in this period seems to have had less to do with the manipulations of business elites than with the party's attempt to respond to a more conservative political climate.

PARTY BUILDING

Increased funding allowed the DNC to begin a modest expansion of its political activities. Its first task following the 1980 election was to prepare for the legislative reapportionment process in 1981 and 1982. Under the leadership of Political Director Ann Lewis, the DNC began to consult with Democratic governors, state legislators, and congressmen in order to coordinate reapportionment strategies.[108]

The DNC also began various efforts to help state parties. According to Lewis this was a very important activity for the DNC. Not only had many of the state parties declined substantially, but relations between the state and national parties had been strained during the 1980 election when the Carter campaign refused to work with the state parties, even going so far as to charge state parties for polls and then never providing them with the polling data.[109]

In this area the Democrats seem to have caught on to the need for party building that the RNC had so successfully developed. In 1981, Lewis told the DNC: "We have an absolute commitment to working with Democrats from the grassroots up at the state and local level. We know that means nuts and bolts services and we think that's what were in business to do."[110]

Lewis's use of the phrase *nuts and bolts* is interesting. The term was Ray Bliss's favorite, and during his tenure and Bill Brock's it became the standard label for the RNC's organizational efforts. In rhetoric at least, the DNC had begun to emulate the RNC.

One aspect of the DNC's new emphasis on party building was the development of a series of campaign seminars. The DNC held the first of these in Des Moines, Iowa, in September 1981, and four more seminars were held through the end of 1981 and early 1982. The sessions focused on training party and campaign workers in fundraising, voter targeting, using union and interest group support, research methods, and media technology.[111] To help spread these techniques beyond the seminars, the DNC also upgraded the party's campaign manuals and made videotapes of the seminar workshops, providing them to party and campaign workers at minimal cost.[112]

In addition to volunteer training, the DNC also began to provide various services to the state parties. One of these was the "State Party Works" program, which gave specific help to the state parties in the areas of organization, communication, and fundraising.[113] In 1982, the DNC also established their first coordinated campaign. In New Mexico, a DNC-employed consultant coordinated a statewide voter registration, targeting, and turnout effort. The costs, and benefits, of the program were shared by the various federal, state, and local campaigns.[114]

Just as with fundraising, the considerations about voice and representation influenced the DNC's political operations. One aspect of this concern was the organizational support that Manatt gave to the black, Hispanic, and women's caucuses on the DNC. According to David Menefee-Libey, Manatt hoped that the resources given to these caucuses would help to increase support and mobilization among their constituencies. In this way, Mannatt hoped to use the DNC as "an arena for party elite coalition building."[115]

The same concerns over voice and representation were even more visible in the DNC's voter registration program. In reviewing the 1980 election results, many Democrats took note of three facts. First, although Reagan had defeated Carter by 10 percentage points, he still just barely won a majority of the vote. Second, in many states, particularly in the South, Reagan won with only a small margin. Finally, voter turnout nationally was only 54 percent, and turnout was even lower for such traditionally Democratic groups as the poor and minorities; in addition, the party had failed to carry out any sort of meaningful voter registration program.[116] Given this set of facts, many in the party hoped that an intensive voter registration and mobilization effort could help the party to win in 1984.

The 1982 midterm election seemed to support such a strategy. In that year, the polarizing influence of the Reagan administration and the worst unemployment since the Great Depression combined to create a surge in voter turnout, especially among the poor, the unemployed, and minorities. In several states, particularly Texas, California, and Illinois, this influx of "have-nots" was seen as a significant factor in the election results.[117]

Sensing an opportunity in the 1980 results and encouraged by the outcome of the 1982 election, the DNC started planning a voter registration strategy for the 1984 election. According to Ann Lewis, who headed the program, there was a sense that the DNC "couldn't do much about who the nominee was, but it could do something about who the voters were." She adds that the effort was based on the idea of constructing a winning coalition based not only on geographic factors, mainly states, but also on demographic factors, such as race, economic status, and gender.[118]

In addition to these political calculations, normative considerations also influenced attitudes toward voter registration. Most Democrats saw voter registration as a means of increasing the voice and representation among groups that had traditionally been excluded from the political process. In 1983, Walter Mondale stated: "These Americans, so crucial to our party, have been explicitly written off by the Republican party. For us to ensure their participation is not only good government, it is also good politics. I am convinced that this registration campaign can make the margin of victory in 1984."[119]

Ron Brown, DNC vice-chairman and head of the party's Voter Participation Task Force, echoed Mondale's perspective in his explanation of his group's work before the DNC: "We started with a rather specific perspective, and that is that not only in the elimination of all barriers to full participation in the political process right and just and fair and in compliance with the law, but the fact is that there is no single activity more important to Democratic victories in 1984 and beyond than bringing those who have been systematically excluded from the process into the process."[120]

Initial planning for the voter registration program began in December 1982 and envisioned a $3.8 million investment over the next two years. The DNC would contribute $500,000 toward this program, with the rest coming from unions, corporations, foundations, and minority groups.[121] The plan targeted sixteen states for extensive registration efforts according to the following criteria:

1.) Concentration of minority populations. Blacks in states with *one* million or more. Hispanics in states with 300,000 or more.

2.) Key electoral states.

3.) Governors and mayoral races in 1983.

4.) Key Senate and House races in 1984.

5.) Marginal Democratic losing states in 1980, where defeat was 5% or lower.[122]

Following the success of voter registration efforts in electing black mayors in Chicago and Philadelphia in the spring of 1983, the DNC increased the total voter registration effort to $5 million and expanded it to twenty-six states.[123] The program envisioned three DNC-paid regional voter registration coordinators, voter registration training sessions for party workers, production and broadcasting of public service announcements urging people to register and vote, lobbying for changes in state laws to make voter registration easier, and production and distribution of voter registration manuals, posters, and handbills.[124]

Despite this sweeping plans, the DNC's voter registration plan fizzled; 1984 did not see a vastly changed electorate and the changes that did take place were insufficient to offset the Reagan landslide. Why did the DNC voter registration program fail? Ferguson and Rogers claim that the DNC, controlled by business elites, did not make extensive voter registration efforts for fear of upsetting the economic status quo.[125] The facts, however, belie this interpretation. Herbert Alexander reports that the DNC transferred $1.8 million in soft money to twenty-eight states for voter registration and $1.6 million to twenty-two states for get-out-the-vote efforts. This $3.4 million represents 56 percent of the $6 million in soft money raised by the DNC for the 1984 presidential campaign, 16 percent of the $20.3 million in total funds raised by the party in 1984, and nearly 45 percent of the amount spent by the party on political activities during the 1984 presidential election campaign. Furthermore, the DNC assisted several unions in raising $1.7 million for voter registration and turnout activities and channeled $1.3 million from Democratic contributors to various nonprofit groups that were formally nonpartisan but were nonetheless carrying out registration campaigns designed to disproportionately aid the Democrats.[126]

Moreover, any limitations on the DNC's voter registration efforts were financial and not political. Ferguson and Rogers cite Ann Lewis as the principal proponent of the voter registration strategy and Manatt as the one responsible for stifling such efforts.[127] Lewis, however, directly contradicts their claim. According to her, Manatt "supported registration wholeheartedly," but the DNC did not have the resources to mount a larger effort.[128]

Ferguson and Rogers correctly state that the DNC's voter registration efforts failed, but their reasons are inaccurate. Instead, the efforts of the DNC, sizable by Democratic party standards, were overwhelmed by the better-financed and more sophisticated registration efforts of the Republican party. In 1984, the RNC, more concerned with getting the maximum number of votes for its party than with giving voice to the voiceless, spent $5.6 million on voter registration and mobilization, while conservative religious and business groups spent at least another $1.5 million.[129] Not only did the Republicans start earlier than the Democrats, but they followed up with a more intensive program of getting newly registered voters out to the polls on election day.[130] Finally, the Democrats' voter registration efforts were up against a tidal wave of popular support for Ronald Reagan and, among the newly registered, only blacks supported the Democrats.[131]

THE STRATEGY COUNCIL

In addition to an organizational response, Manatt hoped to establish a policy council. Manatt, who had been chairman of the Young Democrats in the late 1950s, admired Paul Butler's policy efforts with the DAC and sought to achieve a similar result.[132] According to Eugene Eidenberg, DNC executive director from 1981 to 1982, Manatt believed that without the White House the party needed a policy council as an "incubator for developing new ideas and policies." In a situation similar to the creation of party policy councils in 1956 and 1976, both men saw the congressional leadership as inadequate for this task, since it was too involved in the day-to-day chores of legislation. They believed that only the DNC had the capacity for a forward-looking approach to policy development.[133]

Soon after his election by the DNC, Manatt hired Harold Kwalwasser, an associate of his from California, to develop the council. Unfortunately for both men, Manatt had failed to discuss the idea with the congressional leadership. According to one account: "Hal . . . went charging up to see [Senate Minority Leader, Robert] Byrd and [Speaker] O'Neill . . . and started talking about how the chairman had this hot idea . . . to create this policy council and lay out the 'Democratic alternative.' Well, it took him about one week, and the Democratic leadership was up in flames. They were all saying what the hell is this new guy Manatt doing. Doesn't he know that Democratic policy is made by House Democrats and Senate Democrats?"[134]

Faced with this criticism, Manatt had two choices: develop a party council independent of the congressional leadership as Butler had done and as Manatt had originally intended, or, avoid bruising the egos of Byrd and O'Neill and possibly further dividing an already fractured party (conservative southern "boll weevils" were already aligning with Republicans in Congress to support Reagan's economic program) by scaling back the council to accommodate its congressional critics. Manatt chose the latter. He substantially limited the policy council so that it would not offend congressional sensibilities and made sure that it was composed solely of elected officials. In deference to Senator Byrd, Manatt even dropped the word *policy* from its title, calling it instead, the Democratic Strategy Council.[135] The council first met in October 1981, but, as one would expect of a council of elected officials, it failed to engage in a very substantive discussion of the party's programmatic plight. The Strategy Council sputtered on, holding hearings at the 1982 midterm convention in Philadelphia, but never seriously attempting to formulate a Democratic policy alternative.

This incident points out the difficulties in developing a successful policy response for an out-party. Even when there is strong support in the party for such an effort—Eugene Eidenberg claims that outside of Congress, support was very strong—it is very difficult for a party chairman to upset the congressional leadership.[136] Manatt's experience serves to highlight Paul Butler's successful leadership strategy:despite strong congressional opposition, he was able to organize an effective policy council.

Having failed to provide a serious forum for discussing and developing party policy, the Democrats went about policy-making in the usual manner for out-parties—through their congressional parties and their presidential candidates. Obviously such an approach had many problems. Throughout the early 1980s the Democratic congressional party was deeply divided and uncertain of how best to contend with the Reagan administration.

The three principal presidential candidates in 1984 seemed no better at policy formulation. Jesse Jackson spoke mostly to the symbolic aspirations of blacks and thus never formulated a coherent policy agenda. Gary Hart did attempt to engage in serious policy discussion, but these issues became distorted in the heat of the campaign ("Where's the beef?"), an outcome that might have been avoided through a more formalized process of policy discussion prior to 1984. The Mondale campaign's policy discussion consisted of bargaining with various Democratic party interest groups—a good way to line up support for the party's nomination but a very problematic method for devising a viable agenda for governing the country. Failing to think through a set of policies spelled disaster for the Democratic party. Most voters in 1984 seem to have identified Mondale with the promise to raise taxes and redistribute the proceeds to various special interest groups. Perhaps no set of policies, no matter how well formulated, could have persuaded the country to reject a popular president in a time of peace and prosperity, but this package seemed assured to do exactly the opposite—which it did.

ASSESSING THE RESPONSE

Determining the exact nature of the DNC's response to the 1980 election is difficult. The party mounted both its usual procedural response, the Hunt Commission, but it also responded by improving its organizational capacities as the RNC had done so successfully. Which one was more important? Different people have varying assessments, but I am forced to agree with Charles Manatt. When asked which of the two responses the party emphasized more, he could not differentiate between the two. In his mind, the organizational and procedural responses were of equal priority and necessity.[137]

Manatt's assessment is illuminating. On the one hand it indicates that the Democrats, influenced by a clear rejection at the polls and by Bill Brock's success at the RNC, responded to defeat by copying the Republicans' organizational tactics. Much of the discussion within the party immediately following the defeat focused on the need for organizational rebuilding and for making the party more like their more successful counterpart. Consequently, the DNC selected a new chairman who was devoted to such a rebuilding process and who pointedly set out "to do the kind of job that Bill Brock did." This move seems to provide some evidence that parties under extreme stress will attempt to incorporate new responses that seem more successful.

Parties, however, are often creatures of habit, and this period shows the limitations confronting a Democratic organizational response. Despite the DNC's best intentions of concentrating on organizational matters, it could not avoid attempting once again to see its problems in procedural terms. The Hunt Commission diverted a significant amount of time, energy, and resources from organizational to procedural matters, thereby limiting what the DNC could do in the former area.

The work of the Hunt Commission is important also in the way that it highlights Democratic attitudes toward organizational renewal. The commission's reforms were seen not only for their procedural outcome (increasing party leaders' influence in the nominating process), but also for their organizational outcomes (helping to rebuild the party organizations). Hence the Democrats saw procedure as an important component of organizational renewal, as opposed to the Republicans who went about organizational renewal with purely technical and financial means.

In addition to the focus on a procedural responses, the DNC's lack of resources also hampered its efforts at organizational renewal. Though the party had managed to reduce much of the 1968 debt that had been such a burden in the past, the debt left over from the 1980 campaign and the need to reinvest direct-mail proceeds back into the prospecting lists, severely limited the DNC's party-building efforts. In 1981, though the party raised $6,108,090, this was not even enough to pay for the DNC's fixed costs (fundraising, overhead, and administrative expenses) of $6,113,589. This forced the DNC to borrow to pay for its meager outlay of $296,647 for political activities.[138] By 1984 the situation had improved, but not by much. In that year, the DNC's Victory Fund raised $20.3 million for the fall campaign, but after subtracting various administrative, overhead, and debt costs, only $7.7 million remained to spend on campaign activities.[139] This sum pales in comparison to that spent by the RNC.[140]

For all the talk of a new emphasis on state and local party building, the number of state parties actually assisted by the DNC was quite small. One survey in this period showed that only a very few states were able to obtain assistance in the important areas of financial aid and fundraising assistance. Once again, the Republicans far outspent the Democrats.[141]

Anecdotal evidence also supports the notion that the DNC's organizational efforts were done on a shoestring. Ann Lewis claims that as political director in this period, she "always assumed that there wouldn't be any money" for her activities and was always looking for ways to economize and to find outside sources of funding for her programs.[142] For example, the DNC actually charged participants at its training seminars since it could not bear their costs alone.

Thus, even if the DNC had concentrated solely on organizational matters, the party lacked the funds for a major rebuilding operation. But the Democrats' organizational problems, however, went beyond the financial. Just as the party, through the Hunt Commission reforms, saw procedure as a component of organizational renewal, they also saw organizational methods as a means of achieving procedural goals. The various DNC fundraising councils present an example of how the party's procedural concerns influenced its organizational efforts. By all accounts, the DNC established these councils not just as fundraising vehicles, but also as a means of giving greater voice and representation to various interests within the Democratic coalition.

Even more so than the fundraising councils, the DNC's voter registration efforts show how procedural concerns influenced organizational decisions. Though most political experts (including some who were at the DNC at the time) disagree with Ann Lewis's belief that the party could alter the composition of the national electorate through a massive voter registration strategy, the Democrats still made serious efforts in this direction. Here the party seems to have been guided more by a normative desire to increase the representation of those traditionally excluded from the political process than by any rational calculation of the best organizational techniques for the party to undertake. As a result, the DNC's voter registration efforts were unfocused attempts at registering massive numbers of people in extremely broad categories without much consideration to identifying likely Democratic registrants and voters. By contrast, the RNC's voter registration efforts not only were much more sophisticated in their targeting but were based on the purely political calculation of responding to the Democrats' effort rather than on any grandiose and normative attempts to open up the political system or reshape the whole of the electorate.[143]

To some extent, the response of the Democrats after their 1980 loss is an exception, since, unlike previous responses, the party concentrated on organizational matters. But this exception is a limited one at best. Even Chuck Manatt, the chairman who vowed to do what Bill Brock had done for the RNC, saw organization and procedural concerns on an equal footing. Furthermore, the DNC not only attempted organizational renewal through procedural methods with the Hunt Commission reforms, but its organizational efforts were often influenced by procedural concerns. If exceptions cannot prove rules, then the exceptional experience of the DNC in this period at least supports the rule that the Democrats tend to respond with changes in procedure rather than in organization.

9

OUT-PARTY

RESPONSES

SINCE 1984

This chapter examines the three most recent responses to presidential election losses: the Democrats after 1984 and 1988 and the Republicans after 1992. I have combined these cases into one chapter, since the lack of perspective, material, and willingness of participants to reflect at length on such recent experiences precludes the more thorough treatment given the other cases, particularly for the Republicans since 1992, whose response is still ongoing. Still, I believe that there is enough information to gain an accurate sense of the activities of the out-parties in these periods and to classify their responses to losing.

THE DEMOCRATS: 1984–1988

Their defeat in the 1984 election left most Democrats demoralized and uncertain about their future. Most Democrats saw previous defeats as temporary aberrations, resulting from the apolitical appeal of Dwight Eisenhower (1952 and 1956), factional divisions (1968), or exceedingly weak nominees (1972 and 1980). Despite these defeats, most Democrats still believed that the majority of public identified with the basic values of their party. Such was not the case after the 1984 debacle, when Walter Mondale, a man who was emblematic of all that the Democratic party had stood for and accomplished since the New Deal, lost forty-nine states to Ronald Reagan, the most ideologically conservative president since Calvin Coolidge.[1]

Once again, procedural questions of voice and representation within the party dominated discussions about the party's loss and its strategy for the future. Underlying these discussions was a belief that the public now perceived the Democrats as the party of "special interests." At a deeper level, Mondale's abysmal showing among white males, particularly in the South, caused many Democrats to fear they were no longer seen as the party of the common person, but rather as the vehicle for the political expressions of liberal interest groups, union bosses, feminists, homosexuals, and, most important, blacks and other minorities. According to Dick Lodge, Tennessee's Democratic party chairman, "Technically and organizationally, the party's in good shape. The problem is the public's perception of the Democrats. The perception is that we are the party that can't say no, that caters to special interests and that does not have the interests of the middle class at heart."[2] One party leader claimed, "We ought to be just as concerned with the farmer on the tractor as that guy with an earring in his left ear."[3] On the perceived influence of blacks in the party, former LBJ aide, Harry McPherson bluntly declared, "Blacks own the Democratic Party. . . . White Protestant male Democrats are an endangered species."[4]

To rectify this perceived problem, many in the party sought ways to expand the party, its leadership, its policies, and its nominating system to include the voices of middle-class whites, particularly the Reagan Democrats, who had traditionally voted Democratic and now held the balance of power between the two parties. Some, like Florida governor Bob Graham, suggested that the party once again revamp its nominating process by instituting national or regional primaries. Otherwise, he warned: "As long as we put candidates on endless march from Iowa to California you are forcing them to appeal to one special-interest group after another and by the time they are nominated, they have been politically emasculated . . . non-electable."[5]

Other Democrats spoke of the need to revamp the internal structure of the DNC by reducing the influence of various constituency caucuses. Two of the leading candidates to succeed Charles Manatt as DNC chair voiced this attitude. According to Paul Kirk, the attitude of the DNC to organized constituencies was, "Got a cause, get a caucus. As a result, white male Americans say, 'Do we have to have a caucus to have a vote in the party?' Enough is enough." Added Nancy Pelosi, another candidate for DNC chair, Democrats "must have a basic, fundamental attitude of addressing people as individuals, not as groups."[6]

Still others thought that the party needed to reformulate its policies. "We have no post-welfare program," declared Stuart Eizenstat, a former advisor to Jimmy Carter.[7] Some even went so far as to suggest that the party's focus on procedural reforms since 1968 had prevented it from developing new programs and policies that would appeal to the electorate. According to DNC political director, Ann Lewis, "We don't need to spend the next two years rewriting the rules. We need to spend the next two years learning how to talk to voters."[8]

As in past defeats, arguments about how to best respond soon centered on the selection of a new party chairman. This time the Democrats sought someone who could reidentify the party with the political center, both in ideological and demographic terms, and free it from its image as the party of "special interests." According to one journalist, "The long resume reads something like this: former elected official from outside Washington with good ties with the various power blocs of the party but who can speak to new voters in the growth areas of the country, and—by the way—someone who looks and sounds great on television. The short form is more crudely put: white, southern male."9

Leading the search for such a candidate were several Democratic governors and state party chairmen, mostly from the South and the West, headed by Governors Bruce Babbitt of Arizona and Chuck Robb of Virginia. After failing to persuade such prominent Democrats as Scott Matheson, governor of Utah; James Hunt, governor of North Carolina; and former transportation secretary, Neil Goldschmidt to enter the race for DNC chair, Robb, Babbitt, and the other governors gave up the search and instead called for the DNC to establish a policy council to "refurbish the party's image."10

With this failure to entice a high-profile candidate into the race to replace Manatt, the DNC chairman's race boiled down to a competition between Kirk, a former aide to Senator Edward Kennedy with strong support from the AFL-CIO; Pelosi, former chair of the California Democratic party; and Terry Sanford, out-going president of Duke University, former governor of North Carolina, and head of the party charter commission from 1972 to 1974.11 After some controversy centering on the heavy-handed tactics employed by the AFL-CIO to help Kirk, the DNC voted 203.07 to 150.93 to elect Kirk over Sanford.12

As DNC chairman, Paul Kirk faced a daunting task. He needed to reestablish the party's credibility with moderate voters, while making sure not to alienate its traditional supporters among liberals, blacks, and other minorities. One way Kirk sought to do this was through a "nuts and bolts" organizational strategy, typical of the Republican party. Such a strategy had several virtues for the Republican party, not the least of which was that an emphasis on organizational resources allowed the party to avoid bitter factional battles. The Republicans had found that providing money and computers and campaign assistance helped to keep everyone in the party happy, or at least not vocally critical, and such a strategy also seemed useful for the Democrats as they sought to reintegrate the various factions of the party.

To accomplish this task, Kirk made a vigorous effort to build upon the organizational changes begun by Charles Manatt. He moved to expand both the DNC's direct-mail program and its contributions from large donors. With direct mail, Kirk decided to lower the DNC's costs by running the operation "in-house," rather than contracting the services of an outside party. In addition to lowering costs, the DNC expanded its base of direct-mail donors. By 1986, the DNC was bringing in $600,000 a month.13

Efforts with large donors were even more successful. Kirk aggressively sought large donations from wealthy individuals, and moved to increase the flow of "soft money" from PACs, corporations, and unions into party coffers, including a $1 million soft-money donation from Joan Kroc, owner of the San Diego Padres and widow of McDonald's founder Ray Kroc.14 Though many complained that such fundraising, especially from corporate and business interests, ran counter to the Democrats' traditional role as the party of the poor and working class, by 1988 the

DNC succeeded in bringing in $20 million dollars for use in the presidential election campaign.[15]

Kirk's fundraising efforts were an unparalleled success. His success at raising soft money contributions helped the Democrats to reach parity with the Republicans during the 1988 presidential campaign.[16] Moreover, at the end of the 1988 campaign, the DNC was debt free and had $3 million in the bank, quite an achievement for a party burdened by a massive debt and little revenue for most of the previous twenty years.[17]

Kirk's fundraising success allowed him to expand the services that the DNC could provide to candidates and state and local parties. Among his party-building efforts were an expansion of the Democratic Training School, establishing a system of regional field coordinators to assist state parties, developing an Office of Party Outreach to work with elected officials at the state and local level, sending a Democratic Party Election Force of field workers to assist local candidates in 1986, and Project 500, an effort to win five hundred additional legislative seats in key states prior to the 1990 reapportionment through DNC-sponsored polling and the development of improved voter lists and computer assistance for the state parties.[18]

Kirk's organizational efforts were prodigious to be sure, but the DNC did not utterly refashion itself in the Republican image. Procedural concerns, reflecting the party's traditional desire to make sure all of its elements had fair and adequate voice and representation within the party, still played an important role in how the party responded to its 1984 defeat. Kirk and other Democrats believed that the party had gone overboard in its efforts over the previous twenty years to ensure representation for various organized interests, particularly blacks and other minorities, to the point where other groups, moderate whites especially, felt that they no longer had a voice in the party. Throughout his tenure, Kirk sought various ways of showing that the DNC represented ordinary voters, not just organized interests, and more moderate whites, not just minorities and feminists.

In many ways, the election of Paul Kirk, former chief of staff to Senator Edward Kennedy, Washington lawyer, and candidate of party liberals and the AFL-CIO, as chairman of the DNC ran directly counter to the desire to change the image and direction of the Democratic party. In fact, Kirk's election exasperated many of the more moderate members of the DNC. Texas Democratic chairman Bob Slagle summed up these attitudes when he said, "I doubt seriously that the people of Texas will think electing a Kennedy chief of staff as party chairman is a moderate signal."[19] "One more meeting like this," commented a DNC member from Arizona, "and I'm going home and hang myself."[20] Disappointment over Kirk's election was also viewed as instrumental in the creation of the Democratic Leadership Council (DLC), a group of Democratic elected officials, mostly from the South and the West, who hoped to move the party in a more conservative direction.[21]

Recognizing the potential threats within the DNC, and the DLC's potential threat from without, Kirk moved swiftly to indicate that he would not conduct business as usual and that the party's traditional organized constituencies would carry less influence. In his acceptance speech, he told the DNC: "You have honored me today with your confidence. . . . I ask also for your trust. . . . Without mutual trust, each of us will be tempted to make unreasonable demands on one another—to protect our particular cause or to advance our own special agenda. If we let that happen, we will be viewed as nothing more than a collection of narrow groups looking inward in conflict and dividing ourselves in a struggle for scraps of a declining political party. Thankfully, we have another choice."[22]

Moving quickly from rhetoric to reality, Kirk then broke with tradition by refusing to endorse the DNC black caucus's choice for party vice-chair, Mayor Richard Hatcher of Gary, Indiana. Instead, he let the DNC decide between Hatcher and Roland Burris, Illinois state controller, whom Hatcher had beaten for the endorsement of the black caucus. According to David Broder, "Burris beat Hatcher by 50 votes, with his strongest support coming from the same organization states . . . and the labor-dominated at-large delegation, which provided Kirk with his biggest blocks of votes."[23]

If Kirk's failure to support Hatcher was designed to send a strong message that the party was attempting to reduce the influence of its organized constituencies, then the effort certainly succeeded, for better or for worse. Commentator Michael Barone stated, "Kirk's refusal to let the Black Caucus choose the party's vice chairman is a sign that the Democrats may finally be moving away from caucuses and toward a potential majority coalition."[24] Jesse Jackson, however, claimed that the Hatcher-Burris controversy was part of an effort by Kirk and others in the party "to prove its manhood to whites by showing its capacity to be unkind to blacks" and called on blacks to "reassess their relationship with the party."[25]

Kirk's efforts to reorient the makeup of the DNC did not stop here, as he soon began to reduce the influence of constituency caucuses within the DNC. Organized caucuses had been part of the DNC structure since the adoption of a party charter in 1974. That document gave formal recognition to the black, Hispanic, and women's caucuses, giving each a seat on the DNC's executive committee. In 1982, the DNC established a formal mechanism for recognizing additional constituency caucuses and provided staff support for all recognized caucuses. To be recognized as a caucus, all one needed to do was obtain the signatures of thirty-eight DNC members, 10 percent of the total membership, and submit a statement of purpose.[26] Soon, Asian-Pacific, Liberal-Progressive, Lesbian and Gay, and Business and Professional caucuses were granted official status, while others, Native Americans, farmers, Israel supporters, the disabled, European ethnics, and an "All-American" caucus of white males, clamored for recognition and seats on the executive committee.[27]

Kirk, and many others in the party, believed that the caucuses had contributed to the idea that "the parts of the Democratic party were bigger than the whole" and the impression of the Democrats as the "captive of special interests" that had done so much to defeat Walter Mondale. He would later recall that the situation had become so absurd that it seemed, "left-handed carpenters from western Mississippi" wanted a caucus.[28] With this in mind, Kirk asked, and the DNC Executive Committee agreed in May 1985, to remove formal recognition from all party caucuses, though the black, Hispanic, and women's caucuses retained their seats on the executive committee.

Just as with the Hatcher-Burris controversy, the message entailed in Kirk's action was heard, as the DNC's move against the caucuses drew much attention, both good and bad. The *Washington Post* editorialized: "[The caucus system] has not drawn diverse constituencies together; it has fragmented them. . . . The caucus system has made the Democrats an object of ridicule. Put in place to build a party, it became an instrument in the weakening and even wrecking of the party. Mr. Kirk's Democrats showed good sense in moving toward abolishing it."[29]

Others were not so positive, Ron Walters, Jesse Jackson's deputy campaign manager in 1984, wrote in the *Nation*: "The D.N.C.'s swipe at the party caucuses, together with attacks on Jackson's influence at the meeting, smacked of scapegoating. Such treatment makes one wonder how long blacks and other minority groups will continue to play an organized role in the party."[30]

In addition to attacking the caucuses, Kirk also moved to play down the position of organized labor in the Democratic party, despite having been elected with their strong support. He publicly asked the AFL-CIO to refrain from endorsing a candidate prior to the party conventions. Kirk's move was a reaction to the AFL-CIO's preprimary season endorsement of Walter Mondale, a move that did much to reinforce the idea of Mondale and the Democrats as the creatures of "special interests." AFL-CIO president Lane Kirkland reacted angrily to Kirk's suggestion, but ultimately his organization waited until after the 1988 conventions before endorsing a candidate.[31]

In another effort to help remove the "special interest" label, Kirk moved to deny various party interest groups one of their most visible public platforms—the midterm party convention. First established by the party charter in 1974, many had come to believe that the midterm convention offered no real benefits to the party and merely served as an opportunity to highlight Democratic disunity. In recognition of this, and of the high cost a midterm convention would place on the still financially strapped party, in June 1985 the DNC approved Kirk's motion to cancel the 1986 midterm convention. According to Kirk, "I just think it's wrong to spend a lot of money on . . . what becomes an exercise in damage control."[32]

The final procedural undertaking of the DNC under Kirk's leadership was the Fairness Commission, the latest in the DNC's quadrennial revampings of the party's delegate selection rules. The Fairness Commission was mandated by the 1984 national convention in response to the protests of Jesse Jackson and Gary Hart that the nominating system, particularly the rules mandating a 20 percent threshold for winning delegates and a large number of nonelected "superdelegates," had been stacked against them.[33] Though not a direct outgrowth of the 1984 loss, the ultimate composition and work of the Fairness Commission would be influenced by the prevailing view that the party had lost because it was the captive of special interests and as such soon became a part of the DNC's response to its defeat.

Kirk and others recognized that Jesse Jackson, who to many people had come to embody the notion of "special interests" within the Democratic party, and his supporters formed the most vocal, if not only, constituency for using the Fairness Commission to radically reform the party's nominating system and that doing so would be perceived as another example of the party kowtowing to the demands of its constituencies. According to one southern state chair, "We can't allow Southern officeholders to walk away from this thing because they believe it has been orchestrated by Jesse Jackson."[34] To prevent such a split, Kirk rejected Jackson's demand that former Atlanta mayor Maynard Jackson be appointed to head the Fairness Commission. Instead, he appointed Don Fowler, a veteran of the party's many rules battles and a white, moderate southerner, and made sure that party regulars would control the selection of commission members.

Thus, to no one's surprise, the Fairness Commission rejected the proposals of Jackson and others for a major overhaul in the party's delegate selection rules and undertook only a modest tinkering, albeit in the direction of making the nominating system more open. The major change instituted by the commission was to reduce the delegate threshold from 20 to 15 percent to ensure greater representation for minority candidates. The commission did, however, move to enhance representation for party officials by including all 372 DNC members as convention delegates and increasing the percentage of congressional Democrats selected as delegates from 60 to 80 percent, but it moved the date of their selection from January to March, thus giving them less impact on the delegate race.[35]

The effort to establish a southern regional primary, known as "Super Tuesday," was perhaps the biggest change in the party's delegate selection procedures for 1988. Super Tuesday developed out of the belief that the party's nominating system had been reduced to mounting dog sleds and chasing liberal interest groups through the snows of Iowa and New Hampshire, thus deterring more conservative (or less acclimated) candidates from running. To offset the influence of Iowa and New Hampshire, and, consequently, liberal interest groups, the southern Democratic elected officials, and the DLC encouraged all southern states to hold their primaries on the same day early in the primary season. They hoped that grouping all of the southern primaries together at such a strategic time in the nomination process would make it more attractive for a more conservative Democrat to run for president or, at the very least, to force more liberal candidates to moderate their appeals in the early primaries in order to better compete on Super Tuesday.

While not established by the DNC, Super Tuesday had to have at least its tacit support, since previous party rules reforms had established the preeminence of the national party in this area. Rather than stopping Super Tuesday, Kirk gave the effort his support since it provided the party with another way to help shed its "special interest" label and also allowed the constituency served by the DCL, southern, white moderates, to believe that the party was responsive to their demands.[36]

Though supporters of Super Tuesday succeeded in convincing the legislatures in most of the South to hold their primaries on the same day, the effort did not live up to expectations. Not only did it fail to entice a prominent conservative Democrat into the 1988 race, but Super Tuesday's biggest winners were Jesse Jackson and Michael Dukakis!

The efforts of the DNC under Paul Kirk to revamp the public image of the Democratic party did not rest solely on formal procedures. The DNC also undertook a policy effort in response to its 1984 defeat. Soon after his election, Kirk set up the Democratic Policy Commission (DPC) to help develop and project a new party program. The purpose of this effort was twofold. First and most obviously, the Democratic party desperately needed to rethink the substance of its program, especially in light of their drubbing at the polls in 1984. To that end, the DPC, under the leadership of Scott Matheson, established various policy councils to rethink and reformulate the party's stands on a variety of issues. The DPC's final report was distinctly more moderate in tone than most past party policy statements. On economic policy, the DPC stressed the concerns of the middle-class more than those of the poor and stated a preference for "public-private partnerships" over government programs.[37] On foreign policy, the DPC struck a distinctly conservative note, twice calling the Soviet Union "the greatest threat to world peace and freedom," and acknowledging that U.S. national security required "foremost, military strength . . . constant vigilance and a strong conventional and nuclear arsenal."[38]

In addition to the substantive policy stands that it took, the DPC also had a procedural purpose. From its inception, the DPC was seen by Kirk and others within the party as a voice for party moderates and elected officials. Providing these voices with a forum and a vehicle for expressing themselves would help to combat the perception of the party as the tool of special interests, as well as moderating the party's image.[39] Perhaps more important, by providing more conservative Democrats and elected officials with a platform, Kirk hoped to undercut the efforts of the DLC (which Jesse Jackson alternately called "Democrats for the Leisure Class" or the "white boys caucus") to claim that it, and not the DNC, was the "true" voice of the party.[40]

Though the DPC was intended to moderate the image of the Democratic party, there were, however, limits to how far Kirk and others in the party were willing to go to reorient its policies. Soon after his election as chair, Kirk authorized spending $250,000 (a huge amount of money for the cash-strapped DNC) to poll voters on the reasons for Mondale's loss and their attitudes toward the parties and the political system. The poll consisted of two parts, a general survey of five thousand voters and a series of thirty-three focus groups with key demographic groups. The results of the poll, particularly the focus groups done with middle-class whites, were highly disturbing. These voters interpreted politics through the prism of race, viewing the Democratic party as controlled by blacks, minorities, and fringe social groups. Moreover, they saw the Democrats as committed to providing special privileges for these groups at their expense. In short, when the Democrats spoke of fairness, the party's principal slogan in the Reagan years, these voters saw it as fairness for "them," not "us."[41]

The poll called into question the political efficacy of some of the Democratic party's basic premises and its commitment to the advancement of minorities and the poor. Despite whatever truths might have been uncovered by the poll, Kirk rejected them, saying, "I don't want to be the chairman of a party that would leave these people [minorities and the poor] behind," and he ordered the DNC not to release the poll's results and publicly disputed a summary of its findings given at a meeting of the Democratic state chairmen.[42]

Labelling the Democrats' response to the 1984 election is somewhat problematic. While most of the activities undertaken by the DNC under Paul Kirk were procedural, some argue that they were in the direction of downplaying, if not eliminating, the party's traditional concern with voice and representation, and remaking the DNC into a more hierarchical and campaign-centered organization like the RNC.[43] Accordingly, one should then label this as an organizational response, in light of Kirk's strenuous and largely successful efforts to improve the DNC's finances and support for candidates. Yet, such an interpretation does not seem completely accurate. The Democrats' response did have a strong organizational component, but procedure was of equal importance since Kirk's efforts in this area were intended not to wholly eliminate procedural concerns from the DNC, but merely to alter party procedures in order to achieve a better and more accurate balance of voices and representation within the party.

Two points bear this out. First, Kirk did not interpret Mondale's loss as the result of insufficient organization efforts by the DNC. Rather, he saw Mondale's loss stemming in large part from the perception of the Democratic party as the party of "special interests" and the captive of its most vocal and extreme elements. As chairman, his principal efforts were to alter this image, by introducing a more "commonsense" approach of speaking with a national voice, rather than the voice of "the last special interest group that gets to your ear." While organizational concerns did not conflict with this goal, they were of secondary importance.[44]

Second, several times as chairman, Kirk rejected efforts that were seen as attempts to repudiate the party's traditional concern with providing adequate voice and representation for all groups. In the case of the "fairness survey," several of Kirk's assistants wanted to use the poll as a means to eliminate the influence of constituency groups in the party. According to Brian Lunde, the DNC's executive director, the poll "could have been the platform for real changes in the party, but Kirk didn't want to do them."[45]

Even when Kirk did attempt to rein in the constituency caucuses, the effort seems to have been little more than symbolic. Kirk rejected efforts to go further and completely eliminate the caucuses. In a confidential memo, Lunde claimed that "our trouble began when we started giving *Party* offices to *special interest* representatives," and urged Kirk to "*eliminate all special privileges for all Democratic groups* and to do it *formally in our Charter and By-Laws through restructuring the Executive Committee.*"[46] Such a move not only would have ended official recognition and support of the caucuses but would also have meant revising the party charter to remove representatives of the black, Hispanic, and women's caucuses from the DNC's executive committee—the formal means of caucus influence and minority representation on the DNC.

Kirk's action, ending official recognition of the caucuses, but allowing the black, hispanic, and women's caucuses to retain their executive committee seats, fell far short of Lunde's proposal. In fact, the move did little to change the underlying role of the caucuses at the DNC. According to Sandra Perlmutter, assistant secretary of the DNC at the time, Kirk's action was purely symbolic; while not *formally* recognized and supported, the caucuses still made *informal* use of DNC staff and resources.[47]

In a final instance of Kirk's unwillingness to eliminate procedural concerns from the DNC, he categorically rejected eliminating delegate-selection quotas for the 1988 convention, as demanded by Edward Vrdolyak, Cook County Democratic chairman and member of the Chicago City Council where he led a faction of white aldermen opposed to Mayor Harold Washington.[48] Since 1972, the party had required that all convention delegates adequately represent the proportion of women and minorities in their state's population. According to Kirk, "That [eliminating the quotas] is not what the Democratic Party is all about. I don't think we can turn our back on our heritage. . . . one of the great strengths of our party is diversity."[49] Such a statement seems unlikely to have come from a DNC chairman intent on abandoning the party's tradition of concern for adequate voice and representation for all of its elements.

Each of these instances, the "fairness poll," the attack on the caucuses, and the rejection of efforts to end delegate quotas, provide evidence of the continuing importance of procedural concerns to the Democratic party. As in the response to their defeat in 1980, the Democrats made important organizational advances, yet procedural concerns, questions of the optimal way to structure the party and its nominating system in order to best represent and balance the voices of the party's constituents, remained of equal importance.

THE DEMOCRATS: 1988–1992

In 1988, the Democratic party lost its third straight presidential election. In fact, to many Democrats losing presidential elections seemed to be becoming a routine occurrence, much like cycles of nature or the swallows returning to San Juan Capistrano. As a result, the response fashioned by the party seemed to be much less active or intense than in past years, almost as though the party were saying, "Oh, what the Hell! It doesn't matter what we do."

This listlessness seemed to carry over into the battle for the party chairmanship. Some in the party wanted to see Paul Kirk remain as head of the DNC, in recognition of his success in helping the party upgrade its organization and in making the party appear to be more than the sum of its parts. But Kirk declined to run again, and the DNC soon settled on Ron Brown to succeed him. To many, Brown seemed exactly the wrong candidate to lead the party for the next four years. As a black, a former aide to Ted Kennedy, an advisor to Jesse Jackson, and a wealthy Washington lawyer/lobbyist, Brown had the credentials to alienate just about every faction in the party and to reinforce the electorate's image of the Democrats as a collection of special interest pleaders. Yet, no other serious contenders entered into the race and Brown won an easy victory over Rick Wiener, chairman of the Democratic party in Michigan.

Under Brown, the DNC engaged in a response similar to what followed their defeats in 1980 and 1984—increasing the organizational capacity of the DNC and continuing traditional concerns with party procedures—albeit both at a lower level of energy and visibility than in the past.[50] In addition to maintaining and expanding the organizational efforts begun by Manatt and Kirk, the DNC began to develop the apparatus to help it run the general election campaign of the party nominee. This response stemmed directly from the 1988 election loss, which many believed resulted in part from the incompetence of the Dukakis campaign. Not only did the Dukakis organization fail to mount an effective media and field operation after the convention, but by concentrating decision making at its Boston headquarters and by sending its own operatives to run the show in the states, it succeeded in alienating Democratic party officials and activists at the state and local levels. The result was a campaign that was confused, divided, and disorganized. According to one DNC official involved in the new effort, "There was not in place a coordinated campaign strategy post-convention. You can't decide on a national strategy when the Republicans were planning Willie Horton, the Pledge of Allegiance and Boston Harbor 12 to 18 months before."[51]

Brown and others in the party hoped to avoid a repeat situation in 1992 by establishing a "generic" general election campaign at the DNC, similar to the effort undertaken by Bill Brock at the RNC in 1979 and 1980.[52] Under this strategy, the DNC, in close consultation with the state parties, would lay the groundwork for issues development, field operations, resource targeting, and staffing decisions prior to the national convention. Consequently, whoever received the Democratic nomination could then go into the general election without having to build a campaign apparatus from scratch.[53] Brown recalled telling the prospective Democratic candidates, "We want you to designate us as your general election agents, so while you're fighting it out in the primaries, there's somebody focused on the general election period."[54] Moreover, the DNC also hoped to avoid a repeat of the acrimony that arose between the Dukakis campaign and the state and local parties, by relying much more on the latter to run campaigns in their states. As Alice Travis, DNC director of programs, noted, the 1988 campaign showed that "people from Boston were not by birth better able to run campaigns in Montana than people from Montana."[55]

To some extent this effort succeeded. During the 1992 general election campaign, several DNC staffers assumed key positions in the Clinton campaign. Additionally, the state-by-state targeting strategy developed in 1991 by Paul Tully, the DNC's political director, served as the blueprint for the Clinton campaign and as a remarkable predictor of ultimate Electoral College outcome. All in all, the DNC's efforts seemed to have helped the Democrats run their best general election campaign in nearly thirty years.[56]

Procedural concerns were also an important focus of the DNC after 1988. While the party, for the first time since 1964, did not have an official commission to deal with its delegate selection procedures, the DNC could still not resist tinkering with the nominating rules. The most important of these that related to the 1988 loss was the effort to convince California to move its primary from June to March.[57] As in the past, many Democrats believed that their nominating system was too heavily weighted, especially in the crucial early tests in Iowa and New Hampshire, toward liberal activists, and resulted in unelectable nominees. The nomination of Michael Dukakis and his defeat in November added to this concern.

To help redress this imbalance, several Democrats hit upon the idea of moving the California primary up to early March, immediately after the Iowa caucuses and the New Hampshire primary. Not only would this overshadow Iowa and New Hampshire, but by putting delegate-rich California near the beginning of the process rather than at the very end, it would make it easier for a front-running candidate to wrap up the nomination early, or so the thinking went.[58]

To encourage California to move its primary, Brown and the DNC rules committee agreed to open the party's primary season "window" (dates between which states, other than the traditional early starters of Iowa, New Hampshire, and Maine, can select their delegates) on the first, rather than second Tuesday in March. The new rules would have allowed California to hold its primary on March 3, one week after the New Hampshire primary and fifteen days after the Iowa caucuses.[59] Despite this urging, the California state legislature was unable to produce the legislation necessary to move the primary, in part because of concerns that the redistricting of congressional and legislative seats would not be completed in time for the early primary and in part because Republican legislators were reluctant to agree to a move so desired by the DNC.[60]

On policy matters, as in organization and procedure, the DNC undertook little formal activity and did not establish an official policy council. The absence of such activity was a departure for the DNC, which in each of its previous losses had set up a policy council of some sort. Granted, most of these past out-party policy efforts by the Democrats were merely pro forma, but the party saw at least some benefit in showing the public that it was attempting to think about its program. Not so under Brown, when the only noticeable policy activity by the DNC, aware of how Republican charges that the Democrats were the party of higher taxes had helped to undo the Mondale and Dukakis campaigns, was to endorse a proposal by Democratic Senator Daniel Patrick Moynihan of New York to slash the withholding taxes on Social Security.[61]

Why the lack of policy activity? Two interpretations seem plausible. Perhaps Brown recognized the limited utility of such councils or the potential that a policy council might only further polarize an already divided party, though endorsing the Moynihan tax cut proposal against the wishes of the party's congressional leadership seemed unlikely to help unify the party. Another possible interpretation is that Brown realized that in the new age of media "punditocracy," a policy commission would be ignored, whereas a smooth and articulate party chairman, such as himself, making the rounds of the political talk shows would have a far greater impact on public perceptions of the Democratic party. Certainly Brown succeeded in gaining greater media visibility as a party spokesperson than any previous national chairman.[62]

All of this indicates that the Democrats' response to their 1988 loss was not a policy one, but some mix of organization and procedure. Which of the two was more important is difficult to determine. The DNC put only limited efforts into both responses, and the press paid only scant attention to them. Perhaps future analyses, with greater information and hindsight, will yield a more definitive judgment, but for now it seems that the DNC's response, as in its two previous losses, should be viewed as equal parts procedure and organization.

THE REPUBLICANS: 1992–PRESENT

In November 1992, the Republican party found itself in unusual circumstances— out of power. The party had controlled the White House for twelve years, but in attempting to fashion a response to their defeat, the Republicans acted as though the out-party experiences of Ray Bliss and Bill Brock had occurred only yesterday. Just as they had after their defeats in 1964 and 1976, the Republican party spoke of the need to minimize factional disputes and focus on "grass-roots" rebuilding and "nuts and bolts" organizational work. Most Republicans believed that such efforts were needed because the party had become too much of an inside-the-beltway party, unaware of the concerns of average voters around the country. In addition, many thought that Republican failures below the presidency, particularly the inability to elect Republican majorities in Congress, had created political gridlock that had contributed to Bush's loss.

Despite this emphasis on organizational rebuilding, many observers believed that factional disputes between traditional conservatives and New Right religious activists would dominate the party's reaction to defeat, particularly when the RNC set out to replace outgoing chairman, Rich Bond.[63] Yet, such factional concerns were notably absent in the RNC chairmanship battle. According to one report, the RNC contest was "not so much a battle for the soul of a battered political party as a contest over who has the practical skills to repair it."[64]

Specifically, the members of the RNC sought a chairman who could reorient the party away from Washington, harmonize its factions, and lead an organizational renewal. Ohio state chairman, Robert Bennett claimed that when the party controls the White House, "the RNC becomes a support group for the president. Now, the emphasis switches back to building the strongest national party you can."[65] "Debating societies are great," declared California state chairman Jim Dignan, "but I'm not viewing any of them [candidates for the RNC post] on ideology. When it comes down to it, what I'm looking at is who can keep the party together and who can raise the money."[66]

All of the major candidates for RNC chair—Haley Barbour, RNC member from Mississippi and former Reagan White House political director; Howard "Bo" Callaway, former Colorado state chair and congressman from Georgia; John Ashcroft, former governor of Missouri; Spencer Abraham, outgoing head of the National Republican Congressional Committee and former head of the Republican party in Michigan; and Craig Berkman, Oregon GOP chairman—stressed their ability to help the party organization.[67] Callaway even admitted, "All of us are saying the same things: we'd go grass roots and be responsive."[68]

The focus on nonideological party building led each of the contenders to soft-peddle the divisive social issues, particularly abortion, that threatened to rend the party. RNC chair Rich Bond helped to set this tone in his farewell address, saying, that Republicans must resist making litmus tests of abortion or other social issues and that they "not cling to zealotry masquerading as principle and the stale ideas of the dead and dying past."[69] In addition, all of the contenders spoke of the Republican party as a "big tent," open to both pro-choice and pro-life activists.

Even the most conservative and liberal of the candidates for Bond's position emphasized organization over ideology. Ashcroft, the contender most clearly aligned with the party's more conservative elements and a staunch pro-lifer, cited his support from pro-choice Republicans, like Kansas senator Nancy Kassebaum and Massachusetts governor William Weld.[70] Berkman, a pro-choice moderate who had battled to keep the Oregon party out of the hands of conservative religious activists, said that the top criteria for the next chair were "strong, political organizational skills" and downplayed his support for abortion rights, saying only that the party needed to do more to assure "women and young" that the party "is open to them and their ideas."[71]

The emphasis on nonideological leadership was not limited to the chairmanship contenders. While one conservative declared, "The party needs to be organized differently and have an eloquent spokesman for its views. Our party needs to stand for values and articulate the future," most Republican conservatives, and liberals for that matter, made clear that their desire was for nonideological leadership. According to one analysis of the race, "ideological groups (e.g., Christian Coalition on the right and National Republican Coalition for Choice on the left) are not endorsing candidates—and the . . . decision [on the chairmanship] is more likely to be made on questions such as: 'Who can raise the money? Who can bring techniques for organization?' "[72]

By the time the RNC met in St. Louis in late January, the race settled into a contest between Barbour and Abraham. With all of the candidates agreeing on the need for organizational renewal, the race turned on personality and which candidate was least tied to the party's feuding factions and potential candidates for 1996.[73] Barbour was slammed for his lobbying activities, while Abraham was condemned for his ties to the former vice-president and potential 1996 contender, Dan Quayle.[74] In the end, the race went to Haley Barbour on the third ballot, by a vote of 90 to 57.

In his campaign for chairman, Barbour made it clear that he intended to follow the same organizational path chosen by his Republican out-party predecessors. In a manifesto used during his campaign for the chairmanship, he stated, "The Chairman must be a nuts and bolts organizational leader like Ray Bliss or Bill Brock. The Chairman must develop and effectively manage programs to accomplish our organizational, communications and financial goals."[75] In fact, the parallels with the past were so striking that David Broder described Barbour as the "Third B" of Bliss, Brock, and Barbour.[76]

Broder's assessment seems accurate, as Barbour has undertaken the same type of organizational response that Bliss and Brock did. In his first year in office, Barbour sought to increase the use of advanced communications technology by state and local parties by trying to provide each state party with a satellite dish for better access to local media outlets. He also focused on rebuilding the RNC's direct mail program, which had begun to slip in recent years as its donor base got older and because many contributors were disenchanted with George Bush.[77]

The most interesting of the RNC's recent organizational efforts are in the area of public relations. In July 1993, the RNC began a $110,000 campaign of radio advertisements attacking President Clinton's budget package. The ads were targeted at swing Democratic districts in the hopes of persuading their House members to vote against the budget.[78] In a follow-up campaign in December 1993, the RNC ran radio spots attacking fifteen Democratic House members (mostly first termers) who had supported the president's economic proposals.[79] While both the RNC and the DNC have often run political advertising, both these campaigns were unusual in that they came well before the election season, and the first campaign was intended to defeat a legislative proposal rather than influence election outcomes.

Along with this advertising campaign, the RNC has also achieved another organizational innovation in January 1994 with the broadcast of its own weekly television program, "Rising Tide." The one-hour show offers a mixture of "news" reports, interviews with prominent Republicans, calls from viewers, and commercials for Republican campaign seminars and party memberships. According to the RNC, the program is broadcast to "more than 950 groups at down link locations in 49 states" in addition to the more than thirty cable systems that broadcast the show as part of their regular programming.[80]

"Rising Tide" appears innovative not only because it uses advanced media and satellite technology, but because it is the first attempt in decades to provide a regular source of information to adherents of a political party. One might have to go back to the party newspapers of the early years of the century to find a similar effort. As one reporter commented about "Rising Tide": "The political parties have been in decline for years, but now the new technologies may help bring them back to life."[81]

In addition to its organizational efforts, the RNC has also begun a significant attempt at policy development to, in Barbour's words, "regain our position as the party of principle and do a better job of explaining what we're for."[82] In June 1993, Barbour announced the creation of the National Policy Forum (NPF). This organization, consisting of twenty policy councils covering a range of subjects, will organize a series of town hall meeting with Republican elected officials to solicit, discuss, and offer ideas on important issues.

The NPF appears to be a clone of the RNC policy councils started by Bill Brock in 1977. Not only is the NPF headed by Michael Baroody, who led the RNC policy councils in the late 1970s, but the NPF has also stated that it will revive *Commonsense,* the "Republican journal of thought and opinion" issued by the RNC under Bill Brock.

The NPF is ostensibly a nonpartisan organization and therefore exempt from both taxes and campaign finance regulations, allowing it to accept large contributions to finance its $4 million yearly budget. According to NPF president Michael Baroody, "It's 'A Republican Center for the Exchange of Ideas.' But it is pointedly not, 'A Center for the Exchange of Republican Ideas.'" Baroody's semantics aside, it is obvious that the NPF is an RNC operation; the elected officials involved are

Republicans, the foundation's counsellor to the chairman and director of strategic planning is a former RNC staff member and manager of Haley Barbour's campaign for RNC chair, and, according to one reporter, "the Republican National Committee's phone list sits on the receptionist's desk."[83]

Although it is still to early to determine how successful these efforts will be, the RNC's efforts in the development and communication of party policy are significant and appear to be the result of several factors. The first is that since the late 1980s, the Republican party has lacked a unifying and viable policy agenda. The party program of the Reagan years, lower taxes, reduced government, and a militaristic foreign policy, no longer has the same appeal with a public that is increasingly concerned about reduced economic opportunities, increased social problems, and the challenges and opportunities of a post–Cold War world. The bareness of the Republicans programmatic and intellectual cupboard, combined with the absence of presidential leadership, has provided the RNC with an important opportunity to significantly influence the party's policy agenda for the future.

A second set of factors behind the RNC's policy efforts relate to changes in media technology and consumption of information through the electronic media. The development of accessible and low-cost video equipment, satellite technology, and cable networks has broken the broadcast networks' monopoly on the production and distribution of televised information. Consequently, the ability of other groups and institutions to communicate via the television airwaves has vastly increased, allowing the development of programs like "Rising Tide."

The decentralization of media technology has also whetted the appetites of voters eager to seek out alternative sources of political information. Instead of relying solely on network news programs, the 1992 campaign showed the increased use of talk radio, cable call-in shows, televised town meetings, C-SPAN, and thirty-minute and one-hour campaign advertisements as sources of political information. Programs like "Rising Tide" are another way to appeal to those searching for different sources of information about politics.

The final, and perhaps most important, reason for the direction of the RNC's efforts is Ross Perot. During the 1992 campaign, Perot mounted a strong challenge to the political parties, arguing that they lacked clear and viable policy alternatives, no longer provided meaningful vehicles for citizen participation, and, ultimately, failed to serve any positive purpose in our political system. In many ways, the efforts of the RNC can be seen as an attempt to meet this challenge by attracting the votes of Perot's followers and justifying the continued viability and usefulness of political parties. The RNC's radio ads, "Rising Tide," and the NPF all represent efforts to develop party policy, articulate it to the voters, and directly involve citizens in this process. As Haley Barbour said of the NPF, "One of the things Ross

Perot's campaign showed us is that if you give people something to be for, and a chance to participate, they'll knock down your door."[84]

Although it is still too early to say with certainty what the RNC's response to the 1992 election will be, early indications strongly suggest that it will be an organizational response with a secondary emphasis on policy development. In choosing this response, Haley Barbour will be following in the footsteps of his predecessors, Ray Bliss and Bill Brock.

10

PARTY CULTURE

AND OUT-PARTY

BEHAVIOR

THE DESIRE FOR VICTORY

The pattern of responses of out-party national organizations between 1956 and the present does not provide strong evidence that national parties behave according to models of victory-oriented party behavior. As mentioned in Chapter 1, one indication that parties might be behaving according to these theories is for the pattern of responses to vary across time, as the parties attempt to accommodate changes in political circumstances and technology by using whatever response is considered most efficient for winning the next election. Table 16 shows that these variations do occur— all three types of responses appear at different times. But a closer examination reveals that this variation is attributable to which party was out of power. It is extremely unlikely that the need to select a procedural response would arise only when the Democrats lost or that the necessity of an organizational response would appear only when the Republicans lost.

Second, one might expect victory-oriented parties to pay close attention to successful responses employed by previous out-parties and show a willingness to reject responses that had been tried in the past and failed. Such behavior should be most evident following a landslide defeat when there is clearer evidence of failed methods and greater ability to make decisive and thorough changes. Once again, this pattern does not seem to exist. The parties are usually reluctant to adopt responses employed by their opponents, usually the possibility is not even discussed. Only after 1980 did the DNC engage in a serious discussion about emulating the response of its opponent.

Nor do the national committees often discard past responses that have proven unsuccessful, despite the magnitude of loss. For example, the Republicans lost in 1960 by a mere 0.2 percent and by more than 22 percent in 1964, but in each case the party relied on an organizational response. Furthermore, the Republicans after 1960 rejected a policy response of the sort employed by the Democrats prior to their success in

TABLE 16.

OUT-PARTIES, 1956–PRESENT: CIRCUMSTANCES AND RESPONSES.

Period	Losing Party	Margin of Defeat	Response
1956–1960	Democrats	15.5%	Policy
1960–1964	Republicans	0.2%	Organizational
1964–1968	Republicans	22.6%	Organizational
1968–1972	Democrats	0.7%	Procedural
1972–1976	Democrats	23.2%	Procedural
1976–1980	Republicans	2.1%	Organizational
1980–1984	Democrats	9.7%	Procedural/Organizational
1984–1988	Democrats	18.2%	Procedural/Organizational
1988–1992	Democrats	7.8%	Procedural/Organizational
1992–1996	Republicans	5.6%	Organizational?

1960. A similar pattern exists for the Democrats, who lost by a narrow margin in 1968 and by a landslide in 1972, but who selected a procedural response in both instances, dismissing the organizational response used by the Republicans before their 1968 victory.

Third, with the exception of the Democrats after 1956, strong policy efforts are noticeably lacking from these cases. If parties are truly victory-oriented, then it seems likely that the parties would have seen a policy response as the best way to respond to their defeat at least once since 1960.

Moreover, even when a party did employ a policy response, it did not pursue the direction that victory-oriented models would predict. After 1956 the Democrats mounted a policy response, but this response deliberately moved them away from, not toward, the perceived political center. Liberals like Paul Butler and Adlai Stevenson sought to sharpen rather than blur the distinctions between the two parties. Such behavior directly contradicts the predictions of victory-oriented party behavior.

Finally, responses geared solely toward winning the next presidential election are not nearly as prevalent as Downs and other proponents of victory-oriented parties would have us believe. Instead, the parties, although not excluding attempts to win the next presidential election, often select strategies only indirectly related to a strategy for winning the next presidential election, such as rebuilding the party's grass roots as the Republicans sought to do after 1964 and 1976, altering the long-term balance of power between the parties as the Republicans tried after 1960, or achieving internal party democracy as the Democrats attempted after 1968.

IDEOLOGICAL ORIENTATION

These case studies show some, but not overwhelming, support for the characterization of parties as ideologically oriented. As one might expect from parties motivated by ideological concerns, the Democrats and Republicans rarely attempt to change their ideologies and frequently reject such efforts. In most instances where the parties did engage in some form of a policy response, the attempt was less to change their ideological message, than to repackage it in a more palatable form as the Republicans did after 1964 and 1976. The Democrats after 1956 stand out as the only example of a party relying primarily upon a policy response.

Still, in some circumstances the parties have shown a willingness to move away from previous ideological positions. For example, in the aftermath of the 1960 election, the Republican party radically altered its position on civil rights. Reversing a century-long progressive stand on civil rights, the Republicans quickly raised the standard of states' rights in order to garner the votes of white southerners. Though not as dramatically or as suddenly as the Republicans did four years later, the Democrats after 1956 also changed their position on civil rights to attract northern blacks. The same is true for the Deomcrats after 1984, for they attempted to move the party to the right on foreign policy.

Not only have the parties occasionally engaged in ideological turnabouts, but it is also striking how little discussion was given to policy matters within the parties and how often ideological considerations took a back seat to organizational or procedural concerns. Following their defeats of 1968 and 1972, very little of the discussion within the Democratic party focused on programmatic concerns, though this period was as ideologically charged as any this century. Instead, the party was obsessed with procedural reform.

One can argue (and many have) that these reforms were merely a cover for the real intention of altering the party's ideology, but this seems unlikely. First, the period between 1968 and 1976 is not known as a period of taciturnity in Democratic party discourse. It is unlikely that the reform Democrats, usually displaying a blunt openness on every matter of concern to them, would have desired or been able to pull off such a ruse. Second, the Democratic reformers did not possess a unified stand on party policy. They were a diverse coalition, united only in their approach to party reform.

Finally, despite the sound and fury generated by the battles over party reform, there seems to have been very little disagreement between reformers and counter-reformers on most matters of party policy; hindsight has diminished the differences between George McGovern and George Meany, and one suspects, given his later stands, George Wallace. Though not without policy implications, the Democratic party reform battles were not so much over program and ideology as over power and procedure. The reform controversy was over who would make the decisions for the party, not what those decisions would be.

PARTY CULTURES

Instead of behaving as organizations motivated solely by concerns of victory or ideology, the response of parties to losing presidential elections seems to result chiefly from factors unique to each party. As table 16 shows, each party responded clearly and consistently, as would be expected from predictions based upon the existence of party cultures. The Republicans employed an organizational response. The Democrats, however, in all but one case, relied upon procedural responses. At no time in this period did the Republicans employ a procedural response, and only during the 1980s did the Democrats attempt to combine an organizational response with their procedural responses, but at a much lower level of enthusiasm and success than their Republican counterparts.

The case studies also bear out this party-based explanation for the selection of responses. The parties not only failed to select responses used by the other party, they rarely even considered doing so. Instead of engaging in a "rational" search for the most efficient means of responding to their defeat, objectively assessing the causes of their loss and considering all possible responses on their merits the parties tended to assess their defeats in ways that led them to rely on the measures that they had employed in the past. Rather than selecting the most appropriate response for the cause of their defeat, the parties usually selected the cause of defeat most appropriate for their traditional response.

What might account for the tendency for each party to rely on a unique set of responses? One factor is the difference in resources between the parties. The components of a modern and sophisticated political organization—direct-mail fundraising, survey research, media operations, and computerized databases—are extremely expensive and thus more readily adopted by the wealthier Republican party organization. In contrast, the prohibitive cost of these organizational components might have caused the perennially cash-starved Democrats to look to other, cheaper methods with which to respond to defeat.

Moreover, as David Price points out, for the Democrats in the 1960s and 1970s: "The pressures to develop aggressive political and financial strategies were not as strong. The Democratic party still controlled Congress; its members retained access to extensive staff resources and often to reliable financial support from labor and/or from PACs inclined to ingratiate themselves with incumbents. The need that Republican members felt for assistance from their party and for concerted party efforts to capture marginal seats was much less intense on the Democratic side."[1]

Republicans undoubtedly saw these Democratic advantages as a reason to emphasize organizational rebuilding. At RNC meetings Ray Bliss constantly warned that the AFL-CIO was actively organizing Democrats and that the Republicans had no alternative but to respond.[2] Under Bill Brock, the RNC began extensive programs to train campaign managers, a necessary task, since, according to Brock's assistant, Ben Cotton, union organizers provided Democratic campaigns with a cadre of professional workers on which to draw, while Republican campaigns were forced to use amateurs with little or no experience.[3]

The difference in resources available to each party has certainly created opportunities and constraints for each that are reflected in their responses. The most significant example of this was the Democrats' inability to develop an effective direct-mail fundraising program during the late 1960s and 1970s. Though the party sought to build such a program, its precarious financial situation forced it to use what direct-mail funds it did raise for general expenses rather than for the necessary reinvestment back into the program. Without such a fundraising program, the DNC continually lacked the means to begin to emulate the RNC's organizational improvements. Only after Chuck Manatt succeeded in developing a direct-mail program in the early 1980s could the DNC begin to contemplate organizational responses, but even then only on a very limited basis. Moreover, the differing economic bases of the two parties make it unlikely that the Democrats will ever be able to develop and sustain a corps of small contributors as well as the Republicans.

Still, one cannot attribute the differences between the parties solely to finances. Even in the cash-strapped aftermath of the 1960 election and prior to the development of its direct-mail program, the Republicans still focused on an organizational response. Nor does one suspect that the Republicans would have been any less adamant about their party-building activities if COPE had never existed. Furthermore, in these cases one does not observe the Democrats looking wistfully at their wealthier Republican counterparts, forcing themselves to be content with less expensive, and presumably less desirable, procedural responses. Instead, one sees the Democrats going about their procedural tasks with fervor and commitment, often paying scant attention to their party's financial and organizational decline, which was abundantly evident by the late 1960s even considering the advantages of incumbency and union resources. Even in the 1980s when the DNC began to gain financial sufficiency, it seemed just as committed to procedural reforms as to organizational renewal.

Rather than the difference in money, the difference in patterns, rules, traditions, and mores described by models of party culture appears to best account for the pattern of out-party responses. Each national party organization possesses a unique culture that influences its selection of responses to losing presidential elections. With the GOP, there is a preponderant tendency to view party activities in organizational terms, or, to use Ray Bliss's apt and revealing phrase, the Republicans concentrate more on the "nuts and bolts"—the technical and organizational aspects of a political party's functions when out of power. The Democrats, however, have a culture that focuses on procedure, making it a much more "democratic" party. They are continually concerned about voice and representation within the party and they tend to see the party as both the arena and arbiter for such questions after their losses.

The Republicans: The Culture of Organization

Where do these party cultures come from? One important influence in the development of the parties' cultures is the composition of the parties. The parties do not draw their members from a random cross section of American society; rather, each party tends to recruit from a particular section of society. In this respect, the Republicans are the party of business. The relationship between Republicans and the business world has traditionally been understood in ideological terms, but that relationship encompasses more than just supporting the political agenda of the business community. Much more so than Democrats, Republicans tend to come from business backgrounds, they associate with business people, they admire and emulate the efficiency of business organizations, and, as a result, their party culture shows a marked similarity with that of the business world.[4] Dwight Eisenhower typified the Republican attitude toward business: "We have been called the party of business. Well, I for one am proud of that allegation for the simple reason that the people who become successful in business have shown qualities of organization and leadership; they have led their businesses into positions of existence if not of preeminence."[5]

One aspect of the business-like culture of the Republicans is their reliance on business technology and methods. Throughout each of the Republican cases in this study, the party used techniques first developed and perfected by the private sector—direct-mail solicitation, computerized data bases, professional consultants, marketing research, and television advertising. Democrats, on the other hand, tend to lack familiarity with such techniques. Where Republicans often seek to copy technological and managerial innovations from the private sector, Democrats have usually viewed such methods as extraneous to the more expressive purposes political activity.

This business orientation has been evident since at least the 1950s, when Hugh Bone observed that the Republicans were explicit in their desire to run the RNC "like a corporation," and he quotes Stewart Alsop's description of the RNC looking like the "home of a large and successful business concern." In contrast, he found the Democrats to be much more informal and disorganized.[6] In 1960, Alexander Heard observed, "A visitor to the headquarters of a well-organized Republican finance committee senses the same atmosphere that pervades a giant philanthropic drive."[7] He added that the reason for this was that the same businesspeople who ran many charity campaigns, also ran the fundraising for the Republican party. This contrasted with the Democratic party, which, in Heard's description, "has traditionally been typified by informality and confusion. . . . Neither at the national level nor elsewhere has the Democratic party made use of professional fund-raisers on anything like the scale the Republicans have done."[8] A few years later, Cotter and Hennessy made a similar observation, stating that while each of the Democratic national committees does "what it damn well pleases," the "Republicans approach the problem of national party financing with business-like matter-of-factness."[9]

Though made thirty years ago, these observations still provide an accurate description of current differences between the parties. In a more recent analysis of national party activity in congressional races, Paul Herrnson states that Democratic party staff members "work in a highly politicized environment which lacks the business-like ethos of its Republican counterpart."[10] According to John Bibby: "The observer of DNC and RNC meetings is immediately struck by the fact that the differences between the two committees go well beyond their respective sizes. Differences in style of operation and party constituencies are apparent. Republican National Committee meetings are extremely well organized and professionally staffed. There is an air of formality and relative order about the conduct of the meetings. DNC meetings are less well organized, informal, and have a rather ad hoc character. Orderliness prevails in RNC sessions, while confusion is common at DNC meetings."[11]

My own observations of the national party operations and staff reinforce this view. On several visits to both party headquarters, I was struck by the comparatively more modern and efficient operation of the Republicans, in contrast with the more informal and less organized Democrats. To me, a trip to the RNC was like visiting a law office or investment bank, while going to DNC was akin to stopping by the offices of junior faculty members at a small college.[12]

In addition to using business technology and methods, the Republicans also seem to speak of politics in much the same terms as business people speak of an industry or a market. One of the best examples of how Republicans use business terms to describe politics comes from a 1962 speech by Dwight Eisenhower:

> We [the Republican party] have a good bill of fare, or you might say, stock of goods on the shelf, but the trouble is that we think that because they are good in the cans and packages, we can let them get dusty on the shelves.
>
> . . . the Democrats have less value in their goods, but they paint up the can, tidy up the store, and then they have a better, more appealing idea to put before a prospective customer.
>
> Now, I think we ought to read this very objectively and see wherein we are weak and wherein we are strong, and if we are happy with the package . . . I think we should find out whether this [the Republican program] is saleable and we ought to use salesmanship in getting it before the public.[13]

Throughout my interviews with the leadership and staff of the Republican party, I frequently heard such business and managerial language, whereas the Democrats almost never used such expressions. The Republicans constantly relied on terms and phrases such as, "make the sale," "marketing" a candidate or an idea, the "corporate wheel" of the party, and "distribution system." Indicative of this reliance on business terms is the campaign manifesto used by Haley Barbour in his successful race for RNC chair, which describes the RNC as a "Board of Directors" with the chairman as the "CEO" and "manager" who must "ensure productivity, accountability and quality control" by relying on "good business practice."[14]

Among Republicans, the most commonly used term is Ray Bliss's favorite expression, "nuts and bolts." Nearly every Republican that I interviewed for this project reached for this phrase to describe the efforts and purpose of the RNC. Additionally, in 1993, each of the contenders for the RNC chairmanship sought to use the "nuts and bolts" label to characterize their proposed efforts. Certainly Bliss's success and high regard within the party help to account for the common and continued use of this term, but it also seems likely that the term accurately reflects the technical and business-oriented nature of the Republican party.

In addition to their role as the "party of business," the high degree of homogeneity within the Republican party is another likely reason for its organizational orientation. According to Jo Freeman, the social homogeneity of the Republican party helps to create a sense of trust among party members: "People normally trust those who are like them to think like them and to do what they do. People understand others who are like themselves. Organizations or communities whose members trust each other function more smoothly and take direction more willingly than those where trust is more limited. Republicans trust their party and their leaders to do what they think is right more than Democrats do, because they are socially homogeneous."[15]

As a result of the trust created by this homogeneity, Freeman claims: "The Republican party sees itself as an organic whole whose parts are interdependent. Republican activists are expected to be good soldiers who respect leadership and whose only important political commitment is to the Republican party."[16]

In turn, this centralization and hierarchy creates an environment hospitable to the organizational activities used by the Republicans. In her words, a party "which is hierarchical, unitary and in which power flows downward" will be better "able to use more of its resources for attaining its goals and direct them more efficiently."[17]

The Republicans' experience as a minority party also seems to have helped shape their party culture, contributing to their affinity for organizational responses. Perhaps following an example from the private sector, as is their wont, the Republicans have emulated Avis Rental Cars by acting according to the claim, "We're number two, so we try harder." According to Cotter and Hennessy, the behavior of the Republican party might be explained as "the frugality of the minority party aware that organization may compensate for numbers."[18] Since their banishment to minority party status in the 1930s, the Republicans have often operated on the assumption that while they might be out-numbered by the Democrats, their emphasis on organization would serve as an equalizer. As one study of contemporary party organizations states: "The Republicans, in the first years of the New Deal, preached organization for the out party as the key to mitigating the adverse consequences of Democratic hegemony. In subsequent decades they practiced organization as a key to reversing electoral adversity. In short, the national party organizational elites in the 1920s and 1930s perceived a relationship between long-term electoral trends and organizational strength."[19]

The role of important leaders has also reinforced the RNC's organizational orientation. Leaders often have an influential role in developing and maintaining an organization's culture, particularly when they develop successful strategies for dealing with crises. Leaders often derive such strategies from their previous experiences and their continued success imbeds them in the organization's culture.[20] Such was the case with the two most important Republican party leaders of this period: Ray Bliss and Bill Brock. Each came from predominantly Democratic areas where superior organization was the Republican party's only hope and each first succeeded by building political organizations that could successfully compete with the numerically larger Democrats. Bliss first began in politics in Akron, Ohio, where the Democratic party, bolstered by the political organization of the rubber workers' union, dominated local elections. He eventually moved on to the larger stage of Ohio state politics, but here, once again, the Democrats had an edge in voter registration. Bill Brock began his political career in the then still solidly Democratic South, becoming the first Republican elected to Congress from Chattanooga, Tennessee, since the 1920s.

While serving as RNC chairman, both Bliss and Brock emphasized the importance of party organization that they had gained from their previous experiences. In both cases the strategy was perceived as successful since the Republican party won the White House during their tenure. As a result, Ray Bliss and Bill Brock are held in high esteem by their colleagues and successors, who often refer to them in tones best described as reverential, and their methods are still used although they have long since relinquished their leadership positions.[21]

As much as Bliss and Brock might have influenced the culture of the Republican party, it is also reasonable to see these two leaders as products of that same party culture. Organizations with strong cultures tend to recruit members who share their values.[22] According to organizational theorist Edgar Schein, an "organization is likely to look for new members who already have the 'right' set of assumptions, beliefs, and values."[23] One can see evidence of this process at work in the selection of Bliss and Brock as RNC chairman. Both men had reputations as nonideological leaders who would emphasize organization over factional maneuvering, characteristics that not only suited the perceived needs of the party at the time, but that also fit well with the existing culture of the Republican party.

THE DEMOCRATS: THE CULTURE OF DEMOCRACY

While Republicans have a cultural affinity toward business, the primary cultural referents for Democrats outside of their party are interest and constituency groups. Many of these Democratic groups—women, minorities, gays and lesbians, labor, and others—have traditionally perceived themselves as disempowered or locked out of America's important social and political decision-making processes. According to Jo Freeman, Democrats "do not think of themselves as the center of society. The party's components think of themselves as outsiders pounding on the door seeking programs that will facilitate entry into the mainstream. Thus the party is very responsive to any groups, including such social pariahs as gays and lesbians, that claim to be left out."[24]

These groups view the Democratic party as an arena and a vehicle for achieving the representation and power denied them by other societal groups and institutions.[25] Freeman adds that representing these groups: "does not mean the articulation of a single coherent program for the betterment of the nation but the inclusion of all relevant groups and viewpoints. Their concept of representation is delegatory, in which accurate reflection of the parts is necessary to the welfare of the whole."[26]

This analysis is supported by the observations of a recent DNC official, who states that the Democratic party allows these groups to "express their heart and soul." Moreover, in her view, the Democratic party is the only instrument for this expression, since the Republican party is "not big enough to give them any power."[27]

Attempting to achieve an "accurate reflection of the parts" leads to the Democrats' stress upon procedural reforms. These reforms make sure that each of the party's constituent elements achieves the amount of representation in party circles that they deserve. The various party reform battles detailed in previous chapters show how the various Democratic constituencies have used the DNC as an arena to determine the proper representation due to them. In short, the Democratic party is devoted to being a democratic party.

While Democrats revel in such procedural matters, Republicans approach them with a distinctly different attitude. The Republican party has not engaged in significant procedural reform since 1912, and when current Republicans are asked why they did not undertake procedural reforms similar to those of the Democrats, their responses fall into one of two categories. One answer is in the form of a question, usually along the lines of, "Why the Hell would we want to do something like that for?" The second is not so much an answer as an uncomprehending stare, much as one might get if you had asked them why the Republican party had not called for a confiscatory tax system, a command economy, unilateral disarmament, or legalization of child pornography. Both responses show that procedural reforms are simply not a part of the Republican party's nature.[28]

When the Republicans are forced to undertake even minor procedural changes, they tend to keep the efforts as controlled and limited as possible. Commenting upon changes in Republican rules in the early 1970s, William Crotty observed:

> Their approach to [procedural] problems appears to reflect an innate restraint, a sense of order and disciplined change, a quest for efficiency, and a belief in appearances. Innumerable committees deal with and evaluate questions, recommendations are passed on to other committees and superiors, and out of this over a period of time modest change in line with the party's values is expected to emerge. The atmosphere is dignified and the entire process is decorous, not unlike the local gentry who view with alarm the modifications of traditions that have served them so well. Constructive, reasoned change moderately indulged in may have its place. Tempestuous excesses instituted on short notice are confined to their more unruly counterparts in the Democratic party.[29]

The quest for inclusiveness that spurred much of the Democrats' procedural efforts is not absent in the Republican party. Many, if not most, Republicans want to broaden their party, particularly regarding women and minorities, but they are willing to do so only as long as these new entrants act as individual Republicans, rather than as organized groups. According to an organizer of the Republican Women's Task Force at the 1976 convention, the Republican party is not "an interest group party. And consequently the Republican Women's Task Force is viewed with skepticism. Party regulars have a hard time adjusting to the presence of an organized interest."[30] Not surprisingly, constituency groups within the Republican party seem unwilling to challenge this attitude and, therefore, usually do not attempt to voice their demands within party circles.[31]

In comparison, the Democratic party seems much more attractive to new groups since the Democrats do not require group loyalties to be replaced by party loyalties. The culture of the Democratic party is such that interest and constituency groups are allowed, even encouraged, to organize and pressure the party. Furthermore, the Democrats often offer new groups, by virtue of their legitimacy as a group, direct representation and power in the party decision-making process. Even Paul Kirk's celebrated, but ultimately symbolic, attack on the DNC's caucuses could not change this basic orientation.

John Bibby best summed up the two parties' different approaches to organized interest groups:

> The major subunits of RNC gatherings are meetings of state chairmen and regional associations. There are also informal meetings of various ideological and candidate factions. The DNC has all of these types of subunits and factions, but in addition has active caucuses for blacks, Hispanics, and women which have played a major role in DNC meetings. . . . There is no

comparable specialized representational structure—formal or informal—within the RNC. This no doubt reflects the important role which organized interest groups have traditionally played within the Democratic coalition. By contrast, the Republicans, with their more homogeneous constituency and middle class orientation, have had a less extensive and explicit relationship with organized groups.[32]

Just as the Republican party's homogeneity bolsters its organizational tendencies and reduces the role of interest groups within the party, the Democrats' heterogeneity reinforces their affinity for procedural matters. In Jo Freeman's words:

> Heterogeneity facilitates misunderstanding. People with different backgrounds, different values, different styles, and different modes of expression interpret the world differently and often misrepresent each other. A great deal of communication, clarification, and reassurance is necessary to maintain working relationships among diverse allies. In a highly heterogeneous organization people with one group identity are reluctant to trust those with another to act as their leaders or adequately represent their interests. Instead they demand consultation, representation, and participation. The heterogeneous nature of the Democratic party requires that time and energy be devoted to intraparty relationships and that identifiable groups feel that they have as much say as they want.[33]

Party procedure provides the Democrats with the "consultation, representation, and participation" required of a heterogeneous party and is therefore an expression of cultural makeup of the Democratic party. On the other hand, as the more homogeneous party, Republicans need less "consultation, representation, and participation," and, consequently, are less disposed to tinker with their party procedures.

The Democrats' heterogeneity also limits their ability to carry out organizational reforms as easily as the Republicans. Without the bonds of trust established by a homogeneous membership, it becomes very difficult to institute the centralization and hierarchy necessary for a businesslike organization. Organizational decisions are scrutinized, not only for their effectiveness, but also for the impact they will have on the representation of the party's constituencies, which often makes those decisions more difficult to implement.

This difference between the parties comes out in discussions with members and staffs of the national committees. With the Republicans, one gets the impression that the national chairman is given great latitude to make and implement decisions for the party. These decisions do not necessarily have unanimous agreement, but most Republicans seem willing to defer to the judgment of the party leadership. In interviews with Democrats, however, one constantly hears of how decisions, even those regarding relatively minor matters, must be cleared with important constituency groups. For example, after Paul Kirk became chairman in 1985, the DNC took great efforts to ensure that minority-owned businesses received an adequate proportion of DNC business.[34] One DNC staffer commented, anonymously, "Working at the DNC is a Noah's Ark kind of thing. You have to make sure to have two of everybody before you do anything."

Since the 1930s, the Democrats have viewed themselves as the majority party, a perception that has also aided their predilection for procedure. As the majority party, the Democrats will naturally win every election so long as they are united and procedure provides the means by which the party can achieve unity, or so the thinking goes for many Democrats. The history of Democratic party reforms provides testimony for this reasoning. The Democrats have attempted continually to devise a procedure for nominating presidential candidates that satisfies the desires of all party constituencies and thus keeps them unified for the general election. After 1968 the party reformed itself to bring back the McCarthy supporters who had defected or stayed at home. After 1972 they took steps to give greater say to the state and local party officials and union leaders who had abandoned McGovern. After 1980 the Democrats created the superdelegates to give more representation to elected officials. After 1984 the DNC supported "Super Tuesday" to give conservative whites more influence over the nomination. The Democrats seem to operate under the assumption that if only they can construct an ideal nomination system that properly represents each of the party's constituencies, then the perfect nominee will emerge, leading a unified party to victory. To some extent the party's 1992 nominee, Bill Clinton, succeeded in this effort, though it is uncertain how much the Democrats' nominating system influenced his selection and success.

A final reinforcement to the procedural impulse in the Democratic party is the impact of the 1968 election. How an organization deals with critical incidents, such as a challenge to authority, has a strong influence on its culture. According to Edgar Schein: "One can see in [organizations] how norms and beliefs arise around the way members respond to critical incidents. Something emotionally charged or anxiety producing may happen, such as an attack by a member on the leader. Because everyone witnesses it and because tension is high when the attack occurs, the immediate next set of behaviors tends to create a norm."[35]

The events of 1968, if nothing else, were "emotionally charged and anxiety producing" for the Democratic party, and the Democratic party's response to those events had an important impact on its culture. In 1968 liberal insurgents challenged the traditional leadership of the Democratic party. The party leadership, seeking unity in the aftermath of Humphrey's loss, responded to that challenge by beginning a series of procedural reforms that would open up the party to insurgent groups. This helped to create a cultural norm in which the party used procedural reforms as a method of unifying the party over the next twenty years.

PARTY CULTURE AND OUT-PARTY BEHAVIOR

Although party culture has a significant influence on the behavior of the out-parties, it does not always determine a party's response to defeat. Parties usually respond to defeat according to the dictates of their culture, but at times other factors outweigh this instinct. For example, after the 1956 election, the Democrats employed a policy response. In this case, the Democrats' response resulted from a unique set of circumstances in which the party's sharp ideological divisions closely matched the structural division between the national and the congressional parties—liberals dominated the national committee while conservatives dominated the leadership of the congressional party leadership. This meant that the national committee, which possessed a strong and relatively coherent notion of what party policy should be, had no way of advancing its views other than through a party council. Such a situation has not repeated itself for the Democrats since then because the DNC and the congressional leadership have been much more unified on policy issues than they were in the late 1950s.

Party culture also fails to explain fully the Democrats' behavior during the 1980s. Although it engaged in its traditional procedural responses after all three of its defeats in this decade, the DNC, contrary to what might be predicted from relying solely on a party culture explanation, also instituted organizational efforts. In these instances it seems that the Democrats began to behave somewhat more like a victory-oriented party. Stunned by their landslide losses, confronted with a party apparatus suffering from twenty years of neglect, and finally emerging from the under the debt that had hampered it in the past, the Democratic party implemented several of the organizational improvements used so successfully by their Republican counterparts.

These Democratic exceptions suggest the limitations of a party culture explanation across time. One might argue that the Democrats' procedural emphasis is a short-term tendency resulting from the social upheavals of the 1960s and 1970s and the party crisis of 1968. As for the Republicans, it could be said that their organizational responses reflect the revolution in campaign and fundraising technology since the early 1960s.

An analysis of the parties prior to 1956 does provide examples of previous responses that seem uncharacteristic of the party cultures observed in this study. As mentioned before, procedural issues dominated the Republican party after their 1912 convention. With the Democrats, organizational strength was always a high priority among the urban party machines of the late nineteenth and early twentieth century. And organizational responses are not unknown even for the national committee. Cordell Hull mounted a vigorous organizational effort while DNC chairman from 1921 to 1924.[36] After the 1928 election, millionaire businessman John J. Raskob, sought to bring "business principles" to the DNC.[37] Aided mightily by his own large contributions, he put the DNC on a sound financial footing and established several organizational efforts, the most famous of which was the work of the Publicity Division which unleashed a relentless assault on President Herbert Hoover after the stock market crash of 1929.[38] Finally, the movement toward organizational responses by the DNC in the 1980s suggests the time-bound nature of the Democrats' procedural responses in this period.

Still, one should not go so far as to characterize the responses found in this study merely as artifacts of the times. Rather, they reflect long-standing historical concerns and traditions within their respective parties. The businesslike culture of the Republicans is not new. The impact of business has been evident in the culture of the Republican party since at least the days of Mark Hanna. Matthew Josephson's description of Hanna's efforts in 1896 clearly illustrates the organizational style evident in the GOP nearly one hundred years ago: "Hanna set up a complete machinery for modern political warfare. The Republican National Committee, which he headed, instead of being a sort of clearinghouse, a kind of central agency (chiefly for receiving appeals for funds from State bosses worried about their districts), became the general staff of the whole army. Its orders were carried out by the State committees automatically, as if they were the branch offices of one of the modern, centralized industrial Trusts in oil, steel, or sugar."[39]

Hanna's methods persisted after his tenure, and the RNC, particularly under the out-party leadership of Will Hays (1919–1921), John C. Hamilton (1936–1940), and Herbert Brownell (1944–1946), has often led the way in applying business techniques to the functions of the party.[40] In his analysis of the national party committees from their inception until 1960, Ralph Goldman concludes: "In general, Republicans, somewhat more so than Democrats, seem to have selected party chairmen with organizational and managerial skills and experience. These individuals have been recruited from such positions as state party chairmen, chairmen of congressional campaign committees, national committee staff and membership, and corporate executives. Republicans have manifest a concern, particularly after the Hanna and Hays regimes, for 'business-like' efficiency at national party headquarters."[41]

In contrast, throughout their history, the Democrats have displayed nearly the opposite inclinations. According to Goldman, as the RNC was developing organizational prowess under Hanna and his successors, the DNC served more as a forum for representing factional and geographic conflicts, "most often manifesting themselves in disputes over the size of representation on various committees, strategic instructions to chairman [sic] or subcommittees, and the selection of time, site and other arrangements for a forthcoming national convention." In addition to these procedural disputes, the DNC was usually, if not almost always, hobbled by debt and disorganization.[42]

Just as the Republicans have a long history of organizational emphasis, concerns about voice and representation have played an important role in the Democratic party since its origins. The out-group nature of the Democratic party extends to its earliest days under Thomas Jefferson when, according to Ralph Goldman, it was comprised of such out-groups as: "the frontier settler, the small farmer, the unskilled laborer, the craftsman, the enlisted soldier, the immigrant, the English dissenter, the debtor, the poor, and the disenfranchised. From the outset, these constituencies were where the discontented, the angry, and the resigned could most often be found."[43]

This coalition of the resentful carried over into the 1820s when Andrew Jackson, attacking elitist privilege in the form of "King Caucus" and the National Bank, founded the modern Democratic party. Lawrence Frederick Kohl best sums up Jacksonian Democracy as, "the collective cry of men who felt the world was not treating them fairly," adding, "One of the strongest bonds uniting the disparate elements of forming the Democratic party [in the age of Jackson] was the common perception of living outside society's dominant sources of power and acceptance. Other men seemed, in a multitude of ways, to be 'insiders,' while the Jacksonian felt himself to be on the outside looking in. Even many Democratic leaders, including Jackson himself, felt themselves on the defensive against more powerful men who controlled affairs."[44]

Class formed one component of this sentiment. As Wilfred Binkley states, the Jacksonians were "the enemy of special privilege. The whoop and hurrah of the movement afforded a wholesome psychological release of the accumulated resentments of Western small farmers and Eastern urban underlings. Everywhere the less prosperous had been wont to attribute their ill fortune to the ruling oligarchy that had run the government in its own interest. . . . 'Equal rights for all, special privileges for none,' became the appropriate slogan for the party."[45]

But the Jacksonians' resentment of privilege had a cultural as well as an economic component. According to historian Robert Kelley: "Whether Democrats were attacking the wealthy or the moralists, they were attacking essentially the same people. Thus it made sense on cultural as well as economic grounds for the ethnic outgroups to be Democrats. They were workers and consumers for whom the Democratic economic ideology was desirable, and they were either strangers in the land or long-resident non-Yankee peoples like the Dutch who needed protection from Yankee cultural imperialism."[46]

The tradition of the Democrats as the party of out-groups continued on after the Jacksonian era. Following the Civil War, the base of the Democratic party was the South—a region that viewed itself as socially, economically, politically, and militarily put upon by the North. In addition to the South, the Democratic party also drew strength from urban immigrants, particularly Catholics, another group that believed itself locked out of the upper reaches of American society, and, after the 1890s, western farmers who saw themselves at the mercy of the railroads and eastern bankers. To these groups the New Deal added urban workers, particularly those associated with organized labor.

Although the Democrats might have represented the out-groups within their coalition, they did not always attempt to include all of society's out-groups. From the days of Jefferson to the 1930s, the Democrats conspicuously and vehemently excluded blacks, an out-group by any definition. Yet even this barrier began to give way in the 1930s, as Democratic liberals began to question their party's racism and more pragmatic politicians in the North began to see blacks as a potentially important base of support. Since then the party has made great efforts to open itself up, not only to blacks and other racial and ethnic minorities, but also to such out-groups as gays and lesbians, feminists, and many others.

The out-group nature of the Democratic party has historically given it a greater concern for procedural matters. In fact, the Jacksonian Democrats founded the first modern political parties because they believed that parties offered a superior means of popular representation as compared to the personal cliques and factions that preceded the rise of parties. According to Michael Wallace's analysis of the Albany Regency, these predecessors of the Jacksonians believed that "personal factions were bad: they were aristocratic and concerned only with enriching their leader. But parties were good: they allowed all members an equal voice; gave all members an equal chance to rise to positions of leadership and to receive party nominations for important elective positions; and provided all members with an equal chance at receiving patronage, now no longer disposed at the whim of an arbitrary leader."[47] Many people viewed such an egalitarian organization enthusiastically. According to Douglas Jaenicke, "The party's attraction for Democrats derived from its role as defender of equal opportunity."[48]

The Jacksonian Democratic party instituted several political innovations that helped to make it representative of its constituent elements, primarily the national nominating convention and the two-thirds rule. The rise of the nominating convention represented and reinforced the democratic impulse of the Democrats. In historian James Chase's assessment, "The convention prevailed over the nominating methods because it best satisfied the ideological demands of the Jacksonian era that government should be responsive to the people's direction."[49] Of conventions, Andrew Jackson said, "This is the only mode by which the people will be able long to retain in their own hands, the election of the President and Vice-President."[50]

The two-thirds rule, adopted in 1832, furthered the idea that the party should represent all of its voices by ensuring that no significant minority constituency of the party could be shut out of the nomination decision. According to Jaenicke, the two-thirds rule was the "best known example" of how "the Democratic party carefully sought to protect intra-party minorities by granting them effective veto power within the party's councils."[51]

Procedural issues were a recurrent theme in the Democratic party over the next century. As mentioned earlier, Ralph Goldman claims that they bedeviled the DNC in the late nineteenth and early twentieth century. In 1919, the DNC provided women with equal representation in its membership, one year prior to the passage of the Nineteenth Amendment that established women's suffrage and five years before a similar move by the RNC.[52] In the 1920s, several progressive Democrats, Franklin Roosevelt most notably, attempted unsuccessfully to reform party procedures to help bridge the party's bitter division between its liberal urban and conservative agrarian wings.[53] As president, Roosevelt again sought to transform the DNC by making it more participatory and democratic, mainly through the creation and expansion of special divisions within the national committee "to cultivate the electoral support of specific voting blocs and interest groups, namely women, blacks, labor, and young voters."[54] Roosevelt also eliminated the two-thirds rule, which, by giving veto power to a minority, came to be seen as a hindrance to effective representation.

Procedural issues became increasingly important to the Democratic party during the 1950s. After the election of 1952, the question of "loyalty oaths" captured the party's attention as it attempted to deny convention representation to turncoat conservative southerners. The 1950s also witnessed the rise of liberal "amateurs" who challenged the urban machines to follow more democratic procedures. According to James Q. Wilson, one of the principal concerns of these amateurs was "that participation in the management of the affairs of the party ought to be widespread and in accord with strictly democratic procedures."[55] Even the controversy over the Democratic Advisory Council of the late 1950s had a procedural component to it, in that it represented a division over which element of the party, liberals or conservatives, should provide its voice and leadership.

By the 1960s, most Democrats had concluded that intraparty democracy meant little so long as the party sought to systematically exclude blacks and other minorities. As a result, the Democrats began a series of reforms that sought to make the party more representative, but also more participatory and inclusive. Since 1968, the Democrats have given important constituencies, such as minorities, labor, elected officials, and women, official status within the party through delegate quotas and DNC positions. The party opened up the nomination process to give rank-and-file members a direct mechanism for making their preferences known and moved the delegate apportionment system toward proportional representation to make sure that those preferences were equally weighted. Today the Democratic party prides itself on its inclusive nature, often contrasting it with the perceived exclusiveness of the Republicans.

Although the DNC's procedural efforts during the period of this study may have been more extensive than in the past, they are not uncharacteristic. Nor does it appear that the Democrats will soon evolve beyond this historic concern for voice and representation. Even in the 1980s and early 1990s, as the DNC focused on more organizational efforts, procedural issues still occupied equal, if not greater, positions of importance.

It is not altogether surprising to find that most deviations from the influence of party culture have occurred in the Democratic party. The Democratic party is a very loose and heterogeneous organization and, consequently, its party culture offers a less rigid constraint on the party's behavior. The Republicans, on the other hand, being a more hierarchical and homogeneous party, have a stronger sense of cultural constraints that, in turn, exert a tighter influence over party behavior. The Democratic and Republican parties differ not only in their cultures but also in the impact that those cultures have on their behavior.

Finally, while advances in campaign technology and social upheaval may have influenced the parties' recent responses, these changes were not limited to only one of the two parties. Democrats also had access to advanced technologies, and Republicans were not immune to society's changes—they merely chose not focus on them when selecting their responses. The parties simply chose to emphasize those changes that mirrored their party's cultural traditions and strengths, and to de-emphasize those that did not.

Party culture significantly influences the behavior of the national committees. Although party culture is not necessarily determinative, explanations of how the national committees respond to defeat in presidential elections based upon party culture are much more complete and insightful than those offered by theories of victory-oriented party behavior or of ideologically-driven parties. Rather than symmetrical organizations possessed by the single-minded purpose of winning the next election or advancing an ideological agenda, the national committees appear to act more as distinct entities motivated by a variety of influences unique to each party's culture. While this study is limited to the responses of national party committees to presidential election losses, the results seem applicable to a wider range of party organizations and activities. For example, party culture might provide a better understanding of how other party organizations behave, or how party affiliation influences the behavior of activists, candidates, and elected officials. By taking party culture into account, perhaps future research can provide richer and more realistic explanations of party behavior.

NOTES

CHAPTER 1

1. Robert Dahl, ed., *Political Opositions in Western Democracies* (New Haven: Yale University Press, 1966), xiii.

2. Robert Harmel, ed., *Presidents and Their Parties: Leadership or Neglect?* (New York: Praeger Publishers, 1984), 83, and Robert Harmel, Kenneth Janda, Uk Heo, and Alexander Tan, "Performance, Leadership, Factions, and Party Changes: An Empirical Analysis" (Paper presented at the 1993 Annual Meeting of the American Political Science Association, Washington, D.C.)

3. Walter Lippmann, *A Preface to Politics* (New York: Mitchell Kennerley, 1914), 26.

4. Theodore Lowi, "Toward Functionalism in Political Science: The Case of Innovation in Party Systems," *American Political Science Review* 57 (September 1963): 582.

5. Paul T. David, Ralph M. Goldman, and Richard C. Bain, *The Politics of National Party Conventions* (Washington D.C.: Brookings Institution, 1960), 49–74, and John F. Bibby, *Politics, Parties, and Elections in America,* 2d ed. (Chicago: Nelson-Hall, 1992), 88–89.

6. Sidney Milkis, "Franklin D. Roosevelt and the Transcendence of Partisan Politics," *Political Science Quarterly* 100 (Fall 1985): 481. Also see Theodore J. Lowi, *The Personal President: Power Invested, Promise Unfulfilled* (Ithaca, N.Y.: Cornell University Press, 1985), 71–79.

7. Nixon even went so far as to admit this strategy to Theodore White during the campaign. See White's, *The Making of the President: 1972* (New York: Atheneum, 1973), 299–304.

8. Lowi, *Personal President,* 79.

9. Quoted in Michael J. Malbin, "The Past and Future Parties," *National Journal,* February 5, 1977, 214.

10. Milkis, "Franklin D. Roosevelt," 502. For more about Bailey's lack of power under Johnson, see Joseph I. Lieberman, *The Power Broker: A Biography of John M. Bailey, Modern Political Boss* (Boston: Houghton Mifflin, 1966), esp. 319–20.

11. James L. Sundquist, *Politics and Policy: The Eisenhower, Kennedy, and Johnson Years* (Washington D.C.: Brookings Institution, 1968), 415.

12. Most of the work in this area concentrates on opposition to regimes, as opposed to loyal opposition, or on the social conditions that give rise to political opposition. See Robert Dahl, ed., *Regimes and Oppositions* (New Haven: Yale University Press, 1973), and Dahl, ed., *Political Oppositions in Western Democracies* (New Haven: Yale University Press, 1966). One exception to this tendency is Max Beloff, "The Leader of the Opposition," *Parliamentary Affairs* 11 (Spring 1958): 155–62.

13. The singular exception to this is Charles O. Jones, *The Minority Party in Congress* (Boston: Little, Brown, and Company, 1970).

14. Quoted in Stephen Hess and David S. Broder, *The Republican Establishment: The Present and Future of the GOP* (New York: Harper and Row, 1967), 16.

15. Samuel Lubell, *The Future of American Politics* (New York: Harper, 1951), 191–92.

16. Cornelius P. Cotter and Bernard C. Hennessy, *Politics without Power: The National Party Committees* (New York: Atherton, 1964), 98.

17. Ibid., 101 and 103.

18. The seminal article in this literature is that written by Cornelius P. Cotter and John F. Bibby, "Institutional Development of Parties and the Thesis of Party Decline," *Political Science Quarterly* 95 (Spring 1980): 1–27. Also see Gerald M. Pomper, ed., *Party Renewal in America: Theory and Practice* (New York: Praeger, 1980); Cornelius P. Cotter et al., *Party Organizations in American Politics* (New York: Praeger, 1984); David E. Price, *Bringing Back the Parties* (Washington D.C.: Congressional Quarterly Press, 1984); Xandra Kayden and Eddie Mahe, Jr., *The Party Goes On: The Persistence of the Two-Party System in the United States* (New York: Basic Books, 1985); Paul S. Herrnson, *Party Campaigning in the 1980s* (Cambridge: Harvard University Press, 1988); Herrnson, "Reemergent National Party Organizations," in L. Sandy Maisel, ed., *The Parties Respond: Changes in the American Party System* (Boulder, Colo.: Westview Press, 1990), 41–66; Herrnson and David Menefee-Libey, "The Dynamics of Party Organizational Development," *Mid-South Journal of Political Science* 11 (Winter 1990): 3–30; Gary Wekkin, *Democrat versus Democrat: The National Party's Campaign to Close the Wisconsin Primary* (Columbia: University of Missouri Press: 1984); Ralph M. Goldman, *The National Party Chairmen and Committees: Factionalism at the Top* (Armonk, N.Y.: Sharpe, 1990); and Stephen E. Frantzich, *Political Parties in the Technological Age* (New York: Longman, 1989).

19. Tim Hames, "Power without Politics: The Republican National Committee in American Political Life and the Debate over Party Renewal" (Unpublished manuscript, 1990).

20. These explanations of party behavior are vast and growing. The most influential work in this corpus is by Anthony Downs, *An Economic Theory of Democracy* (New York: Harper and Row, 1957). A more recent general statement appears in Joseph A. Schlesinger, *Political Parties and the Winning of Office* (Ann Arbor: University of Michigan Press, 1991). Also see Joseph A. Schumpeter, *Capitalism, Socialism, and Democracy* (New York: Harper and Brothers, 1942), and R. T. McKenzie, *British Political Parties: The Distribution of Power within the Conservative and Labour Parties* (New York: Praeger, 1964).

21. Ian Budge and Hans Keman, *Parties and Democracy: Coalition Formation and Government Functioning in Twenty States* (Oxford: Oxford University Press, 1990), 158 and 205.

22. Henry W. Chappell, Jr., and William R. Keech, "Policy Motivation and Party Differences in a Dynamic Spatial Model of Party Competition," *American Political Science Review* 80 (September 1986): 897.

23. Alan M. Kantrow, *The Constraints of Corporate Tradition* (New York: Harper and Row, 1984), x.

24. William Crotty, *Party Reform* (New York: Longman, 1983), 205–6.

25. Jo Freeman, "The Political Culture of Democratic and Republican Parties," *Political Science Quarterly* 101 (June 1986): 327–56. Also see Denise L. Baer and David A. Bositis, *Politics and Linkage in a Democratic Society* (Englewood Cliffs, N.J.: Prentice-Hall, 1993), 139–44.

26. Byron E. Shafer, "Republicans and Democrats as Social Types: Or, Notes toward an Ethnography of the Political Parties," *Journal of American Studies* 20 (December 1986): 341–54.

27. Mildred A. Schwartz, *The Party Network: The Robust Organization of Illinois Republicans* (Madison: University of Wisconsin Press, 1990), 281–82.

28. J. Steven Ott, *The Organizational Culture Perspective* (Chicago: Dorsey Press, 1989),

74–87, and Edgar H. Schein, "Organizational Culture," *American Psychologist* 45 (February 1990): 115.

29. Downs, *Economic Theory,* 109.

30. Kantrow, *Constraints of Corporate Tradition,* 2.

31. There are some exceptions to this generalization, most notably in the aforementioned work of Mildred A. Schwartz.

32. Michael Owen Jones, Michael Dane Moore, and Richard Christopher Snyder, eds., *Inside Organizations: Understanding the Human Dimension* (Newbury Park, Calif.: Sage Publications, 1988), 27. Also see Schein, "Organizational Culture," 109–19.

CHAPTER 2

1. Hays quoted in David E. Price, *Bringing Back the Parties* (Washington D.C.: Congressional Quarterly Press, 1984), 264.

2. Hays quoted in American Political Science Association Committee on Political Parties, *Toward a More Responsible Two-Party System* (New York: Rhinehart, 1950), 55.

3. Ralph M. Goldman, *The National Party Chairmen and Committees: Factionalism at the Top* (Armonk, N.Y.: Sharpe, 1990), 292–93.

4. Frank quoted in Cornelius P. Cotter and Bernard C. Hennessy, *Politics without Power: The National Party Committees* (New York: Atherton, 1964), 194.

5. Goldman, *National Party Chairmen,* 405–8.

6. Ibid., 482; Cotter and Hennessy, *Politics without Power,* 195; Price, *Bringing Back the Parties,* 265; and Richard Norton Smith, *Thomas E. Dewey and His Times* (New York: Touchstone, 1982), 384–87. The council appears to have involved a rather eclectic group; Groucho Marx was among those who corresponded with the Post-War Advisory Council. See Booth Tarkington to Groucho Marx, June 30, 1943, in *The Groucho Letters: Letters From and To Groucho Marx* (New York: Simon and Schuster, 1967), 295–97. Unfortunately for posterity, there is no record of Groucho's response.

7. Hugh A. Bone, *Party Committees and National Politics* (Seattle: University of Washington Press, 1958), 12–13.

8. Quoted in Doris Kearns, *Lyndon Johnson and the American Dream* (New York: Harper and Row, 1976), 154.

9. Quoted in ibid., 155.

10. Quoted in Douglass Cater, "Who Will Speak For the Democrats?" *Reporter,* November 29, 1956, 22.

11. Quoted in Kearns, *Lyndon Johnson,* 155.

12. The term *Inner Club* comes from William S. White's *Citadel: The Story of the U.S. Senate* (New York: Vintage Books, 1956). Other than Richard Russell (Ga.), the Inner Club's acknowledged leader, the membership of this body was nebulous. Among those most commonly mentioned are, James Eastland (Miss.), Harry F. Byrd (Va.), Carl Hayden (Ariz.), A. Willis Robertson (Va.), Allen Ellender (La.), Walter George (Ga.), and Tom Connally (Tex.).

13. Sidney Hyman, "Can a Democrat Win in '60?" *Reporter,* March 5, 1959, 12.

14. Kearns, *Lyndon Johnson,* 139.

15. Ibid., 141.

16. Quoted in James Q. Wilson, *The Amateur Democrat: Club Politics in Three Cities* (Chicago: University of Chicago Press, 1962), 3.

17. Porter McKeever, *Adlai Stevenson: His Life and Legacy* (New York: Morrow, 1989), 314.

18. John Kenneth Galbraith to Adlai E. Stevenson, September 23, 1953, Democratic Party,

Finletter Group, July 23, 1953–February 15, 1954 folder, Galbraith Papers, General Correspondence, box 34, John F. Kennedy Library (hereafter referred to as JFKL).

19. Ibid.

20. Adlai E. Stevenson to John Kenneth Galbraith, October 16, 1953, Democratic Party, Finletter Group, July 23, 1953–February 15, 1954 folder, Galbraith Papers, General Correspondence, box 34, JFKL. Bevanism refers to the radical positions associated with Aneurin Bevan, the fiery British Labor party politician of the 1950s.

21. Thomas K. Finletter, *Can Representative Government Do the Job?* (New York: Reynal & Hitchcock, 1945), esp. part 3.

22. John Bartlow Martin, *Adlai Stevenson and the World: The Life of Adlai Stevenson* (Garden City, N.Y.: Doubleday, 1977), 84.

23. John Frederick Martin, *Civil Rights and the Crisis of Liberalism: The Democratic Party 1945–1976* (Boulder, Colo.: Westview Press, 1979), 120.

24. Wilson, *Amateur Democrat,* 174.

25. James L. Sundquist, *Politics and Policy: The Eisenhower, Kennedy, and Johnson Years* (Washington, D.C.: Brookings Institution, 1968), 406; and Paul T. David, Ralph M. Goldman, and Richard C. Bain, *The Politics of National Party Conventions* (Washington D.C.: Brookings Institution, 1960), 108.

26. Quoted in D. B. Hardeman and Donald C. Bacon, *Rayburn: A Biography* (Lanham, Md.: Madison Books, 1987), 407.

27. Quoted in John B. Oakes, "Visit with Private Citizen Stevenson," *New York Times Magazine,* November 25, 1956, 30.

28. Gary W. Reichard, "Divisions and Dissent: Democrats and Foreign Policy, 1952–1956," *Political Science Quarterly* 93 (Spring 1978): 66–69.

29. Quoted in Kenneth S. Davis, *A Prophet in His Own Country: The Triumphs and Defeats of Adlai E. Stevenson* (New York: Doubleday, 1957), 439.

30. Quoted in McKeever, *Adlai Stevenson,* 392.

31. Sundquist, *Politics and Policy,* 395.

32. Quoted in Reichard, "Divisions and Dissent," 69.

33. Hubert H. Humphrey to Averell Harriman, November 27, 1956, Democratic folder, Averell Harriman Papers, Special Files: Public Service, New York Files, 1950–1960, Gubernatorial, box 391, Library of Congress (hereafter referred to as LOC).

34. Quoted in Kearns, *Lyndon Johnson,* 140–41.

35. Sidney Hyman, "The Collective Leadership of Paul M. Butler," *Reporter,* December 24, 1959, 9; Herbert S. Parmet, *The Democrats: The Years after FDR,* (New York: Macmillan, 1976), 147; and James L. Sundquist, *Dynamics of the Party System: Alignment and Realignment of the Political Parties in the United States,* 2d ed. (Washington D.C.: Brookings Institution, 1983), 263–68, for an analysis of the national impact of this group.

36. Wilson, *Amateur Democrat,* 113; Evelyn Nieves, "Paul Ziffren, Democratic Leader in California in 1950s, Dies at 77," *New York Times,* June 3, 1991, B10; and Kenneth Reich, "Paul Ziffren, Democratic Power in State, Dies at 77," *Los Angeles Times,* June 1, 1991, 1 and 32.

37. Quoted in Wilson, *Amateur Democrat,* 152.

38. Hyman, "Can a Democrat Win in '60?" 12–13.

39. Ibid., 13.

40. American Political Science Association Committee on Political Parties, *Toward a More Responsible Two-Party System,* 1–2.

41. Ibid., 43.

42. George C. Roberts, *Paul M. Butler: Hoosier Politician and National Political Leader* (Lanham, Md.: University Press of America, 1987), esp.chaps. 2–3.

43. Draft of Butler proposal quoted in ibid., 37.

44. Quoted in ibid., 38.

45. Ibid., 38–39, and Daniel M. Ogden, Jr., "Paul Butler, Party Theory, and the Democratic Party," in John E. Kersell and Marshall W. Conley, eds., *Comparative Political Problems: Britain, United States, and Canada* (Scarborough, Ontario: Prentice-Hall of Canada, 1968), 118.

46. Quoted in Bone, *Party Committees and National Politics,* 67–68.

47. Ibid., 62, and Roberts, *Paul M. Butler,* 104.

48. John J. Sparkman and Wright Patman to Paul M. Butler, August 9, 1956, including "Report on the Condition of Small Business," Democratic National Committee Advisory Committee on Small Business, Democratic folder, Harriman Papers, Special Files: Public Service, New York Files, 1950–1960, Gubernatorial, box 390, LOC.

49. Bone, *Party Committees and National Politics,* 62–63.

50. Quoted in Arlene Lazarowitz, *Years in Exile: The Liberal Democrats, 1950–1959* (New York: Garland, 1988), 128 and 74–76. Also see David, Goldman, and Bain, *Politics of National Party Conventions,* 89, and Rowland Evans and Robert Novak, *Lyndon B. Johnson: The Exercise of Power* (London: George Allen and Unwin: 1966), 160.

51. Interview with Charles Tyroler, June 11, 1991.

52. DNC Executive Committee Resolution, November 27, 1956, DNC Advisory Council Organization Papers, November 27, 1956–September 28, 1957 folder, Galbraith Papers, General Correspondence, box 23, JFKL.

53. Quoted in Bone, *Party Committees and National Politics,* 219.

54. DNC Executive Committee Resolution, November 27, 1956, DNC Advisory Council Organization Papers, November 27, 1956–September 28, 1957 folder, Galbraith Papers, General Correspondence, box 23, JFKL.

55. Russell Baker, "Democrats Name 20 to Chart Program," *New York Times,* December 6, 1956, 31.

56. Russell Baker, "Johnson Spurns Advisory Group," *New York Times,* December 13, 1956, 22.

57. Price, *Bringing Back the Parties,* 267.

58. Quoted in Dwayne Lee Little, "The Political Leadership of Speaker Sam Rayburn, 1940–1961," (Ph.D. dissertation, University of Cincinnati, 1970), 340.

59. Quoted in ibid., 340.

60. Quoted in ibid., 343.

61. Quoted in Bone, *Party Committees and National Politics,* 220.

62. Quoted in Little, "Political Leadership of Speaker Sam Rayburn," 344.

63. Quoted in ibid., 221.

64. Quoted in Lazarowitz, *Years in Exile,* 121.

65. Quoted in ibid., 154.

66. Joseph P. Lasch, *Eleanor: The Years Alone* (New York: Norton, 1972), 202.

67. "Statement by Paul M. Butler, Chairman of the Democratic National Committee," December 18, 1956, DNC Advisory Council Organization Papers, November 27, 1956–September 28, 1957 folder, Galbraith Papers, General Correspondence, box 23, JFKL.

68. Quoted in Goldman, *National Party Chairmen,* 460.

69. Paul M. Butler to Lyndon B. Johnson, Johnson folder, 1960 Chairman Butler's Files (Loretta Larkin, Secretary), DNC Records, box 441, JFKL.

70. "Statement on Its Purposes by the Democratic Advisory Council," January 4, 1957, DNC Advisory Council Organization Papers, November 27, 1956–September 28, 1957 folder, Galbraith Papers, General Correspondence, box 23, JFKL.

71. Quoted in Goldman, *National Party Chairmen,* 460.

72. Sundquist, *Politics and Policy,* 407.

73. "Statement by the Democratic Advisory Council on the Action to Provide for Reasonable Limitation of Debate in the United States Senate," January 4, 1957, DAC Policy Statements, November 27, 1956–September 15, 1957 folder, John F. Kennedy Papers, Senate Files, Pre-Presidential Papers, box 924, JFKL.

74. Bone, *Party Committees and National Politics,* 223.

75. "Resolution on Civil Rights Adopted by the Democratic Advisory Council," February 16, 1957, DAC Policy Statements, November 27, 1956–September 15, 1957 folder, Kennedy Papers, Senate Files, Pre-Presidential Papers, box 924, JFKL.

76. "DNC Resolution on Advisory Council," February 15, 1957, DNC Advisory Committee Organization Papers, November 27, 1956–September 28, 1957 folder, Galbraith Papers, General Correspondence, box 23, JFKL.

77. Bone, *Party Committees and National Politics,* 224.

78. Interview with Charles Tyroler, June 11, 1991.

79. J. B. Martin, *Adlai Stevenson,* 400; DNC Internal Memo, Finance Committee, Fund Raising folder, 1960 Chairman Butler's Files (Loretta Larkin, Secretary), DNC Records, box 440, JFKL, and DNC Internal Memo, Charles Tyroler II to Paul M. Butler, March 5, 1959, Charles Tyroler folder, 1960 Chairman Butler's Files (Evelyn Chavoor, Administrative Assistant), DNC Records, box 446, JFKL.

80. Roberts, *Paul M. Butler,* 58–59, 112; Parmet, *Democrats,* 154; and Cotter and Hennessey, *Politics without Power,* 224.

81. Dean Acheson to Harry S. Truman, June 5, 1957, in David S. McLellan and David C. Acheson, eds., *Among Friends: Personal Letters of Dean Acheson* (New York: Dodd, Mead, 1980), 123–24.

82. Interview with John Kenneth Galbraith, December 20, 1990; interview with Charles Tyroler, June 11, 1991; Walter Isaacson and Evan Thomas, *The Wise Men: Six Friends and the World They Made* (New York: Simon and Schuster, 1986), 583; and Lazarowitz, *Years in Exile,* 142.

83. Dean Acheson to Mrs. Jack Chadderdon, November 4, 1957, quoted in Douglas Brinkley, "After the Creation: Dean Acheson and American Foreign Policy" (Unpublished manuscript), chap. 2.

84. "The Democratic Approach to Foreign Policy and United States Defense," DAC Statement, October 19, 1957, DAC Policy Statements, October 11, 1957–February 16, 1958 folder, Kennedy Papers, Senate Files, Pre-Presidential Papers, box 924, JFKL.

85. Lawrence Freedman, *The Evolution of Nuclear Strategy* (New York: St. Martin's Press, 1983), 139–140.

86. "Statement on President Eisenhower's Security Speeches," DAC Statement, November 16, 1957, p. 1, DAC Policy Statements, October 11, 1957–February 16, 1958 folder, Kennedy Papers, Senate Files, Pre-Presidential Papers, box 924, JFKL.

87. Ibid., 5.

88. "America's Present Danger and What We Must Do About It," DAC Statement, February 1, 1958, Advisory Council Press Releases, 1957–1958 folder, 1960 Chairman Butler's Files (Evelyn Chavoor, Administrative Assistant), DNC Records, box 449, JFKL. In an interesting historical parallel, the term *present danger* would be used again in the late 1970s by the Committee on the Present Danger. This group was established by, among others, Paul Nitze, vice-chairman of the DAC's foreign policy committee, and Charles Tyroler II, the DAC's executive director, to criticize what they considered to be the inadequate foreign and military policies of the Carter administration. The committee also operated out of the same offices as the DAC.

89. The Advisory Council of the Democratic National Committee, *Democratic Programs for*

Action: Foreign and Military Policy for Peace and Security, pamphlet 1, "Where We Are: The World of Today and How It Got That Way," May 1958, 8, Advisory Council Pamphlets and Brochures, 1954–1960 folder, 1960 Chairman Butler's Files (Evelyn Chavoor, Administrative Assistant), DNC Records, box 449, JFKL.

90. "The Decision in 1960: The Need to Elect a Democratic President," DAC Statement, December 6, 1959, DAC Policy Statements, August 19, 1959–March 15, 1960 folder, Kennedy Papers, Senate Files, Pre-Presidential Papers, box 924, JFKL.

91. The Advisory Council of the Democratic National Committee, *Democratic Programs for Action: Foreign and Military Policy for Peace and Security,* pamphlet 4, "The Military Forces We Need and How to Get Them," July 1959, DAC Policy Statements, April 30, 1958–June 17, 1959 folder, Kennedy Papers, Senate Files, Pre-Presidential Papers, box 924, JFKL and U.S. Department of Commerce, *Historical Statistics of the United States: Colonial Times to 1970,* pt. 2 (Washington, D.C.: Government Printing Office, 1976), 1116.

92. Interview with John Kenneth Galbraith, December 20, 1990.

93. Stevenson quoted in Lazarowitz, *Years in Exile,* 143.

94. Interview with John Kenneth Galbraith, December 20, 1990. In his memoirs, Galbraith says that Harriman told Acheson, "You know, Dean, I don't agree with your declarations of war" (Galbraith, *A Life in Our Times* [Boston: Houghton Mifflin, 1981], 359). Acheson was often assisted in these battles by Truman, who still had great prestige and respect in the party. According to Charles Tyroler, the DAC met during the weekend and most foreign policy discussions came up on Sundays. Often, Truman would get up and say, "I'm going to church with the boss [Mrs. Truman]. You go ahead and talk about this [Acheson's statement], but I read it on the train out here and I thought it was just fine. But you guys go ahead and chew on it." Only occasionally would other members of the DAC wish to disagree with the former president (Interview with Charles Tyroler, June 11, 1991).

95. See Galbraith, *A Life in Our Times,* 358–60, and Arthur M. Schlesinger, Jr., *A Thousand Days: John F. Kennedy in the White House,* (Boston: Houghton Mifflin, 1965), 299–301.

96. J. B. Martin, *Adlai Stevenson,* 402.

97. The Advisory Council of the Democratic National Committee, *Democratic Programs for Action: Foreign and Military Policy for Peace and Security,* pamphlet 5, "A Policy for the West toward Underdeveloping Countries," April 1960, DAC Policy Statements, April 8–May 22, 1960 folder, Kennedy Papers, Senate Files, Pre-Presidential Papers, box 924, JFKL.

98. "The United Nations and Disarmament," DAC Administrative Committee Statement, August 19, 1959, DAC Policy Statements, August 19, 1959–March 15, 1960 folder, Kennedy Papers, Senate Files, Pre-Presidential Papers, box 924, JFKL.

99. The Committee on Science and Technology of the Democratic Advisory Council, *Science and Technology,* pamphlet 4, "Nuclear Tests and National Security," 9 and 3, March 1960, DAC Policy Statements, August 19, 1959-March 15, 1960 folder, Kennedy Papers, Senate Files, Pre-Presidential Papers, box 924, JFKL.

100. The Committee on Science and Technology of the Democratic Advisory Council, *Science and Technology,* pamphlet 1, "A National Peace Agency," 7–8, December 1959, DAC Policy Statements, August 19, 1959–March 15, 1960 folder, Kennedy Papers, Senate Files, Pre-Presidential Papers, box 924, JFKL.

101. Interview with John Kenneth Galbraith, December 20, 1990.

102. Lazarowitz, *Years in Exile,* 156–57; Iwan Morgan, *Eisenhower versus "The Spenders": The Eisenhower Administration, the Democrats, and the Budget* (New York: St. Martin's Press, 1989), 34–37, 154–56, 162–163; Gary W. Reichard, "The Domestic Politics of National Security," in Norman A. Graebner, ed., *National Security: Its Theory and Practice, 1945–1960* (New York: Oxford University Press, 1986), 266; Schlesinger, *A Thousand Days,* 300–301; Steven M.

Gillon, *Politics and Vision: The ADA and American Liberalism, 1947–1985* (New York: Oxford University Press, 1987), 120–21; and Kent M. Beck, "What Was Liberalism in the 1950s?" *Political Science Quarterly* 102 (Summer 1987): 249–58.

103. Morgan, *Eisenhower versus "The Spenders,"* 42.

104. "Economic Growth, Tight Money, and the Cost of Living," DAC Statement, October 20, 1957, 6–7, DNC Advisory Council Press Releases, 1957 folder, Galbraith Papers, General Correspondence, box 23, JFKL.

105. "The Democratic Task during the Next Two Years," DAC Statement, December 7, 1958, 7, DNC Advisory Council Organization Papers, October 1–December 31, 1958 folder, Galbraith Papers, General Correspondence, box 23, JFKL.

106. "A Program to Meet the Recession," DAC Statement, April 30, 1958, DNC Advisory Council Press Releases, 1958 folder, Galbraith Papers, General Correspondence, box 23, JFKL.

107. Morgan, *Eisenhower versus "The Spenders,"* 43.

108. "Can America Afford Increased Federal Expenditures for Essential National Purposes?" DAC Statement, February 13, 1958, 5, DNC Advisory Committee Press Releases, 1958 folder, Galbraith Papers, General Correspondence, box 23, JFKL.

109. Morgan, *Eisenhower versus "The Spenders,"* 45.

110. John Kenneth Galbraith to Leon H. Keyserling, April 15, 1958, DNC Advisory Council, March 1–June 30, 1958 folder, Galbraith Papers, General Correspondence, box 22, JFKL. Emphasis in original.

111. Leon H. Keyserling to John Kenneth Galbraith, April 18, 1958, DNC Advisory Council, March 1–June 30, 1958 folder, Galbraith Papers, General Correspondence, box 22, JFKL.

112. Leon H. Keyserling to Paul Ziffren, April 30, 1958, DNC Advisory Council, March 1–June 30, 1958 folder, Galbraith Papers, General Correspondence, box 22, JFKL.

113. Ibid.

114. For a fuller explanation of this debate, see Gillon, *Politics and Vision,* 124–27.

115. Morgan, *Eisenhower versus "The Spenders,"* 46.

116. For an explanation of Keyserling's views, see Morgan, *Eisenhower versus "The Spenders,"* 47; Leon Keyserling, "Growth without Inflation: What We Must Do Because We Can," Draft Submitted to the DAC Economic Advisory Committee, March 5, 1959, DNC Advisory Committee, Economic Policy Committee Draft Statements, June 4–September 15, 1959 folder, Galbraith Papers, General Correspondence, box 23, JFKL; and Leon H. Keyserling to Charles Tyroler II, March 10, 1959, Leon Keyserling, January 6–September 24, 1959 folder, Galbraith Papers, General Correspondence, box 38, JFKL.

117. The sections of the Galbraith Papers concerned with the DAC are littered with letters criticizing Keyserling on this point. See the Leon Keyserling, January 6–September 24, 1959 folder, box 38, and the Economic Policy Committee Draft Statements, June 4–September 15, 1959, General Correspondence, box 23, JFKL.

118. Morgan, *Eisenhower versus "The Spenders,"* 127–51, esp. 134–36.

119. Interview with Charles Tyroler, June 11, 1991.

120. Lazarowitz, *Years in Exile,* 151; and Morgan, *Eisenhower versus "The Spenders,"* 172.

121. Morgan, *Eisenhower versus "The Spenders,"* 48. Also see pp. 173 and 180–81.

122. Gary W. Reichard, "Democrats, Civil Rights, and Electoral Strategies," *Congress and the Presidency* 13 (Spring 1986): 60–61, 63–65.

123. Quoted in ibid., 64.

124. Ibid., 63.

125. Hubert H. Humphrey to Paul M. Butler, February 7, 1956, Humphrey folder, 1960 Chairman Butler's Files (Loretta Larkin, Secretary), DNC Records, box 441, JFKL.

126. Harold W. Stanley and Richard G. Niemi, eds., *Vital Statistics on American Politics,* 2d ed. (Washington, D.C.: Congressional Quarterly Press, 1990), 98.

127. Charles A. H. Thomson and Frances M. Shattuck, *The 1956 Presidential Campaign* (Washington, D.C.: Brookings Institution, 1960), 352–53.

128. Thomas L. Stokes, "Revolt of Northern Democrats," *Washington Evening Star,* December 11, 1956, quoted in Reichard, "Democrats, Civil Rights, and Electoral Strategies," 66.

129. Roberts, *Paul M. Butler,* 92.

130. Quoted in Reichard, "Democrats, Civil Rights, and Electoral Strategies," 65.

131. "Statement by the Democratic Advisory Council on the Action to Provide for Reasonable Limitation of Debate in the United States Senate," January 4, 1957, DAC Policy Statements, November 27, 1956–September 15, 1957 folder, Kennedy Papers, Senate Files, Pre-Presidential Papers, box 924, JFKL.

132. Reichard, "Democrats, Civil Rights, and Electoral Strategies," 68.

133. Robert Frederick Burk, *The Eisenhower Administration and Black Civil Rights* (Knoxville: University of Tennessee Press, 1984), 177–85.

134. Dissenting from this statement were the three Southerners on the DNC Executive Committee who served ex oficio on the DAC : Benjamin Everett of North Carolina, Mrs. Lennard Thomas of Alabama, and Camille F. Gravel, Jr., of Louisiana.

135. Allen Drury, "Democrats Term President Remiss," *New York Times,* September 16, 1957, 1, 21.

136. "Statement by the Democratic Advisory Council on the Little Rock School Controversy," September 15, 1957, Advisory Committee Press Releases, April 11, 1957–July 16, 1958 folder, 1960 Chairman Butler's Files (Evelyn Chavoor, Administrative Assistant), DNC Records, box 449, JFKL.

137. Reichard, "Democrats, Civil Rights, and Electoral Strategies," 69.

138. "Statement on the Civil Rights Act of 1957," DAC Statement, October 20, 1957, DAC Policy Statements, October 11, 1957–February 16, 1958 folder, Kennedy Papers, Senate Files, Pre-Presidential Papers, box 924, JFKL.

139. "The Current Legislative Situation," DAC Statement, June 15, 1959, DAC Policy Statements, April 30, 1958–June 17, 1959 folder, Kennedy Papers, Senate Files, Pre-Presidential Papers, box 924, JFKL.

140. "Civil Rights in the Second Session of the 86th Congress," DAC Statement, March 15, 1960, DAC Policy Statements, August 19, 1959–March 15, 1960 folder, Kennedy Papers, Senate Files, Pre-Presidential Papers, box 924, JFKL.

141. "Civil Rights," DAC Advisory Committee on Civil Rights Statement, April 22, 1960, DAC Policy Statements, April 8–May 22, 1960 folder, Kennedy Papers, Senate Files, Pre-Presidential Papers, box 924, JFKL.

142. Interview with Charles Tyroler, June 11, 1991.

143. Parmet, *Democrats,* 159.

144. Quoted in Lazarowitz, *Years in Exile,* 152.

145. Sundquist, *Politics and Policy,* 414.

146. Lazarowitz, *Years in Exile,* 154.

147. Cotter and Hennessey, *Politics without Power,* 168; and Ithiel de Sola Pool and Robert Abelson, "The Simulmatics Project," *Public Opinion Quarterly* 25 (Summer 1961): 167–83.

148. Daniel M. Ogden, Jr., "Party Theory and Political Reality Inside the Democratic Party" (Paper delivered at the 1960 Annual Meeting of the American Political Science Association, New York City; available from Ann Arbor, Mich.: University Microfilm), 5–7; and Roberts, *Paul M. Butler,* 133–46.

149. Sundquist, *Politics and Policy,* 411.

150. Ibid., 411–15.

151. Interview with John Kenneth Galbraith, December 20, 1990.

152. Parmet, Democrats, 161.

153. Charles Tyroler to Averell Harriman, November 12, 1956, Democratic Advisory Council folder, Harriman Papers, Special Files: Public Service, New York Files, 1950–1960, Gubernatorial, box 390, LOC.

154. Quoted in Cotter and Hennessy, *Politics without Power,* 223.

155. Charles Tyroler to Averell Harriman, November 12, 1956, Democratic Advisory Council folder, Harriman Papers, Special Files: Public Service, New York Files, 1950–1960, Gubernatorial, box 390, LOC.

156. Parmet, *Democrats,* 161.

157. Ogden, "Party Theory and Political Reality."

158. Interview with Orville Freeman, December 11, 1990.

CHAPTER 3

1. Stephen E. Ambrose, *Nixon: The Education of a Politician, 1913–1962* (New York: Simon and Schuster, 1987), chaps. 9–14.

2. A. James Reichley, "Party Politics and American Democracy" (Unpublished manuscript). Reichley, *The Life of the Parties: A History of American Political Parties* (New York: The Free Press, 1992) offers a revised version of this manuscript.

3. Reichley, "Party Politics and American Democracy."

4. Quoted in Lewis Chester, Godfrey Hodgson, and Bruce Page, *An American Melodrama: The Presidential Campaign of 1968* (New York: The Viking Press, 1969), 746. Actually, a switch of just 12,000 in five states (Hawaii, Illinois, Missouri, New Mexico, and Nevada) would have thrown the election to Nixon (Republican National Committee Research Division, "The 1960 Elections," April 1961, *Papers of the Republican Party,* pt. 2: Research Division Reports, Paul L. Kesaris, ed., [Frederick, Md.: University Publications of America], reel 2, frames 1000–1053; hereafter referred to as *PRP,* pt. 2).

5. Virginius Dabney, "What the GOP Is Doing in the South," *Harper's,* May 1963, 94. For a more detailed explanation of this strategy, see Robert D. Novak, *The Agony of the GOP, 1964* (New York: Macmillan Co., 1965), 8.

6. Thruston B. Morton, "Leadership Problems in the Opposition Party," in Paul T. David, ed., *The Presidential Election and Transition, 1960–1961* (Washington, D.C.: Brookings Institution, 1961), 292.

7. Ambrose, *Nixon,* 606–7 and Reichley, "Party Politics and American Democracy." One analysis of the various Illinois election recounts concludes that although Nixon was undercounted in Chicago, it was not by enough to have swung the outcome. In fact, most of the voting irregularities occurred in the Cook County State Attorney's race, a position of far more importance to the Chicago machine than president of the United States. See Edmund F. Kallina, "Was the 1960 Presidential Election Stolen? The Case of Illinois," *Presidential Studies Quarterly* 15 (Winter 1985): 113–18.

8. Minutes of the RNC Executive Committee, Executive Session, January 5, 1961, Washington D.C., *Papers of the Republican Party,* pt. 1: Meetings of the Republican National Committee, 1911–1980; Series B: 1960–1980, Paul L. Kesaris, ed. (Frederick, Md.: University Publications of America), reel 1, frames 130–38 (hereafter referred to as *PRP,* pt. 1).

9. Ibid., frame 89.

10. David W. Reinhard, *The Republican Right since 1945* (Lexington: University Press of Kentucky, 1983), 168.

11. Minutes of the RNC Meeting, January 6, 1961, Washington D.C., *PRP,* pt. 1, reel 1, frame 309.

12. Vera Glasser, "Republicans Stage Non-Partisan Political Relations Program That Works," *Public Relations Journal,* November 1961, 26. Though the pamphlet was officially nonpartisan, most examples of voter fraud came from Chicago newspapers, a point that was probably not lost by many.

13. Robert L. Johnson, "Republican Problem: 'We've Got to Wake Up in the Big Cities,'" *U.S. News and World Report,* April 23, 1962, 68–69. Also see, Minutes of the RNC Meeting, January 6, 1961, Washington D.C., *PRP,* pt. 1, reel 1, frames 299–306.

14. Interview with Sylvia Hermann, February 8, 1991.

15. Interview with William Prendergast, February 28, 1991.

16. Interviews with Robert Novak, March 13, 1991, and with Arthur Peterson, March 27, 1991.

17. Minutes of the RNC Meeting, January 6, 1961, Washington D.C., *PRP,* pt. 1, reel 1, frame 300.

18. Ibid., frame 299.

19. Johnson, "Republican Problem," 69.

20. Minutes of the RNC Meeting, January 6, 1961, Washington D.C., *PRP,* pt. 1, reel 1, frames 307–8.

21. Ibid., frame 308.

22. This seems to have begun with his expulsion from college for stuffing the ballot box in a campus May Queen contest (Joel Marshall Fisher, "The Role of the National Party Chairman in American Politics" [Ph.D. dissertation, Claremont University, 1969], 147).

23. Jonathan Rose, "GOP in Ohio: Anatomy of a Victory," *Advance,* April 1961, 20, and David S. Broder, "Bliss Rides the Elephant," *New York Times Magazine,* March 21, 1965, 52.

24. He was Barry Goldwater's first choice to become RNC chair when Thruston Morton stepped down later in 1961.

25. Ray C. Bliss, "The Role of the State Chairman," in James M. Cannon, ed, *Politics U.S.A.: A Practical Guide to the Winning of Public Office* (Garden City, N.Y.: Doubleday, 1960), 161.

26. John H. Fenton, *Midwest Politics* (New York: Holt, Rinehart, and Winston, 1966), 133.

27. Ray C. Bliss, "Report of the Committee on Big City Politics," Minutes of the RNC Meeting, June 1, 1961, Chicago, Illinois, *PRP,* pt. 1, reel 1, frames 464–67.

28. Ibid., frame 464. COPE (Committee on Political Education) is the political arm of the AFL-CIO.

29. Ibid., frame 468.

30. "Report of the Committee on Big City Politics: Summary of Major Recommendations," State Chairman's Advisory Council Files, 1963–1967, box 91, RNC Papers, National Archives (photocopy).

31. Quoted in Novak, *Agony of the GOP, 1964,* 56.

32. Ibid.

33. Quoted in ibid., 57.

34. Ibid., 59.

35. Quoted in ibid., 58.

36. Ibid.

37. Ibid., 59.

38. Ibid., 65.

39. Nicol C. Rae, *The Decline and Fall of the Liberal Republicans: From 1952 to the Present* (New York: Oxford University Press, 1989), 69.

40. Bernard Cosman, "Presidential Republicanism in the South, 1960," *Journal of Politics* 24 (May 1962): 303. Kennedy's share of the southern vote may have been lower than indicated by the rough totals, since in Alabama the total Democratic vote of 324,050 represents the combined vote for five Kennedy electors and six unpledged electors who eventually gave their support to Senator Harry F. Byrd. See Svend Petersen, *A Statistical History of the American Presidential Elections* (New York: Frederick Ungar, 1963), 112–13.

41. George L. Grassmuck, "Emerging Republicanism in the South" (Paper delivered at the 1964 Annual Meeting of the American Political Science Association, Chicago, Illinois), 10–11.

42. Novak, *Agony of the GOP, 1964,* 14.

43. Minutes of the RNC Meeting, January 6, 1961, Washington D.C., *PRP,* pt. 1, reel 1, frame 283. Actually, Goldwater had planned a scathing criticism of how liberal Republicans had lost the election but was persuaded to tone down his presentation in the interests of party unity (Novak, *Agony of the GOP, 1964,* 38–39).

44. V. O. Key, Jr., *Southern Politics in State and Nation* (Knoxville: University of Tennessee Press, 1949), 277.

45. Ibid., 292.

46. Paul T. David, Ralph M. Goldman, and Richard C. Bain, *The Politics of National Party Conventions* (Washington D.C.: Brookings Institution, 1960), 166–67.

47. Ibid., 167–68, 180–81.

48. Reichley, "Party Politics and American Democracy."

49. George F. Gilder and Bruce K. Chapman, *The Party That Lost Its Head* (New York: Knopf, 1966), 58.

50. Interview with Clarke Reed, February 22, 1991.

51. Interview with Hal Dunham, March 11, 1991.

52. Quoted in John H. Kessel, *The Goldwater Coalition: Republican Strategies in 1964* (Indianapolis: Bobs-Merrill, 1968), 40. These efforts at extolling the virtues of a two-party system were said to have unintended consequences. Virginia Hooper, a former RNC member from Mississippi, tells the story that during one election her husband, also a Republican party official, was asked to give a speech at Bradley Box, a small crossroads general store and post office that served as the local polling place. Mr. Hooper was surprised to find that nearly every voter in the district turned out to hear him discuss why two parties were better than one. On election night, Mr. Hooper, interested to see if his speech had had any effect on the voters of Bradley Box, called up the local election official to get the results. The official replied, "It's the strangest thing. None of the votes counted. They all voted for two parties" (Interview with Virginia Hooper, February 25, 1991).

53. Interview with Clarke Reed, February 22, 1991.

54. Theodore H. White, *The Making of the President, 1964* (New York: Antheneum, 1965), 136.

55. Interview with Hal Dunham, March 11, 1991.

56. Grassmuck, "Emerging Republicanism in the South," 13.

57. Interviews with Clarke Reed, February 22, 1991, and with Virginia Hooper, February 25, 1991.

58. Interview with Virginia Hooper, February 25, 1991.

59. Ibid; interview with Ellie Peterson, February 22, 1991; and Jane Kottmeir, "Operation Dixie Far from Being Passe," *Washington Star,* October 6, 1957, D18–19.

60. Interview with Virginia Hooper, February 25, 1991.

61. Interviews with Clarke Reed, February 22, 1991, and with Wirt Yerger Jr., former Mississippi Republican state chairman, February 25, 1991.

62. Karl A. Lamb, "Under One Roof: Barry Goldwater's Campaign Staff," in Bernard

Cosman and Robert J. Huckshorn, eds., *Republican Politics: The 1964 Campaign and Its After-math for the Republican Party* (New York: Praeger, 1968), 14; Grassmuck, "Emerging Republicanism in the South," 13; and interview with Hal Dunham, March 11, 1991, and Grassmuck, "Emerging Republicanism in the South," 13.

63. Philip S. Wilder, Jr., "Meade Alcorn and the 1958 Election," in Paul Tillet, ed., *Cases on Party Organization* (New York: McGraw-Hill, 1963), 104. For a detailed analysis of the development of a local Republican party organization in the South during the 1950s, see Kenneth N. Vines, "Two Parties for Shreveport," in Tillett, ed. *Cases on Party Organization,* 183–210.

64. Theodore H. White, *The Making of the President, 1960* (New York: Antheneum, 1961), 202–5.

65. Quoted in ibid., 204.

66. Quoted in Gilder and Chapman, *The Party That Lost Its Head,* 52.

67. Republican National Committee Research Division, "The 1960 Elections" April 1961, *PRP,* pt. 2, frame 981.

68. Ibid.

69. Quoted in White, *Making of the President, 1964,* 89.

70. For a detailed, insider account of this process, see F. Clifton White, *Suite 3505: The Story of the Draft Goldwater Movement* (New Rochelle, N.Y.: Arlington House, 1967). A more analytic account is provided in Kessel, *Goldwater Coalition.*

71. "Goldwater Supporters Hold Key Professional GOP Posts," *Congressional Quarterly,* October 11, 1963, 1770.

72. Rae, *Decline and Fall of the Liberal Republicans,* 68–69.

73. Reinhard, *The Republican Right since 1945,* 168, and Numan V. Bartley and Hugh D. Graham, *Southern Politics and the Second Reconstruction* (Baltimore: Johns Hopkins University Press, 1975), 95–97.

74. Quoted in Gilder and Chapman, *The Party That Lost Its Head,* 56–57.

75. Interview with Bruce Chapman, February 25, 1991.

76. Interview with John Kessel, March 5, 1991.

77. "Republicans Look to South," *U.S. News and World Report,* December 11, 1961, 79–80; Meg Greenfield, "Senator Goldwater and the Negro," *Reporter,* October 8, 1964, 27; Barbara Carter, "Who Was Bill Miller?" *Reporter,* November 5, 1964, 24; and John F. Bibby, *The Republicans and the Metropolis: The Role of National Party Leadership* (Chicago: Center for Research in Urban Government, Loyola University, 1967), 16.

78. Lamb, "Under One Roof," 16. Gilder and Chapman state that in 1963, Miller claimed to have spent $600,000 on the project. The data on RNC internal budgets is spotty at best, so it is impossible to determine which claim is correct (Gilder and Chapman, *The Party That Lost Its Head,* 61). Lamb also reports that in this same period only $250,000 was spent on the Big City Program (Lamb, "Under One Roof," 14).

79. Document from the Republican National Finance Committee Meeting, Chicago, Illinois, January 21, 1965 (photocopy). I am indebted to Herbert Alexander for providing me with this document.

80. Grassmuck, "Emerging Republicanism in the South," 12.

81. Interview with Hal Dunham, March 11, 1991.

82. Grassmuck, "Emerging Republicanism in the South," 12–13.

83. "Political Parties Plan New Strategies," *Nation's Business,* December 1963, 50–51.

84. Interview with Wirt Yerger, Jr., February 25, 1991.

85. Gilder and Chapman, *The Party That Lost Its Head,* 63.

86. Ward Just, "'This Schizophrenia Business' Comes to the GOP," *Reporter,* December 20, 1962, 23.

87. Bartley and Graham, *Southern Politics and the Second Reconstruction,* 101.

88. Walter Dean Burnham, "The Alabama Senatorial Election of 1962: Return of Inter-Party Competition," *Journal of Politics* 26 (November 1964): 812.

89. Reinhard, *The Republican Right since 1945,* 169.

90. Quoted in Just, "'This Schizophrenia Business,'" 23.

91. Quoted in Reinhard, *The Republican Right since 1945,* 167–69.

92. Quoted in Just, "'This Schizophrenia Business,'" 24.

93. Minutes of the RNC Meeting, December 7, 1962, Washington D.C., *PRP,* pt. 1, reel 2, frame 538.

94. Ibid., frames 538–39.

95. "Goldwater Supporters Hold Key Professional GOP Posts," 1771.

96. Quoted in George Brown Tindall, *The Disruption of the Solid South* (New York: Norton, 1972), 60.

97. Quoted in Bartley and Graham, *Southern Politics and the Second Reconstruction,* 97.

98. Quoted in Burnham, "Alabama Senatorial Election of 1962," 810.

99. Quoted in Just, "'This Schizophrenia Business,'" 24.

100. Snodgrass and other Georgia moderates were deposed by more conservative and segregationist Goldwater supporters at the 1964 state party convention. (Stephen Hess and David S. Broder, *The Republican Establishment: The Present and Future of the GOP* [New York: Harper and Row, 1967], 335–36).

101. Lee Potter, "GOP's Southern Drive," *New York Times,* May 2, 1963, 36. Potter himself seems to have had divided feelings on the race issue. At the same time that he was encouraging and supporting segregationist candidates, he was also working to elect racially liberal Republicans like A. Linwood Holton. Holton, who ran unsuccessfully for governor of Virginia in 1965 and successfully in 1969, recalls that Potter would go with him to campaign in black neighborhoods but that Potter would always stay on the other side of the street while he mingled with the voters (Interview with A. Linwood Holton, December 12, 1990).

102. Just, "'This Schizophrenia Business,'" 24.

103. Quoted in David S. Broder, "Strategists for '62 and '64," *New York Times Magazine,* October 15, 1961, 118.

104. Interview with Clarke Reed, February 22, 1991.

105. Quoted in "A Special Correspondent," "Mississippi Challenge: The Republicans against History," *Advance,* Fall 1963, 26.

106. Novak, *Agony of the GOP, 1964,* 177–79.

107. Cornelius P. Cotter and Bernard C. Hennessy, *Politics without Power: The National Party Committees* (New York: Atherton, 1964), 177, and Herbert Alexander, *Financing the 1960 Election* (Princeton, N.J.: Citizens' Research Foundation, 1962), 85.

108. This pattern is described in Alexander Heard, *The Costs of Democracy* (Chapel Hill: University of North Carolina Press, 1960), 69.

109. Minutes of the RNC Executive Committee, February 23–24, 1962, Washington D.C., *PRP,* pt. 1, reel 1, frame 945.

110. See Heard, *Costs of Democracy,* 249–58, and Dom Bonafede, "Part Science, Part Art, Part Hokum, Direct Mail Now a Key Campaign Tool," *National Journal,* July 31, 1982, 1332–36, for various descriptions of these programs.

111. The RNFC was the umbrella finance committee for the RNC and both Republican congressional campaign committees.

112. Cotter and Hennessy, *Politics without Power,* 185.

113. That the mailings were sent to states only in the South and the West might suggest that the RNC was trying to find sources of funds outside of the more liberal East.

114. Cotter and Hennessy, *Politics without Power*, 185.

115. "Report on the Sustaining Membership Program," Minutes of the RNC Executive Committee, January 8, 1964, Washington, D.C., *PRP*, pt. 1, reel 3, frame 264.

116. Ibid.

117. Hess and Broder, *The Republican Establishment*, 60, and Herbert Alexander, *Financing the 1964 Election* (Princeton, N.J.: Citizens' Research Foundation, 1966), 71. The list of car wash cloth buyers was the most successful of those used by the RNC, even more so than lists of registered Republicans, businessmen, prominent conservatives, or wealthy individuals. The reason is that the people on the list were mostly upper-income suburbanites who had already proven responsive to direct mail appeals (Richard Armstrong, *The Next Hurrah: The Communications Revolution in American Politics* [New York: Beech Tree Books, 1988], 77–78).

118. Heard, *Costs of Democracy*, 289–90.

119. Ibid., 51, and Hess and Broder, *The Republican Establishment*, 61.

120. Heard, *Costs of Democracy*, 288, and document from the Republican National Finance Committee Meeting, Chicago, Illinois, January 21, 1965 (photocopy).

121. The national parties in this period did not usually release information about their quotas. Bone states that they were based upon six factors: electoral vote, Republican vote in last presidential election, population, personal income tax, number of occupied dwellings, and purchasing power. Quotas based upon these criteria would tend to place a heavier assessment on the large, northeastern states (Hugh A. Bone, *Party Committees and National Politics* [Seattle: University of Washington Press, 1958], 98–99). Heard reports that in the 1950s, New York's quota contribution was about 15 percent of the national Republican party total (Heard, *Costs of Democracy*, 215). For various descriptions of the prominence of East Coast financiers in Republican fundraising, see Heard, *Costs of Democracy*, esp. 265–66 and 340; and George Thayer, *Who Shakes the Money Tree?: American Campaign Finance Practices from 1789 to the Present* (New York: Simon and Schuster, 1973).

122. Interview with J. William Middendorf, April 3, 1991.

123. Hess and Broder, *The Republican Establishment*, 61.

124. Quoted in Cotter and Hennessy, *Politics without Power*, 164.

125. Gilder and Chapman, *The Party That Lost Its Head*, 59.

126. Ibid., 60

127. Greenfield, "Senator Goldwater and the Negro," 27.

128. Interview with Grant Reynolds, March 13, 1991.

129. Greenfield, "Senator Goldwater and the Negro," 28.

130. Quoted in Just, "'This Schizophrenia Business,'" 24.

131. Quoted in George Bailey, "A Republican Footnote," *Reporter*, May 23, 1963, 14.

132. Interview with Grant Reynolds, March 13, 1991.

133. Ralph M. Goldman, *The National Party Chairmen and Committees: Factionalism at the Top* (Armonk, N.Y.: Sharpe, 1990), 530.

134. Quoted in Novak, *Agony of the GOP, 1964*, 39.

135. Russell Baker, "The GOP Faces a Three-Headed Dilemma," *New York Times Magazine*, May 7, 1961, 120.

136. Minutes of the RNC Meeting, January 6, 1961, Washington D.C., *PRP*, pt. 1, reel 1, frame 206.

137. Ibid., frame 402.

138. Ibid., frames 396–403.

139. Felix Belair, Jr., "Eisenhower Group Will Scrutinize Kennedy Policies," *New York Times*, May 12, 1961, 1, 11.

140. Reinhard, *The Republican Right since 1945*, 165.

141. Stephen E. Ambrose, *Eisenhower: The President* (New York: Simon and Schuster, 1984), 644–45.

142. Quoted in Tom Wicker, "Eisenhower Bids Business Aid GOP as Its Party," *New York Times,* July 1, 1962, 4.

143. Minutes of the All-Republican Conference, Gettysburg, Pennsylvania, June 30, 1962, *PRP,* pt. 1, reel 2, frames 467–469.

144. Novak, *Agony of the GOP, 1964,* 75.

145. Quoted in Cotter and Hennessy, *Politics without Power,* 205.

146. Quoted in Gilder and Chapman, *The Party That Lost Its Head,* 100. Goldwater's image of being "led down the path" to destruction recalls Everett Dirksen's famous speech at the 1952 convention where he publicly admonished Thomas Dewey for leading the Republican party down the path to defeat.

147. Ambrose, *Eisenhower,* 644–45, and Rae, *Decline and Fall of the Liberal Republicans,* 67–68.

148. Quoted in Cotter and Hennessy, *Politics without Power,* 208.

149. Quoted in Hess and Broder, *The Republican Establishment,* 337.

150. Reichley, "Party Politics and American Democracy."

CHAPTER 4

1. Dewey wrote the FBI report on the urban riots that Johnson used to help defuse the law-and-order thrust of the Goldwater campaign. See Kenneth O'Reilly, "The FBI and the Politics of the Riots, 1964–1968," *Journal of American History* 75 (June 1988): 91–114.

2. Quoted in Joseph R. L. Sterne, "The Old Guard Returns," *Reporter,* February 11, 1965, 28.

3. Karl Hess, *In A Cause That Will Triumph* (Garden City, N.Y.: Doubleday, 1967), 135.

4. Stephen Hess and David S. Broder, *The Republican Establishment: The Present and Future of the GOP* (New York: Harper and Row, 1967), 39; Jerald Ter Horst, "The Grenier Plan for the GOP," *Reporter,* October 8, 1964, 24–26; and Karl A. Lamb, "Under One Roof: Barry Goldwater's Campaign Staff," in Bernard Cosman and Robert J. Huckshorn, eds., *Republican Politics: The 1964 Campaign and Its Aftermath for the Republican Party* (New York: Praeger, 1968), 21–40.

5. Ter Horst, "Grenier Plan for the GOP," 24, and Lamb, "Under One Roof," 23–24.

6. Quoted in Ter Horst, "Grenier Plan for the GOP," 26.

7. "Moderate Republicans Organize as Campaign Ends," *Congressional Quarterly,* October 30, 1964, 2579–80.

8. Lamb, "Under One Roof," 43.

9. Quoted in Cabell Phillips, "Burch's Removal Sought in Capital," *New York Times,* November 6, 1964, 20.

10. Quoted in "Republican Attacks on Party Leadership Intensify," *Congressional Quarterly,* November 13, 1964, 2673.

11. Quoted in "Alcorn Declares GOP Must Start To Rebuild 'Image'," *New York Times,* November 6, 1964, 21.

12. Quoted in "Republican Attacks on Party Leadership Intensify," 2671.

13. Earl Mazo, "$1.2 Million Left in GOP Treasury after Campaign," *New York Times,* November 10, 1964, 1, 20.

14. Joseph A. Loftus, "Fund Cutoff Charged," *New York Times,* November 10, 1964, 20, and "Republican Attacks on Party Leadership Intensify," 2673.

15. Quoted in "Republican Infighting," *Congressional Quarterly,* November 20, 1964, p. 2712.

16. The following account of the battle over the RNC chairmanship relies, except where indicated, on the recollections of Donald Ross (Interview with Donald Ross, February 5, 1991). Ross's account is corroborated by Hess and Broder, *Republican Establishment,* 41–42.

17. Efforts to hide the role of eastern liberals in the Dump Burch movement went to absurd lengths when Craig Truax, the liberal chairman of the Pennsylvania Republican party, checked into a hotel under an assumed name while attending one plotting session (Rowland Evans and Robert Novak, "The Ordeal of Ray Bliss," *Saturday Evening Post,* November 6, 1965, 34).

18. Ray C. Bliss, "The Role of the State Chairman," in James M. Cannon, ed., *Politics U.S.A: A Practical Guide to the Winning of Public Office* (Garden City, N.Y.: Doubleday, 1960), 160.

19. See chapter 2 for a description of Butler's conception of his role as party chairman. For more on Bliss, see chapter 3.

20. Quoted in Earl Mazo, "GOP Governors Demand Shake-Up in Party Control," *New York Times,* December 6, 1964, 33. Ross claims that the governors originally intended to release a much harsher statement that named Burch directly but that he persuaded them to tone it down.

21. Quoted in ibid.

22. Quoted in ibid.

23. Quoted in "Political Notes: Goldwater Letter," *Congressional Quarterly,* January 1, 1965, 14.

24. Quoted in "Political Notes: Republican Debate Continues," *Congressional Quarterly,* December 18, 1964, 2829.

25. Hess and Broder, *Republican Establishment,* 41.

26. Alan L. Otten and Charles B. Seib, "The Minor Masterpiece of Ray C. Bliss," *Reporter,* February 10, 1966, 36.

27. Edward G. Janeway to Barry Goldwater, January 4, 1965, Post-Election Correspondence, reel 1, Barry Goldwater Papers, Cornell University Library; hereafter referred to as CUL (microfilm).

28. Roland E. Meidinger to Barry Goldwater, December 17, 1964, Post-Election Correspondence, reel 1, Goldwater Papers, CUL.

29. Stanley K. Hathaway to Barry Goldwater, December 28, 1964, Post-Election Correspondence, reel 1, Goldwater Papers, CUL.

30. Quoted in "Burch Will Yield GOP Job April 1; Bliss To Get Post," *New York Times,* January 13, 1965, 38.

31. Minutes of the RNC Executive Committee, January 21, 1965, Chicago, Illinois, *Papers of the Republican Party,* pt. 1: Meetings of the Republican National Committee, 1911–1980; Series B: 1960–1980, Paul L. Kesaris, ed. (Frederick, Md.: University Publications of America), reel 4, frames 379–80 (hereafter referred to as *PRP,* pt. 1). At the Chicago meeting, Bliss, known for his less than enlightened attitude toward women in politics, was also questioned about his willingness to tolerate the activities of women on the RNC. See ibid., frames 380–82.

32. Quoted in "Political Notes: Republican National Committee Meeting," *Congressional Quarterly,* January 29, 1965, 137.

33. Quoted in "Political Notes: Republicans," *Congressional Quarterly,* June 18, 1965, 1186.

34. Quoted in Cabell Phillips, "Bliss Denounces Goldwater Unit As Peril To Party," *New York Times,* June 19, 1965, 1.

35. Cabell Phillips, "Bliss Dismisses a Top Assistant Accused of Raiding GOP File," *New York Times,* June 24, 1965, 17. The raid turned up a list of $1,000 contributors to the Goldwater campaign; five prints of the campaign film "Choice" that Goldwater, believing it to be racist, vetoed showing; and 435,000 address plates (Cabell Phillips, "Kelly Says Bliss Backed Files Raid," *New York Times,* June 25, 1965, 12).

36. Ray C. Bliss, "The Role of the State Chairman," in James M. Cannon, ed., *Politics U.S.A:*

A Practical Guide to the Winning of Public Office (Garden City, N.Y.: Doubleday, 1960), 161; interview with Arthur Peterson, March 27, 1991; and minutes of the RNC Executive Session, June 29, 1965, Washington, D.C., *PRP,* pt, 1, reel 4, frames 885–87.

37. Walter Pincus, "The Fight over Money," *Atlantic Monthly,* April 1966, 73; Herbert Alexander, *Financing the 1964 Election* (Princeton, N.J.: Citizens' Research Foundation, 1966), 108–9; and Alexander, *Money in Politics* (Washington D.C.: Public Affairs Press, 1972), 108.

38. David Broder, "GOP Seeks Clay as Finance Chief," *New York Times,* June 5, 1965, 16.

39. Evans and Novak, "Ordeal of Ray Bliss," 34.

40. Quoted in Pincus, "Fight over Money," 73.

41. Evans and Novak, "Ordeal of Ray Bliss," 34, and Alexander, *Financing the 1964 Election,* 110.

42. Otten and Seib, "Minor Masterpiece of Ray C. Bliss," 36.

43. Even Bliss was intimidated by Clay, reportedly the only man for whom Bliss ever cleaned off his desk (Interview with Arthur Peterson, March 27, 1991).

44. Interview with J. William Middendorf, April 3, 1991.

45. Hess and Broder, *Republican Establishment,* 47; Pincus, "Fight over Money," 73–74; David S. Broder, "GOP Backs Bliss on Raising Funds," *New York Times,* June 30, 1965, 15; and Broder, "Clay Is Moving to Centralize GOP Fund-Raising Groups," *New York Times,* July 16, 1965, 7.

46. Pincus, "Fight over Money," 74, and "Eisenhower Host to GOP Donors," *New York Times,* August 20, 1965, 11.

47. Document from the Republican National Finance Committee Meeting, Chicago, Illinois, January 21, 1965 (photocopy). See chapter 3 for more on the development of the RNC's direct mail fund-raising program.

48. Minutes of the RNC Executive Session, January 31, 1966, Washington, D.C., *PRP,* pt. 1, reel 5, frame 54, and John Herbers, "Republicans Hail Direct Mail Plea," *New York Times,* February 20, 1966, 47.

49. Alexander, *Money and Politics,* 109.

50. Interview with J. William Middendorf, April 3, 1991.

51. Robert B. Semple, Jr., "Skill Replaces Ideology at GOP Headquarters under Bliss" *New York Times,* February 1, 1968, 24.

52. Herbert Alexander, *Financing the 1968 Election* (Lexington, Mass.: D.C. Heath, 1971), 146.

53. Republican National Committee Research Division, "The 1964 Elections: A Summary Report with Supporting Tables," October 1965, *Papers of the Republican Party,* pt. 2: Research Division Reports, Paul L. Kesaris, ed. (Frederick, Md.: University Publications of America), reel 4, frame 381 (hereafter referred to as *PRP,* pt. 2).

54. Quoted in "How Ray Bliss Plays the Cards for GOP," *Business Week,* March 9, 1968, 28. Also see David S. Broder, "GOP Shifts Focus under Bliss Rule," *New York Times,* January 31, 1966, 16.

55. Quoted in John F. Bibby and Robert J. Huckshorn, "Out-Party Strategy: Republican National Committee Rebuilding Politics, 1964–1966," in Bernard Cosman and Robert J. Huckshorn, eds., *Republican Politics: The 1964 Campaign and Its Aftermath for the Republican Party* (New York: Praeger, 1968), 214.

56. Quoted in "How Ray Bliss Plays the Cards for GOP," 30.

57. Quoted in A. James Reichley, "The Rise of the National Parties," in John E. Chubb and Paul Peterson, eds., *The New Directions in American Politics* (Washington D.C.: Brookings Institution, 1985), 186–87.

58. Quoted in "Election Aftermath: How Republicans See the Future," *U.S. News and World Report,* November 15, 1965, 34–36.

59. Bibby and Huckshorn, "Out-Party Strategy," 227.

60. Minutes of the RNC Executive Committee meeting, January 28, 1966, Washington, D.C., *PRP,* pt. 1, reel 5, frame 102.

61. John F. Bibby, *The Republicans and the Metropolis: The Role of National Party Leadership* (Chicago: Center for Research in Urban Government, Loyola University, 1967), 17, and Bibby and Huckshorn, "Out-Party Strategy," 230.

62. Bibby and Huckshorn, "Out-Party Strategy," 227; interview with Arthur Peterson, March 27, 1991; minutes of the RNC Executive Session, June 20, 1966, Washington, D.C., *PRP,* pt. 1, reel 5, frames 378–79; minutes of the RNC Executive Session, January 23, 1967, New Orleans, Louisiana, *PRP,* pt. 1, reel 5, frames 830–31.

63. Minutes of the RNC Executive Session, June 20, 1966, Washington, D.C., *PRP,* pt. 1, reel 5, frame 376.

64. Interview with Arthur Peterson, March 27, 1991.

65. See chapter 3 for more on the Big City Committee and the RNC's failure to implement its recommendations.

66. David S. Broder, "Republicans Intensifying Efforts in Big Cities as Democrats Cut Back Their Urban Staff," *New York Times,* December 29, 1965, 19, and Minutes of the RNC Executive Committee meeting, January 28, 1966, Washington, D.C., *PRP,* pt. 1, reel 5, frame 102.

67. Bibby, *Republicans and the Metropolis,* 18.

68. Tim Hames, "Power without Politics: The Republican National Committee in American Political Life and the Debate over Party Renewal" (Unpublished manuscript), 71.

69. Interview with Arthur Peterson, March 27, 1991.

70. Bliss, "Role of the State Chairman," 165.

71. David S. Broder, "Bliss Helped Nudge Lindsay," *Washington Star,* May 14, 1965, 1, 8.

72. Interview with A. Linwood Holton, December 12, 1990.

73. George H. Mayer, *The Republican Party, 1854–1966* (New York: Oxford University Press, 1967), 314.

74. David S. Broder, "Bliss Proves a Good GOP Caretaker," *Washington Post,* November 15, 1966.

75. Quoted in Nicol C. Rae, *The Decline and Fall of the Liberal Republicans: From 1952 to the Present* (New York: Oxford University Press, 1989), 74.

76. "Statement by Governors," *New York Times,* December 6, 1964, 32.

77. Minutes of the RNC Executive Committee Meeting, February 1965, Washington, D.C., *PRP,* pt. 1, reel 4, frame 720.

78. Quoted in "Republican Research Report: Activities of the Republican Coordinating Committee, 1965–1967," January 30, 1968, *PRP,* pt. 2, reel 5, frame 838.

79. For more on the DAC , see chapter 2.

80. Republican Coordinating Committee, *Choice for America: Republican Answers to the Challenge of Now; Reports of the Republican Coordinating Committee, 1965–1968* (Washington, D.C.: Republican National Committee, 1968), 473–74.

81. Jack M. Pitney, "Republican Alternatives to the Great Society" (Paper presented at the Conference on Grassroots Politics and Party Organizations: The Leadership Model of Ray C. Bliss, University of Akron, September 1991).

82. Bibby and Huckshorn, "Out-Party Strategy," 222. Also see Pitney, "Republican Alternatives to the Great Society."

83. Ibid., 223, and interview with Arthur Peterson, March 27, 1991.

84. Interview with Donald Ross, February 5, 1991.

85. *PRP,* pt. 2, reels 2–7.

86. Interview with Arthur Peterson, March 27, 1991; and Minutes of the RNC Executive Committee Meeting, June 20, 1986, Washington, D.C., *PRP,* pt. 1, reel 5, frames 449–59.

CHAPTER 5

1. In the other chapters I have provided a detailed and comprehensive account of the responses of the national committees, since there are no thorough treatments of recent party history. However, for the principal subject of this chapter, the Democrats' procedural reforms from 1968 to 1972, the detailed historical groundwork has already been provided by other sources. The most thorough account of the reform process is provided in Byron E. Shafer, *Quiet Revolution: The Struggle for the Democratic Party and the Shaping of Post-Reform Politics* (New York: Russell Sage Foundation, 1983). Though lacking Shafer's immense detail and use of primary sources, William Crotty's *Decision for the Democrats: Reforming the Party Structure* (Baltimore; Johns Hopkins University Press, 1978) is also a good account of the Democratic reforms and provides a less critical assessment than Shafer. Other useful treatments of the procedural reforms in this era are Crotty's, *Party Reform* (New York: Longman, 1983) and Nelson W. Polsby, *Consequences of Party Reform* (Oxford: Oxford University Press, 1983). In this chapter I will try to avoid reiterating these accounts and instead focus on explaining how the 1968 loss influenced the Democrats' reform efforts.

2. James Q. Wilson, *The Amateur Democrat: Club Politics in Three Cities* (Chicago: University of Chicago Press, 1962), 128.

3. Quoted in James MacGregor Burns, *The American Experiment: The Crosswinds of Freedom,* vol. 3 (New York: Vintage, 1989), 381. Unfortunately, television coverage of Hamer's testimony was interrupted when Johnson called a White House press conference (Robert Weisbrot, *Freedom Bound: A History of America's Civil Rights Movement* [New York: Plume, 1990], 119).

4. Carol F. Casey, "The National Democratic Party," in Gerald M. Pomper, ed., *Party Renewal in America: Theory and Practice* (New York: Praeger, 1980), 87.

5. Quoted in Burns, *American Experiment,* 381–82.

6. Humphrey and his protege, Walter Mondale, played key roles in trying to broker a deal with the MFDP at the 1964 convention. See Steve Gillon, *The Democrats' Dilemma: Walter F. Mondale and the Liberal Legacy* (New York: Columbia University Press, 1992).

7. McCarthy supporters claimed that McGovern's candidacy was an attempt to deny McCarthy the nomination by preventing the Kennedy delegates from moving to him, while many Humphrey supporters believed that McGovern joined the race only in an attempt to keep Kennedy delegates from supporting the vice-president.

8. Congressional Quarterly, *Guide to U.S. Elections* (Washington, D.C.: Congressional Quarterly, 1985), 210.

9. Ibid., 210 and 419; and William R. Keech and Donald R. Matthews, *The Party's Choice* (Washington D.C.: Brookings Institution, 1977), 199.

10. Polsby, *Consequences of Party Reform,* 27.

11. Congressional Quarterly, *Guide to U.S. Elections,* 210 and 417–19.

12. Shafer, *Quiet Revolution,* 13–15.

13. Theodore White, *The Making of the President: 1972* (New York: Atheneum, 1973), 20; and Shafer, *Quiet Revolution,* 528.

14. White, *Making of the President: 1972,* 35.

15. Theodore H. White, *The Making of the President, 1968* (New York: Atheneum, 1969), 442–43.

16. McCarthy made it clear that he preferred Humphrey only as the lesser of two evils, saying at one point, "I'm voting for Humphrey and I think you should suffer with me" (Lewis Chester, Godfrey Hodgson, and Bruce Page, *An American Melodrama: The Presidential Campaign of 1968* [New York: The Viking Press, 1969], 745).

17. Quoted in Steven V. Roberts, "Aides of M'Carthy Protest His Plans to Back Humphrey," *New York Times*, November 1, 1968, 50.

18. Chester, Hodgson, and Page, *American Melodrama*, 737–38. This account, reflecting popular perception at the time, believed that the opposition or indifference of many McCarthy supporters cost Humphrey the election. Converse, et al., however, claim that even if McCarthy had given Humphrey his wholehearted support, it is unlikely that Humphrey would have won the election. See Philip E. Converse, Warren E. Miller, Jerrold G. Rusk, and Arthur C. Wolfe, "Continuity and Change in American Politics: Parties and Issues in the 1968 Election," *American Political Science Review* 63 (December 1969): 1083–1105.

19. Chester, Hodgson, and Page, *American Melodrama*, 645.

20. Stewart R. Mott to Hubert H. Humphrey, October 13, 1968, reprinted in Herbert Alexander, *Financing the 1968 Election* (Lexington, Mass.: D.C. Heath, 1971), 263–65.

21. Ibid., 157 and 255.

22. Ibid., 84; Sidney Milkis, "Franklin D. Roosevelt and the Transcendence of Partisan Politics," *Political Science Quarterly* 100 (Fall 1985): 502–3; Rowland Evans and Robert Novak, *Lyndon B. Johnson: The Exercise of Power* (New York: New American Library, 1966), 572; and Hubert H. Humphrey, *The Education of a Public Man: My Life and Politics* (Garden City, N.Y.: Doubleday, 1976), 364–68.

23. Interview with William Welsh, June 7, 1991.

24. Ibid.; White, *Making of the President: 1968*, 420–22 and 453–54; and Alexander, *Financing the 1968 Election*, 85–86, 156–57, and 191–96.

25. For more on the Bliss program, see chapter 4.

26. Alexander, *Financing the 1968 Election*, 216–17. The DNC did not assume the debt remaining from the McCarthy campaign, although there was pressure to do so. According to Vick French, a DNC staffer at the time, after the DNC agreed to take on the Kennedy and Humphrey debts, a McCarthy aide called him wanting to know the conditions for assuming the McCarthy debt. The McCarthy aide said, "Gene wants to know what's the principle involved here. Do you have to be dead? How about from Minnesota? Gene says he's not dead, but he is from Minnesota you know." The DNC refused to take on the debt since McCarthy, unlike Humphrey and Ted Kennedy, refused to help reduce all of the DNC's debts (Interview with Verrick O. French, June 5, 1991).

27. Ibid., 156; and interview with Fred Harris, May 6, 1991.

28. Interview with Verrick O. French, June 5, 1991.

29. Shafer, *Quiet Revolution*, 52.

30. Interview with Verrick O. French, June 5, 1991.

31. Ibid; interviews with Olga "Bobbie" Gechas, June 7, 1991, and with Fred Harris, May 6, 1991; and Fred R. Harris, *Now Is the Time: A New Populist Call to Action* (New York: McGraw-Hill, 1971), 46 and 86–87.

32. Interview with Fred Harris, May 6, 1991; Harris, *Now Is the Time*, 46 and 86–87; and interview with Olga "Bobbie" Gechas, June 7, 1991.

33. Interview with Olga "Bobbie" Gechas, June 7, 1991.

34. Alexander, *Financing the 1968 Election*, 220.

35. R. W. Apple, Jr., "Democrats' Purse Starved At Fete," *New York Times*, February 6, 1970, 14; and interview with Verrick O. French, June 5, 1991.

36. According to Vick French, there was a sense of relief in the party over Harris's decision. When he told Bob Strauss of Harris's intention, Strauss replied, "Not a fucking minute too soon" (Interview with Verrick O. French, June 5, 1991).

37. R. W. Apple, Jr., "O'Brien Is Gloomy On 1972 Prospect," *New York Times,* March 29, 1970, 1 and 42.

38. Alexander, *Financing the 1968 Election,* 221; and R. W. Apple, Jr., "Democrats Fight Money Problems," *New York Times,* November 15, 1970, 1 and 39.

39. *New York Times,* February 7, 1972, 23.

40. Interview with Kitty Halperin Bayh, June 5, 1991.

41. Alexander, *Financing the 1968 Election,* 305–6; Steven V. Roberts, "Democrats Try to Talk Way Out of Debt," *New York Times,* July 6, 1972, 28; and "Democrats End TV Fund Appeal," *New York Times,* July 10, 1972, 23.

42. John W. Ellwood and Robert J. Spitzer, "The Democratic National Telethons: Their Successes and Failures," *Journal of Politics* 41 (August 1979): 835.

43. Crotty, *Decision,* 28.

44. The best analysis of the O'Hara Commission is in ibid., 148–221. Crotty's analysis contrasting the O'Hara and McGovern-Fraser Commissions offers a useful portrait of the path not taken by the DNC.

45. Shafer, *Quiet Revolution,* 47.

46. Interview with William Welsh, June 7, 1991.

47. Interview with Verrick O. French, June 5, 1991.

48. Interview with Fred Harris, May 6, 1991. On how reform factored into Harris's personal ambitions, see Shafer, *Quiet Revolution,* 50–60.

49. Shafer, *Quiet Revolution,* 56–61.

50. Interview with George McGovern, May 28, 1991.

51. The following summary is adapted from David E. Price, *Bringing Back the Parties* (Washington D.C.: Congressional Quarterly Press, 1984), 148–49.

52. Ibid., 149.

53. Shafer, *Quiet Revolution,* 264.

54. Ibid., 267.

55. Lawrence F. O'Brien, *No Final Victories: A Life in Politics From John F. Kennedy to Watergate* (Garden City, N.Y.: Doubleday, 1974), 273.

56. Quoted in John G. Stewart, *One Last Chance: The Democratic Party, 1974–1976* (New York: Praeger, 1974), 48.

57. Shafer, *Quiet Revolution,* 250.

58. Ibid., 367–95.

59. E. W. Kenworthy, "Harris Named National Chairman by Democrats," *The New York Times,* January 15, 1969, 22.

60. Harris, *Now Is the Time,* 43–45; interview with Fred Harris, May 6, 1991; and interview with John Stewart, May 10, 1991.

61. Interview with Verrick O. French, June 5, 1991.

62. Interview with John Stewart, May 10, 1991.

63. Democratic Policy Council, *Alternatives "72: A Report by the Democratic Policy Council* (Washington, D.C.: Democratic National Committee, 1972).

64. Interview with Arthur Krim, July 9, 1991.

65. "Members of the Advisory Council of the Democratic National Committee," June 1960, Advisory Council Committees folder, Chairman Jackson's Files, box 471, Democratic National Committee Records, John F. Kennedy Library.

66. Warren Weaver, Jr., "Democrats Set Up Policy Unit; Humphrey Named Chairman," *New York Times*, September 17, 1969, 17.

67. Interview with John Stewart, May 10, 1991.

68. Quoted in R. W. Apple, Jr., "Democratic Council Asks Pullout within 18 Months," *New York Times*, February 10, 1970, 1.

69. Democratic Policy Council, *America in the 1970s* (Washington, D.C.: Democratic National Committee, 1970), 13.

70. Democratic Policy Council, *Alternatives "72*, 138.

71. Ibid., 140.

72. MIRV missiles have several warheads, each capable of striking separate targets.

73. Democratic Policy Council, *America in the 1970s*, 23.

74. Interview with John Stewart, May 10, 1991.

75. Quoted in Price, *Bringing Back the Parties*, 270–71.

CHAPTER 6

1. Byron E. Shafer, *Quiet Revolution: The Struggle for the Democratic Party and the Shaping of Post-Reform Politics* (New York: Russell Sage Foundation, 1983), 541.

2. Quoted in William Crotty, *Decision for the Democrats: Reforming the Party Structure* (Baltimore: Johns Hopkins University Press, 1978), 148.

3. Quoted in Theodore White, *The Making of the President: 1972* (New York: Atheneum, 1973), 178.

4. The most comprehensive accounts of the unseating of the Chicago delegation are by William Crotty in *Party Reform* (New York: Longman, 1983), 155–202, and his "Anatomy of a Challenge: The Chicago Delegation to the Democratic National Convention," in Robert L. Peabody, ed., *Cases in American Politics* (New York: Praeger, 1984), 111–58.

5. Crotty, *Decision*, 222–23.

6. Transcript of the Commission on Delegate Selection and Party Structure Meeting, September 22, 1973, Washington, D.C., DNC Office of the Secretary Files, box 90–06, Democratic National Committee Papers, National Archives (hereafter referred to as DNCP).

7. Steven V. Roberts, "Democrats Face Fight for Control," *New York Times*, November 9, 1972, 1; and "Wallace Seeks Changes," *New York Times*, November 15, 1972, 28.

8. Quoted in "Wallace Seeks Changes," 25.

9. David Broder, "Democrats' Dilemma," *Atlantic Monthly*, March 1974, 33.

10. Quoted in Christopher Lydon, "Renewed Strife of the Democrats," *New York Times*, December 12, 1972, 25.

11. Christopher Lydon, "Democrats' Chief Given New Rebuff," *New York Times*, November 16, 1972, 25; and Lydon, "Muskie Suggests Chairman Leave," *New York Times*, November 17, 1972, 27.

12. Christopher Lydon, "M'Govern Aides Back Muskie Ally as Head of Party," *New York Times*, November 20, 1972, 1 and 28; Lydon, "McGovern Opposing Dismissing Chairman, But Not Resigning," *New York Times*, November 21, 1972, 1 and 28; interviews with Jean Westwood, June 3, 1991; and with George McGovern, May 28, 1991.

13. Crotty, *Decision*, 223.

14. Christopher Lydon, "Governors Back Westwood Rival," *New York Times*, December 4, 1972, 11; Lydon, "Daley Associate Favors Strauss as Democratic Chief," *New York Times*, December 6, 1972, 27; and Lydon, "Strauss Elected Democrats' Head and Vows Unity," *New York Times*, December 10, 1972, 1 and 39.

15. Molly Ivins, "Whither the Democratic National Committee," *Texas Observer,* December 1, 1972, 1 and 3.

16. Christopher Lydon, "Strauss Foes in Texas Seeking to Block Bid for Party Post," *New York Times,* December 7, 1972, 26.

17. Quoted in Lydon, "Democrats' Chief Given New Rebuff," 25.

18. Ibid.

19. Herbert E. Alexander, *Financing the 1972 Election* (Lexington, Mass.: Lexington Books, 1976), 299.

20. Quoted in "Democrats: After the Fall," *Newsweek,* November 13, 1972, 33.

21. Interview with Jean Westwood, June 3, 1991.

22. Lydon, "Strauss Foes in Texas Seeking to Block Bid for Party Post," 26.

23. George Lardner, Jr., "Strauss: Blacks Due 9 New Seats," *Washington Post,* December 13, 1972, A7; and interview with Jean Westwood, June 3, 1991.

24. Interview with Jean Westwood, June 3, 1991. Newspaper reports of the DNC meeting support Westwood's view that some of the votes in her favor were conditional on the agreement she then step down. These reports do not identify which votes went to her under this condition, however. See Lardner, "Strauss."

25. Marvin L. Madeson, "New Democratic Chairman," *New York Times,* December 17, 1972, E10; and Crotty, *Decision,* 307. Opponents of reform jibed that the group's initials, NDC, stood for "November Doesn't Count."

26. Interview with Alan Baron, June 18, 1991.

27. Quoted in "Democratic Party: Start of a Big Repair Job," *Congressional Quarterly,* December 2, 1972, 3098.

28. Crotty, *Decision,* 229–30.

29. Interview with Robert Keefe, June 12, 1991.

30. Ibid.; and interview with Mark Siegel, June 5, 1991.

31. Quoted in Lydon, "Strauss Foes in Texas Seeking to Block Bid for Party Post," 26.

32. Ibid.

33. Ivins, "Whither," 3.

34. Quoted in Paul R. Wieck, "Chairman Strauss' Hot Seat," *New Republic,* April 20, 1974, 17.

35. Quoted in "Democrats: Mellower Mood," *Time,* January 1, 1973, 26.

36. Interview with Mark Siegel, June 5, 1991. The address refers to the location of the AFL-CIO's Washington headquarters.

37. Quoted in Wieck, "Chairman Strauss' Hot Seat," 17.

38. Interview with Mark Siegel, June 5, 1991; and Broder, "Democrats' Dilemma," 35.

39. Quoted in John G. Stewart, *One Last Chance: The Democratic Party, 1974–1976* (New York: Praeger, 1974), 171.

40. Quoted in Linda Charlton, "M'Govern Urges Better Reforms," *New York Times,* April 11, 1973, 15.

41. Crotty, *Decision,* 230.

42. Surveys of convention delegates and party activists taken at the time also suggest that the reforms had broad support within the party. See Robert A. Hitlin and John S. Jackson, III, "Change and Reform in the Democratic Party," *Polity* 11 (Summer 1979): 617–33.

43. Quoted in "Strauss Journeys to Meet Wallace on Party Unity," *New York Times,* December 22, 1972, 13.

44. Broder, "Democrats' Dilemma," 34.

45. Quoted in Wieck, "Chairman Strauss' Hot Seat," 18.

46. Broder, "Democrats' Dilemma," 34.

47. Commission on Delegate Selection and Party Structure, *Democrats All* (Washington, D.C.: Democratic National Committee, 1973), 5.

48. Interview with Alan Baron, June 18, 1991.

49. Interview with Mark Siegel, June 5, 1991.

50. Shafer, *Quiet Revolution,* 301.

51. Ibid.

52. Report of the Democratic Executive Committee, February 6, 1973, DNC 1973 Folder, DNC Research Library Files, 1981–1984, box 1, DNCP.

53. "Woodcock Leaves Democratic Post," *New York Times,* January 21, 1973, 32.

54. Interviews with Mark Siegel, June 5, 1991; and with Robert Keefe, June 12, 1991.

55. Interview with Mark Siegel, June 5, 1991.

56. Quoted in Crotty, *Decision,* 308–9. Crotty claims that this incident shows that Strauss "was prepared to go to extreme and unorthodox ends to repudiate the newly instituted reform rules of 1972." But based on the recollections of those involved, both pro- and anti-reform, Strauss never really wanted to undo the reforms, and his statements on this issue probably served only to warn the Mikulski Commission that it needed to produce a set of rules that everyone in the party could accept (Interviews with Mark Siegel, June 5, 1991; and with Alan Baron, June 18, 1991).

57. Transcript of the Commission on Delegate Selection and Party Structure Meeting, October 27, 1973, Washington, D.C., DNC Office of the Secretary Files, box 90–06, DNCP.

58. Ibid.

59. Commission on Delegate Selection and Party Structure, *Democrats All,* 22.

60. Ibid.

61. Ibid., 19.

62. Ibid., 12.

63. Ibid., 17 and 19.

64. David E. Price, *Bringing Back the Parties* (Washington D.C.: Congressional Quarterly Press, 1984), 151–52.

65. Commission on Party Structure and Delegate Selection, *Mandate for Reform,* (Washington, D.C.: Democratic National Committee, 1970), 44–45.

66. The 1988 Illinois Democratic presidential primary provides a good illustration of this latter point. Illinois Senator Paul Simon received 79 percent of the state's 173 delegates with only 42 percent of the total vote, since his support was distributed relatively evenly throughout the state. On the other hand, Jesse Jackson, received only 21 percent of the delegates, despite winning 32 percent of the vote, since his support was concentrated in Chicago's heavily black congressional districts. Michael Dukakis received no delegates, despite winning 16 percent of the primary vote (*Congressional Quarterly,* March 19, 1988, 741). The DNC, due in part to the objections of Jackson and his supporters, eliminated the congressional district loophole primary for 1992.

67. Commission on Delegate Selection and Party Structure, *Democrats All,* 11–12.

68. Quoted in Crotty, *Decision,* 234.

69. Interview with Mark Siegel, June 5, 1991.

70. Commission on Delegate Selection and Party Structure, *Democrats All,* 22.

71. Jonathan Cottin, "Optimistic Democrats Solving Leftover Disputes, Predict 1974 Gains," *National Journal,* January 5, 1974, 10.

72. Quoted in "Democrats: Pitfalls in Path of Pulling It Together," *Congressional Quarterly,* February 9, 1974, 298.

73. Quoted in Cottin, "Optimistic Democrats," 10.

74. Quoted in ibid.

75. Quoted in ibid.

76. Quoted in ibid. Strauss would eventually use this value-neutral (the less charitable might call it unprincipled) approach to achieve great fame and wealth as a Washington lawyer. This led to the joke that for $10,000 Bob Strauss will tell you how to undo the advice that he gave to the last person who paid him $10,000.

77. Quoted in Wieck, "Chairman Strauss' Hot Seat," 19.

78. "Democrats Plan Warily for 1974 National Conference," *Congressional Quarterly,* June 16, 1973, 1501.

79. Quoted in ibid.

80. Crotty, *Decision,* 40.

81. Quoted in David S. Broder, "Democratic 'Reforms' under Ax," Washington Post,March 1, 1973, A24.

82. "Democrats Plan Warily for 1974 National Conference," 3.

83. Interview with Mark Siegel, June 5, 1991.

84. "Charter of the Democratic Party of the United States," *Official Proceedings of the 1974 Conference on Democratic Party Organization and Policy, Kansas City, Missouri, December 1974* (Washington D.C.: Democratic National Committee, 1974), 238–45.

85. William Crotty, *Political Reform and the American Experiment* (New York: Crowell, 1977), 249–50.

86. Quoted in "Strauss Defeats Reform Group, Tightens Grip on Party's Panel," *New York Times,* August 16, 1974, 14.

87. David S. Broder, "Discord among the Democrats," *Washington Post,* August 21, 1974, A14.

88. David S. Broder, "Democratic Regulars Drop 3 Major Reforms," *Washington Post,* August 18, 1974, A8.

89. David S. Broder, "Rift Ends Charter Session," *Washington Post,* August 18, 1974, 1 and 4.

90. Quoted in ibid.

91. Brown quoted in ibid.

92. Ibid., 4.

93. Crotty, *Decision,* 244–46.

94. Broder, "Discord among the Democrats," A14; and interview with Mark Siegel, June 5, 1991.

95. Interview with Alan Baron, June 18, 1991.

96. Christopher Lydon, "McGovern Foes Say They Prevail on Democratic Charter Issues," *New York Times,* November 24, 1974, 48; and "Democrats: Striving to Avert a Midterm Blowup," *Congressional Quarterly,* November 30, 1974, 3209.

97. "Dissidents Leave Democratic Unit," *New York Times,* August 19, 1974, 11.

98. Broder, "Discord among the Democrats."

99. Christopher Lydon, "Democratic Governors Uphold Compromise on the Make-Up of Conventions," *New York Times,* November 24, 1974, 24; and "Democrats: Striving To Avert a Midterm Blowup," 3212.

100. "Democrats: Striving To Avert a Midterm Blowup," 3212.

101. Interview with Alan Baron, June 18, 1991.

102. Ibid.; and Damon Stetson, "Meany Is Fearful of A Depression," *New York Times,* September 1, 1974, 1 and 29.

103. Quoted in "COPE's Barkan: Worried about a 1976 Repeat of 1972," *Congressional Quarterly,* February 9, 1974, 298.

104. Austin Scott, "Compromise Averts Black Walkout," *Washington Post,* December 8, 1974, A14.

105. Ibid.; and Rowland Evans and Robert Novak, "Capitulation at Kansas City," *Washington Post,* December 11, 1974, A19.

106. Myra MacPherson, "Mr. Chairman," *Potomac: Washington Post Magazine,* January 5, 1975, 7.

107. "Democratic Party: Start of a Big Repair Job," *Congressional Quarterly,* December 2, 1972, 3096.

108. Interview with Mark Siegel, June 5, 1991.

109. Warren Weaver, Jr., "Ebullient Democratic Chairman," *New York Times,* July 12, 1976, C20; Wieck, "Chairman Strauss' Hot Seat," 17; and Broder, "Democrats' Dilemma," 35.

110. Robert Kuttner, "Ass Backward," *New Republic,* April 22, 1985, 18.

111. John W. Ellwood and Robert J. Spitzer, "The Democratic National Telethons: Their Successes and Failures," *Journal of Politics* 41 (August 1979): 828–64.

112. "Shaking the Money Tree," *Congressional Quarterly,* February 9, 1974, 299.

113. Interview with Robert Keefe, June 12, 1991.

114. "Shaking the Money Tree," 299; "DNC's $2 Million Debt 'Manageable'," *National Journal,* January 5, 1974, 11; and interview with Olga "Bobbie" Gechas, June 7, 1991.

115. "DNC's $2 Million Debt 'Manageable'," 11.

116. Ibid.; Herbert Alexander, *Financing the 1976 Election* (Washington, D.C.: Congressional Quarterly Press, 1979), 360; and interview with Olga "Bobbie" Gechas, June 7, 1991.

117. *DNC Chairman's Report, January 1974,* 9–10, DNC 1975 Folder, DNC Research Library Files, 1981–1984, box 1, DNCP.

118. Interview with Terry Straub, June 12, 1991.

119. Ibid.

120. Jules Witcover, *Marathon: The Pursuit of the Presidency, 1972–1976* (New York: Viking, 1977), 117–18.

121. Interview with Terry Straub, June 12, 1991.

122. Ibid.; and interview with Robert Keefe, June 12, 1991.

123. *DNC Chairman's Report, January 1974,* 2. Emphasis added.

124. Price, *Bringing Back the Parties,* 271.

125. Broder, "Democrats' Dilemma," 40; and interview with Robert Keefe, June 12, 1991.

126. Quoted in Broder, "Democrats' Dilemma," 39.

127. Interview with Mark Siegel, June 5, 1991.

128. Quoted in Price, *Bringing Back the Parties,* 271.

129. Interview with Robert Keefe, June 12, 1991.

130. Ibid.; and interview with Mark Siegel, June 5, 1991.

131. Interview with Arthur Krim, July 9, 1991.

132. Crotty, *Decision,* 229–30; and Lydon, "McGovern Foes Say They Prevail on Democratic Charter Issues," 48.

133. Quoted in David S. Broder, "What Is a Democrat?," *Washington Post,* September 16, 1973, C6; and Broder, "Democrats' Dilemma," 40.

134. Broder, "Democrats' Dilemma," 40.

135. Quoted in Price, *Bringing Back the Parties,* 271.

CHAPTER 7

1. A. James Reichley, "The Rise of the National Parties," in John E. Chubb and Paul Peterson, eds., *The New Directions in American Politics* (Washington D.C.: Brookings Institution, 1985), 187.

244

2. Warren Weaver, Jr., "Politicians Find GOP Fighting for Its Survival," *New York Times,* November 24, 1976, 1.

3. Ibid., 1 and 15.

4. Minutes of the RNC Meeting, January 15, 1977, Washington, D.C., *Papers of the Republican Party,* pt. 1: Meetings of the Republican National Committee, 1911–1980; Series B: 1960–1980, Paul L. Kesaris, ed., (Frederick, Md.: University Publications of America), reel 14, frames 808–12 (hereafter referred to as *PRP,* pt. 1); and Tom Wicker, "The Republicans Try to Get Their Act Together," *New York Times Magazine,* February 12, 1978, 13.

5. Interview with Mary Louise Smith, February 27, 1991.

6. Quoted in Warren Weaver, Jr., "Mrs. Smith Quits as GOP Head; Party Fight Foreseen," *New York Times,* November 23, 1976, 1.

7. Quoted in Weaver, "Politicians Find GOP Fighting for Its Survival," 1.

8. Ibid., 15; "Republican Party Chairmanship Still Uncertain," *Congressional Quarterly,* December 11, 1976, 3312; and Interview with Robert Carter, April 2, 1991.

9. Warren Weaver, Jr., "Struggle in GOP Appears on 2 Fronts," *New York Times,* November 30, 1976, 20.

10. "Republican Party Chairmanship Still Uncertain," *Congressional Quarterly,* December 11, 1976, 3312.

11. Interview with Ben Cotton, April 2, 1991.

12. Ibid.

13. Quoted in "Republican Party Chairmanship Still Uncertain," 3312.

14. Interview with Roger Semerad, April 3, 1991.

15. Rhodes Cook, "Brock Chosen to Lead Rebuilding of GOP," *Congressional Quarterly,* January 22, 1977, 142.

16. Interview with Ben Cotton, April 2, 1991.

17. Rhodes Cook, "Brock: Skilled Organizer and Campaigner," *Congressional Quarterly,* January 22, 1977, 143; and interview with Eddie Mahe, May 16, 1991.

18. Interview with Robert Carter, April 2, 1991.

19. Quoted in Cook, "Brock Chosen to Lead Rebuilding of GOP," 142.

20. Ibid.; and interview with Ben Cotton, April 2, 1991.

21. Quoted in Warren Weaver, Jr., "Brock Takes Lead for GOP Chairman," *New York Times,* January 14, 1977, 8.

22. Warren Weaver, Jr., "Republicans Select Brock as Party Head," *New York Times,* January 15, 1977, 9.

23. Interview with Ben Cotton, April 2, 1991.

24. Tim Hames, "Power without Politics: The Republican National Committee in American Political Life and the Debate over Party Renewal" (Unpublished manuscript), 76.

25. Interview with Mary Louise Smith, February 27, 1991.

26. Quoted in Cook, "Brock Chosen to Lead Rebuilding of GOP," 143.

27. Ibid, 142.

28. Minutes of the RNC Meeting, January 14, 1977, Washington, D.C., *PRP,* pt. 1, reel 14, frame 735.

29. Charles W. Hucker, "GOP Makes Significant Gains in Legislatures," *Congressional Quarterly,* November 18, 1978, 3301.

30. Minutes of the RNC Meeting, January 14, 1977, Washington, D.C., *PRP,* pt. 1, reel 14, frame 737.

31. See Paul S. Herrnson and David Menefee-Libey, "The Dynamics of Party Organizational Development," *Mid-South Journal of Political Science* 11 (Winter 1990): 3–30. As a result of these varied purposes, Bliss was eventually dumped by Nixon and faded into the background.

Brock, despite the strong wishes of the Reagan campaign, managed to retain his position through the 1980 campaign and was eventually rewarded with an appointment as U.S. Trade Representative.

32. Herbert Alexander, *Financing the 1976 Election* (Washington, D.C.: Congressional Quarterly Press, 1979), 710.

33. In January 1977, the DNC reported a deficit of $3.5 million (Ibid., 703).

34. Timothy B. Clark, "The RNC Prospers, the DNC Struggles as They Face the 1980 Elections," *National Journal,* September 27, 1980, 1617–21.

35. Xandra Kayden, "The Nationalizing of the Party System," in Michael J. Malbin, ed., *Parties, Interest Groups, and Campaign Finances* (Washington D.C.: American Enterprise Institute, 1980), 257; Paul S. Herrnson, "Reemergent National Party Organizations," in L. Sandy Maisel, ed., *The Parties Respond: Changes in the American Party System* (Boulder, Colo.: Westview Press, 1990), 49; and R. Kenneth Godwin, *One Billion Dollars of Influence: The Direct Marketing of Politics* (Chatham, N.J.: Chatham House, 1988).

36. Quoted in A. James Reichley, "The Rise of the National Parties," in John E. Chubb and Paul Peterson, ed., *The New Directions in American Politics* (Washington D.C.: Brookings Institution, 1985), 187.

37. Quoted in Clark, "The RNC Prospers," 1618.

38. Ibid.; and David Adamany, "Political Parties in the 1980s," in Michael Malbin, ed., *Money and Politics in the United States* (Chatham, N.J.: Chatham House, 1984), 76,

39. Clark, "The RNC Prospers," 1618.

40. Herbert Alexander, *Financing the 1980 Election* (Lexington, Mass.: D.C. Heath, 1983), 300–301.

41. Larry J. Sabato, *The Rise of the Political Consultants: New Ways of Winning Elections* (New York: Basic Books, 1981), 294.

42. Interview with Ben Cotton, April 2, 1991; and Xandra Kayden and Eddie Mahe, Jr., *The Party Goes On: The Persistence of the Two-Party System in the United States* (New York: Basic Books, 1985), 73.

43. Interview with Ben Cotton, April 2, 1991.

44. Sabato, *Rise of the Political Consultants,* 294.

45. Clark, "The RNC Prospers," 1618; and Alexander, *Financing the 1980 Election,* 301. In comparison, the DNC in 1980 raised only 20 percent of its revenues from its direct mail program and had to rely on large contributions for 61 percent of its funds (Alexander, *Financing the 1980 Election,* 326).

46. Adamany, "Political Parties in the 1980s," 76.

47. Alexander, *Financing the 1980 Election,* 300–301.

48. Ibid., 300.

49. Federal law limits PAC contributions to the national committees to $15,000, but allows PACs to spend an unlimited amount on candidates, as long as donations to any one candidate do not exceed $5,000.

50. Interview with Ben Cotton, April 2, 1991; and Christopher J. Bailey, *The Republican Party in the U.S. Senate, 1974–1984* (New York: St. Martin's, 1987), 47–48.

51. Interview with Ben Cotton, April 2, 1991; and Elizabeth Drew, *Politics and Money: The New Road to Corruption* (New York: Macmillan, 1983), 20–21. For a description of the efforts of the National Republican Congressional Committee to shift PAC support from Democrats to Republicans and the response of the Democratic Congressional Campaign Committee, see Brooks Jackson, *Honest Graft: Big Money and the American Political Process* (New York: Knopf, 1988), 70–94.

52. John F. Bibby, "Party Renewal in the National Republican Party," in Gerald M. Pomper,

ed., *Party Renewal in America* (New York: Praeger, 1980), 108; and Minutes of the RNC Executive Committee Meeting, March 12, 1977, Washington, D.C., *PRP*, pt. 1, reel 15, frame 6.

53. Bibby, "Party Renewal in the National Republican Party," 109–10.

54. Ibid., 109.

55. Ibid., 108–9; and transcript of the RNC Executive Committee Meeting, March 12, 1977, Washington, D.C., *PRP*, pt. 1, reel 15, frame 6.

56. John F. Bibby, "Political Parties and Federalism: The Republican National Committee Involvement in Gubernatorial and Legislative Elections," *Publius* 9 (Winter 1979): 233; and Minutes of the RNC Executive Committee Meeting, March 12, 1977, Washington, D.C., *PRP*, pt. 1, reel 15, frame 6.

57. David E. Price, *Bringing Back the Parties* (Washington D.C.: Congressional Quarterly Press, 1984), 40.

58. M. Margaret Conway, "Republican Political Party Nationalization, Campaign Activities, and Their Implications for the Political System," *Publius* 13 (Winter 1983): 5.

59. Clark, "The RNC Prospers," 1619.

60. Interview with Ben Cotton, April 2, 1991; Thomas E. Mann and Norman J. Ornstein, "The Republican Surge in Congress," in Austin Ranney, ed., *The American Elections of 1980* (Washington D.C.: American Enterprise Institute, 1981), 265; and Sabato, *Rise of the Political Consultants,* 291.

61. Margaret K. Latimer, "'No-Party' Politics at the End of the Wallace Era," *Publius* 9 (Winter 1979): 219.

62. Conway, "Republican Political Party Nationalization," 6.

63. Ibid., 5.

64. Bibby, "Party Renewal in the National Republican Party," 110–11; and Bibby, "Political Parties and Federalism," 233–34.

65. Bibby, "Political Parties and Federalism," 231–32.

66. Conway, "Republican Political Party Nationalization," 6.

67. Maxwell Glen, "Republicans Set Their Sights on State Legislative Elections," *National Journal,* September 8, 1979, 1480–83.

68. Christopher Buchanan, "National GOP Pushing Hard to Capture State Legislatures," *Congressional Quarterly,* October 25, 1980, 3192.

69. Ibid.

70. Kayden and Mahe, *The Party Goes On,* 79–801; and Sabato, *Rise of the Political Consultants,* 294.

71. Conway, "Republican Political Party Nationalization," 7; Adamany, "Political Parties in the 1980s," 21; Buchanan, "National GOP Pushing Hard," 3189.

72. Hames, "Power without Politics," 89.

73. Paul S. Herrnson, *Party Campaigning in the 1980s* (Cambridge: Harvard University Press, 1988), 39.

74. Interview with Ben Cotton, April 2, 1991.

75. Hames, "Power without Politics," 90–91; and Rhodes Cook, "National Committee Given Major Role in Fall Campaign," *Congressional Quarterly,* July 19, 1980, 2011.

76. Conway, "Republican Political Party Nationalization," 7.

77. Clark, "The RNC Prospers," 1620.

78. Coordinated expenditures involve activities over which both the party and the candidate have some control.

79. Morton Kondracke, "The GOP Gets Its Act Together," *New York Times Magazine,* July 13, 1980, 56.

80. Adamany, "Political Parties in the 1980s," 85.

81. Kondracke, "The GOP Gets Its Act Together," 44; and interview with Ben Cotton, April 2, 1991.

82. Interview with Ben Cotton, April 2, 1991.

83. Kayden and Mahe, *The Party Goes On*, 78–79.

84. Ibid., 79.

85. Quoted in Charles W. Hucker, "Blacks and the GOP: A Cautious Courtship," *Congressional Quarterly*, April 29, 1978, 1045–51.

86. Interview with Michael Baroody, April 10, 1991.

87. Quoted in Kondracke, "The GOP Gets Its Act Together," 45.

88. For more on the Republican reform efforts, see William Crotty, *Party Reform* (New York: Longman, 1983) and Bibby, "Party Renewal in the National Republican Party."

89. Adam Clymer, "Jesse Jackson Tells Receptive GOP It Can Pick Up Votes of Blacks," *New York Times*, January 21, 1978, 4.

90. Hucker, "Blacks and the GOP," 1048.

91. John F. Bibby, "Political Parties and Federalism," 233; and Kondracke, "The GOP Gets Its Act Together," 45.

92. Rhodes Cook, "Bill Brock Concentrates on the Grass Roots, But Conservatives Are Critical," *Congressional Quarterly*, April 28, 1979, 775; Irwin B. Arieff, "Republican Party Converges on Detroit," *Congressional Quarterly*, July 12, 1980, 1923; and John Herbers, "GOP Ends Its National Meeting with an Optimistic View of 1980," *New York Times*, June 27, 1979, 14.

93. Interview with Roger Semerad, April 3, 1991.

94. Interview with Ben Cotton, April 2, 1991.

95. Weaver, "Struggle in GOP Appears on 2 Fronts," 20; and Philip Shabecoff, "Ford Sees Connally, Reagan, Rockefeller," *New York Times*, December 10, 1976, 1 and 17.

96. "A 'Shadow Cabinet' Suggested by Ford," *New York Times*, January 16, 1977, 18.

97. Interview with Roger Semerad, April 3, 1991.

98. Interview with Michael Baroody, April 10, 1991.

99. Interview with Roger Semerad, April 3, 1991.

100. Interview with Eddie Mahe, May 16, 1991.

101. Interview with Roger Semerad, April 3, 1991.

102. Interview with Eddie Mahe, May 16, 1991.

103. Interview with Roger Semerad, April 3, 1991.

104. Quoted in Price, *Bringing Back the Parties*, 272.

105. Ibid.

106. Interview with Michael Baroody, April 10, 1991.

107. For an early explanation of this theory, see Jude Wanniski, "Taxes, Revenues, and the 'Laffer Curve'," *Public Interest*, Winter 1978, 3–16.

108. Michael Malbin, "The Conventions, Platforms, and Issue Activists," in Austin Ranney, ed., *The American Elections of 1980* (Washington D.C.: American Enterprise Institute, 1981), 102.

109. Interview with Roger Semerad, April 3, 1991.

110. Malbin, "The Conventions, Platforms, and Issue Activists," 102.

111. Interview with Michael Baroody, April 10, 1991.

112. Ibid.

113. Ibid; Peter L. Berger, "Mediating Structures: The Missing Link of Politics," *Commonsense* 1 (Summer 1978): 1–9; and Michael Novak, "Prescription for Republicans," *Commonsense* 1 (Summer 1978): 27–33.

114. "Reagan: 'Time to Recapture Our Destiny'," *Congressional Quarterly*, July 19, 1980, 2063.

115. Ibid., 2066.

116. "1980 Republican National Convention Platform," *Congressional Record,* 96th Cong., 2d sess., July 31, 1980.

117. Quoted in Kayden and Mahe, *The Party Goes On,* 77.

118. Bailey, *Republican Party in the U.S. Senate,* 48; and Sabato, *Rise of the Political Consultants,* 292–93.

119. Adamany, "Political Parties in the 1980s," 82. The NRCC and the NRSC contributed $3.4 million to this effort.

120. Sabato, *Rise of the Political Consultants,* 129–31 and 293–294; and Adamany, "Political Parties in the 1980s," 82.

121. Sabato, *Rise of the Political Consultants,* 293. The worker publicly recanted his support of the GOP in a 1982 ad for the Democratic party.

122. Warren Weaver, Jr., "GOP Starting $5 Million Drive with TV Spots," *New York Times,* January 30, 1980, 18.

123. Bailey, *Republican Party in the U.S. Senate,* 49.

124. Weaver, "GOP Starting $5 Million Drive with TV Spots," 18; and Adamany, "Political Parties in the 1980s," 82.

125. Adamany, "Political Parties in the 1980s," 82; and Conway, "Republican Political Party Nationalization," 9.

126. These years seem the best for comparison, since in 1968 the Republican party was able to raise huge sums through large (and often illegal) contributions to the Nixon campaign, something the campaign finance laws prevented the RNC from doing in 1980. Still, the RNC in 1980 managed to raise $36 million (independent of the Reagan campaign) versus only $26 million for the combined RNC and Nixon campaign in 1968.

127. Interview with Roger Semerad, April 3, 1991.

128. The term *nationalization* comes from Cornelius P. Cotter and John F. Bibby, "Institutional Development of Parties and the Thesis of Party Decline," *Political Science Quarterly* 95 (Spring 1980): 1–27.

129. Adam Clymer, "For the Democrats, a Need to Catch Up," *New York Times,* May 28, 1978, E4.

130. Quoted in Bibby, "Party Renewal in the National Republican Party," 112.

131. Quoted in ibid., 111.

132. Kayden and Mahe, *The Party Goes On,* 75–76.

133. Herrnson, *Party Campaigning in the 1980s.*

134. Quoted in Cook, "Bill Brock Concentrates on the Grass Roots," 776.

135. Kondracke, "The GOP Gets Its Act Together," 42.

CHAPTER 8

1. Tom Wicker, "Democrats in Search of Ideas," *New York Times Magazine,* January 25, 1981, 30.

2. Quoted in Dom Bonafede, "For the Democratic Party, It's a Time for Rebuilding a Seeking New Ideas," *National Journal,* February 21, 1981, 320.

3. Quoted in ibid., 319.

4. Quoted in ibid., 319–20.

5. Quoted in Wicker, "Democrats in Search of Ideas," 40; and Rhodes Cook, "Chorus of Democratic Voices Urges New Policies, Methods," *Congressional Quarterly,* January 17, 1981, 137. If Mondale's optimism—calling the 1980 defeat "a priceless opportunity"—seems a bit

extreme, then one must remember that he was the protege of Hubert Humphrey who, in the maelstrom of 1968, spoke of the "politics of joy."

6. Wicker, "Democrats in Search of Ideas," 32; Bonafede, "For the Democratic Party,," 319; and Cook, "Chorus of Democratic Voices," 139.

7. Irvin Molotsky, "Moynihan Vows to Resist a 'Cadre' of Kennedy Backers from the Left," *New York Times,* November 12, 1980, A1.

8. Quoted in Cook, "Chorus of Democratic Voices," 137.

9. Adam Clymer, "Democrats Seek Party Chairman in Bid for Unity," *New York Times,* November 12, 1980, A1.

10. Cook, "Chorus of Democratic Voices," 140.

11. Quoted in Adam Clymer, "15 Governors Want Shift by Democrats," *New York Times,* December 9, 1980, B18.

12. Cook, "Chorus of Democratic Voices," 140.

13. Quoted in Bonafede, "For the Democratic Party," 319.

14. Ibid., 320; and Cook, "Chorus of Democratic Voices," 139.

15. Bonafede, "For the Democratic Party," 318.

16. Quoted in Cook, "Chorus of Democratic Voices," 139.

17. Quoted in Bonafede, "For the Democratic Party," 320.

18. Quoted in ibid., 317.

19. Quoted in ibid., 319.

20. Quoted in ibid., 317.

21. Quoted in Adam Clymer, "4 Major Democrats to Seek Party Unity," *New York Times,* November 12, 1980, A27.

22. Adam Clymer, "4 in Intense Race for Post as Democratic Chairman," *New York Times,* February 9, 1981, A13.

23. Adam Clymer, "Democrats Select Manatt as Chairman," *New York Times,* February 28, 1981, 7.

24. Bonafede, "For the Democratic Party," 317; and Richard D. Lyons, "A New Leader for the Democrats," *New York Times,* February 28, 1991, 7. Some were in fact quite disparaging of Manatt; one person even referred to him as a "Methodist Sammy Glick"—a reference to the manipulative and self-serving protagonist of Bud Schulberg's novel *What Makes Sammy Run?*

25. Adam Clymer, "What Next? Democrats Seek a Way to Rebound," *New York Times,* March 1, 1981, E2.

26. Caroline Arden, *Getting the Donkey Out of the Ditch: The Democratic Party in Search of Itself* (New York: Greenwood, 1988), 26.

27. Quoted in Clymer, "Democrats Select Manatt as Chairman," 7.

28. Quoted in Martin Schram, "Why Can't Democrats Be More Like Republicans? They're Trying," *Washington Post,* March 23, 1982, A2.

29. Interview with Charles Manatt, May 30, 1991.

30. Ibid.

31. Ibid.

32. Quoted in Schram, "Why Can't Democrats Be More Like Republicans?" A2.

33. Arden, *Getting the Donkey Out of the Ditch,* 35.

34. Interview with David Price, May 15, 1991.

35. David E. Price, *Bringing Back the Parties* (Washington D.C.: Congressional Quarterly Press, 1984), 159.

36. Ibid., 160.

37. Ibid., 159.

38. Interview with William Sweeney, June 10, 1991.

39. Ibid.

40. Lanny J. Davis, "Reforming the Reforms: Beware the Law of Unintended Consequences," Miscellaneous Folder, Commission on Presidential Nomination, DNC Office of the Secretary Files, box 90–4, Democratic National Committee Papers, National Archives (hereafter referred to as DNCP), p. 3

41. *Report of the Commission on Presidential Nomination* (Washington, D.C.: Democratic National Committee, 1982), 1.

42. Ibid., 2.

43. Ibid., 17. Obviously, such a result was not easily arrived at, but instead of recounting the various controversies involved in the Hunt Commission's deliberations, I refer readers to David Price's excellent account (Price, *Bringing Back the Parties,* 159–183).

44. *Report of the Commission on Presidential Nomination,* 13.

45. Ibid., 14; and Arden, *Getting the Donkey Out of the Ditch,* 43.

46. Herbert Alexander, *Financing the 1980 Election* (Lexington, Mass.: D.C. Heath, 1983), 300 and 326.

47. Interview with Michael Steed, June 12, 1991.

48. Interview with Peter Kelly, June 11, 1991.

49. Adam Clymer, "$9.3 Million Debt from 1968 Paid Off by Democratic Party," *New York Times,* June 4, 1982, B7.

50. Alexander, *Financing the 1980 Election,* 325. Alexander defines "major contributors and fund-raising events" as "contributions raised by individuals who agreed to solicit $10,000 or contribute a total of $5,000 per year. Contributions received in connection with fund-raising events, such as dinners, are applied to satisfy that commitment."

51. Interview with Roger Craver, June 6, 1991.

52. Interview with Peter Kelly, June 11, 1991.

53. Alexander, *Financing the 1980 Election,* 300 and 326.

54. Transcript of the DNC Executive Committee Meeting, January 14, 1982, Washington, D.C., DNC Office of the Secretary Files, box 90–13, DNCP.

55. According to DNC Counsel, Michael Steed, the DNC made its own direct mail effort in March 1981 with a prospecting letter containing "a roundhouse attack on Ronald Reagan." Unfortunately, for the DNC, the letter hit the mail the same day President Reagan was shot. The incident created a wave of sympathy for Reagan and the letter failed miserably (Interview with Michael Steed, June 12, 1991).

56. Interview with Roger Craver, June 6, 1991; interview with Peter Kelly, June 11, 1991; and interview with Charles Manatt, May 30, 1991.

57. Quoted in Rhodes Cook, "Democrats Develop Tactics; Laying Groundwork for 1984," *Congressional Quarterly,* July 3, 1982, 1595.

58. Ibid.; and Alexander, *Financing the 1980 Election,* 458.

59. Interview with William Sweeney, June 10, 1991.

60. Bill Peterson, "Cash-Short Democrats Cutting Back Staff, Travel," *Washington Post,* July 24, 1982, A2.

61. Transcript of the DNC Executive Committee Meeting, January 14, 1982, Washington, D.C., DNC Office of the Secretary Files, box 90–13, DNCP.

62. Quoted in Price, *Bringing Back the Parties,* 248.

63. DNC fund-raising letter. Copy supplied by Roger Craver. Emphasis in original.

64. Interview with Michael Steed, June 12, 1991.

65. Quoted in "Social Security Appeal by Democrats Assailed," *New York Times,* December 19, 1981, 28.

66. Interview with Michael Steed, June 12, 1991.

67. Quoted in Schram, "Why Can't Democrats Be More Like Republicans?" A2.

68. Interview with Michael Steed, June 12, 1991.

69. Interview with Peter Kelly, June 11, 1991.

70. Arden, *Getting the Donkey Out of the Ditch,* 52.

71. Transcript of the DNC Executive Committee Meeting, February 4, 1983, Washington, D.C., DNC Office of the Secretary Files, box 90–13, DNCP.

72. Transcript of the DNC Executive Committee Meeting, January 30, 1985, Washington, D.C., DNC Office of the Secretary Files, box 90–13, DNCP, p. 16.

73. Ibid.; Alexander, *Financing the 1980 Election,* 300 and 326; and Herbert E. Alexander and Brian A. Haggerty, *Financing the 1984 Election* (Lexington, Mass.: D.C. Heath, 1987), 100–101.

74. Alexander and Haggerty, *Financing the 1984 Election,* 101.

75. Quoted in Martin Schram, "Republicans Using 'Dirty Tricks,' Democrats Charge," *Washington Post,* May 22, 1983, A2.

76. Jay Matthews, "Democrats Hope to Get $6 Million in Telethon," *Washington Post,* May 28, 1983, A2.

77. Martin Schram, "Democrats Trim Telethon Estimate, Blame Hoax Calls," *Washington Post,* June 3, 1983, A3.

78. Tom Shales, "Bombing Out for The Bottom Line," *Washington Post,* May 30, 1983, D1.

79. Schram, "Democrats Trim Telethon Estimate," A3; and Alexander and Haggerty, *Financing the 1984 Election,* 101–2.

80. Transcript of the DNC Executive Committee Meeting, January 14, 1982, Washington, D.C., DNC Office of the Secretary Files, box 90–13, DNCP, p. 51; and interview with Peter Kelly, June 11, 1991.

81. Warren Brown, "Union Heads, Democrats Meet to Strengthen Ties," *Washington Post,* January 4, 1982, A10.

82. Ibid.

83. Transcript of the DNC Executive Committee Meeting, January 30, 1985, Washington, D.C., DNC Office of the Secretary Files, Box 90–13, DNCP, p. 16; and Alexander, *Financing the 1980 Election,* 326.

84. Interview with Michael Steed, June 12, 1991.

85. Interview with Peter Kelly, June 11, 1991.

86. Robert Kuttner, "Ass Backward," *New Republic,* April 22, 1985, 20.

87. Thomas Ferguson and Joel Rogers, *Right Turn: The Decline of the Democrats and the Future of American Politics* (New York: Hill and Wang, 1986), 144–45.

88. Kuttner, "Ass Backward," 20. "Safe harbor leasing" allowed firms with a surplus of tax deductions to sell them to other businesses looking to reduce their tax payments.

89. Ibid. Also see Ferguson and Rogers, *Right Turn,* 138–61.

90. Interview with Peter Kelly, June 11, 1991.

91. Ibid.

92. Rob Gurwitt, "Unions Plan Expanded Efforts to Gain More Political Clout and Elect a President in 1984," *Congressional Quarterly,* September 24, 1983, 1981–85; and interview with William Sweeney, June 10, 1991.

93. Clymer, "4 in Intense Race for Post as Democratic Chairman," A13; "Democrats Entangled in Dispute over Party Positions for Blacks," *New York Times,* February 27, 1981, A17; interview with Frances Kenin, June 26, 1991; interview with Michael Steed, June 12, 1991; and interview with Bob Neuman, June 6, 1991.

94. Interview with Sandra Perlmutter, June 3, 1991.

95. Interview with Michael Steed, June 12, 1991.

96. Interview with William Sweeney, June 10, 1991.

97. Adam Clymer, "Labor and the Democrats," *New York Times,* November 20, 1981, A21.

98. Alexander, *Financing the 1980 Election,* 458.

99. Clymer, "Labor and the Democrats," A21.

100. Interview with William Sweeney, June 10, 1991.

101. Though true for direct contributions, labor's actual giving was probably much higher, since much of it was in the form of unreported "soft money" funneled through the states or used for such party infrastructure as the new DNC building and the equipment inside it. For a detailed description of the used of labor soft money in the Democratic party, see Brooks Jackson, *Honest Graft: Big Money and the American Political Process* (New York: Knopf, 1988), 142–66.

102. Interview with Michael Steed, June 12, 1991.

103. Transcript of the DNC Executive Committee Meeting, January 14, 1982, Washington, D.C., DNC Office of the Secretary Files, box 90–13, DNCP, pp. 36–37.

104. It is interesting to note that Glenn Watts, the chairman of the Labor Council who spoke later at the same meeting, recognized Radaker's gaffe and made light of it. The incident is also referred to several times during later executive committee meetings, as participants joked over Radaker's blunder.

105. Interview with William Sweeney, June 10, 1991.

106. Interview with Sandra Perlmutter, June 3, 1991.

107. Interview with Frances Kenin, June 26, 1991.

108. Transcript of the DNC Executive Committee Meeting, May 8, 1981, Washington, D.C., DNC Office of the Secretary Files, Box 90–13, DNCP, p. 56; and interview with Ann Lewis, June 4, 1991.

109. Interview with Ann Lewis, June 4, 1991.

110. Transcript of the DNC Executive Committee Meeting, May 8, 1981, Washington, D.C., DNC Office of the Secretary Files, Box 90–13, DNCP, p. 60.

111. Arden, *Getting the Donkey Out of the Ditch,* 48.

112. Ibid.; and transcript of the DNC Executive Committee Meeting, May 8, 1981, Washington, D.C., DNC Office of the Secretary Files, Box 90–13, DNCP, p. 61.

113. Cook, "Democrats Develop Tactics," 1594.

114. David S. Broder, "Manatt Rebuilding Democrats, Step by Step, for 1984 Battles," *Washington Post,* February 5, 1983, A3; and interview with Brian Lunde, May 15, 1991.

115. David Menefee-Libey, "Embracing Campaign-Centered Politics at the Democratic Headquarters: Charles Manatt and Paul Kirk in the 1980s" (Unpublished paper, December 1991), 10–11.

116. Preliminary Task Force Report, 1983 Voter Registration Program, "At What Cost Is Victory? A Very Small Cost!" December 27, 1982, Voter Registration Folder, box WF-90–12, DNCP.

117. Rhodes Cook, " 'Have-Not' Surge to Polls: Major Force in 1984 Elections," *Congressional Quarterly,* July 23, 1983, 1503–07.

118. Interview with Ann Lewis, June 4, 1991.

119. Quoted in Milton Coleman, "Democrats Plan a $5 Million Drive to Register Minorities," *Washington Post,* May 28, 1983, A2.

120. Transcript of the DNC Executive Committee Meeting, January 20, 1984, Washington, D.C., DNC Office of the Secretary Files, Box 90–13, DNCP, p. 17.

121. Preliminary Task Force Report, 1983 Voter Registration Program, "At What Cost Is Victory? A Very Small Cost!" December 27, 1982, Voter Registration Folder, box WF-90–12, DNCP.

122. Ibid.

123. Coleman, "Democrats Plan a $5 Million Drive to Register Minorities," A2. The states eventually targeted were California, Arizona, New Mexico, Texas, Louisiana, Mississippi,

Alabama, Georgia, Florida, Tennessee, Missouri, Kentucky, Illinois, Indiana, Minnesota, Wisconsin, North Carolina, Ohio, Virginia, Pennsylvania, New York, New Jersey, Colorado, Michigan, Maryland, and Massachusetts.

124. Preliminary Task Force Report, 1983 Voter Registration Program, "At What Cost is Victory? A Very Small Cost!" December 27, 1982, Voter Registration Folder, box WF-90–12, DNCP.

125. Ferguson and Rogers, *Right Turn*, 160.

126. Alexander and Haggerty, *Financing the 1984 Election*, 365, 367, and 375–77.

127. Ferguson and Rogers, *Right Turn*, 159–60.

128. Interview with Ann Lewis, June 4, 1991.

129. Alexander and Haggerty, *Financing the 1984 Election*, 357–58.

130. Ibid., 377.

131. Ibid., 378.

132. Interview with Michael Steed, June 12, 1991.

133. Interview with Eugene Eidenberg, May 2, 1991.

134. Quoted in Price, *Bringing Back the Parties*, 273.

135. Arden, *Getting the Donkey Out of the Ditch*, 57.

136. Interview with Eugene Eidenberg, May 2, 1991.

137. Interview with Charles Manatt, May 30, 1991.

138. Alexander, *Financing the 1980 Election*, 458.

139. Alexander and Haggerty, *Financing the 1984 Election*, 375–76.

140. Unfortunately, hard data on RNC spending in the 1984 election is difficult to come by, but it is clear that if they could spend $4–5 million on voter contact and $1.1 just on compiling damaging information about the Democratic candidates, then their total discretionary spending was far in excess of the DNC's $7.7 million. See Alexander and Haggerty, *Financing the 1984 Election*, 354–57.

141. Paul S. Herrnson, *Party Campaigning in the 1980s* (Cambridge: Harvard University Press, 1988), 43.

142. Interview with Ann Lewis, June 4, 1991.

143. Ferguson and Rogers, *Right Turn*, 190–91.

CHAPTER 9

1. For an excellent treatment of Mondale's career, the 1984 campaign, and Mondale's place in the modern Democratic party, see Steven M. Gillon, *The Democrats' Dilemma: Walter F. Mondale and the Liberal Legacy* (New York: Columbia University Press, 1992).

2. Quoted in Dan Balz, "Democrats Chart the Way Back," *Washington Post*, November 19, 1984, A1.

3. Quoted in Bill Peterson and Dale Russakoff, "Democrats Worry," *Washington Post*, November 12, 1984, A16.

4. Quoted in James R. Dickenson, "Democrats Seek Identity after Loss," *Washington Post*, December 17, 1984, A6.

5. Quoted in James R. Dickenson, "Democrats and Republicans Map Ways to Overcome Deficiencies," *Washington Post*, November 8, 1984, A47.

6. Quoted in Balz, "Democrats Chart the Way Back," A4.

7. Quoted in Dickenson, "Democrats Seek Identity after Loss," A6.

8. Quoted in Balz, "Democrats Chart the Way Back," A4.

9. Dan Balz, "Democrats Search for a Chairman," *Washington Post*, December 3, 1984, A5.

10. Dan Balz, "Group Ends DNC Chairman Search," *Washington Post*, December 17, A7.

11. Robert Keefe, a Washington political consultant and a DNC staff member under Robert Strauss; Duane Garrett, an official in Mondale's presidential election campaign; Sharon Pratt Dixon, national committee member from the District of Columbia; and former representative John Cavanaugh of Nebraska also entered the race, but none ever proved a viable contender.

12. Dan Balz, "Kirk Elected Democratic Chairman," *Washington Post*, February 2, 1985, A1. The DNC's willingness to divide votes down to the hundredth seems a further indication of the party's efforts to ensure the maximum possible representation.

13. David Menefee-Libey, "Embracing Campaign-Centered Politics at the Democratic Head-quarters: Charles Manatt and Paul Kirk in the 1980s" (Unpublished paper, December 1991), 16.

14. Herbert E. Alexander and Monica Bauer, *Financing the 1988 Election* (Boulder, Colo.: Westview Press, 1991), 81.

15. Menefee-Libey, "Embracing Campaign-Centered Politics," 16.

16. Alexander and Bauer, *Financing the 1988 Election*, 41.

17. Peter Brown, *Minority Party: Why the Democrats Face Defeat in 1992 and Beyond* (Washington, D.C.: Regnery Gateway, 1991), 207.

18. Menefee-Libey, "Embracing Campaign-Centered Politics," 19–21.

19. Quoted in Balz, "Kirk Elected Democratic Chairman," A1.

20. Quoted in David S. Broder, "Democrats Remain in Doldrums," *Washington Post*, February 3, 1985, A1.

21. Jack W. Germond and Jules Witcover, "It's Alive! It's Alive!" *Washingtonian*, November 1985, 111; and interview with George Burger, May 15, 1991.

22. Quoted in David S. Broder, "The Truth about Paul Kirk," *Washington Post*, February 6, 1985, A19.

23. David S. Broder, "Democrats Voted Like a House Divided," *Washington Post*, February 2, 1985, A5.

24. Michael Barone, "Smart Move, Kirk," *Washington Post*, February 17, 1985, D7.

25. Quoted in Juan Williams, "Jackson Rips Democratic Chiefs," *Washington Post*, February 11, 1985.

26. James R. Dickenson, "DNC Withdraws Recognition of 7 Caucuses," *Washington Post*, May 18, 1985, A7.

27. Ibid.; and Paul M. Barrett, "The Caucus-Happy Democrats," *Washington Monthly*, April 1985, 25.

28. Interview with Paul Kirk, May 30, 1991.

29. "Abolishing the Caucuses," *Washington Post*, May 22, 1985, A20.

30. Ron Walters, "Black Democrats: Time for a Third Party?" *Nation*, November 2, 1985, 440.

31. Fred Barnes, "Majority Complex," *New Republic*, August 5, 1985, 13.

32. Quoted in David S. Broder, "Kirk to Seek Cancellation of Midterm Convention," *Washington Post*, May 10, 1985.

33. Elaine Ciulla Kamarck, "Democrats Look Ahead: Fight over Delegate Rules for '88," *Nation*, March 2, 1985, 220.

34. Quoted in Ronald Grover and Stephen W. Wildstrom, "The Democrats' War with Jesse Jackson," *Business Week*, February 25, 1985.

35. Phil Gailey, "Democrats Propose Shift in Rules for Presidential Nomination, *New York Times*, October 19, 1985, A11; and Rhodes Cook, "Democrats Alter Rules Slightly in Effort to Broaden Party Base," *Congressional Quarterly*, October 26, 1985, 2158. For a comprehensive analysis of the Fairness Commission, see John F. Bibby, "Political Party Trends in 1985: The Continuing but Constrained Advance of the National Parties," *Publius* 16 (Summer 1986): 79–91.

36. Bibby, "Political Party Trends in 1985," 86; Andrew Mollison, "Maestro of the Democrats," *New Leader,* June 27, 1988, 4, and interview with Paul Kirk, May 30, 1991.

37. Andrew Mollison, "Guidebook for the Democrats," *New Leader,* September 22, 1986, 3–4.

38. Quoted in Morton Kondracke, "The Democrats' 'Yes, But' Foreign Policy," *New Republic,* October 20, 1986, 21.

39. Interview with Paul Kirk, May 30, 1991.

40. Interview with Brian Lunde, May 15, 1991; interview with George Burger, May 15, 1991; Germond and Whitcover, "It's Alive! It's Alive!" 110; and Andrew Mollison, "Maestro of the Democrats," *New Leader,* June 27, 1988, 4. Though publicly the DNC did not criticize the DLC, internal memos indicate that the DNC saw the DLC as a strong potential rival and often discussed ways to better compete with it. See memo from Wally Chalmers to Paul Kirk, April 26, 1987, and memo from Jean B. Dunn to Paul Kirk, July 29, 1986, Democratic Leadership Council Folder, DNC General Files, box 86–80, Democratic National Committee Papers, National Archives (hereafter referred to as DCNP).

41. Thomas Byrne Edsall and Mary D. Edsall, *Chain Reaction: The Impact of Race, Rights, and Taxes on American Politics* (New York: Norton, 1991), 182–84; and Brown, *Minority Party,* 196–203.

42. Quoted in Brown, *Minority Party,* 201; and Paul Taylor, "Democrats Are Divided over 'Fairness' Survey," *Washington Post,* December 14, 1985, A8.

43. This argument is best made by Menefee-Libey, "Embracing Campaign-Centered Politics."

44. Interview with Paul Kirk, May 30, 1991.

45. Interviews with Brian Lunde, May 15, 1991, and with George Burger, May 15, 1991.

46. Confidential memo from Brian Lunde to Paul Kirk, March 11, 1985, unmarked folder, DNC General Files, box 88–61, DCNP. Emphasis in original.

47. Interview with Sandra Perlmutter, June 3, 1991.

48. Vrdolyak, in perhaps his greatest service to the Democratic party, eventually became a Republican.

49. Quoted in Keven Klose, "DNC Chief Rejects Vrdolyak's Demand to End Delegate Quotas," *Washington Post,* April 27, 1985, A5.

50. One reason for the slow pace of organizational efforts was the DNC's lack of fund-raising success until 1992. In part, this stemmed from the reluctance of some Jewish donors to contribute to Brown, whom they saw as too closely tied to Jesse Jackson. See Douglas Harbrecht, "Ron Brown May Be Just What the Democrats Don't Need," *Business Week,* June 18, 1990, 30; and Paul Taylor, "Party Chairman Brown Finds Democrats in Robust Health and 'On a Roll,'" *Washington Post,* June 30, 1990, A6. The surge in George Bush's popularity following the Gulf War also made it difficult to raise money. Not until 1992, when Bush's popularity had slipped and the Democrats again seemed competitive in the presidential race, did money begin to flow into party coffers.

51. Quoted in Gwen Ifill, "Democrats Meet to Plot Strategy for the '92 Election," *New York Times,* June 15, 1991, A11.

52. See chapter 7 for more information on the RNC's activity in this area.

53. Thomas B. Edsall and Dan Balz, "DNC Poised to Play Role in Late Starting Campaign," *Washington Post,* September 23, 1991, A6; and James A. Barnes, "Ron Brown's Fast Start," *National Journal,* May 6, 1989, 1103–7.

54. Quoted in Jack W. Germond and Jules Witcover, *Mad as Hell: Revolt at the Ballot Box, 1992* (New York: Warner Books, 1993), 87.

55. Interview with Alice Travis, May 29, 1991.

56. Germond and Witcover, "It's Alive! It's Alive!" 373–75, 438–40.

57. The DNC also revised several rules that were part of the compromise between the Dukakis and Jackson forces agreed to at the 1988 national convention. These compromises included abolishing the 15 percent threshold and selecting delegates according to a strict proportional representation and eliminating DNC members as "super delegates." After the election, the DNC altered this somewhat by reinstituting the 15 percent threshold, while maintaing proportional representation for candidates above that mark, and reinstating DNC members as "super delegates." These procedural changes, though undertaken after the 1988 loss, do not appear to have resulted directly from that loss. As such, I have not included them as a part of the DNC's response.

58. Rhodes Cook, "Bid to Move Primary to March Draws Wary GOP Response," *Congressional Quarterly,* February 17, 1990, 542; and Rhodes Cook, "Democratic Party Rules Changes Readied for '92 Campaign," *Congressional Quarterly,* March 17, 1990, 847–49.

59. Paul Taylor and Maralee Schwartz, "Jackson's Unity Address Baffles, Irk Some Moderate Democrats," *Washington Post,* March 25, 1990, A10; and Paul Taylor, "California's Early Primary a Move with Pitfalls," *Washington Post,* February 27, 1990, A11.

60. Dan Balz, "California Governor Balks at Bill for Early Primary," *Washington Post,* August 24, 1991, A8.

61. Dan Balz, "DNC Endorses Moynihan Social Security Tax Rollback Plan," *Washington Post,* March 25, 1990, A11; and George Will, "A Party Starting to Get Interesting," *Washington Post,* March 29, 1990, A27.

62. A less charitable interpretation suggests that Brown realized that a policy council would detract from his ability to use the media to raise his own political status.

63. James M. Perry, "Republicans' Next Contest Is Strictly Internal as Party Fights to Avoid Democrats' Fate in '70s," *Wall Street Journal,* November 5, 1992, A20.

64. Quoted in "National Briefing—RNC Chair: Emphasis on Organization, Not Ideology," *American Political Network Hotline* (hereafter referred to as *APN Hotline*), January 11, 1993.

65. Quoted in "Race Heats Up for RNC Chair," *Congressional Quarterly,* January 16, 1993, 147.

66. Quoted in Richard L. Berke, "Rarity for the Republicans: Party Leadership Race," *New York Times,* January 13, 1993.

67. Thomas B. Edsall and David S. Broder, "5 Candidates for RNC Post Compete Fiercely But Shun Ideological Rifts," *Washington Post,* January 29, 1993, A7.

68. Quoted in Richard L. Berke, "GOP Braces for Fight over Party Chairman's Post," *New York Times,* January 29, 1993, A7.

69. Quoted in "National Briefing—RNC: Bond's 'Stinging' Farewell," *APN Hotline,* February 1, 1993.

70. "National Briefing—RNC Chair: And Then There Were Five," *APN Hotline,* January 6, 1993; and "National Briefing—RNC Chair: Firing Up the Ashcroft Bandwagon," *APN Hotline,* January 7, 1993.

71. Quoted in "National Briefing—RNC Chair: Berkman Video Hits the Charts," *APN Hotline,* January 11, 1993; and "National Briefing—RNC Chair: The Candidates Report from St. Louis," *APN Hotline,* January 27, 1993.

72. Quoted in "National Briefing—RNC: Meet Me in St. Looie, Looie—Meet Me At the War!," *APN Hotline,* January 11, 1993.

73. Rowland Evans and Robert Novak, "Republicans at Bay," *Washington Post,* February 1, 1993, A19; and interview with Paula Nowakowski, June 3, 1993.

74. "National Briefing—RNC Chair: New Party Leader Emerges Today," *APN Hotline,* January 29, 1993.

75. Haley Barbour, RNC Chairmanship Campaign Manifesto, January 1993, photocopy, p. 1. I am indebted to Paula Nowakowski for a copy of this document.

76. David S. Broder, "Barbour: The GOP's 'Third B,'" *Washington Post,* February 3, 1993,

A17.

77. Barbour, "RNC Chairmanship Campaign Manifesto," 2 and 8.

78. Richard L. Berke, "At GOP Meeting, an Uninvited Guest," *New York Times*, July 9, 1993, A18; and "National Briefing—RNC Meeting: Radio Ad Set for 30 Markets," *APN Hotline*, July 9, 1993.

79. "One the House—RNC: GOP Targets Mostly Frosh Reps with Radio Ads," *APN Hotline*, December 8, 1993.

80. Quoted in "National Briefing—RNC: Weekly Satellite TV Show Premieres Tonight," *APN Hotline*, January 27, 1994; and "National Briefing—GOP-TV: RNC Goes Live with Slick Weekly TV Show," *APN Hotline*, January 28, 1994.

81. Quoted in "National Briefing—GOP-TV: RNC Goes Live with Slick Weekly TV Show."

82. Quoted in Richard L. Berke, "GOP Hopes New Group Can Attract Support from Outsiders," *New York Times*, November 15, 1993, B8; "National Briefing—The GOP: Policy Foundation Launched," *APN Hotline*, June 22, 1993; and "National Briefing—The GOP: Barbour Gambling on Policy Foundation," *APN Hotline*, June 17, 1993. The foundation is also similar to a DNC-sponsored, tax-exempt, nonpartisan foundation to lobby for President Clinton's health care proposals. The Democrats' program, however, was scrapped amidst complaints that is was a thinly veiled effort to avoid campaign finance regulations (Berke, "GOP Hopes New Group Can Attract Support from Outsiders").

83. Quoted in Richard L. Berke, "GOP Hopes New Group Can Attract Support from Outsiders;" and "National Briefing—The GOP: Policy Foundation Launched."

84. Quoted in "National Briefing—The GOP: Policy Foundation Launched."

CHAPTER 10

1. David E. Price, *Bringing Back the Parties* (Washington D.C.: Congressional Quarterly Press, 1984), 43.

2. Ray C. Bliss, "Report of the Committee on Big City Politics," Minutes of the RNC Meeting, June 1, 1961, Chicago, Illinois, *Papers of the Republican Party*, pt. 1: Meetings of the Republican National Committee, 1911–1980; Series B: 1960–1980, Paul L. Kesaris, ed., (Frederick, Md.: University Publications of America), reel 1, frames 464–67 (hereafter referred to as *PRP*, pt. 1).

3. Interview with Ben Cotton, April 2, 1991.

4. Xandra Kayden and Eddie Mahe, Jr., *The Party Goes On: The Persistence of the Two-Party System in the United States* (New York: Basic Books, 1985), 69.

5. Minutes of the All-Republican Conference, Gettysburg, Pennsylvania, June 30, 1962, *PRP*, pt. 1, reel 2, frame 355 .

6. Hugh A. Bone, *Party Committees and National Politics* (Seattle: University of Washington Press, 1958), 44–45.

7. Alexander Heard, *The Costs of Democracy* (Chapel Hill: University of North Carolina Press, 1960), 220–21.

8. Ibid., 224–25.

9. Cornelius P. Cotter and Bernard C. Hennessy, *Politics without Power: The National Party Committees* (New York: Atherton, 1964), 176–78.

10. Paul S. Herrnson, "National Party Decision-Making, Strategies, and Resource Distribution in Congressional Elections," *Western Political Quarterly* 42 (September 1989): 317–18.

11. John F. Bibby, *Politics, Parties, and Elections in America*, 2d ed. (Chicago: Nelson-Hall, 1992), 85–86.

12. Although I am a junior faculty member at a small college, I intend no value judgment with this observation; indeed, my wife works for an investment bank. Not surprisingly, she is a Republican and I am a Democrat.

13. Minutes of the All-Republican Conference, Gettysburg, Pennsylvania, June 30, 1962, *PRP,* pt. 1, reel 2, frames 354–55.

14. Haley Barbour, "RNC Chairmanship Campaign Manifesto," January 1993 (photocopy), 1–3.

15. Jo Freeman, "The Political Culture of Democratic and Republican Parties," *Political Science Quarterly* 101 (Fall 1986): 351.

16. Ibid., 339. Byron Shafer observed such attributes in the guest gallery at the Republican national convention. Republicans who saw someone occupying their assigned seat would not directly confront the interloper. They instead would seek out a person in authority to resolve the matter for them. When confronted by an authority figure, the squatter would yield quickly and quietly. Democrats in a similar situation would immediately confront the person in their seat, who would then argue heatedly with the claimant and with any authorities who intervened (Byron E. Shafer, "Republicans and Democrats as Social Types: Or, Notes toward an Ethnography of the Political Parties," *Journal of American Studies* 20 (December 1986): 345).

17. Freeman, "Political Culture," 345. Also see Stephen E. Frantzich, *Political Parties in the Technological Age* (New York: Longman, 1989), 90.

18. Cotter and Hennessy, *Politics without Power,* 183.

19. Cornelius P. Cotter, James L. Gibson, John F. Bibby, and Robert J. Huckshorn, *Party Organizations in American Politics* (New York: Praeger, 1984), 164. Also see Dom Bonafede, "Laxalt's RNC Follows a Simple Rule: A Minority Must Be Better Organized," *National Journal,* June 18, 1983, 1270–73.

20. Edgar H. Schein, "The Role of the Founder in Creating Organizational Culture," *Organizational Dynamics* (Summer 1983): 14–28.

21. In the pantheon of party gods, Ray Bliss is the Republicans' Zeus. Not only do past and present Republican party operatives recite his term *nuts and bolts* in mantra-like fashion, but the University of Akron (from which Bliss was suspended for stuffing ballot boxes during the campus May Queen contest) is now home to the Ray C. Bliss Institute of Applied Politics. It was here in 1991 that several nationally prominent academics, politicians, and journalists held a conference to proclaim Bliss's work and "leadership model."

22. J. Steven Ott, *The Organizational Culture Perspective* (Chicago: Dorsey Press, 1989), 87–89.

23. Edgar H. Schein, "Organizational Culture," *American Psychologist* 45 (February 1990): 115.

24. Freeman, "Political Culture," 338.

25. At times, the Democrats take their effort to be the party of the "the little people" to absurd and literal lengths. See the exchange of letters between Billy Barty and the 1988 Platform Committee concerning "people of small stature," Billy Barty Foundation Folder, DNC 1988 Platform Committee Files, box 88–9, Democratic National Committee Papers, National Archives (hereafter referred to as DNCP).

26. Freeman, "Political Culture," 337.

27. Interview with Alice Travis, May 29, 1991.

28. For more on the coalitional differences between the parties, see Warren E. Miller and M. Kent Jennings, *Parties in Transition: A Longitudinal Study of Party Elites and Party Supporters* (New York: Russell Sage Foundation, 1986), 219 and 246.

29. William Crotty, *Party Reform* (New York: Longman, 1983), 206.

30. Quoted in Jeffrey L. Pressman, "Groups and Group Caucuses," *Political Science Quarterly* 92 (Winter 1977–1978): 682.

31. Ibid.

32. Bibby, *Politics, Parties, and Elections in America,* 86.

33. Freeman, "Political Culture," 351.

34. Memo from Terry Michael to Paul Kirk, April 18, 1986, Rainbow Coalition Folder, DNC General Files, box 88–82, DNCP.

35. Schein, "Organizational Culture," 115.

36. Douglas B. Craig, *After Wilson: The Struggle for the Democratic Party, 1920–1934* (Chapel Hill: University of North Carolina Press, 1992), 78–79; Ralph M. Goldman, *The National Party Chairmen and Committees: Factionalism at the Top* (Armonk, N.Y.: Sharpe, 1990), 310–11; and David Burner, *The Politics of Provincialism: The Democratic Party in Transition, 1918–1932* (New York: Norton, 1967), 146–47.

37. Craig, *After Wilson,* 181.

38. Ibid., 181–87.

39. Matthew Josephson, *The Politicos: 1965–1896* (New York: Harcourt, Brace, and World, 1938), 695.

40. Goldman, *National Party Chairmen,* 291–95, 401–9, and 487–88.

41. Ibid., 555.

42. Ibid., 559–61, and A. James Reichley, "Party Politics in a Federal Polity," in John Kenneth White and Jerome M. Mileur, eds., *Challenges to Party Government* (Carbondale: Southern Illinois University Press, 1992), 50.

43. Ralph M. Goldman, *Dilemma and Destiny: The Democratic Party in America* (Lanham, Md.: Madison Books, 1986), 58–59.

44. Lawrence Frederick Kohl, *The Politics of Individualism: Parties and the American Character in the Jacksonian Era* (New York: Oxford University Press, 1989), 21 and 34–35.

45. Wilfred Binkley, *American Political Parties: Their Natural History,* 2d ed. (New York: Knopf, 1954), 129–30.

46. Robert Kelley, *The Cultural Pattern in American Politics: The First Century* (New York: Knopf, 1979), 163.

47. Michael Wallace, "Changing Concepts of Party in the United States: New York, 1815–1828," *American Historical Review* 74 (December 1968): 460.

48. Douglas Walter Jaenicke, "American Ideas of Political Party as Theories of Politics: Competing Ideas of Liberty and Community" (Ph.D. diss., Cornell University, 1981), 200.

49. James Staton Chase, "Jacksonian Democracy and the Rise of the Nominating Convention," *Mid-American: An Historical Review* 45 (October 1963): 231.

50. Harry L. Watson, *Liberty and Power: The Politics of Jacksonian America* (New York: Hill and Wang, 1990), 174.

51. Jaenicke, "American Ideas of Political Party," 225.

52. Edward McChesney Sait, *American Parties and Elections,* rev. ed. (New York: D. Appleton-Century Company, 1939), 363–64.

53. Sean J. Savage, *Roosevelt: The Party Leader, 1932–1945* (Lexington: University Press of Kentuck, 1991), 4–7; Burner, *The Politics of Provincialism,* 142–53; and Craig, *After Wilson,* 75–91. Craig points out that in the 1920s, southern and western progressives considered creating their own party organization as a counterweight to the more conservative DNC. Sixty years later, acting with the same impulse but in a different ideological direction, Southern and western Democrats established the DLC to provide a more conservative alternative to the DNC.

54. Sean Savage, "Franklin D. Roosevelt and the Democratic National Committee" (Paper delivered at the 1991 Midwest Political Science Association Meeting, Chicago, Illinois); and Savage, *Roosevelt,* chap. 4.

55. James Q. Wilson, *The Amateur Democrat: Club Politics in Three Cities* (Chicago: University of Chicago Press, 1962), vii–viii.

SELECT BIBLIOGRAPHY OF PRIMARY SOURCES

ARCHIVAL SOURCES

Democratic National Committee Papers, 1968–1988, National Archives, Washington, D.C.

Democratic National Committee Records, 1953–1963, John F. Kennedy Presidential Library, Boston, Massachusetts.

John Kenneth Galbraith Papers, John F. Kennedy Presidential Library, Boston, Massachusetts.

Averell Harriman Papers, Library of Congress, Washington, D.C.

John F. Kennedy Papers, John F. Kennedy Presidential Library, Boston, Massachusetts.

Republican National Committee Papers, National Archives, Washington, D.C.

Arthur M. Schlesinger, Jr., Papers, John F. Kennedy Presidential Library, Boston, Massachusetts.

MICROFILM SOURCES

Barry M. Goldwater Papers, Post-Election Correspondence. Cornell University Library, Ithaca, N.Y.

Paul L. Kesaris, ed. *Papers of the Republican Party*. Pt. 1: Meetings of the Republican National Committee, 1911–1980, and Pt. 2: Research Division Reports. Frederick, Md.: University Publications of America, 1986.

PARTY DOCUMENTS

Commission on Delegate Selection and Party Structure. *Democrats All*. Washington, D.C.: Democratic National Committee, 1973.

Commission on Party Structure and Delegate Selection. *Mandate for Reform*. Washington, D.C.: Democratic National Committee, 1970.

Commission on Presidential Nominations. *Report of the Commission on Presidential Nomination*. Washington D.C.: Democratic National Committee, 1982.

Democratic National Committee. *Official Proceedings of the 1974 Conference on Democratic Organization and Policy, Kansas City, Missouri, December 1974*. Washington, D.C.: Democratic National Committee, 1975.

Democratic Policy Council. *America in the 1970s*. Washington, D.C.: Democratic National Committee, 1970.

Democratic Policy Council. *Alternatives '72: A Report by the Democratic Policy Council.* Washington, D.C.: Democratic National Committee, 1972.

Republican Coordinating Committee. *Brief Position Papers and Other Documents Relating to the Republican Coordinating Committee.* Washington D.C.: Republican National Committee, 1967.

Republican Coordinating Committee. *Choice for America: Republican Answers to the Challenge of Now, Reports of the Republican Coordinating Committee, 1965–1968.* Washington, D.C.: Republican National Committee, 1968.

Republican Coordinating Committee. *The Development of National Party Policy between Conventions.* Washington D.C.: Republican National Committee, 1967.

Republican National Committee. *The Development of National Party Policy between Conventions.* Washington D.C.: Republican National Committee, 1966.

Republican National Committee. *The Elements of Victory.* Washington D.C.: Republican National Committee, 1966.

Republican National Committee, Committee on Big City Politics. *Report of the Committee on Big City Politics.* Washington D.C.: Republican National Committee, 1962.

INTERVIEWS

PERSONAL INTERVIEWS

Alan Baron, Washington, D.C., June 18, 1991.
Michael Baroody, Washington, D.C., April 10, 1991.
William Brock, Washington, D.C., June 17, 1991.
Joel Broyhill, Arlington, Virginia, February 27, 1991.
George Burger, Alexandria, Virginia, May 15, 1991.
Wally Chalmers, Washington, D.C., June 5, 1991.
Ben Cotton, Washington, D.C., April 2, 1991.
Roger Craver, Falls Church, Virginia, June 6, 1991.
Hal Dunham, Rockville, Maryland, March 11, 1991.
Eugene Eidenberg, Washington, D.C., May 2, 1991.
Jeff Ely, Washington, D.C., June 21, 1991.
Verrick O. French, Washington, D.C., June 5, 1991.
John Kenneth Galbraith, Cambridge, Massachusetts, December 20, 1990.
Sylvia Hermann, Bethesda, Maryland, February 8, 1991.
A. Linwood Holton, Washington, D.C., December 12, 1990.
Robert Huckshorn, Washington, D.C., February 15, 1991.
Robert Keefe, Washington, D.C., June 12, 1991.
Arthur Krim, New York City, New York, July 9, 1991.
Brian Lunde, Alexandria, Virginia, June 10, 1991.
George McGovern, Washington, D.C., May 28, 1991.
Eddie Mahe, Washington, D.C., May 16, 1991.
Charles Manatt, Washington, D.C., May 30, 1991.
Thomas E. Mann, Washington, D.C., June 26, 1991.
Richard Murphy, Washington, D.C., June 5, 1991.
Bob Neuman, Washington, D.C., June 6, 1991.
Paul Nitze, Washington, D.C., February 14, 1991.
Robert Novak, Washington, D.C., March 13, 1991.
Paula Nowakowski, Washington, D.C., June 3, 1993.

Patrick O'Connor, Washington, D.C., June 14, 1991.
Rima Parkhurst, Washington, D.C., June 10, 1991.
Sandra Perlmutter, Washington, D.C., June 3, 1991.
William Prendergast, Washington, D.C., February 28, 1991.
David Price, Washington, D.C., May 15, 1991.
Roger Semerad, Washington, D.C., April 3, 1991.
Georgiana Sheldon, Washington, D.C., February 6, 1991.
Mark Siegel, Washington, D.C., June 5, 1991.
Terry Straub, Washington, D.C., June 12, 1991.
Strom Thurmond, Washington, D.C., March 1, 1991.
Alice Travis, Washington, D.C., May 29, 1991.
Charles Tyroler, Washington, D.C., June 11, 1991.
William Welsh, Washington, D.C., June 7, 1991.

Telephone Interviews

John Bibby, March 22, 1991.
Kitty Bayh, June 5, 1991.
Howard "Bo" Calloway, March 8, 1991.
Robert Carter, April 2, 1991.
Carol F. Casey, June 25, 1991.
Bruce Chapman, February 25, 1991.
Evelyn Chavoor, June 5, 1991.
William Cramer, February 22, 1991.
Marta David, June 5, 1991.
Harry Dent, February 28, 1991.
Maureen Drummy, February 25, 1991.
Don Fowler, June 3, 1991.
Donald Fraser, June 3, 1991.
Orville Freeman, December 11, 1990.
Olga "Bobbie" Gechas, June 7, 1991.
George Gilder, February 26, 1991.
Vera Glasser, February 5, 1991.
Josephine Good, February 22, 1991.
Fred Harris, May 6, 1991.
Virginia Hooper, February 25, 1991.
Peter Kelly, June 11, 1991.
Frances Kenin, June 26, 1991.
John Kessel, March 5, 1991.
Paul Kirk, May 30, 1991.
Ann Lewis, June 4, 1991.
Charles McWhorter, February 8, 1991.
J. William Middendorf, April 3, 1991.
Jeremiah Milbank, February 7, 1991.
Arthur Peterson, March 27, 1991.
Ellie Peterson, February 22, 1991.
Clarke Reed, February 22, 1991.
Grant Reynolds, March 13, 1991.

Donald Ross, February 5, 1991.
Terry Sanford, May 29, 1991.
Fred Scribner, February 27, 1991.
Claire Williams Shank, February 5, 1991.
Mary Louise Smith, February 27, 1991.
Neil Staebler, June 10, 1991.
Michael Steed, June 12, 1991.
John Stewart, May 10, 1991.
Jean Sullivan, February 22, 1991.
William Sweeney, June 10, 1991.
Richard Vigurie, March 15, 1991.
Jean Westwood, June 3, 1991.
F. Clifton White, February 26, 1991.
Wirt Yerger Jr., February 25, 1991.

INDEX